Lecture Notes in Computer Science

Vol. 352: J. Díaz, F. Orejas (Eds.), TAPSOFT '89. Volume 2. Proceedings, 1989. X, 389 pages. 1989.

Vol. 353: S. Hölldobler, Foundations of Equational Logic Programming. X, 250 pages. 1989. (Subseries LNAI).

Vol. 354: J.W. de Bakker, W.-P. de Roever, G. Rozenberg (Eds.), Linear Time, Branching Time and Partial Order in Logics and Models for Concurrency. VIII, 713 pages. 1989.

Vol. 355: N. Dershowitz (Ed.), Rewriting Techniques and Applications. Proceedings, 1989. VII, 579 pages. 1989.

Vol. 356: L. Huguet, A. Poli (Eds.), Applied Algebra, Algebraic Algorithms and Error-Correcting Codes. Proceedings, 1987. VI, 417 pages. 1989.

Vol. 357: T. Mora (Ed.), Applied Algebra, Algebraic Algorithms and Error-Correcting Codes. Proceedings, 1988. IX, 481 pages. 1989.

Vol. 358: P. Gianni (Ed.), Symbolic and Algebraic Computation. Proceedings, 1988. XI, 545 pages. 1989.

Vol. 359: D. Gawlick, M. Haynie, A. Reuter (Eds.), High Performance Transaction Systems. Proceedings, 1987. XII, 329 pages. 1989.

Vol. 360: H. Maurer (Ed.), Computer Assisted Learning – ICCAL '89. Proceedings, 1989. VII, 642 pages. 1989.

Vol. 361: S. Abiteboul, P.C. Fischer, H.-J. Schek (Eds.), Nested Relations and Complex Objects in Databases. VI, 323 pages. 1989.

Vol. 362: B. Lisper, Synthesizing Synchronous Systems by Static Scheduling in Space-Time. VI, 263 pages. 1989.

Vol. 363: A.R. Meyer, M.A. Taitslin (Eds.), Logic at Botik '89. Proceedings, 1989. X, 289 pages. 1989.

Vol. 364: J. Demetrovics, B. Thalheim (Eds.), MFDBS 89. Proceedings, 1989. VI, 428 pages. 1989.

Vol. 365: E. Odijk, M. Rem, J.-C. Syre (Eds.), PARLE '89. Parallel Architectures and Languages Europe. Volume I. Proceedings, 1989. XIII, 478 pages. 1989.

Vol. 366: E. Odijk, M. Rem, J.-C. Syre (Eds.), PARLE '89. Parallel Architectures and Languages Europe. Volume II. Proceedings, 1989. XIII, 442 pages. 1989.

Vol. 367: W. Litwin, H.-J. Schek (Eds.), Foundations of Data Organization and Algorithms. Proceedings, 1989. VIII, 531 pages. 1989.

Vol. 368: H. Boral, P. Faudemay (Eds.), IWDM '89, Database Machines. Proceedings, 1989. VI, 387 pages. 1989.

Vol. 369: D. Taubner, Finite Representations of CCS and TCSP Programs by Automata and Petri Nets. X. 168 pages. 1989.

Vol. 370: Ch. Meinel, Modified Branching Programs and Their Computational Power. VI, 132 pages. 1989.

Vol. 371: D. Hammer (Ed.), Compiler Compilers and High Speed Compilation. Proceedings, 1988. VI, 242 pages. 1989.

Vol. 372: G. Ausiello, M. Dezani-Ciancaglini, S. Ronchi Della Rocca (Eds.), Automata, Languages and Programming. Proceedings, 1989. XI, 788 pages. 1989.

Vol. 373: T. Theoharis, Algorithms for Parallel Polygon Rendering. VIII, 147 pages. 1989.

Vol. 374: K.A. Robbins, S. Robbins, The Cray X-MP/Model 24. VI, 165 pages. 1989.

Vol. 375: J.L.A. van de Snepscheut (Ed.), Mathematics of Program Construction. Proceedings, 1989. VI, 421 pages. 1989.

Vol. 376: N.E. Gibbs (Ed.), Software Engineering Education. Proceedings, 1989. VII, 312 pages. 1989.

Vol. 377: M. Gross, D. Perrin (Eds.), Electronic Dictionaries and Automata in Computational Linguistics. Proceedings, 1987. V, 110 pages. 1989.

Vol. 378: J.H. Davenport (Ed.), EUROCAL '87. Proceedings, 1987. VIII, 499 pages. 1989.

Vol. 379: [...] lations of Compute [...] 989.

Vol. 380: [...] ntals of Computation Theory. Proceedings, 1989. XI, 493 pages. 1989.

Vol. 381: J. Dassow, J. Kelemen (Eds.), Machines, Languages, and Complexity. Proceedings, 1988. VI, 244 pages. 1989.

Vol. 382: F. Dehne, J.-R. Sack, N. Santoro (Eds.), Algorithms and Data Structures. WADS '89. Proceedings, 1989. IX, 592 pages. 1989.

Vol. 383: K. Furukawa, H. Tanaka, T. Fujisaki (Eds.), Logic Programming '88. Proceedings, 1988. VII, 251 pages. 1989 (Subseries LNAI).

Vol. 384: G. A. van Zee, J. G. G. van de Vorst (Eds.), Parallel Computing 1988. Proceedings, 1988. V, 135 pages. 1989.

Vol. 385: E. Börger, H. Kleine Büning, M. M. Richter (Eds.), CSL '88. Proceedings, 1988. VI, 399 pages. 1989.

Vol. 386: J.E. Pin (Ed.), Formal Properties of Finite Automata and Applications. Proceedings, 1988. VIII, 260 pages. 1989.

Vol. 387: C. Ghezzi, J. A. McDermid (Eds.), ESEC '89. 2nd European Software Engineering Conference. Proceedings, 1989. VI, 496 pages. 1989.

Vol. 388: G. Cohen, J. Wolfmann (Eds.), Coding Theory and Applications. Proceedings, 1988. IX, 329 pages. 1989.

Vol. 389: D. H. Pitt, D. E. Rydeheard, P. Dybjer, A. M. Pitts, A. Poigné (Eds.), Category Theory and Computer Science. Proceedings, 1989. VI, 365 pages. 1989.

Vol. 390: J.P. Martins, E.M. Morgado (Eds.), EPIA 89. Proceedings, 1989. XII, 400 pages. 1989 (Subseries LNAI).

Vol. 391: J.-D. Boissonnat, J.-P. Laumond (Eds.), Geometry and Robotics. Proceedings, 1988. VI, 413 pages. 1989.

Vol. 392: J.-C. Bermond, M. Raynal (Eds.), Distributed Algorithms. Proceedings, 1989. VI, 315 pages. 1989.

Vol. 393: H. Ehrig, H. Herrlich, H.-J. Kreowski, G. Preuß (Eds.), Categorical Methods in Computer Science. VI, 350 pages. 1989.

Vol. 394: M. Wirsing, J.A. Bergstra (Eds.), Algebraic Methods: Theory, Tools and Applications. VI, 558 pages. 1989.

Vol. 395: M. Schmidt-Schauß, Computational Aspects of an Order-Sorted Logic with Term Declarations. VIII, 171 pages. 1989 (Subseries LNAI).

Vol. 396: T. A. Berson, T. Beth (Eds.), Local Area Network Security. Proceedings, 1989. IX, 152 pages. 1989.

Vol. 397: K.P. Jantke (Ed.), Analogical and Inductive Inference. Proceedings, 1989. IX, 338 pages. 1989 (Subseries LNAI).

Vol. 398: B. Banieqbal, H. Barringer, A. Pnueli (Eds.), Temporal Logic in Specification. Proceedings, 1987. VI, 448 pages. 1989.

Vol. 399: V. Cantoni, R. Creutzburg, S. Levialdi, G. Wolf (Eds.), Recent Issues in Pattern Analysis and Recognition. VII, 400 pages. 1989.

Vol. 400: R. Klein, Concrete and Abstract Voronoi Diagrams. IV, 167 pages. 1989.

Vol. 401: H. Djidjev (Ed.), Optimal Algorithms. Proceedings, 1989. VI, 308 pages. 1989.

Vol. 402: T. P. Bagchi, V. K. Chaudhri, Interactive Relational Database Design. XI, 186 pages. 1989.

Vol. 403: S. Goldwasser (Ed.), Advances in Cryptology – CRYPTO '88. Proceedings, 1988. XI, 591 pages. 1990.

Vol. 404: J. Beer, Concepts, Design, and Performance Analysis of a Parallel Prolog Machine. VI, 128 pages. 1989.

Vol. 405: C. E. Veni Madhavan (Ed.), Foundations of Software Technology and Theoretical Computer Science. Proceedings, 1989. VIII, 339 pages. 1989.

Vol. 406: C. J. Barter, M. J. Brooks (Eds.), AI '88. Proceedings, 1988. VIII, 463 pages. 1990 (Subseries LNAI).

Vol. 407: J. Sifakis (Ed.), Automatic Verification Methods for Finite State Systems. Proceedings, 1989. VII, 382 pages. 1990.

Lecture Notes in Computer Science

Edited by G. Goos and J. Hartmanis

464

J. Dassow   J. Kelemen (Eds.)

Aspects and Prospects of Theoretical Computer Science

6th International Meeting of Young Computer Scientists
Smolenice, Czechoslovakia, November 19–23, 1990
Proceedings

Springer-Verlag
Berlin Heidelberg New York London
Paris Tokyo Hong Kong Barcelona

Editors

Jürgen Dassow
Sektion Mathematik, Technische Universität Magdeburg
Postfach 124, O-3010 Magdeburg, FRG

Jozef Kelemen
Department of Artificial Intelligence, Comenius University
Mlynská dolina, 842 15 Bratislava, Czechoslovakia

CR Subject Classification (1987): D.2, F.1−4, I.2−4

ISBN 3-540-53414-8 Springer-Verlag Berlin Heidelberg New York
ISBN 0-387-53414-8 Springer-Verlag New York Berlin Heidelberg

Printing and binding: Druckhaus Beltz, Hemsbach/Bergstr.
2145/3140-543210 – Printed on acid-free paper

Foreword

This volume contains the text of the tutorial lecture, the texts of five invited lectures and the texts of twenty short communications contributed for presentation at the Sixth International Meeting of Young Computer Scientists, IMYCS'90, held at Smolenice Castle, Czechoslovakia, November 19-23, 1990.

The IMYCSs have been organized biennially since 1980 by the Association of the Slovak Mathematicians and Physicists in cooperation with Comenius University, Bratislava, and with other institutions. The aim of the meetings is threefold: (1) to inform on newest trends, results, and problems in theoretical computer science and related fields through a tutorial and invited lectures delivered by internationally distinguished speakers, (2) to provide a possibility for beginners in scientific work to present and discuss their results, and (3) to create an adequate opportunity for establishing first professional relations among the participants.

Short communications included in this proceedings were selected from 47 papers submitted in response to the call for papers. The selection was made on the basis of originality and relevance of presented results to theoretical computer science and related fields by the Programme Committee. The members of the Programme Committee were E. Csuhaj-Varjú (Budapest), J. Dassow (chairman, Magdeburg), S. K. Dulin (Moscow), K. P. Jantke (Leipzig), J. Karhumäki (Turku), A. Kelemenová (Bratislava), M. Křivánek (Prague), K. J. Lange (Munich), J. Sakarovitch (Paris), and M. Szijártó (Györ). The editors wish to thank all of them as well as to subreferees G. Asser, A. Brandstaedt, M. Broy, V. Diekert, C. Dimitrovici, P. Ďuriš, H. Giessmann, D. Hernandez, J. Hromkovič, J. U. Jahn, I. Kalaš, J. Kelemen, I. Korec, V. Koubek, M. Kráľová, M. Krause, F. Kröger, A. Kučera, M. Kunde, L. Kühnel, S. Lange, R. Letz, P. Mikulecký, M. Pawlowski, J. Procházka, H. Reichel, W. Reisig, G. Riedewald, E. Ružický, P. Ružička, S. Schönherr, K. Schultz, M. Tegze, E. Tiptig, J. Vyskoč, R. Walter, J. Wiedermann, R. Wiehagen, H. Wolter, T. Zeugmann, and maybe some others not mentioned here who assisted the members of the Programme Committee in evaluating the submissions.

On behalf of all the participants of IMYCS'90 we express our gratitude to the members of the organizational staff of the Meeting, especially to Peter Mikulecký for chairing the Organizing Committee.

The editors are highly indebted to all contributors for preparing their texts carefully and on time. We would like to acknowledge gratefully the support of the organizing institutions: Association of Slovak Mathematicians and Physicists, Institute of Computer Science and Department of Artificial Intelligence of the Comenius University, Bratislava, Department of Computers of the Slovak Institute of Technology, Bratislava, and the Mathematical Institute of the Slovak Academy of Sciences, Bratislava.

We highly appreciate the excellent cooperation with Springer-Verlag in the publication of this volume.

Jürgen Dassow
Jozef Kelemen

Contents

Part I: Tutorial 1
  K. Culik II, S. Dube
  Methods for Generating Deterministic Fractals and Image Compression 2
Part II: Invited Lectures 29
  B. Cong, Z. Miller, I. H. Sudborough
  Optimum Simulation of Meshes by Small Hypercubes 30
  Y. Kodratoff
  Seven Hard Problems in Symbolic Background Knowledge Acquisition 47
  Ch. Reutenauer
  Subsequential Functions: Characterizations, Minimization, Examples 62
  I. Sain
  Past Proves More Invariance Properties But Not PCA's 80
  J. Wiedermann
  Complexity Issues in Discrete Neurocomputing 93
Part III: Communications 109
  M. Anselmo
  Two-Way Reading on Words 110
  J. L. Coquidé, R. Gilleron
  Proofs and Reachability Problem for Ground Rewrite Systems 120
  C. Damm
  Problems Complete for +L 130
  M. Fraňová
  Constructive Matching – Explanation Based Methodology
  for Inductive Theorem Proving 138
  A. Goerdt, H. Seidl
  Characterizing Complexity Classes by Higher Type Primitive Recursive Definitions,
  Part II 148
  D. Gomm, R. Walter
  The Distributed Termination Problem: Formal Solution and Correctness
  Based on Petri Nets 159
  M. Loebl
  Greedy Compression Systems 169
  M. Mňuk
  A div(n) Depth Boolean Circuit for Smooth Modular Inverse 177
  M. F. Møller
  Learning by Conjugate Gradients 184
  M. Pelletier
  Monoids Described by Pushdown Automata 195

P. Rajčáni
Optimal Parallel 3-colouring Algorithm for Rooted Trees and its Application 204

K. Reinhardt
Hierarchies over the Context-Free Languages 214

L. Santean
A Hierarchy of Unary Primitive Recursive String-Functions 225

P. Séébold, K. Slowinski
Minimizing Picture Words 234

P. Škodný
Remarks on the Frequency-Coded Neural Nets Complexity 244

R. Stiebe
Picture Generation Using Matrix Systems 251

Ch. B. Suttner
Representing Heuristic-Relevant Information for an Automated
Theorem Prover 261

K. Unger
A New Method for Proving Lower Bounds in the Model
of Algebraic Decision Trees 271

J. Waczulík
Area Time Squared and Area Complexity of VLSI Computations is
Strongly Unclosed Under Union and Intersection 278

I. Walukiewicz
Decision Procedure for Checking Validity of PAL Formulas 288

Part I
Tutorial

Methods for Generating Deterministic Fractals and Image Compression *

Karel Culik II

Dept. of Computer Science
University of South Carolina
Columbia, SC 29208, USA

Simant Dube

Dept. of Computer Science
University of South Carolina
Columbia, SC 29208, USA

Abstract

We survey recently developed methods for generating deterministic fractals that have the potential for compression of arbitrary (practical) images. They are the Iterative Function Systems developed by Barnsley, the probabilistic finite generators, and probabilistic mutually recursive systems that generalize both former methods. We briefly introduce the formal notion of an image both as a compact set (of black points) and as a measure on Borel sets (specifying greyness or colors). We describe the above mentioned systems for image generation, some mathematical properties and discuss the problem of image encoding.

1 Introduction

Recently, the fractal geometry introduced by B. Mandelbrot [19] is getting increased attention in relation to the study of deterministic chaos (complex systems) [16]. The relation of fractal geometry to classical geometry is similar to the relation of classical physics, which handles primarily phenomena described by linear differential equations, to the new "chaos" physics. "Chaos" physics studies complex phenomena, mathematically described by nonlinear differential equations, like the flow of gases. Classical geometry handles well "man-made" objects like polygons, circles, etc. The new "fractal" geometry should handle well all the classical objects as well as those of fractal (recurrent) type. Examples are H-trees, Sierpinski triangles and also all natural objects like plants, trees, clouds, mountains, etc. The study of fractal geometry was pioneered by B. Mandelbrot [19] and the study of practical "computational fractal geometry" by M. Barnsley [1]. He introduced the Iterative Function Systems (IFS) that are used to define an object (an image) as the limit (attractor) of a "chaotic process." He has used IFS to generate exclusively Deterministic fractals. Voss et al. have considered techniques to generate Random fractals [4]. Barnsley's hyperbolic IFS [1] is specified by several affine transformations, and the attractor is the limit of the sequence generated from an arbitrary starting point by randomly choosing and applying these affine transformations.

---

*This research was supported by the National Sciences Foundation under Grant No. CCR-8702752.

A number of various methods for generating both deterministic and random fractals have been developed, here we will concentrate on those that have potential to be used for efficient encoding of a wide variety of images. Besides Barnsley's IFS we will discuss rational expressions (probabilistic finite generators), affine expressions, (probabilistic) affine automata, and (probabilistic) mutually recursive IFS.

Barnsley's collage theorem [1] gives the mathematical basis for infering concise IFS-description of any given image, which includes texture or color. We will discuss how this can be done also for finite generators. Collage theorem can be extended also to affine automata and mutually recursive IFS, even if presently we do not have any efficient methods of encoding arbitrary images by these methods.

Encoding of images by IFS and other methods have tremendous potential for practical applications because they allow drastic compressing of data and their efficient processing. For example, from an IFS description of an image it is possible to regenerate effectively not only the original image but also its various modifications, e.g. a view from a different angle. Applications of this are studied not only to computer graphics [3] but also to compression of videos, to medical imaging, to high-resolution TV, etc.

We first discuss the formal notions of an image in Section 2. A black and white image is formalized as a compact set and texture (color) image is formalized as a normalized measure (greyness density). Then we introduce Barnsley's IFS method to generate fractals.

In [9], automata-theoretic techniques have been developed for image representation, manipulation and generation, which we describe in Section 3. A similar approach to represent patterns by finite automata has been independently taken in [5]. Our approach in [9] is more general as we have defined images in terms of languages of infinite words, rather than finite words, and we have also considered textures. Images here are sets of points in n-dimensional space (or sometimes functions on this space specifying the level of grey or color). Points are represented by coordinates, i.e. n-tuples of rational numbers. In turn, rational numbers are represented by strings of bits usually in binary notation (e.g. string 011 represents number 0.011 in binary notation). Hence an n-tuple of strings can be interpreted as a point in the n-dimensional space $< 0, 1 >^n$, and a relation $\rho \subseteq \underbrace{\Sigma^* \times \ldots \times \Sigma^*}_{n-times}$ as a set of points, i.e. an object (image). Similarly, an ω-string is interpreted as a real number in the interval $< 0, 1 >$.

It has been known for more than twenty years that, for example, the Cantor Set (as subset of $< 0, 1 >$) can be represented in ternary notation by regular expression $\{0 + 2\}^+$ [15,17]. We can show how most "regular" 2-dimensional geometrical objects (both classical and fractal) can be represented by simple rational expressions. Unlike Barnsley's IFS the rational expressions allow to build complex images from simple ones by set and other operations. We can convert the rational expressions into probabilistic finite generators that are used to generate images much like the Barnsley's Chaos Game algorithm. We also have a method to automatically infer the probabilistic generator from an arbitrary given image. This is based on the quad tree representation of images that has already been used in Computer Graphics for compressing data [18] and computing the Hausdorff dimension of images [24]. Hence, much like Barnsley, we can concisely represent objects (both fractal and classical) and regenerate them in the original or modified version.

In addition to considering images as compact sets, we can define "texture" images, which are formalized in terms of probabilistic measures. A finite approximation of such a texture image on a computer screen will be a matrix of pixels which are assigned grey tones (or colors).

Considering the practical descriptive power, our rational expressions (probabilistic generators) are incomparable with Barnsley's IFS [9].

In Section 4, we briefly discuss a generalization of Barnsley's IFS called Affine Expressions which define a bigger class of images of more complex geometries [8]. Intuitively, an affine expression generates an image based on a finite set of affine transformations that are applied in an order controlled by a regular set.

We consider two more generalizations of IFS in Sections 5 and 6. The first one is probabilistic affine automaton (PAA), which is informally probabilistic finite generator whose input symbols are affine transformations. PAA are equivalent to recurrent IFS, as introduced in [2], under certain assumptions [8]. Fractal dimension of recurrent IFS is computed in [14]. The other one is called mutually recursive IFS (MRIFS) and is given by a number of "variables" which are defined in terms of each others as unions under affine transformations. We consider both deterministic and probabilistic variations of MRIFS. Barnsley's Collage Theorem can be generalized to PAA and MRIFS, and provides for the basis of the algorithm to automatically synthesize a PAA (or a MRIFS) for a given image.

Rational expressions are special case of affine expressions. This allows one to efficiently implement rational expressions (probabilistic finite generators) by PAA and PMRIFS. This implementation does not use the bit-by-bit approach and hence yields algorithms that using standard (numerically oriented) software and hardware are almost as fast as Barnsley's.

All these generalizations of IFS—affine expressions, PAA and MRIFS, are equivalent in their power to generate images (as compact sets).

In Section 7, we consider another approach to generate interesting images, which is based on L-systems (string rewriting systems). We give two examples illustrating that certain L-systems can be simulated by MRIFS.

Finally, we conclude the paper by briefly discussing the problem of an image encoding.

2 Preliminaries

2.1 Two Notions of an Image

Following [1] we introduce two different formalizations of an image:

(1) Given a complete metric space (X, d), an image is a compact subset of X. The quality of an approximation for such images is measured by the Hausdorff metric $h(d)$ on the complete metric space $\mathcal{K}(X)$ of the nonempty compact subsets of X. This is a formalization of such an image as consisting of black and white regions. A finite approximation of such an image on the computer screen is an assignment of 0 (white) or 1 (black) to each pixel of a matrix of pixels.

(2) Given a complete metric space (X, d), an image is a normalized invariant measure on X, that is an additive function f defined on the Borel subsets of X such that $f(X) = 1$ (see [1] for more details). The quality of an approximation for such images is measured by the Hutchinson metric d_H on the complete metric space of all the normalized measures on X. This is a formalization of an image as a texture, either of various tones of grey or

colors. A finite approximation of such an image on the computer screen is an assignment of grey tones (or colors) to each pixel. Here each pixel represents a small subsquare of the space X.

2.2 Iterative Function Systems

A space X together with a real-valued function $d : X \times X \to R$, which measures the *distance* between pairs of points x and y in X, is called a *metric space*. In this paper, we will be concerned with metric spaces $(R^n, Euclidean)$, where $n \geq 1$ and R is the set of real numbers.

A 2-dimensional *affine transformation* $w : R^2 \to R^2$ is defined by

$$w \begin{bmatrix} x \\ y \end{bmatrix} = \begin{bmatrix} a_{11}x + a_{12}y + b_1 \\ a_{21}x + a_{22}y + b_2 \end{bmatrix}$$

where a_{ij}'s and b_i's are real constants [1]. Similarly, a 1-dimensional affine transformation $w : R \to R$ is defined by $w(x) = ax + b$, where a and b are real constants.

A transformation $f : X \to X$ on a metric space (X, d) is called a *contractive mapping* if there is a constant $0 \leq s < 1$ such that

$$d(f(x), f(y)) \leq s.d(x, y) \text{ for all } x, y \in X.$$

Any such number s is called a *contractivity factor* for f.

Let (X, d) be a complete metric space. Then $\mathcal{K}(X)$ denotes the space whose points are the compact nonempty subsets of X. Let $x \in X$, and $B \in \mathcal{K}(X)$. The distance from the point x to the set B is defined to be

$$d(x, B) = \min\{d(x, y) : y \in B\}.$$

Now, let $A \in \mathcal{K}(X)$. The distance from the set A to the set B is defined to be

$$d(A, B) = \max\{d(x, B) : x \in A\}.$$

The *Hausdorff distance* between the sets A and B is defined by

$$h(A, B) = \max\{d(A, B), d(B, A)\}.$$

It can be shown that $(\mathcal{K}(X), h(d))$ is a complete metric space [1].

A (hyperbolic) *iterated function system*(IFS) consists of a complete metric space (X, d) together with a finite set of contractive mappings $w_n : X \to X$, with respective contractive factors s_n, for $n = 1, 2, \ldots, N$. The notation for the IFS defined is $\{X; w_n, n = 1, 2, \ldots, N\}$ and its contractivity factor is $s = \max\{s_n : n = 1, 2, \ldots, N\}$. We will also consider probabilistic IFS, in which a probability $p_i > 0$ is associated with each mapping w_i, such that $\sum_1^N p_i = 1$.

For its applications to the fractal geometry, the metric spaces are $([0, 1], Euclidean)$ and $([0, 1]^2, Euclidean)$, for 1-D and 2-D images respectively, and the mappings are affine transformations. The transformation $W : \mathcal{K}(X) \to \mathcal{K}(X)$ defined by

$$W(B) = \bigcup_{n=1}^{N} w_n(B)$$

for all $B \in \mathcal{K}(X)$, is a contraction mapping on the complete metric space $(\mathcal{K}(X), h(d))$, where $h(d)$ is the Hausdorff distance. Its unique fixed point, $A \in \mathcal{K}(X)$, is called the *attractor* of the IFS, and is the geometric object defined by the IFS. This geometric object could be self-similar, and hence a fractal may be defined by an IFS [1].

This basic mathematical characterization of a fractal to be the attractor of an IFS, provides two algorithms to generate fractals [1]. Let $\{X; w_1, w_2, \ldots, w_N\}$ be an IFS with probability p_i associated with w_i for $i = 0, 1, \ldots, N$.

The *Deterministic* Algorithm starts by choosing a compact set $A_0 \subset X$. Then, one computes successively $A_n = W^n(A_0)$ according to

$$A_{n+1} = \bigcup_{j=1}^{N} w_j(A_n) \text{ for } n = 1, 2, \ldots .$$

The sequence $\{A_n\}$ converges to the attractor of the IFS in the Hausdorff metric. Note that the probabilities assigned to the mappings play no role in the Deterministic Algorithm.

The Random Iteration (or Chaos Game) Algorithm starts by choosing a point $x_o \in X$. Then, one chooses recursively and independently,

$$x_n \in \{w_1(x_{n-1}), w_2(x_{n-1}), \ldots, w_N(x_{n-1})\} \text{ for } n = 1, 2, 3, \ldots,$$

where the probability of the event $x_n = w_i(x_{n-1})$ is p_i. The collection of points $\{x_n\}_{n=0}^{\infty}$ converges to the attractor of the IFS. This algorithm also defines the texture of an image as an invariant mesaure on Borel subsets of X [1].

Example: The Sierpinski Triangle, a subset of $[0, 1]^2$, is the attractor of the IFS specified by the affine transformations $w_1(x, y) = (0.5x, 0.5y)$, $w_2(x, y) = (0.5x + 0.5, 0.5y)$ and $w_3(x, y) = (0.5x, 0.5y + 0.5)$. The output of the Deterministic Algorithm after 8 iterations is shown in Fig. 1(a).

Example: Fig. 1(b) shows a self-similar fern, generated by 80000 iterations of the Chaos Game Algorithm on the IFS specified by the four affine transformations

$$
\begin{aligned}
w_1(x, y) &= (0, 0.16y), \\
w_2(x, y) &= (0.85x + 0.04y, -0.04x + 0.85y + 1.6), \\
w_3(x, y) &= (-0.15x + 0.28y, 0.26x + 0.24y + 0.44), \\
w_4(x, y) &= (0.2x - 0.26y, 0.23x + 0.22y + 1.6).
\end{aligned}
$$

The corresponding probabilities are $0.01, 0.85, 0.07$ and 0.07, respectively.

2.3 Languages of Infinite Words

We assume that the reader is familiar with basic formal language theory, in which languages are defined as sets of *finite* words. This computation domain can be extended by adding the set of infinite strings Σ^ω [7,11]. Formally, Σ^ω denotes all infinite (ω-length) strings $\sigma = \prod_{i=1}^{\infty} a_i, a_i \in \Sigma$, over Σ. An element σ of Σ^ω is called an *ω-word* or *ω-string*. An *ω-language* is any subset of Σ^ω. The set of both finite and infinite strings is denoted by $\Sigma^\infty = \Sigma^* \cup \Sigma^\omega$. The superscript ω means infinite repitition, e.g. $(00)^*1^\omega$ denotes an ω-set of strings which have an even number of zeroes followed by an infinite number of

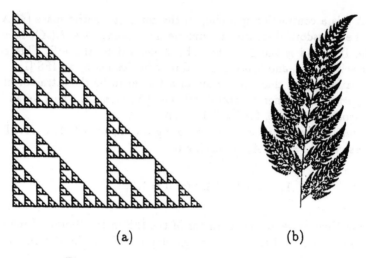

(a) (b)

Figure 1: Examples of Images Generated by IFS

consecutive ones. Later we will interpret finite strings as rational numbers and ω-strings as real numbers.

For any language $L \subseteq \Sigma^*$, define

$$L^\omega = \{\sigma \in \Sigma^\omega | \sigma = \prod_{i=1}^\infty x_i, \forall i, x_i \in L\}.$$

Therefore, L^ω consists of all ω-strings obtained by concatenating words from L in an infinite sequence.

For any family $\mathcal{L}$ of languages over alphabet Σ, the ω-Kleene closure of $\mathcal{L}$, denoted by ω-KC($\mathcal{L}$), is given by

$$\omega - \mathrm{KC}(\mathcal{L}) = \{L \subseteq \Sigma^\omega | L = \cup_{i=1}^k V_i W_i^\omega \text{ for some } V_i, W_i \in \mathcal{L}, i = 1, 2, \ldots, k; k = 1, 2, \ldots\}$$

If $\mathcal{L}$ is the family of regular languages, then ω-KC($\mathcal{L}$) is called the family of ω-regular languages [7]. In a straightforward generalization, we may define ω-rational expressions for ω-rational relations.

The ω-regular languages are exactly the languages accepted by the ω-finite automata, which are defined in the following paragraph.

An ω-finite automaton(ω-FA) is a 5-tuple $(Q, \Sigma, \delta, q_0, F)$, where Q is the finite set of states, Σ is the input alphabet, δ is a mapping from $Q \times \Sigma$ to 2^Q, q_0 is the initial state and F is the set of final states.

An ω-word is accepted by an ω-FA if on reading the input ω-word the ω-FA enters a final state infinitely many times.

The class of ω-regular languages are closed under all Boolean operations. For any ω-regular languages L_1 and L_2, effectively given, it is decidable whether (1) L_1 is empty, finite or infinite; (2) $L_1 = L_2$; (3) $L_1 \subseteq L_2$; (4) $L_1 \cap L_2 = \phi$ [7].

An ω-*finite transducer* T is a 6-tuple $(Q, \Sigma, \Delta, \delta, q_0, F)$ where Q is the finite set of states, Σ is the input alphabet, Δ is the output alphabet, δ is a mapping from $Q \times (\Sigma \cup \{\epsilon\})$ to finite subsets of $Q \times \Delta^*$, q_0 is the initial state and F is the set of final states.

An ω-word τ is an output on an input ω-word σ under ω-finite transducer T if there exists a run of T on σ which produces τ. The relation defined by an ω-finite transducer is called an ω-*rational relation*. The ω-rational relations are exactly the ω-rational expressions. The family of ω-regular sets is closed under ω-rational relations.

An ω-word τ is called an *adherence* of a language L, if τ has infinitely many prefixes such that each of these prefixes is also a prefix of some word in L. Formally, define $\text{Prefix}(y) = \{x \in \Sigma^* | x \text{ is a prefix of y}\}$. Note that y can be both a finite or an infinite word. An ω-word τ is an adherence of L iff $\text{Prefix}(\tau) \subseteq \text{Prefix}(L)$. The set of all adherences of L, denoted by $adherence(L)$, is called the adherence set of L. The adherence set of any regular language is ω-regular [6,11]. Note that the adherence set of a language L, which is accepted by an FA M, is accepted by an ω-FA M' which is obtained from M by discarding all those states which do not have an outgoing transition and by making every state a final state.

3 Rational Expressions and Finite Generators

In this section, we study rational expressions as a tool to represent images. For more details and for the omitted proofs see [9].

Let $\Sigma = \{0, 1, \dots, n-1\}$ be an alphabet of n symbols. A word in Σ^* can be interpreted as a rational number in the interval $[0, 1]$. More precisely, a string $w = w_1 w_2 \dots w_m$ represents a coordinate with "numeric value" equal to the rational number $(.w_1 w_2 \dots w_m)_n$, which is nothing but the number obtained by placing the radix point to the left of the word and treating the number in notation with radix n. For example, if $\Sigma = \{0, 1\}$, then the string $w = 0110$ represents the binary number $(.0110)_2$, which is equal to 0.375 in decimal notation. In a similar manner, an ω-word in Σ^ω can be interpreted as a real number e.g. the ω-word $(01)^\omega$ over $\Sigma = \{0, 1\}$ represents the binary number $0.010101\dots$ in binary notation.

Formally, we define an *interpretation function* $I : \Sigma^\infty \to [0, 1] \times [0, 1]$ which maps a finite or infinite string to its "numeric value." An n-tuple of words can be interpreted as a point in $[0, 1]^n$, where each component word is interpreted individually as a coordinate value i.e. $I(x_1, x_2, \dots, x_n) = (I(x_1), I(x_2), \dots, I(x_n))$, where $n \geq 1$.

A compact subset of n-dimensional Euclidean space, where $n \geq 1$, is a formalization of an n-dimensional image (without texture). Therefore, a topologically closed ω-relation $L \subseteq \underbrace{\Sigma^\omega \times \dots \times \Sigma^\omega}_{n-times}$ can be interpreted as an image $X = I(L) \subseteq [0, 1]^n$.

The notion of adherence allows one to specify an image by a language of finite words. Let $L \subseteq \Sigma^*$. Then the image represented by L, denoted by $A(L) \subseteq [0, 1]$, is given by

$$A(L) = \{I(\sigma) | \sigma \in adherence(L)\}.$$

In other words, $A(L) = I(adherence(L))$.

To represent images in more than one dimension, we consider n-ary relations and extend the definition of adherence from languages to relations. We need to only extend the definition of the Prefix operation from finite words to ω-words. An n-tuple $(x_1, x_2, \ldots, x_n)$, where $x_i \in \Sigma^*$ is a prefix of $(y_1, y_2, \ldots, y_n)$, where all y_i's are in Σ^* or all y_i's are in Σ^ω, if x_i is a prefix of y_i, $1 \leq i \leq n$. Also, if ρ is an n-ary relation, we will denote $\rho.\underbrace{(0, 0, \ldots, 0)}_{n-times}{}^*$ by shorthand $\rho.0^*$.

Theorem 1 *Let ρ be an n-ary relation over some alphabet Σ. Then $A(\rho.0^*)$ is the closure of $I(\rho)$ i.e. $A(\rho) = I(\rho) \cup \{$limit points of $I(\rho)\}$.*

Note that the interpretation function I may not be injective, when its domain is restricted to some language $L \subseteq \Sigma^\omega$. For example, $I(01^\omega)$ and $I(10^\omega)$ both are equal to the same binary number 0.1. In general, a number might have two different representations. If $\Sigma = \{0, 1, \ldots, n-1\}$, then the *left canonical representation* is the one with trailing 0's, while the *right canonical representation* is the one with trailing $(n-1)$'s. If for every point which is in the image represented by a given language and which has two representations, the language has both the representations then the language is called to be in the *canonical form*.

Example: The Cantor Set is obtained by starting with the interval $[0, 1]$ and successively deleting the middle third open subinterval. The n-th iteration is represented by the regular language $\{0 + 2\}^n \Sigma^*$, where $\Sigma = \{0, 1, 2\}$. The Cantor Set C is the limit of this recursive process. This set can be represented by languages as follows.

$$C = A(\{0 + 2\}^*) = I(\{0 + 2\}^\omega).$$

Note that $\{0 + 2\}^\omega$ represents the Cantor Set but is not canonical because the point $x = 0.333\ldots$ has two representations—02^ω and 10^ω, and only the first representation is in the language. □

3.1 Interpreting Rational Expressions as Images

A remarkable variety of images can be represented by considering rational expressions (and topologically closed ω-rational relations).

We consider only a normal length-preserving form of rational expressions (rational relations), as this allows us to treat a (binary) rational relation ρ over alphabet Σ as a language over alphabet $\Sigma \times \Sigma$. This is not an essential restriction because practically one does not specify the value of one coordinate much more precisely than that of the other coordinate. Moreover, if there is a bounded difference in the precision of different coordinate values, then the lengths of their representations can be made exactly equal by suffixing zeroes.

A rational relation ρ is called *almost length-preserving* if for every $(x_1, x_2) \in \rho$, $||x_1| - |x_2|| < c$, where c is a fixed positive constant. Alternatively, let M be a finite transducer. If every loop in M is exactly length-preserving, then M is called almost length-preserving. A rational relation is almost length-preserving if there exists an almost length-preserving finite transducer accepting the rational relation.

A rational relation ρ is called *(exactly) length-preserving* if for each $(x_1, x_2) \in \rho$, $|x_1| = |x_2|$. A length-preserving finite transducer is a Mealy machine (which produces exactly one output symbol for every input symbol).

These definitions can be generalized to ω-rational relations in a straightforward manner. An ω-rational relation is almost length-preserving if it is accepted by an ω-finite transducer which is exactly length-preserving on all of its loops. An ω-rational relation is (exactly) length-preserving if it is accepted by an ω-finite transducer which is length-preserving on all of its transitions.

Now we show a normal form of our rational relations.

Theorem 2 *Let ρ be an almost length-preserving ω-rational relation. Then, there exists another ω-rational relation δ, such that δ is exactly length-preserving and both ρ and δ represent the same image.*

Since adherence set of a regular set is an ω-regular set, we may work only with ω-regular sets as image representations. The following lemma states that this holds for relations too.

Lemma 1 *Let ρ be an almost length-preserving rational relation. Then, the adherence set of ρ is a length-preserving ω-rational relation.*

Moreover, we can work with canonical representations.

Lemma 2 *Let an image be represented by a length-preserving ω-rational relation. Then, there exists an ω-rational relation which is a canonical representation of the same image.*

Several results from the theory of ω-regular languages can be used to show the decidability of different questions about images.

Theorem 3 *The membership problem of a rational point, effectively given as an ω-word, in an image given by a rational expression, is decidable.*

Theorem 4 *For two images A and B (compact sets) given by rational expressions it is decidable whether:*
(i) $A = B$ (equivalence problem)
(ii) $A \subseteq B$ (inclusion problem)
(iii) $A \cap B = \phi$ (overlap problem)

Theorem 5 *Given two images A and B, effectively given, it is decidable whether the Hausdorff distance $h(A, B)$ between them is less than or equal to ϵ.*

Proof: (Outline) We first construct an ω-finite transducer ρ, which computes the ϵ-neighborhood of an image. More precisely, for some image C,

$$\rho(C) = \{x | h(x, C) \le \epsilon\}.$$

Then,

$$h(A, B) \le \epsilon \text{ iff } B \subseteq \rho(A) \wedge A \subseteq \rho(B).$$

Since, ω-regular sets are closed under ω-finite transduction and the inclusion problem for w-regular sets is decidable, it follows that it is decidable to test if $h(A, B) \le \epsilon$. $\qquad\square$

In the above proof, the underlying metric d for the Hausdorff metric is assumed to be $d((x_1, y_1), (x_2, y_2)) = \max\{|x_1 - x_2|, |y_1 - y_2|\}$. This metric is topologically equivalent to the Euclidean metric.

3.2 Operations on Images

One of the reasons why the representation of images by languages turns out to be concise is that a number of operations on images can be concisely described by language operations. First note that the boolean operations of union, intersection and complementation have straightforward graphical interpretation. Therefore, for example, the parts of an image lying outside a window can be clipped by intersecting the language representing the image with the language defining the window. However note that if one is defining images as the interpretation of arbitrary languages then the closure under Boolean operations holds, but in our definition images are compact sets and, therefore, are not closed under complementation.

In this section, we focus mainly on three interesting operations on images—zooming operation, placement operation, and more complicated operations performed by GSM.

We will illustrate these operations on 2-D images. Let $R(x, y), x, y \in \Sigma^*$, denote the rectangular subarea (window) in $[0, 1]^2$ which has its lower left corner at the point $I(x, y)$, and which has sides of lengths $\frac{1}{n^{|x|}}$ and $\frac{1}{n^{|y|}}$, where $n = |\Sigma|$, in the horizontal and vertical directions, respectively i.e.

$$R(x, y) = \{(a, b) \in [0, 1] \times [0, 1] | I(x) \leq a \leq I(x) + \frac{1}{n^{|x|}}, I(y) \leq b \leq I(y) + \frac{1}{n^{|y|}}\}.$$

It is assumed, for the purpose of this definition, that $I(\epsilon) = 0$. Therefore, for example, when $\Sigma = \{0, 1\}$,

$$R(1, \epsilon) = \{(a, b) \in [0, 1]^2 | 0.5 \leq a \leq 1, 0 \leq b \leq 1\}.$$

Zooming: Suppose we are given an image being represented by a language L, and it is desired to zoom into the window $R(x, y)$, for some $x, y \in \Sigma^*$. This operation is accomplished with the *quotient* operation on the relation L,

$$L_{zoom}^{R(x,y)} = (x, y) \backslash L = \{(u, v) | (xu, yv) \in L\}.$$

Clearly, this operation zooms into the image enclosed in the rectangular area $R(x, y)$. To perform more advanced zooming, one may use concatenation and union operation in conjunction with quotient operation. For example, suppose the language is over the binary alphabet, and we want to zoom into the window W given by

$$W = \{(a, b) \in [0, 1]^2 | 0.25 \leq a, b \leq 0.75\}.$$

This zooming is performed by the following more complicated language operation

$$L_{zoom}^W = (0, 0)((01, 01) \backslash L) \cup (0, 1)((01, 10) \backslash L) \cup (1, 0)((10, 01) \backslash L) \cup (1, 1)((10, 10) \backslash L)$$

The zooming operation provides one with a sufficient condition to test the "self-similarity" of an image. Clearly, if $L_{zoom}^W = L$ for some window W, then it implies that there is a scaled down copy of the image in the window W, and therefore the image is self-similar.
Placement: Placement can be viewed as an operation inverse to zooming. We are given an image and a window, and it is desired to place a scaled down copy of the image in the window.

Suppose the given image is represented by a relation L and the window where the image is to be placed is $R(x,y)$ for some $x, y \in \Sigma^*$. Then, concatenating (x,y) with L results in the placement operation

$$L_{place}^{R(x,y)} = \{(x,y)\}.L = \{(xu, yv)|(u,v) \in L\}.$$

Therefore, the simple concatenation operation provides us a mechanism to place images at various positions.

Moreover, it is possible to generate "fractal" images, by placing the copies of a basic image at infinitely many places i.e. by concatenating the language L, which is a representation of the basic image, with an infinite language L', which gives these infinitely many places where the copies of the basic image will be placed.

For example, if $L' = \{(0,0), (0,1), (1,0)\}^*$ then the operation $L'.L$ creates a Sierpinski Triangle type fractal image. Actually, the well-known Sierpinski Triangle happens to be a special case, when $L = L'$.

To perform more advanced placement, one may use quotient and union operations in conjunction with concatenation operation.

GSM operations: Though, simple language operations, like quotient and concatenation operations, can be used to perform important image operations, like zooming and placement, we need more sophisticated automata-theoretic tools to perform more complicated operations. For example, it may be required to rotate or scale or translate an image. In general, it will be interesting to perform an affine transformation on an image. Moreover, for most general zooming and placement operations, in which the window is arbitrary, we need more complex mechanisms than provided by simple language operations.

GSM mappings provide a powerful mechanism to perform more complex operations on images. Since affine transformations have rational constants as their coefficients for practical purposes, they can be implemented by GSM mappings.

The length-preserving normal form of the rational relations allows one to employ GSM on them.

Theorem 6 *Let $\tau : [0,1]^2 \rightarrow [0,1]^2$ be an arbitrary affine transformation. Then τ can be implemented with a GSM M such that*

$$\tau(A(\rho)) = A(M(\rho)),$$

where $\rho \subseteq \Sigma^* \times \Sigma^*$ (and ρ is length-preserving).

The following result extends the result to ω-languages.

Theorem 7 *Let $\tau : [0,1]^n \rightarrow [0,1]^n$ be an arbitrary affine transformation. Then τ can be implemented with an ω-finite transducer M such that*

$$\tau(I(\rho)) = I(M(\rho)),$$

where $\rho \subseteq \Sigma^\omega \times \Sigma^\omega$ (and ρ is length-preserving).

In the above proof, the ω-finite transducer that implements the given affine transformation is synchronous i.e. it reads the two input bits synchronously and produces two output bits synchronously. Such an ω-transducer is called a simple one.

3.3 Texture Images Defined by Finite Generators

So far we have considered only images as compact subsets of n-dimensional Euclidean subspace $[0,1]^n, n \geq 1$, and have used rational expressions as their representations. But in real-world images, an important characteristic of images is their *texture*. An image for which texture is defined will be refered as a texture image. In this section, we show how texture images can be defined by (length-preserving) rational expressions.

From now onwards, we will call a finite automaton accepting a rational expression as a *finite generator*. Note that a finite generator, in each computation step, generates a point independently of the previous points which have been generated.

A straightforward method of defining texture is by assigning probabilities to the transitions of the finite generator such that, for each state, outgoing transitions' probabilities sum to unity. Such a device is nothing but a probabilistic finite generator which generates a point with some probability.

We will illustrate the notion of texture by considering 2-D images over an alphabet Σ, which are subsets of $[0,1]^2$. Let $x, y \in \Sigma^*$ and let $|x| = |y| = n$. Define

$$B(x,y) = \{(a,b) \in [0,1]^2 | I(x) \leq a < I(x) + 1/|\Sigma|^n, I(y) \leq b < I(y) + 1/|\Sigma|^n\}$$

where I, as usual, is the interpretation function. In other words, $B(x,y)$ is the window which has as its lower left corner at the point $(I(x), I(y))$ and has horizontal and vertical dimensions equal to $\frac{1}{|\Sigma|^n}$.

Let $\mathcal{G} = \{B(x,y) | x, y \in \Sigma^*, |x| = |y|\}$.

Let $\mu(B(x,y))$, where $B(x,y) \in \mathcal{G}$ be the probability of generating the tuple (x,y) by the given finite generator. Note that μ so defined is a normalized measure as $\mu([0,1]^2) = 1$ [1].

Define *measure density* $\lambda : \mathcal{G} \rightarrow [0,\infty]$ as follows

$$\lambda(B(x,y)) = \mu((B(x,y))/ \text{ area of B(x,y)}$$

where area of $B(x,y)$ is $1/|\Sigma|^{2n}, n = |x| = |y|$.

The *texture* of an image, represented by a probabilistic finite generator M, is the measure density function $\lambda : \mathcal{G} \rightarrow [0,\infty]$ defined by M. Note that, for practical reasons of displaying "greyness" on a computer screen, we have chosen to consider the area of a "pixel," representing a small subsquare, in the definition of texture. We think that the choice of λ rather than μ as the formalization of texture is better in practice.

An important theoretical result about the problem of testing the equivalence of two texture images follows from the decidability of the equivalence of probabilistic finite automata [25]. A probabilistic finite automaton is an automaton in which for every state s and every input symbol a, the probabilities on the outgoing transitions of the state s on input symbol a sum to unity.

Lemma 3 *Every probabilistic finite generator can be simulated by a probabilistic finite automaton.*

Theorem 8 *It is decidable whether two texture images, effectively given as probabilistic finite generators, are equivalent.*

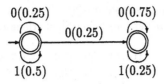

$$0(0.25) \qquad\qquad 0(0.75)$$
$$0(0.25)$$
$$1(0.5) \qquad\qquad 1(0.25)$$

Figure 2: Example of Finite Generator in the Proof of Theorem 13

Proof: The proof follows from Lemma 3 and the decidability of the equivalence problem for probabilistic finite automata [25]. □

Finally, we state the following theorem which says that nondeterminism allows one to define a wider variety of texture images. A deterministic generator below is a probabilistic generator whose underlying finite automaton is deterministic. In a similar way the pumping lemma for regular sets enables us to show proper containment of regular sets in CFL, this following lemma will help us to show the proper containment of texture images defined by deterministic generators in those defined by nondeterministic ones.

Lemma 4 *Let A be a (texture) image defined by a deterministic generator. Then there exists $n \geq 0$, such that by zooming into the window $R(u,v)$ for all possible $(u,v) \in \Sigma^* \times \Sigma^*$, $\mid u \mid = \mid v \mid$ we get at most n distinct (texture) images. Moreover, n can be chosen to be the number of states of the minimal deterministic generator of A.*

Proof: Let $M = (K, \ldots)$ be the minimal deterministic generator of A. Given $(u,v) \in \Sigma^* \times \Sigma^*$, $\mid u \mid = \mid v \mid$, the image obtained by zooming into the window $R(u,v)$ is defined by the deterministic generator obtained from M by replacing its initial state by the one reached by (u,v). Clearly, there are at most $\mid K \mid$ distinct automata obtained this way. □

Theorem 9 *The class of texture images defined by nondeterministic generators is strictly greater than the one defined by deterministic generators.*

Proof: In Fig. 2 an example of a probabilistic nondeterministic finite generator is shown. The texture image defined by it obviously does not satisfy Lemma 4. Thus it cannot be defined by any deterministic generator. □

3.4 Some Examples

Example: Consider the following three rational expressions:

$$\Delta_1 = \{(0,0) + (0,1) + (1,0) + (1,1)\}^*,$$
$$\Delta_2 = \{(0,1) + (1,0)\}^*(0,0)\Delta_1,$$
$$\Delta_3 = \{(0,0) + (1,1)\}^*(1,0)\Delta_1.$$

These expressions represent three simple images X_1, X_2, and X_3, respectively, one being the unit filled square, and the other two being filled triangles:

$$
\begin{aligned}
X_1 &= \{(a,b) \in [0,1]^2 | 0 \leq a, b \leq 1\}, \\
X_2 &= \{(a,b) \in [0,1]^2 | a + b \leq 1\}, \\
X_3 &= \{(a,b) \in [0,1]^2 | a \geq b\}.
\end{aligned}
$$

Example: The Sierpinski Triangle is represented by the rational expression $\{(0,0) + (0,1) + (1,0)\}^*$ over $\Sigma = \{0,1\}$.

Example: In Fig. 3, a self-similar image of diminishing triangles is shown. This image too has a simple rational expression as its representation. Basically, we are placing infinite number of copies of the triangle at the points in the language $\{(0,1) + (1,0)\}^*(0,0)$. The corresponding finite generator is also shown. The probabilities in this generator are chosen in such a way that we obtain a uniform texture.

Example: In Fig. 4, an image with fractal dimension $D = 1.79$ is shown. It is interesting to note that D is exactly between the fractal dimension of Sierpinski Triangle ($D = 1.58$) and that of filled square ($D = 2$). The fractal dimension is computed using the result in [24], according to which it is $\log_2 |\lambda|$, where λ is an eigenvalue, of maximum modulus, of the connection matrix C of the underlying finite automaton (C_{ij} is the number of transitions from state i to state j). In our example, $\lambda = \sqrt{12}$, which gives a dimension of 1.79.

3.5 Inference of Generator for a Given Image

We briefly describe the idea based on which an algorithm to automatically infer a finite generator for a given image can be devised [9]. We will illustrate the idea by considering a "human" approach which can be employed to infer the finite generator shown in Fig. 3(c) for the image of diminishing triangles shown in Fig. 3(a). Denote the image of diminishing triangles by A. Create a state s_0 (which will be the initial state of the resulting finite generator) representing A. Now subdivide the image into four subimages, corresponding to four quadrants. Identify a quadrant by its lower left corner i.e. by (0,0),(0,1),(1,0) and (1,1) (in binary notation). The four subimages are as follows:

B: A filled triangle in quadrant (0,0).
C: Images of diminishing triangles in quadrant (0,1) and (1,0).
D: A totally blank image in quadrant (1,1).

We ignore D as it is totally blank. Since B is not similar to A, an already existing image, we create a new state s_1 for it. We put a transition to s_1 from s_0 labeled (0,0), as B corresponds to quadrant (0,0) of image A. Image C is similar to A, and therefore we do not create any new state for it, and instead have two self-loops at s_0 labeled (0,1) and (1,0). Repeating the above method for image B, results in an image of filled square different from the existing ones (A and B). A new state s_2 is created. Repeating the method once more for s_2, however does not result in any new images, and the algorithm terminates giving us the finite generator as shown in Fig. 3(c).

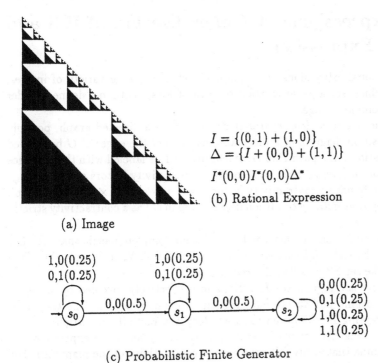

$I = \{(0,1) + (1,0)\}$
$\Delta = \{I + (0,0) + (1,1)\}$

$I^*(0,0)I^*(0,0)\Delta^*$

(b) Rational Expression

(a) Image

1,0(0.25)   1,0(0.25)
0,1(0.25)   0,1(0.25)

0,0(0.25)
0,1(0.25)
1,0(0.25)
1,1(0.25)

0,0(0.5)   0,0(0.5)

s_0 s_1 s_2

(c) Probabilistic Finite Generator

Figure 3: Diminishing Triangles

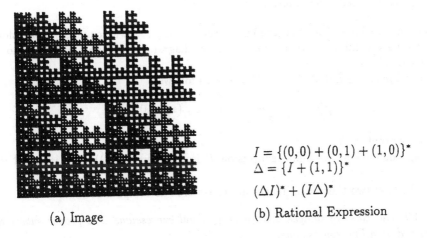

(a) Image

$I = \{(0,0) + (0,1) + (1,0)\}^*$
$\Delta = \{I + (1,1)\}^*$

$(\Delta I)^* + (I\Delta)^*$

(b) Rational Expression

Figure 4: A Variation of Sierpinski Triangle, with fractal dimension $= 1.79$

4 Affine Expressions: A Generalization of IFS and Rational Expressions

Though, IFS and rational expressions are capable of defining a wide variety of images, affine expressions—which are a generalization of both of these methods, define a wider class of much more complex images.

First we define the notion of *loop contractivity*. Let G be a directed graph, possibly representing the transition diagram of a finite automaton. Let the edges of G be labeled with affine transformations. If a path P in G, of length $n \geq 1$, is labeled with the sequence of affine transformations $w_{i_1}, w_{i_2}, \ldots, w_{i_n}$ of respective contractivity factors $s_{i_1}, s_{i_2}, \ldots, s_{i_n}$, then the path P is said to have a contractivity factor of $s = s_{i_1} \times s_{i_2} \times \ldots \times s_{i_n}$. The digraph G is said to satisfy *loop contractivity* condition if every loop in G has a contractivity strictly less than one.

Let $w_1, w_2, \ldots, w_N$ be N affine transformations on some complete metric space X. Let $\Sigma = \{1, 2, \ldots, N\}$ be the *code alphabet*, where symbol $i, 1 \leq i \leq N$, represents the affine transformation w_i. The set Σ^ω is called the *code space*.

An *affine regular set* is a regular set $R \subseteq \Sigma^\omega$, and is effectively specified by an *affine expression*, which is nothing but an ordinary regular expression over Σ. The transition diagram of an FA accepting R is required to satisfy loop contractivity condition.

To justify the following definition of the image defined by an affine expression, we state the following lemma that easily follows from the contractivity of the mappings. For detailed proof see [1].

Lemma 5 *Let $w_1, w_2, \ldots, w_N$ be contractive mappings defined on a complete metric space X. Then, if $w_{i_1}, w_{i_2}, \ldots$ is a sequence of these transformations then for all $x \in X$,*

$$\lim_{j \to \infty} w_{i_1}(w_{i_2}(\ldots(w_{i_j}(x))\ldots))$$

exists and is unique (i.e. independent of x).

This lemma can be extended to the case when $w_{i_1}, w_{i_2}, \ldots$ is a sequence of transformations labeling an infinite path in the transition diagram of an ω-FA satisfying loop contractivity condition [8].

Let $\sigma = \sigma_1 \sigma_2 \sigma_3 \ldots \in \Sigma^\omega$. Define $\varphi : \Sigma^\omega \to X$ as follows

$$\varphi(\sigma) = \lim_{j \to \infty} w_{\sigma_1}(w_{\sigma_2}(\ldots w_{\sigma_j}(x)\ldots))$$

where x is any point in X.

The image defined by an affine expression R is $\varphi(\text{adherence}(R))$, and is called its attractor.

In the following two theorems, images are considered as compact sets.

Theorem 10 *The class of images defined by rational expressions is a proper subset of the one defined by affine expressions.*

Proof: (Outline) We will prove the theorem for 2-D images, defined by rational expressions over binary alphabet. Let R be a rational expression over alphabet $\Sigma = \{0, 1\}$

representing a 2-D image. Consider the four contractive transformations, which map the unit square onto one of the quadrants:

$$w_1(x,y) = (0.5x, 0.5y), \qquad w_2(x,y) = (0.5x, 0.5y + 0.5),$$
$$w_3(x,y) = (0.5x + 0.5, 0.5y), \quad w_4(x,y) = (0.5x + 0.5, 0.5y + 0.5).$$

Let $\Delta = \{1, 2, 3, 4\}$ be the underlying code alphabet. Consider the morphism $h : \Sigma \times \Sigma \to \Delta$, defined as

$$h(0,0) = 1, h(0,1) = 2, h(1,0) = 3 \text{ and } h(1,1) = 4.$$

Now $h(R) \subseteq \Delta^*$ is an affine expression, which defines the same image as the one defined by the rational expression R. For details see [9]. $\qquad \square$

Theorem 11 *The class of images defined by* IFS *method is a proper subset of the one defined by affine expressions.*

Proof: Let $\{X; w_1, w_2, \ldots, w_N\}$ be an IFS. In [1] it is shown that $\varphi(\Sigma^\omega)$ is the attractor of the IFS, where Σ is the underlying code alphabet. Therefore, the affine expression Σ^*, whose adherence is Σ^ω, defines the same image as defined by the given IFS. $\qquad \square$

5 Probabilistic Affine Automata

In Barnsley's Chaos Game Algorithm, in each iteration, the next affine transformation to be applied on the last generated point is chosen from the same fixed set of affine transformations. Moreover, the probability of choosing a particular transformation is always the same in each iteration. A significant improvement can be made on this algorithm, in terms of its capacity to generate images, by changing this set of transformations and the associated probabilities, on each iterative step.

One can therefore think of employing a finite automaton, whose finite control determines the set of transformations and the associated probabilities for each iterative step. Furthermore, one may mark a subset of the states of the automaton as "final" or "display" states, and display only the points generated at these states. One would expect this to give additional power to generate images, but in [8] it is shown later that this division of states into final and non-final states is really not essential. The above idea to generalize the Chaos Game Algorithm is formalized in the definition of probabilistic affine automata.

A *probabilistic affine automaton*(PAA) is a 6-tuple $M = (X, S, \Sigma, \delta, P, F)$, where X is a complete metric space, $Q = \{q_1, q_2, \ldots, q_n\}$ is the set of *states*, Σ is a finite set of affine transformations $w_i : X \to X$, for $i = 1, 2, \ldots, m$, $\delta : Q \times \Sigma \to Q$ is the *state transition function*, such that the loop contractivity is satisfied and the underlying transition diagram is strongly connected, P is an $n \times m \times n$ stochastic matrix such that for each i, $\sum_{k=1}^{n} \sum_{j=1}^{m} P(i, j, k) = 1$, and $F \subseteq Q$ is the set of final states.

The value $P(i, j, k)$ is the probability of the transition from the state q_i to the state q_k by transformation w_j. Note that probabilities of outgoing transitions for each state sum to unity. In other words, a PAA is a probabilistic finite generator whose input alphabet is a set of affine transformations, and which satisfies conditions of strong connectivity and loop contractivity.

A PAA M generates an image on the basis of the following algorithm, which is a generalization of the Chaos Game Algorithm. A point in X is randomly chosen, call it x_0. Any state of M can be randomly chosen to be the initial state. The PAA then generates a *sequence* of points just like in Chaos Game algorithm, the only difference being that at any step, one of the outgoing transitions of the current state of the PAA is chosen according to the associated probabilities, and the affine transformation labeling the chosen transition is applied to the last generated point. The finite control of M then changes its current state and the point is displayed if this new current state is a final state. In other words, if q is the current state and x is the last generated point and if the transition $\delta(q, w) = p$ is chosen, then $w(x)$ is the next point generated, and it is considered to be in the image generated by M if p is a final state.

This process yields a limiting sequence of points, say $S_0 = \{x_0, x_1, x_2, \ldots\}$ generated at final states. This set of points so generated is an approximation to the attractor of the given PAA, denoted by $A(M)$.

To be mathematically precise, a point is in $A(M)$ iff its every neighborhood is visited infinitely many times with almost one probability during the execution of the algorithm. Therefore, if $B(x, \epsilon)$ denotes the closed ball of radius ϵ with center at x,

$$B(x, \epsilon) = \{y \in X | d(x, y) \le \epsilon\},$$

then,

$$A(M) = \{x \in X | \forall \epsilon > 0, \delta > 0, \text{ a point } y \in B(x, \epsilon) \text{ is generated with probability } 1 - \delta\}.$$

In [1], the texture of an image generated by an IFS is defined to be a measure on Borel subsets of X. Mathematically, the set of Borel subsets $\mathcal{B}$ is the σ-field generated by the open subsets of X, and applying the Boolean operations of complementation and countable union, till no more new sets could be added.

A measure on Borel subsets is a real non-negative function $\mu : \mathcal{B} \to [0, \infty)$ such that it is additive on a countable union of pair-wise disjoint Borel sets. We extend this definition of the texture of images to PAA as follows. For details see [1]. Let B be a Borel subset of X. Let $\{x_0, x_1, x_2, \ldots\}$ be a sequence of points generated by a PAA M. Define

$$\mathcal{N}(B, n) = \text{ number of points in } \{x_0, x_1, \ldots, x_n\} \cap B, \text{ for } n = 0, 1, 2, \ldots.$$

Then, with probability one,

$$\mu(B) = \lim_{n \to \infty} \{\mathcal{N}(B, n)/(n + 1)\},$$

for all starting points x_0.

Informally, $\mu(B)$ is the "mass" of B, which is the proportion of iteration steps, when running the Chaos Game Algorithm on M, which produce points in B. Points "fall" at different subsets of X, according to the probabilities on the transitions, and this notion is mathematically formalized in the definition of the texture of an image as a measure.

Therefore, the image defined by a PAA M can be viewed as either as a compact set or as a measure. The result connecting these two definitions, which says the support of the measure defined by an IFS is precisely the compact set defined by the same IFS (see [1]), also holds for PAA.

It is an easy observation that IFS are special case of PAA.

Lemma 6 *Let* $\{X; w_1, w_2, \ldots, w_n\}$ *be an IFS with probabilities* $p_i. 1 \leq i \leq n$. *Then there exists an equivalent PAA defining the same image (both as compact set and measure).*

Proof: The proof follows from the simple observation that an IFS can be implemented by a single-state PAA. The equivalent PAA has one state, which is the only initial as well as final state, with n self-loops as transitions, the i-th transition being labelled with the transformation w_i and probability p_i, for i from 1 to n. This PAA is not only equivalent to the given IFS in terms of the equivalence of their attractors, but also in terms of the texture of the image. □

Now, we show that PAA are closed under invertible affine transformations.

Theorem 12 *The family of images (as compact sets) generated by PAA is closed under invertible affine transformations.*

Proof: Let $M = (X, Q, \Sigma, \delta, P, \rho, F)$, where $\Sigma = \{w_1, w_2, \ldots, w_n\}$, be a PAA and τ an invertible affine transformation. We construct a PAA $M' = (X.Q, \Sigma', \delta, P, \rho, F)$, where $\Sigma' = \{w'_1, w'_2, \ldots, w'_n\}$ with $w'_i = \tau \circ w_i \circ \tau^{-1}$. Now, let $x_0, x_1, x_2, \ldots$ be a sequence generated by M, and let $y_i = \tau(x_i)$ for $i \geq 0$. If $x_{i+1} = w_{j_i}(x_i)$, then $y_{i+1} = \tau(w_{j_i}(\tau^{-1}(y_i))) = \tau(x_{i+1})$ for all $i \geq 0$. Therefore the sequence $y_0, y_1, y_2, \ldots$ can be generated by M' and consequently $A(M') = \tau(A(M))$. □

Theorem 12 is valid also for images as measures assuming natural extension of transformations to measures.

6 Mutually Recursive IFS

In this section, we describe another generalization of IFS, which turns out to be exactly equivalent to PAA and Affine Expressions.

6.1 Deterministic mutually recursive IFS

A *Deterministic mutually recursive* IFS (DMRIFS) M, as studied in [8,20], defines an image on the basis of an algorithm which can be viewed as a generalization of the Deterministic Algorithm for IFS. This generalized algorithm works as follows: Initially, n compact sets $S_i^0 \subseteq X, 1 \leq i \leq n$ are chosen, where $n \geq 1$. (In the case when $n = 1$, a DMRIFS works exactly like IFS.) Each of these n sets is computed from some other sets, in a mutually recursive fashion. In each iterative step of the algorithm, the new sets are computed from the old sets as *unions* of images of the old sets under affine transformations. To be precise, if for some $i, 1 \leq i \leq n$, the *variable* (or set) S_i is defined in terms of, say r, other variables, then S_i is computed iteratively according to the mutually recursive formula of the form

$$S_i^m = w_{i_1}(S_{j_1}^{m-1}) \cup w_{i_2}(S_{j_2}^{m-1}) \cup \ldots \cup w_{i_r}(S_{j_r}^{m-1})$$

where the superscript m indicates the number of the iterative step. There are n such mutually recursive formulas. From this mutually recursive definition, one computes successively S_i^m's, for each $i, 1 \leq i \leq n$, and for iterations $m = 1, 2, 3, \ldots$.

A DMRIFS is required to satisfy loop contractivity (in the following sense) to ensure the existence of a unique attractor. A DMRIFS specified by n mutually recursive definitions can be represented by a digraph having n states and with labels on the edges. Denote the nodes (states) by $s_1, s_2, \ldots, s_n$. For the recursive formula

$$S_i^m = w_{i_1}(S_{j_1}^{m-1}) \cup w_{i_2}(S_{j_2}^{m-1}) \cup \ldots \cup w_{i_r}(S_{j_r}^{m-1})$$

there are r incoming transitions to the node s_i from nodes $s_{j_1}, s_{j_2}, \ldots, s_{j_r}$ labeled with affine transformations $w_{i_1}, w_{i_2}, \ldots, w_{i_r}$ respectively. Note that the set $\{s_i | S_i \in F\}$ is the set of *final* states.

A DMRIFS satisfies loop contractivity iff its underlying digraph satisfies loop contractivity.

A subset F of $\{S_1, S_2, \ldots, S_n\}$ denoting "final" or "display" variables specifies which of the variables $S_1, S_2, \ldots, S_n$ will define the attractor of the given DMRIFS M. Formally, the attractor of M, denoted by $A(M)$, is defined to be

$$A(M) = \lim_{m \to \infty} \bigcup_{S_i \in F} S_i^m.$$

Alternatively, we can characterize the attractor of a DMRIFS as a fixed point. We can define a mapping $W : \mathcal{K}(X^n) \to \mathcal{K}(X^n)$ such that

$$W((S_1^{m-1}, S_2^{m-1}, \ldots, S_n^{m-1})) = (S_1^m, S_2^m, \ldots, S_n^m).$$

Let $(S_1, S_2, \ldots, S_n)$ be the fixed point of W (whose existence follows from loop contractivity). Then, the attractor of the DMRIFS M can be specified in terms of this fixed point

$$A(M) = \bigcup_{S_i \in F} S_i.$$

6.2   Probabilistic Mutually Recursive IFS

Suppose for every mutually recursive formula of a DMRIFS

$$S_i^m = w_{i_1}(S_{j_1}^{m-1}) \cup w_{i_2}(S_{j_2}^{m-1}) \cup \ldots \cup w_{i_r}(S_{j_r}^{m-1})$$

we associate r probabilities $p_{i_1}, p_{i_2}, \ldots, p_{i_r}$, such that $\sum_{k=1}^{r} p_{i_r} = 1$. That is, we specify the weight of the contribution that each of S_{j_k}'s makes in the computation of S_i. In other words, we assign probabilities to the edges of the digraph representing the DMRIFS, such that probabilities assigned to incoming edges for each state sum to unity. (Note that in the case of PAA, the probabilities of *outgoing* transitions summed to unity.) Such a mutually recursive IFS is called a *probabilistic mutually recursive* IFS (PMRIFS).

The attractor of a PMRIFS M can be computed by the following algorithm which is a generalization of the Chaos Game Algorithm on IFS: Initially, n points $x_1^0, x_2^0, \ldots, x_n^0$ in X are chosen randomly. Consider the point x_i^0 to be associated with the state s_i. At each step of the algorithm, each state chooses one of the incoming transitions according to the assigned probabilities. Let, for $1 \leq i \leq n$, the state s_i choose an incoming transition from state s_{j_i} labeled with transformation w_{j_i}. Then, we have

$$x_i^m = w_{j_i}(x_{j_i}^{m-1}), m = 1, 2, 3, \ldots.$$

The collection of points $\cup_{s_i \in F}\{x_i^m\}_{m=0}^{\infty}$ defines the attractor $A(M)$ of the PMRIFS M.

A probabilistic MRIFS defines, in addition to the final attractor, a texture of the image which is determined by the probabilities. This texture is formalized as a mathematical measure, in exactly the same way as for PAA. However, just like IFS, the class of attractors defined by probabilistic MRIFS is same as that defined by deterministic MRIFS.

Theorem 13 DMRIFS *and* PMRIFS *define the same class of images (as compact sets).*

Therefore, from now onwards we will refer to both jointly as MRIFS.

6.3   Equivalence of Affine Expressions, PAA and MRIFS

Interestingly, all the above generalizations of IFS i.e. Affine Expressions, PAA and MRIFS are equivalent in their power to define images (as compact sets). For detailed proof of this claim see [8].

Theorem 14 *Affine expressions,* PAA *and* MRIFS *define the same class of images (as compact sets).*

Proof: Let M be an FA accepting an affine expression R. Note that every state of M has an outgoing transition and there is no need of specifying final states, as the image is defined in terms of the adherence of R, which is the set of limit points of prefixes of words in R. Construct a PMRIFS M' from M as follows. Reverse the directions of the transitions of M and make the initial state of M a final state of M'. Now when we generate the image by running the generalized Chaos Game Algorithm on M', initially we may generate some "stray" points, but soon the generated points get "close" to the attractor and remain so. This follows from Lemma 5. Furthermore, we apply longer and longer sequences of affine transformations on the points stored in the states of M' i.e. starting with some point stored in some state we possibly follow a path in the graph of M', and apply the sequence of affine transformations labeling the path. Consider the reversal of all such finite sequences ending in the final state of M'. Now, each of these reversed sequences is a prefix of some ω-word in adherence(R). Since, each finite path of of M' will be (probabilistically) followed, the adherence of the reversal of these finite sequences (or subwords over code alphabet) is precisely the adherence of R. Therefore, for every $\sigma \in$ adherence(R), its longer and longer prefixes will be applied to some points in the underlying metric space. From Lemma 5, every neighborhood of $\varphi(\sigma)$ will be visited, and applying longer and longer prefixes means visiting smaller and smaller neighborhoods. In this sense, the points generated by M' at its final state are an approximation to the attractor of $R = L(M)$.

On the other hand, if M is a PMRIFS, then construct an FA M' by reversing the directions of the transitions, creating a new initial state which has ϵ-transitions to every final state of M. Then, essentially by the same argument as above, we see that $\sigma \in$ adherence($L(M')$) iff longer and longer prefixes of σ will be (probabilistically) applied, while executing the Chaos Game Algorithm on M, which means visiting smaller and smaller neighborhoods of $\varphi(\sigma)$.

The equivalence of PAA and PMRIFS follows from a similar argument. First note that since for every PMRIFS M there exists an equivalent strongly connected PMRIFS

M' (see [8]), we need to consider only strongly connected PMRIFS. Let M be a PAA (or a PMRIFS). Now, irrespective of whether M is viewed as a PAA or a PMRIFS, the set of finite sequences of affine transformations labeling the paths of M, which are probabilistically traversed while executing the generalized Chaos Game Algorithm on M, is same. Therefore, in both cases, points are generated which approximate the same attractor.   □

Example: As an example illustrating the power of PAA to describe natural objects, see Fig. 5(d) for the generation of a fern. The fern is generated by the PAA shown in Fig. 5(a), in which both the states are possible initial and final states. The numbers in parenthesis are the probabilities. The four affine transformations are the same as given in the last example in Section 3 on IFS, which generated the fern shown in Fig. 1(b). Denote the set of points generated at states s_1 and s_2 by S_1 and S_2, respectively. The sets S_1 and S_2 are shown in Fig. 5(b) and (c), respectively. The attractor is the union of these two sets. Note that the branches of this fern are one-sided. This fern cannot be generated by an IFS. It is possible to generate a "self-similar" fern by an IFS, which has two-sided branches, as shown in Fig. 1(b).

This fern is also defined by an affine expression over code alphabet $\Sigma = \{1, 2, 3, 4\}$, representing the four affine transformations defined above. The affine expression is

$$((1+2)^*3(1+2)^*4)^* + ((1+2)^*4(1+2)^*3)^*.$$

Alternatively, this fern is the attractor of the DMRIFS M

$$S_1^m = w_1(S_1^{m-1}) \cup w_2(S_1^{m-1}) \cup w_4(S_2^{m-1}),$$
$$S_2^m = w_3(S_1^{m-1}) \cup w_1(S_2^{m-1}) \cup w_2(S_2^{m-1}).$$

Let (S_1, S_2) be the fixed point (attractor) of M. The sets S_1 and S_2 are shown in Fig. 5(b) and (c), respectively. The attractor is the union of these two sets. Finally, note that the diagram in Fig. 5(a), also represents a PMRIFS generating the same image, as the requirement that incoming probabilities should sum to unity is satisfied.   □

Example: For another example, see Fig. 5(e) which shows a complex "recursive" image of a tree along with its "shadow." There is a mirror hanging from one of the branches which contains infinitely deep images of the whole image. This image is generated by a six-state PAA. To give the reader an idea how this image is generated, we mention that if a part of an image is generated at a state, say s, then we can create a "shadow" of this part by transiting to a state, say r, where the transition is labeled with an appropriate affine transformation w, which rotates and scales down the part of the image created at the state s. As a programming trick, we then go back to the state s from the state r, by a transition labeled with transformation w^{-1}.   □

7   L-Systems and MRIFS

In this section, we consider another approach to generate fractals, based on L-systems or string rewriting systems, which have been incorporated for applications in computer graphics [21,23]. We show its relationship to MRIFS with the help of two examples. For details see [10].

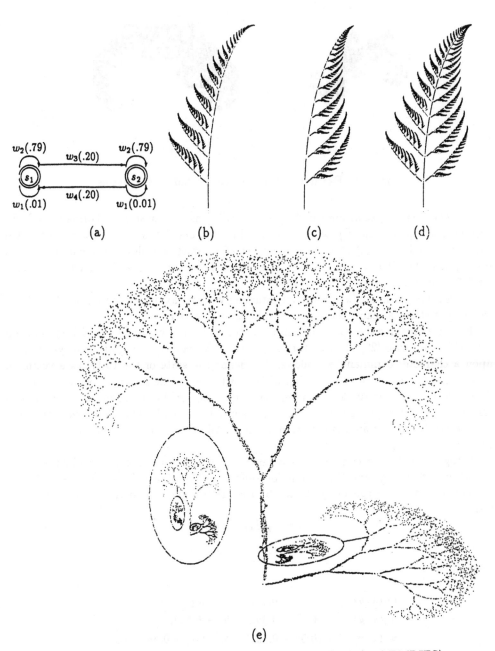

(a) (b) (c) (d)

(e)

Figure 5: Examples of Images Generated by PAA (and PMRIFS)

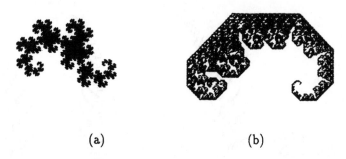

(a) (b)

Figure 6: Examples of Images Generated by L-systems

We consider a special kind of L-systems, called as D0L-systems. Formally, a D0L-system is a triplet (Σ, ω, P), where Σ is an alphabet, $\omega \in \Sigma^*$ is a nonempty word called the axiom and $P \subset \Sigma^* \times \Sigma^*$ is a finite set of production rules. If a pair (c, s) is a production, then it is written as $c \rightarrow s$. For each letter $c \in \Sigma$ there is exactly one word $s \in \Sigma^*$ such that $c \rightarrow s$.

A D0L-system is applied iteratively starting with its axiom as the initial string, and the output string at each iteration is graphically *interpreted*.

First we consider the approach taken by Prusinkiewicz who interpreted L-systems on a LOGO-like turtle [22]. In this turtle approach, the output string of an L-system acts upon a character command as follows. We define the state of the turtle as a vector of three numbers denoting the position of the turtle (x-position and y-position) and the direction in which the turtle is heading (an angle). Let $'F'$ be the command to move one step forward in the present direction and draw the line, and $'+' ('-')$ be the command to turn right (left) by an angle δ given a priori. All other commands are ignored by the turtle.

Using this approach *Dragon curve* is generated by the D0L-system, given by the axiom "X", the angle $\delta = \frac{\pi}{2}$, and the production rules $X \rightarrow X + YF+, Y \rightarrow -FX - Y$.

This fractal curve can be generated by the MRIFS given by mutually recursive definitions

$$S_1 = w_1(S_1) \cup w_4(S_2),$$
$$S_2 = w_2(S_1) \cup w_3(S_2),$$

where

$$
\begin{aligned}
w_1(x, y) &= (0.5x - 0.5y, 0.5x + 0.5y), \\
w_2(x, y) &= (0.5x + 0.5y, -0.5x + 0.5y), \\
w_3(x, y) &= (0.5x + 0.5y + 0.5, -0.5x + 0.5y + 0.5), \\
w_4(x, y) &= (0.5x - 0.5y + 0.5, 0.5x + 0.5y - 0.5),
\end{aligned}
$$

and only S_1 is the final variable. Both S_1 and S_2 are initialized to a horizontal line of unit length, from the origin to the 2-D point (1,0). The output of the above DMRIFS after 14 iterations is shown in Fig. 6(a).

In another approach, Dekking studied the limiting properties of curves generated by L-systems and concentrated on the problem of determining the fractal dimension of the limit set, which he called as "recurrent" set [12,13]. Here we consider one of his graphical interpretations of the the output string of a D0L-system, and explain it using turtle geometry. Each character c in the alphabet represents a vector $(\Delta x, \Delta y)$ and is a command to the turtle to change its current position (x, y) to $(x + \Delta x, y + \Delta y)$.

Using this approach, he has given an example of an interesting spiral curve in [13], given by the D0L-system

$$a \rightarrow abb, b \rightarrow bc, c \rightarrow cd, d \rightarrow dac,$$

where a is the axiom, and the vectors represented by a, b, c and d are $(2, 0), (0, 1), (-1, 0)$ and $(0, -1)$, respectively.

This spiral can be generated by the following MRIFS given by

$$\begin{aligned}
S_1 &= w_1(S_1) \cup w_2(S_2) \cup w_3(S_2), \\
S_2 &= w_1(S_2) \cup w_4(S_3), \\
S_3 &= w_1(S_3) \cup w_4(S_4), \\
S_4 &= w_6(S_1) \cup w_5(S_3) \cup w_1(S_4),
\end{aligned}$$

where

$$\begin{aligned}
w_1(x, y) &= (0.5x + 0.5y + 0.5, -0.5x + 0.5y + 0.5), \\
w_2(x, y) &= (0.25x - 0.25y + 0.25, 0.25x + 0.25y + 0.25), \\
w_3(x, y) &= (0.25x - 0.25y, 0.25x + 0.25y), \\
w_4(x, y) &= (0.5x - 0.5y, 0.5x + 0.5y), \\
w_5(x, y) &= (-0.25x + 0.25y, -0.25x + 0.25y), \\
w_6(x, y) &= (x - y - 0.5, x + y - 0.5),
\end{aligned}$$

and only S_1 is the final variable. Moreover, the Deterministic Algorithm on this MRIFS, in which each of the variables is initialized to a horizontal line from $(0,0)$ to $(1,0)$, simulates the D0L-system iteration by iteration. The output of the above DMRIFS after 14 iterations is shown in Fig. 6(b).

This implementation of D0L-systems with MRIFS is possible under only certain conditions, namely when the variables "grow" at uniform linear rate and angles between vectors representing the characters are correctly preserved. For details see [10].

8   Conclusions

We surveyed recently developed methods to generate deterministic fractals and other images, namely Iterative Function Systems, Finite Generators and Mutually Recursive IFS. We also considered the method based on L-systems, and showed that some of its examples can be implemented by MRIFS.

These methods are of great practical importance as they provide an elegant mechanism to drastically compress images and possibly other forms of data. Therefore, the problem of efficiently infering an IFS or a finite generator or an MRIFS, from a given image is important.

For finite generators, an image can be first encoded as a quad-tree from which a finite generator which defines approximately the given image can be infered [9].

For IFS, Barnsley's Collage Thorem provides the mathematical basis for automatically infering the IFS "code" of a given image [1]. It states that given an image B in $\mathcal{K}(X)$, if an IFS with the contraction mapping W is chosen, and for some $\epsilon > 0$

$$h(B, W(B)) \leq \epsilon$$

then

$$h(B, A) \leq \frac{\epsilon}{1 - s},$$

where A is the attractor of the IFS, and s is the contractivity factor of W.

The theorem can be generalized to the case when we want to infer an MRIFS from a given image [8]. This provides the basis of an interactive trial-and-error method of coming up with an MRIFS for a given image on a computer screen, in which the user "guesses" an MRIFS, whose one iterative step when applied to the image results in an image which is quite "close" to the original image. The Collage Theorem then guarantees that the attractor of the MRIFS will be also quite "close" to the given image.

References

[1] M. F. Barnsley, *Fractals Everywhere*, Academic Press, 1988.

[2] M. F. Barnsley, J. H. Elton and D. P. Hardin, "Recurrent Iterated Function Systems," *Constructive Approximation*, **5** 3-31 (1989).

[3] M. F. Barnsley, A. Jacquin, L. Reuter and A. D. Sloan, "Harnessing Chaos for Image Synthesis," *Computer Graphics*, SIGGARPH 1988 Conference Proceedings.

[4] M. F. Barnsley, R. L. Devaney, B. B. Mandelbrot, H-O. Peitgen, De Saupe, and R. F. Voss, *Science of Fractal Images*, Springer-Verlag, 1988.

[5] J. Berstel and M. Morcrette, "Compact Representation of Patterns by Finite Automata," Proceedings Pixim'89, Paris, pp. 387-402.

[6] L. Boasson and M. Nivat, "Adherences of Languages," *Jour. of Computer. Syst. Sci.*, **20**, 285-309 (1980).

[7] R. Cohen and A. Gold, "Theory of ω-languages," Part I and II, *Jour. of Computer Syst. Sc.*, **15**, 169-208 (1977).

[8] K. Culik and S. Dube, "Image Synthesis using Affine Automata," Technical Report TR90004, Dept. of Computer Science, Univ. of S. Carolina.

[9] K. Culik and S. Dube, "Image Synthesis using Rational Expressions," Technical Report TR90001, Dept. of Computer Science, Univ. of S. Carolina.

[10] K. Culik and S. Dube, "L-systems and IFS", under preparation.

[11] K. Culik and S. Yu, "Cellular Automata, $\omega\omega$-Regular Sets, and Sofic Systems," to appear in *Discrete Applied Mathematics*.

[12] F. M. Dekking, "Recurrent Sets," *Advances in Mathematics*, **44**, 78-104 (1982).

[13] F. M. Dekking, "Recurrent Sets: A Fractal Formalism," Report 82-32, Delft University of Technology, 1982.

[14] D. B. Ellis and M. G. Branton, "Non-Self-Similar Attractors of Hyberbolic IFS," in: J. C. Alexander (Ed.), *Dynamical Systems*, Lecture Notes in Mathematics 1342, pp. 158-171, Springer-Verlag, 1988.

[15] S. Even, "Rational Numbers and Regular Events," *IEEE Transactions on Electronic Computers*, **EC-13**, No. 6, 740-741 (1964).

[16] J.Gleick, *Chaos–Making a New Science*, Penguin Books, 1988.

[17] J. Hartmanis and R. E. Stearns, "Sets of Numbers Defined By Finite Automata," *American Mathematical Monthly*, **74** 539-542 (1967).

[18] G. M. Hunter and K. Steiglitz, "Operations on Images Using Quadtrees," *IEEE Trans. on Pattern Analysis and Machine Intell.*, **1** 145-153 (1979).

[19] B. Mandelbrot, *The Fractal Geometry of Nature*, W. H. Freeman and Co., San Francisco, 1982.

[20] Y. Liu, "Recurrent IFS, ω-orbit Finite Automata, and Regular Set Plotter," M.S. Thesis, Dept. of Comp. Sci., Univ. of S. Carolina, 1990.

[21] P. Prusinkiewicz, "Applications of L-systems to Computer Imagery," in H. Ehrig, M. Nagl, A. Rosenfeld, and G. Rozenberg, editors, *Graph grammars and their application to computer science; Third International Workshop*, pages 534-548, Springer-Verlag, Berlin, 1987. Lecture Notes in Computer Science 291.

[22] P. Prusinkiewicz, "Graphical Applications of L-systems," Proceedings of Graphics Interface'86—Vision Interface'86, 247-253 (1986).

[23] A. R. Smith, "Plants, Fractals, and Formal Languages," *Computer Graphics*, **18**, 1-10 (1984).

[24] L. Staiger, "Quadtrees and the Hausdorff Dimension of Pictures," Workshop on Geometrical Problems of Image Processing, Georgenthal GDR, 173-178 (1989).

[25] W. G. Tzeng, "The Equivalence and Learning of Probabilistic Automata," *FOCS proceedings*, 268-273 (1989).

Part II
Invited Lectures

Optimum Simulation of Meshes by Small Hypercubes

Bin Cong[1], Zevi Miller[2], and I. H. Sudborough[1]

(1) Computer Science Program, University of Texas at Dallas,
Richardson, TX 75083-0688

(2) Department of Mathematics, Miami University, Oxford,
Ohio 45056

Abstract

We consider optimum simulations of large mesh networks by hypercubes. For any arbitrary mesh M, let "M's optimum hypercube" be the smallest hypercube that has at least as many processors as M and, for any $k>0$, let $Q(M/2^k)$ be "M's $1/2^k$-size hypercube", which has $1/2^k$ as many processors as M's optimum hypercube. The ratio $M/Q(M/2^k)$ is called *M's $1/2^k$- density*. We show that (a) for every 2-D mesh M, if M's 1/2-density$\leq$1.828, then M can be embedded into its 1/2-size hypercube with dilation 1 and load factor 2, (b) for every 2-D mesh M, if M's 1/4-density$\leq$3.809, then M can be embedded into its 1/4-size hypercube with dilation 1 and load factor 4, and if M's 1/4-density$\leq$2.8125, then M can be embedded into its 1/4-size hypercube with dilation 1 and load factor 3, (c) If every 2-D mesh M with $1/2^{k_1}$-density$\leq a$ can be embedded into its $1/2^{k_1}$-size hypercube with dilation 1 and load factor l_1, and every 2-D mesh M with $1/2^{k_2}$-density $\leq b$ can be embedded into its $1/2^{k_2}$-size hypercube with dilation 1 and load factor l_2, then we can obtain the densities for load factor $l_1 + l_2$ and load factor $l_1 \times l_2$ based on a, b.

1. Introduction

This work is a continuation of work in [MS], which showed that every two dimensional mesh M can be embedded into its $1/2^k$-size hypercube with dilation 1 and load factor $2^k + 1$. The *dilation* of an embedding f from a graph G (guest) into a graph H (host) is the maximum over all adjacent vertices x and y in G of the distance between f(x) and f(y). The *load factor* of an embedding f is the maximum number of vertices of G that are mapped to the same host vertex. Their result [MS] tells us that when embedding meshes into hypercubes not only adjacencies can be preserved, but also a nearly even distribution of guest points to hypercube processors can be obtained.

However there is still a considerable gap between the results in [MS] and optimum results. For example, using the techniques in [MS] one needs load factor 5 to embed the mesh 25×7 into its ¼-size hypercube, Q(6). But the optimal load factor is

3, since its 1/4-density=$\frac{25\times7}{|Q(6)|}=\frac{175}{64}$ is less than 3. Here we show that the optimum can often be achieved.

We do not know if the optimum can always be achieved. For example, we do not know if the 7×73 mesh, which has 511 points, can be embedded into its 1/2-size hypercube Q(8), which has 256 points, with load factor 2 and dilation 1. However, we can embed the 7×72 mesh, which has 504 points, into its 1/2-size hypercube Q(8) with load factor 2 and dilation 1.

The principal technique used in [MS] is *uniform braiding* , which is a dilation 1, load factor f, for some fixed integer f, embedding of a mesh M onto the vertices of a mesh type subgraph H of a hypercube. Moreover, it has the property that each row is assigned points left-to-right across the columns of H in such a way that load factor f is uniformly obtained. The process is illustrated in Figure 1.1a, where 5 rows are braided onto a representation of a hypercube as a structure with 4 rows (we call the rows of the hypercube structure H *rods* to distinguish them from rows of the mesh). This braiding has cycle length 5, as after 5 columns the rows have all switched rods 3 times and are in the same position relative to each other as they were at the beginning. Therefore, each row of the mesh has 8 of its points embedded per cycle.

Observe how a braiding, such as the one described in Figure 1.1a, yields an embedding of any 5 row mesh into a hypercube. Successive rods are given successive binary string labels that will be a prefix of each hypercube address for the points along the rod. The successive columns along the rods are also given successive binary string labels, say by a binary reflected Gray code. The hypercube address of a mesh point assigned to the third column of a second rod is the product of the prefix used to name the second rod with the binary string naming the third column.

In this paper, a nonuniform braiding technique is developed. This process is illustrated in Figure 1.2, where 13 rows are braided onto 8 rods. One should observe that nearly every point has load factor 2. However, three points received only one guest. This yields an embedding of a 13 row mesh into a hypercube in the same manner as the previously described uniform braiding. Combining uniform and nonuniform braiding techniques we achieve optimum embeddings for both dilation and load factor.

In the next section, we state some general braiding results from [MS]. In section 3, we describe results based on 1/2- and 1/4-densities. We discuss a general $1/2^k$-density theorem in Section 4.

2. Basic Results about Braiding from [MS]

Fact 1 : For all $k>0$, a mesh with 2^k+1 rows can be braided onto 2^k rods with dilation 1 and uniform load factor 2.

Fact 2 : For all $k>0$, if $k=2^i \times p+1$, for some $i>0$ and some p, then a mesh with k rows can be braided onto 2^i rods with dilation 1 and uniform load factor $p+1$.

Fact 3 : If one can braid k rows on a set of rods with dilation 1 and load factor f, then one can braid, for any $i>0$, $k \times 2^i$ rows onto a set of rods with dilation 1 and load factor f.

Fact 4 (Product Theorem) : If k_1 rows can be braided on 2^{t_1} rods with dilation 1 and load factor f_1, and k_2 rows can be braided on 2^{t_2} rods with dilation 1 and load factor f_2, then $m= k_1 \times k_2$ rows can be braided on $2^{t_1+t_2}$ rods with dilation 1 and load factor $f_1 \times f_2$.

One should be aware of a possible *offset* problem when using the product theorem to embed a fixed mesh into a fixed size hypercube.

With the help of these general braiding results and braidings obtained by more exhaustive means, we obtain Table 2.1, it describes our current state of knowledge about uniform braidings.

3. Optimum Embeddings Based on Bounds of 1/2- and 1/4-densities

Theorem 3.1 (1/2-density theorem): If M is a 2-D mesh with 1/2-density at most 1.828, then M can be embedded into its 1/2-size hypercube with dilation 1 and load factor 2.

Proof : Let M be a mesh with m rows and any number of columns. We consider cases based on the ratio of m to $2^{\lfloor \log m \rfloor}$, i.e. $R = \frac{m}{2^{\lfloor \log m \rfloor}}$. Note that R must be in the interval between 1 and 2. We subdivide this interval into subintervals, [8/8, 9/8], [9/8, 10/8], ..., [15/8, 16/8]. In fact, we may further split some subintervals, for example, in this proof, [10/8, 11/8] is subdivided further into the subintervals [20/16, 21/16] and [21/16, 22/16]. If R is in the interval [k/8, k+1/8] where $1 \leq k \leq 15$, then we use a braiding of k+1 rows on 8 rods with load factor 2 and dilation 1. For each braiding used we consider the *average load factor*, A. In every case, as long as A, after a row is deleted, is greater or equal to 1.828 (the stated bound on 1/2-density), the braiding pattern produces the desired embedding. This is so, since A times the number of mesh points gives a lower bound on the number of mesh points embedded. For example, if we have the mesh 21×89, which has 1/2-density < 1.826, the ratio of the number of rows to the next smaller power of 2, which we call R, is 21/16=1.325 ∈ [10/8, 11/8]. We describe in Case (6b) a dilation 1, load factor 2 embedding of a 21×3 mesh into Q(5). Therefore, by partitioning Q(10) into thirty two copies of Q(5) and embedding three successive columns of the 21×89 mesh into each successive copies of Q(5), we get an embedding of the 21×89 mesh into Q(10). Actually, as the reader can easily verify, this process actually embeds the larger 21×96 mesh into Q(10) with dilation 1 and load factor 2. (Whether the 21×97 mesh can be embedded into Q(10) with dilation 1 and load factor 2 is an open question.)

Case (1) : $15/8 \leq R \leq 16/8$.

One braids 2 rows per rod with load factor 2. The rows do not switch from one rod to another, as other rods may have 2 rows already. This gives uniform load factor 2 when there are twice as many rows as rods, but when the ratio is its minimum value, i.e. R=15/8, A is 15/8=1.875. However, this is greater then 1.828.

Case (2) : $14/8 \leq R \leq 15/8$.

Let's consider a 15×17 mesh. Since we already know how to braid 17 rows onto 16 rods with dilation 1 and uniform load factor 2 by Fact 1, one can embed a 15×17 mesh into Q(7). Then one can partition the mesh M into a group of 15×17 submeshes and embed each of them into a copy of Q(7). That is, since any hypercube Q(m), m>7, can be partitioned into some number of Q(7)'s, one obtains an embedding with dilation 1 and load factor 2. Since Q(7) has 128 points, after a row is deleted, A is $\frac{15 \times 17 - 17}{128}$, which is 1.86 and greater than 1.828.

Case (3) : $13/8 \leq R \leq 14/8$.

In this case, we consider the 14×9 mesh. By Fact 1, 9 rows can be braided onto 8 rods with dilation 1 and uniform load factor 2. So, the 9×14 mesh can be embedded into Q(6). This braiding pattern yields an embedding as in case (2). After a row is deleted, A is $\frac{14 \times 9 - 9}{64}$, which is greater than 1.828.

Case (4) : $12/8 \leq R \leq 13/8$.

To achieve the desired density, we divide the interval [12/8, 13/8] into 2 subintervals [24/16, 25/16] and [25/16, 26/16].

Case (4a) : $25/16 \leq R \leq 26/16$.

We know how to braid 13 rows onto 8 rods with dilation 1 and nonuniform load factor 2 (see Figure 1.2), this means one can also braid 26 rows onto 16 rods with load factor 2 and dilation 1 by doubling the 13 row braiding. This braiding has cycle length 5, and after 5 columns the rows have all switched rods exactly 1 time and are in the same position relative to each other as they were at the beginning. The braiding has load factor 2 except for 4 nodes which have load factor 1. After one row is deleted, A is $\frac{32 \times 5 - (4+6)}{5 \times 16}$, which is 15/8 and greater than 1.828.

Case (4b) : $24/16 \leq R \leq 25/16$.

In this case, we embed the 25×5 mesh into Q(6) as 5 rows can be braided onto 4 rods by Fact 1. After one row is deleted, A is $\frac{25 \times 5 - 5}{64}$, which is 15/8 and greater than 1.828.

Case (5) : $11/8 \leq R \leq 12/8$.

As 12=3×4 and 3 rows can be braided onto 2 rods with dilation 1 and load factor 2, one can braid 12 rows onto 8 rods by Fact 3. The cycle length is 3, since after 3 columns the rows have all switched rods exactly one time. After deleting one row, A is $\frac{16 \times 3 - 4}{8 \times 3}$, which is 11/6 and greater than 1.828.

Case (6) : $10/8 \leq R \leq 11/8$.

Figure 3.1 shows how to braid 11 rows onto 8 rods with dilation 1 and nonuniform load factor 2, the cycle length is 9, as after 9 columns, all rows have switched rods exactly 4 times. After one row is deleted, A is $\frac{16 \times 9 - (1+13)}{9 \times 8}$. But this is less than 1.82. So in order to achieve the required density, we divide the interval into two smaller intervals [20/16, 21/16] and [21/16, 22/16].

Case (6a) : $21/16 \leq R \leq 22/16$.

By doubling the 11 row braiding, we get a better average. That is, now, after one row is deleted, A is $\frac{32 \times 9 - (2+13)}{16 \times 9}$, which is 1.9 and greater than 1.828.

Case (6b) : $20/16 \leq R \leq 21/16$.

In this case, the 21×3 mesh can be embedded into Q(5), as 3 rows can be embedded onto 2 rods with dilation 1 and uniform load factor 2. After one row is deleted, A is $\frac{21 \times 3 - 3}{32}$, which is 15/8 and greater than 1.828.

Case (7) : $9/8 \leq R \leq 10/8$.

Again, we divide this interval into two smaller intervals [18/16, 19/16] and [19/16, 20/16] in order to get the desired result.

Case (7a) : $19/16 \leq R \leq 20/8$.

As $20=5\times4$ and 5 rows can be braided onto 4 rods with dilation 1 and uniform load factor 2, 20 rows can also be braided onto 16 rods with dilation 1 and uniform load factor 2 by Fact 3. The cycle length is 5 and after 5 columns the rows have all switched rods 3 times. So, after deleting one row, A is $\frac{32\times5-8}{16\times5}$, which is 1.9 and greater than 1.828.

Case (7b) : $18/16\leq R\leq19/16$.

19 rows can be braided onto 16 rods with dilation 1 and nonuniform load factor 2 (see Figure 3.2). Each row has 5 points assigned per cycle. So, after deleting one row, A is $\frac{32\times3-(1+5)}{16\times3}$, which is 15/8 and greater than 1.828.

Case (8) : $8/8\leq R\leq8/9$.

Case (8a) : $17/16\leq R\leq18/16$.

As $18=9\times2$ and 9 rows can be braided onto 8 rods with dilation 1 and uniform load factor 2 by Fact 1, 18 rows can be braided on 16 rods with dilation 1 and uniform load factor 2 by Fact 3. Each row has 16 points assigned per cycle. So, after deleting one row, A is $\frac{32\times9-16}{16\times9}$, which is 17/9 and greater than 1.828.

Case (8b) : $16/16\leq R\leq17/16$.

17 rows can be braided on 16 rods with dilation 1 and uniform load factor 2, as $17=2^4+1$. Each row has 32 points assigned per cycle. So, after deleting one row, A is $\frac{32\times17-32}{16\times17}$, which is 32/17 and greater than 1.828. $\square$

Theorem 3.2 : Every 2-D mesh M with 1/4-density$\leq$3.809 can be embedded into its 1/4-size hypercube with dilation 1 and load factor 4.

Proof : Let M be a mesh with m rows and any number of columns. We consider cases based on the ratio of m to $2^{\lfloor\log m\rfloor-1}$, i.e. $R=\frac{m}{2^{\lfloor\log m\rfloor-1}}$. Note that R must be in the interval between 2 and 4. We proceed in the same manner as in Theorem 3.1.

Case (1) : $31/8\leq R\leq32/8$

One braids 4 rows per rod with load factor 4. The rows do not switch from one rod to another. This gives uniform load factor 4 when R=32/8, but when R is its minimum value 31/8, A is 31/8, which is 3.875 and greater than 3.809.

Case (2) : $30/8\leq R\leq31/8$

Case (2a) : $61/16\leq R\leq62/16$

We use exactly the same braiding as in case (1). A=61/16 after deleting one row, which is 3.8125.

Case (2b) : $60/16 \leq R \leq 61/16$

Since we know how to braid 33 rows on 32 rods with dilation 1 and load factor 2 by Fact 1, the 33×61 mesh can be embedded into $Q(10)$ with dilation 1 and load factor 2. Then by a simple folding of $Q(10)$, we can obtain an embedding of the 61×33 mesh into $Q(9)$ with dilation 1 and load factor 4. After one row is deleted, A is $\frac{61 \times 33 - 33}{2^9}$, which is 3.867 and greater than 3.809. We partition M into a group of 61×33 submeshes and embed each of them into a copy of $Q(9)$. That is, since any hypercube $Q(m)$, $m > 9$, can be partitioned into some number of $Q(9)$'s, one gets the desired embedding.

Case (3) : $29/8 \leq R \leq 30/8$

From the proof of Theorem 3.1, we know that the 15×17 mesh can be embedded into $Q(7)$ with dilation 1 and load factor 2, so the 30×17 mesh can be embedded into $Q(8)$ with dilation 1 and load factor 2. By folding, we can embed the 30×17 mesh into $Q(7)$ with dilation 1 and load factor 4. After one row is deleted, A is $\frac{30 \times 17 - 17}{2^7}$, which is about 3.86 and greater than 3.809.

Case (4) : $28/8 \leq R \leq 29/8$

Case (4a) : $57/16 \leq R \leq 58/16$

From case (3), we know that the 29×17 mesh can be embedded into $Q(7)$ with dilation 1 and load factor 4, as the 30×17 mesh can be embedded into $Q(7)$ with dilation 1 and load factor 4. By doubling we can embed the 58×17 mesh into $Q(8)$ with dilation 1 and load factor 4. After one row is deleted, A is $\frac{58 \times 17 - 17}{2^8}$, which is about 3.86 and greater than 3.809.

Case (4b) : $56/16 \leq R \leq 57/16$

Figure 3.2 shows how to uniformly braid 19 rows on 16 rods with load factor 2 (except for one point which receives only one guest). By the product theorem we can braid 57 rows on 32 rods with dilation 1 and load factor 4, as $57 = 19 \times 3$. The cycle length is $3 \times 3 = 9$, each row has 20 points assigned per cycle and there are 6 nodes with load factor 2 per cycle in the host hypercube. So after one row is deleted, A is $\frac{32 \times 4 \times 9 - (20 + 12)}{32 \times 9}$, which is about 3.889 and greater than 3.809.

Case (5) : $27/8 \leq R \leq 28/8$

As 7 rows can be braided on 2 rods with dilation 1 and load factor 4 by Fact 2, one can braid 28 rows on 8 rods by quadrupling this braiding. After one row is deleted, A is $\frac{8 \times 4 \times 7 - 8}{8 \times 7} = 27/7$, which is about 3.86 and greater than 3.809.

Case (6) : $26/8 \leq R \leq 27/8$

Since 3 rows can be braided on 2 rods and 9 rows can be braided on 8 rods with dilation 1 and load factor 2, by the product theorem one can braid 27 rows on 16 rods with dilation 1 and load factor 4. After one row is deleted, A is $\frac{16 \times 4 \times 27 - 64}{16 \times 27}$, which is about 3.85 and greater than 3.809.

Case (7) : $25/8 \leq R \leq 26/8$

13 rows can be uniformly braided on 4 rods with dilation 1 and load factor 4 by Fact 2. By doubling one can braid 26 rows on 8 rods with dilation 1 and load factor 4. After one row is deleted, A is 50/13, which is greater than 3.809.

Case (8) : $24/8 \leq R \leq 25/8$

As 5 rows can be braided on 4 rods with dilation 1 and load factor 2, by the product theorem one can braid 25 rows on 16 rods with dilation 1 and load factor 4. After one row is deleted, A is $\frac{64 \times 25 - 64}{16 \times 25}$, which is about 3.84 and greater than 3.809.

Case (9) : $23/8 \leq R \leq 24/8$

As 3 rows can be braided on 2 rods, by Fact 3 we can braid 24 rows on 8 rods with dilation 1 and load factor 4 (We use 8 rods due to doubling to get load factor 4.). After one row is deleted, A is 23/6, which is greater than 3.809.

Case (10) : $22/8 \leq R \leq 23/8$

    Case (10a) : $45/16 \leq R \leq 46/16$

Figure 3.3 shows that 23 rows are braided on 8 rods with dilation 1 and load factor 4 (except 3 points which receive only 3 guests). By doubling, we can braid 46 rows on 16 rods with dilation 1 and load factor 4. After one row is deleted, A is $\frac{16 \times 8 \times 4 - (6 + 11)}{16 \times 8}$, which is about 3.867 and greater than 3.828.

    Case (10b) : $44/16 \leq R \leq 45/16$

As 5 rows can be braided on 4 rods and 9 rows can be braided on 8 rods with dilation 1 and load factor 2, by the product theorem one can braid 45 rows on 32 rods with dilation 1 and load factor 4. After one row is deleted, A is $\frac{32 \times 4 \times 45 - (38 + 90)}{32 \times 45}$, which is about 1.90 and greater than 8.125.

Case (11) : $21/8 \leq R \leq 22/8$

Figure 3.4 shows that 11 rows can be braided on 4 rods with dilation 1 and uniform load factor 4. By doubling one can braid 22 rows on 8 rods with dilation 1 and uniform load factor 4. After one row is deleted, A is $\dfrac{8\times22\times4-(22+10)}{8\times22}$, which is 3.818 and greater than 3.809.

Case (12) : $20/8{\leq}R{\leq}21/8$

Figure 3.5 shows how to braid 21 rows on 8 rods with dilation 1 and uniform load factor 4. After one row is deleted, A is $\dfrac{21\times8\times4-32}{21\times8}$, which is 3.809.

Case (13) : $19/8{\leq}R{\leq}20/8$

Case (13a) : $39/16{\leq}R{\leq}40/16$

As 5 rows can be braided on 4 rods and 8 rows can be braided on 4 rows with dilation 1 and uniform load factor 2, by the product theorem one can braid 40 rows on 16 rods with dilation 1 and uniform load factor 4. After one row is deleted, A is $\dfrac{16\times4\times10-(10+6)}{16\times10}$, which is 3.9 and greater 3.809.

Case (13b) : $38/16{\leq}R{\leq}39/16$

From Case (7), we know that 26 rows can be braided on 8 rods with dilation 1 and uniform load factor 4. This enables us to embed the 26$\times$39 mesh into Q(8), as we can braid 39 columns of these 26 rows onto 32 columns of the 8 rods. After one row is deleted, A is $\dfrac{39\times26-26}{2^8}$, which is about 3.86 and greater than 3.809.

Case (14) : $18/8{\leq}R{\leq}19/8$

Case (14a) : $37/16{\leq}R{\leq}38/16$

Figure 3.6 shows how to braid 19 rows on 8 rods with dilation 1 and uniform load factor 4. By doubling this braiding, we can braid 38 rows on 16 rods with dilation 1 and uniform load factor 4. After one row is deleted, A is $\dfrac{16\times4\times19-(19+13)}{16\times21}$, which is about 3.89 and greater than 3.809.

Case (14b) : $36/16{\leq}R{\leq}37/16$

Case (14b1) : $73/32{\leq}R{\leq}74/32$

By doubling the braiding of 38 rows on 16 rods we can braid 74 rows on 32 rods with dilation 1 and uniform load factor 4. After two rows are deleted, A is the same, which is about 3.89 and greater than 3.809.

Case (14b2) : $72/32{\leq}R{\leq}73/32$

As 7 rows can be braided on 2 rods with dilation 1 and uniform load factor 4 by Fact 2, one can embed the 7$\times$73 into 2 rods and 64 columns, which is a subgraph of Q(7). After one row is deleted, A is about 3.9 and greater than 3.809.

Case (15) : $17/8 \leq R \leq 18/8$

Case (15a) : $35/16 \leq R \leq 36/16$

As 9 rows can be braided on 8 rows with dilation 1 and uniform load factor 2, by quadrupling one can braid 36 rows on 32 rods with dilation 1 and uniform load factor 4. Then we fold this into 16 rods to achieve the braiding of 36 rows on 16 rods with dilation 1 and uniform load factor 4. After one row is deleted, A is $\frac{16 \times 4 \times 36 - (36 + 28)}{16 \times 36}$, which is about 3.89 and greater than 3.809.

Case (15b) : $34/16 \leq R \leq 35/16$

As 5 rows can be braided on 4 rods with dilation 1 and uniform load factor 2 and, and the 7×9 mesh can be embedded into Q(5) with dilation 1 and load factor 2. By using the product theorem, we can braid 35 rows on 16 rods with dilation 1 and load factor 4. The cycle length is 40, and each row has 72 points assigned per cycle. After one row is deleted, A is $\frac{16 \times 4 - (72 + 40)}{16 \times 40}$, which is about 3.825 and greater than 3.809.

Case (16) : $16/8 \leq R \leq 17/8$

Case (16a) : $33/16 \leq R \leq 34/16$

As 17 rows can be braided on 8 rods with dilation 1 and uniform load factor 4, 34 rows can be braided on 16 rods with dilation 1 and uniform load factor 4. After one row is deleted, A is $\frac{16 \times 4 \times 34 - 64}{16 \times 34}$, which is about 3.88 and greater than 3.809.

Case (16b) : $32/16 \leq R \leq 33/16$

As 3 rows can be braided on 2 rods with dilation 1 and uniform load factor 2, and 11 rows can be beaided on 8 rods with dilation 1 and uniform load factor 2 except for one point which has load factor 1, by the product theorem, 33 rows can be braided on 16 rods with dilation 1 and almost uniform load factor 4. This braiding has cycle length 27. After one row is deleted, A is $\frac{16 \times 4 \times 27 - (52 + 6)}{16 \times 27}$, which is about 3.86 and greater than 3.809. $\square$

Theorem 3.3 : Every 2-D mesh M with 1/4-density ≤ 2.8125 can be embedded into its 1/4-size hypercube with dilation 1 and load factor 3.

Proof : (not given here due to space constraints.)

These 3 theorems give us optimum embedding results for both dilation and load factor in most cases. For example, the 127×127 mesh has 16129 points, its 1/4-size hypercube has 4096 points, therefore its 1/4-density is about 3.94. This is greater than the stated bound, but as the braiding described in Case (1) of the proof of Theorem 3.2 yields average density $\frac{127}{32}$=3.97, the embedding of the 127×127 mesh into Q(12) can be done optimally. These density results might easily be improved if one further divides intervals and finds appropriately refined braiding techniques.

4. General Density Theorem

One can clearly embed a 2-D mesh M into its 1/8-size hypercube with dilation 1 and load factor 8 if its 1/8-density is $\leq$ 2×3.809, as the load factor 8 embedding can be obtained by folding the 1/4-size hypercube which is the host for the load factor 4 embedding. Can we obtain the 1/16-density for embedding M into its 1/16-size hypercube with dilation 1 and load factor 12 by combining the 1/4-densities to embed M into its 1/4-size hypercube with dilation 1, load factor 4 as well as load factor 3? The following theorem gives a positive answer.

Theorem 4.1 : If every 2-D mesh M with $1/2^{k_1}$-density$\leq$a can be embedded into its $1/2^{k_1}$-size hypercube with dilation 1 and load factor l_1, and every 2-D mesh with $1/2^{k_2}$-density$\leq$b can be embedded into its $1/2^{k_2}$- size hypercube with dilation 1 and load factor l_2, then every 2-D mesh M with $1/2^k$-density$\leq$a×b can be embedded into its $1/2^k$-size hypercube with dilation 1 and load factor l_1×l_2.

Proof : (deleted for space considerations.)

Using Theorem 4.1, we know that every 2-D mesh M with 1/16-density about 11.3 (which is 2.8125×3.809) can be embedded into its 1/16-size hypercube with dilation 1 and load factor 12.

We have developed techniques to obtain density bound to achieve optimum results for any load factor m, where m$\geq$6, from density bounds for load factor p and q, where m=p+q. Our methods can also be extended to obtain the simulation of multidimensional meshes in small hypercubes. Space limitations prevent full descriptions here.

REFERENCES

[BMS] S. Bettayeb, Z. Miller, and I.H. Sudborough, "Embedding Grids into Hypercubes", *Proc. '88 AWOC: VLSI, Algorithms and Architectures Conf.* (July, 1988), Spring Verlag's Lecture Notes in Computer Science, vol. 327.
[BCLR] S. Bhatt, F. Chung, F. T. Leighton, and A. Rosenberg, "Optimal Simulations

of Tree Machines", *Proc, of 27th Annual IEEE Foundations of Computer Sci. Conf.* (1986), pp.274-282.

[BCHLR] S. Bhatt, F. Chung, J-W. Hong, F. T. Leighton, and A. Rosenberg, "Optimal Simulations by Butterfly Networks", *Proc. of 23rd Annual ACM Theory of Computer Sci. Conf.* (1988), pp 192-204.

[C1] M-Y. Chan, "Dilation 2 Embeddings of Grids into Hypercubes", *Proc. Int. Conf. on Parallel Processing* , August, 1988.

[C2] M-Y. Chan, "Embedding of 3-D Grids into optimal Hypercube", Technical Report (January, 1989), Computer Science Program, University of Texas at Dallas, Richardson, Texas 75083-0688.

[C3] M-Y. Chan, "Embedding of d-D Grids into optimal Hypercubes", Technical Report (January, 1989), Computer Science Program, University of Texas at Dallas, Richardson, Texas 75083-0688.

[DS1] A. Dingle and I.H. Sudborough, "Efficient Uses of Pyramid Networks", Technical Report (January, 1989), Computer Science Program, University of Texas at Dallas, Richardson, Texas 75083-0688.

[DS2] A. Dingle and I.H. Sudborough, "Simulations of Binary Trees and X-trees by Pyramids", Technical Report (January, 1989), Computer Science Program, University of Texas at Dallas, Richardson, Texas 75083-0688

[FS] A. Fiat and A. Shamir, "Polymorphic Arrays: A Novel VLSI Layout for Systolic Computers", *Proc. of 1984 IEEE Foundations of Computer Sci. Conf.* , pp. 37-45.

[GH] A. K. Gupta and S. E. Hambrusch, "Embedding Large Tree Machines into Small Ones", *Proc. of the 5th MIT Conf. on Advanced Research in VLSI* , March, 1988, pp. 179-199.

[HJ] C. T. Ho and S. L. Johnsson. "On the Embedding of Arbitrary Meshes in Boolean Cubes with Expansion Two and Dilation Two", *Proc. 1987 Int. Conf. on Parallel Processing* (August, 1987), pp. 188-191.

[L] J. Lee, "Embedding d-D Meshes into Optimum Size Hypecubes with dilation 4d-1", Technical Report (February, 1989), Computer Science Program, University of Texas at Dallas, Richardson, Texas 75083-0688

[MS] Z. Miller and I. H. Sudborough, "Compressing Meshes into Small Hypercubes", to appear.

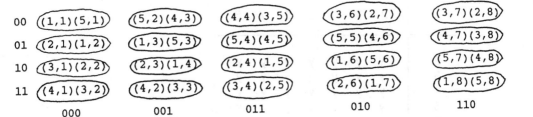

Figure 1.1a. A braiding of 5 rows on 4 rods with dilation 1 and load factor 2.

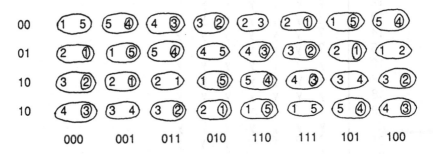

Figure 1.1b. A simple representation of the braiding of Figure 1.1a. All braidings
will be represented in this manner.
(The second point of a row in a column is circled.)

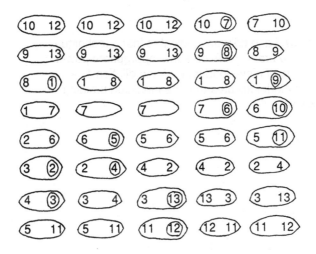

Figure 1.2. A braiding of 13 rows on 8 rods with dilation 1
and load factor 2.

	2	3	4	5	6	7	8
2	y	y	y	y	y	y	y
3	y	y	y	y	y	y	y
4	y	y	y	y	y	y	y
5	y	y	y	y	y	y	y
6	y	y	y	y	y	y	y
7	?	y	y	y	y	y	y
8	y	y	y	y	y	y	y
9	y	y	y	y	y	y	y
10	y	y	y	y	y	y	y
11	?	y	y	y	y	y	y
12	y	y	y	y	y	y	y
13	?	y	y	y	y	y	y
14	?	y	y	y	y	y	y
15	?	y	y	y	y	y	y
16	y	y	y	y	y	y	y
17	y	y	y	y	y	y	y
18	y	y	y	y	y	y	y
19	?	?	y	y	y	y	y
20	y	y	y	y	y	y	y
21	?	?	y	y	y	y	y
22	?	y	y	y	y	y	y
23	?	?	?	y	y	y	y

Table 2.1. A "y" in row i and column j indicates that a technique is known to braid i rows on some appropriate power of 2 rods to achieve load factor j and dilation 1. A question mark indicates that the indicated braiding is unknown.

44

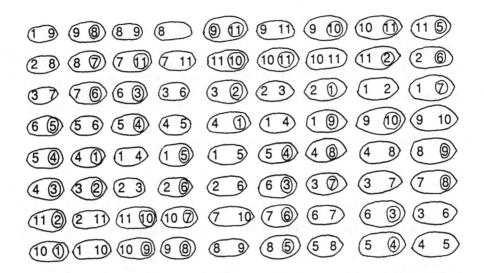

Figure 3.1. A braiding of 11 rows on 8 rods with dilation 1 and load factor 2.

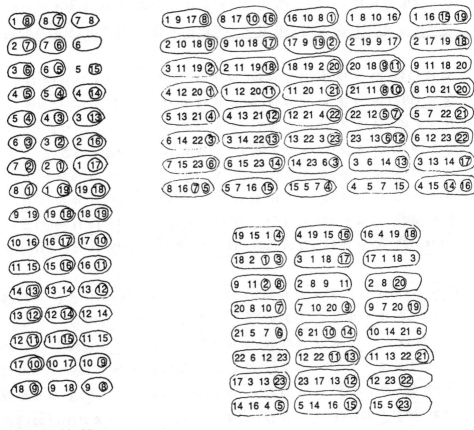

Figure 3.2. A braiding

of 19 rows on 16 rods
with dilation 1 and load
factor 2.

Figure 3.3. A braiding of 23 rows on 8 rods with dilation 1 and load
factor 4.

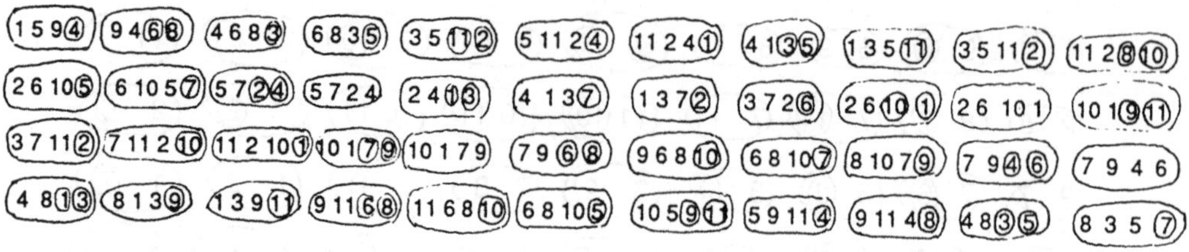

(1 5 9 ④) (9 4 ⑥ ⑧) (4 6 8 ②) (6 8 3 ⑤) (3 5 ⑪ ②) (5 11 2 ④) (11 2 4 ①) (4 1 ③ ⑤) (1 3 5 ⑪) (3 5 11 ②) (11 2 ⑧ ⑩)

(2 6 10 ⑤) (6 10 5 ⑦) (5 7 ② ④) (5 7 2 4) (2 4 ⓪ ③) (4 1 3 ⑦) (1 3 7 ②) (3 7 2 ⑥) (2 6 ⑩ ①) (2 6 10 1) (10 1 ⑨ ⑪)

(3 7 11 ②) (7 11 2 ⑩) (11 2 10 ①) (10 1 ⑦ ⑨) (10 1 7 9) (7 9 ⑥ ⑧) (9 6 8 ⑩) (6 8 10 ⑦) (8 10 7 ⑨) (7 9 ④ ⑥) (7 9 4 6)

(4 8 ⑬ ⑬) (8 13 ⑨) (1 3 9 ⑪) (9 11 ⑥ ⑧) (11 6 8 ⑩) (6 8 10 ⑤) (10 5 ⑨ ⑪) (5 9 11 ④) (9 11 4 ⑧) (4 8 ③ ⑤) (8 3 5 ⑦)

Figure 3.4. A braiding of 11 rows on 4 rods with dilation 1 and load factor 4.

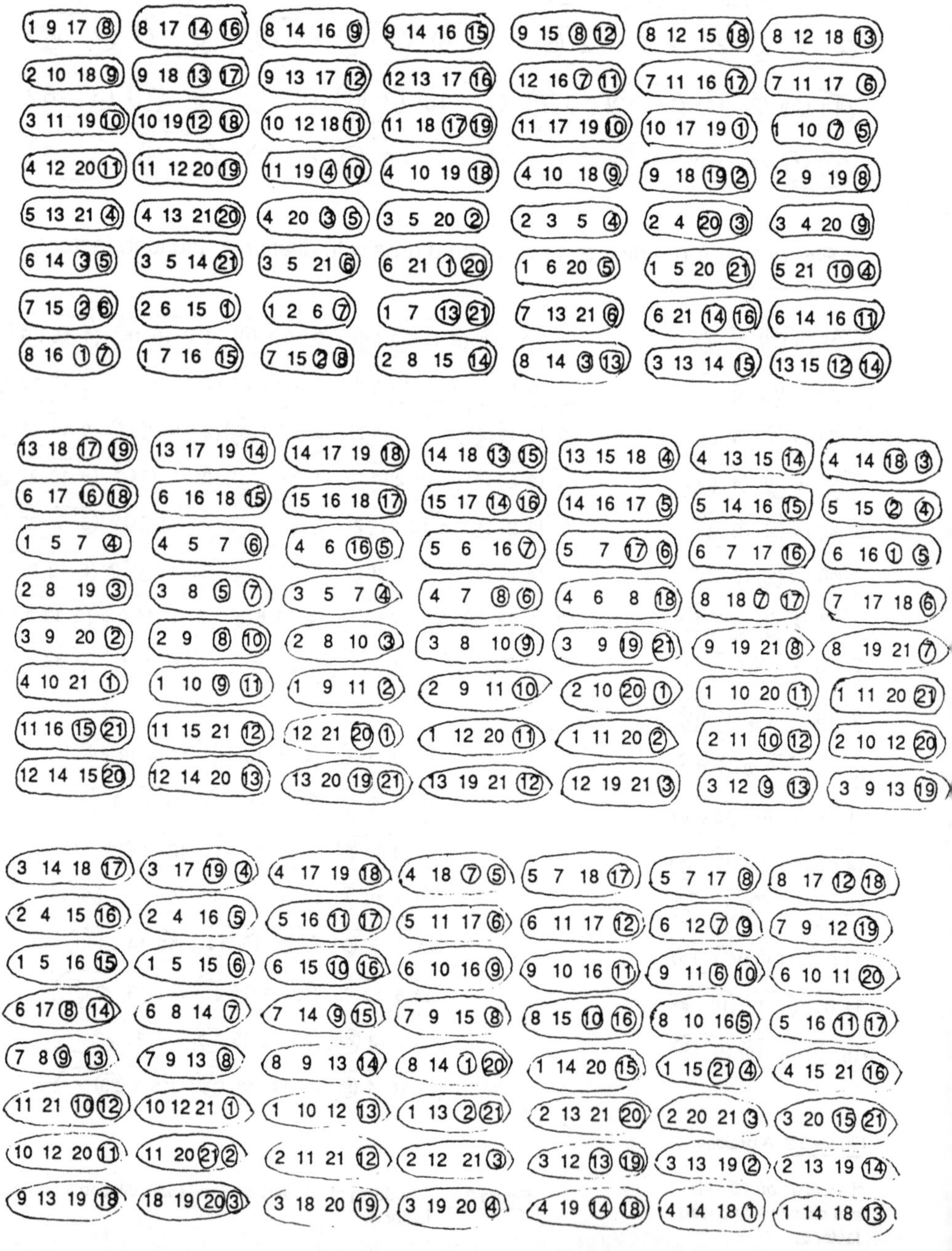

(1 9 17 ⑧) (8 17 ⑭ ⑯) (8 14 16 ⑨) (9 14 16 ⑮) (9 15 ⑧ ⑫) (8 12 15 ⑱) (8 12 18 ⑬)

(2 10 18 ⑨) (9 18 ⑬ ⑰) (9 13 17 ⑫) (12 13 17 ⑯) (12 16 ⑦ ⑪) (7 11 16 ⑰) (7 11 17 ⑥)

(3 11 19 ⑩) (10 19 ⑫ ⑱) (10 12 18 ⑪) (11 18 ⑰ ⑲) (11 17 19 ⑩) (10 17 19 ①) (1 10 ⑦ ⑤)

(4 12 20 ⑪) (11 12 20 ⑲) (11 19 ④ ⑩) (4 10 19 ⑱) (4 10 18 ⑨) (9 18 ⑲ ②) (2 9 19 ⑧)

(5 13 21 ④) (4 13 21 ⑳) (4 20 ③ ⑤) (3 5 20 ②) (2 3 5 ④) (2 4 ⑳ ③) (3 4 20 ⑨)

(6 14 ③ ⑤) (3 5 14 ㉑) (3 5 21 ⑥) (6 21 ① ⑳) (1 6 20 ⑤) (1 5 20 ㉑) (5 21 ⑩ ④)

(7 15 ② ⑥) (2 6 15 ①) (1 2 6 ⑦) (1 7 ⑬ ㉑) (7 13 21 ⑥) (6 21 ⑭ ⑯) (6 14 16 ⑪)

(8 16 ① ⑦) (1 7 16 ⑮) (7 15 ② ⑧) (2 8 15 ⑭) (8 14 ③ ⑬) (3 13 14 ⑮) (13 15 ⑫ ⑭)

(13 18 ⑰ ⑲) (13 17 19 ⑭) (14 17 19 ⑱) (14 18 ⑬ ⑮) (13 15 18 ④) (4 13 15 ⑭) (4 14 ⑱ ③)

(6 17 ⑥ ⑱) (6 16 18 ⑮) (15 16 18 ⑰) (15 17 ⑭ ⑯) (14 16 17 ⑤) (5 14 16 ⑮) (5 15 ② ④)

(1 5 7 ④) (4 5 7 ⑥) (4 6 ⑯ ⑤) (5 6 16 ⑦) (5 7 ⑰ ⑥) (6 7 17 ⑯) (6 16 ① ⑤)

(2 8 19 ③) (3 8 ⑤ ⑦) (3 5 7 ④) (4 7 ⑧ ⑥) (4 6 8 ⑱) (8 18 ⑦ ⑰) (7 17 18 ⑥)

(3 9 20 ②) (2 9 ⑧ ⑩) (2 8 10 ③) (3 8 10 ⑨) (3 9 ⑲ ㉑) (9 19 21 ⑧) (8 19 21 ⑦)

(4 10 21 ①) (1 10 ⑨ ⑪) (1 9 11 ②) (2 9 11 ⑩) (2 10 ⑳ ①) (1 10 20 ⑪) (1 11 20 ㉑)

(11 16 ⑮ ㉑) (11 15 21 ⑫) (12 21 ⑳ ①) (1 12 20 ⑪) (1 11 20 ②) (2 11 ⑩ ⑫) (2 10 12 ⑳)

(12 14 15 ⑳) (12 14 20 ⑬) (13 20 ⑲ ㉑) (13 19 21 ⑫) (12 19 21 ③) (3 12 ⑨ ⑬) (3 9 13 ⑲)

(3 14 18 ⑰) (3 17 ⑲ ④) (4 17 19 ⑱) (4 18 ⑦ ⑤) (5 7 18 ⑰) (5 7 17 ⑧) (8 17 ⑫ ⑱)

(2 4 15 ⑯) (2 4 16 ⑤) (5 16 ⑪ ⑰) (5 11 17 ⑥) (6 11 17 ⑫) (6 12 ⑦ ⑨) (7 9 12 ⑲)

(1 5 16 ⑮) (1 5 15 ⑥) (6 15 ⑩ ⑯) (6 10 16 ⑨) (9 10 16 ⑪) (9 11 ⑥ ⑩) (6 10 11 ⑳)

(6 17 ⑧ ⑭) (6 8 14 ⑦) (7 14 ⑨ ⑮) (7 9 15 ⑧) (8 15 ⑩ ⑯) (8 10 16 ⑤) (5 16 ⑪ ⑰)

(7 8 ⑨ ⑬) (7 9 13 ⑧) (8 9 13 ⑭) (8 14 ① ⑳) (1 14 20 ⑮) (1 15 ㉑ ④) (4 15 21 ⑯)

(11 21 ⑩ ⑫) (10 12 21 ①) (1 10 12 ⑬) (1 13 ② ㉑) (2 13 21 ⑳) (2 20 21 ③) (3 20 ⑮ ㉑)

(10 12 20 ⑪) (11 20 ㉑ ②) (2 11 21 ⑫) (2 12 21 ③) (3 12 ⑬ ⑲) (3 13 19 ②) (2 13 19 ⑭)

(9 13 19 ⑱) (18 19 ⑳ ③) (3 18 20 ⑲) (3 19 20 ④) (4 19 ⑭ ⑱) (4 14 18 ①) (1 14 18 ⑬)

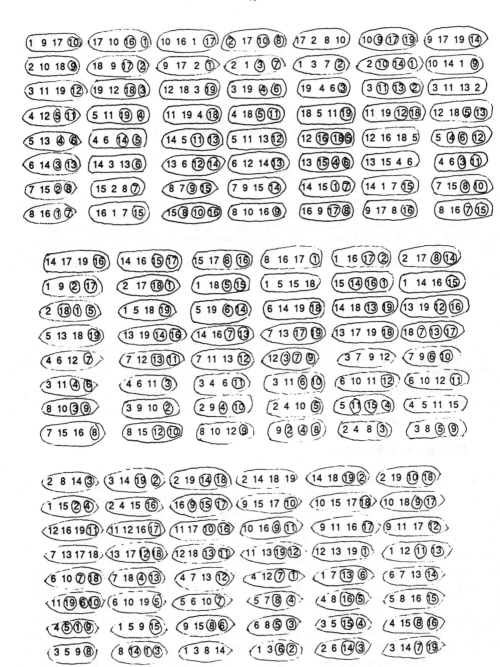

Figure 3.6. A braiding of 19 rows on 8 rods with dilation 1 and load factor 4.

SEVEN HARD PROBLEMS IN SYMBOLIC BACKGROUND KNOWLEDGE ACQUISITION

Yves Kodratoff

CNRS & Université Paris Sud, LRI, Bldg 490, 91405 Orsay, France
George Mason University, AI Center, Fairfax, Virginia 22030, USA

ABSTRACT

By using a special characterization of machine learning algorithms, we first define what is background knowledge, as opposed to case-based, strategic, and explanatory types of knowledge. We oppose also the symbolic to the numeric view of background knowledge. We discuss then what we see as the seven most difficult topics in background knowledge acquisition, namely the detection of implicit implications, first order logic knowledge representation and acquiring "Skolem" functions, uncertain knowledge, weak knowledge, time management and fusion of several sources of knowledge, knowledge for vision, certification of knowledge.

1 - INTRODUCTION

In this paper we shall speak of knowledge acquisition in a general sense, that encompasses both automatic knowledge acquisition as in *machine learning* (ML), and working by interviews with the field experts, as in the sub-field of artificial intelligence (AI) which is called *knowledge acquisition*. Actually, we shall focus our attention on a specific type of knowledge, called *background knowledge* (BK), be it acquired automatically or through interviews.

1.1 Background knowledge

We define BK as follows. The knowledge learned concerns a given domain containing a given set of objects. For instance, the domain of cars contains, say, some of the cars existing in a particular area. This domain is described by a set of descriptors. For instance, the make, color, shape, position, maximum_speed etc. of the set of cars under study. The values of the descriptors[1] give the state in which a particular object is to be found. For instance, for the particular object "my_car", one has make = Peugeot, color = beige, etc. These descriptors show relationships among them, characterizing the particular field under study. These relationships are theorems that hold within this field. For instance, since there are no Peugeot cars of yellow color, one of these theorems can be written as $\forall x\ [peugeot(x) \Rightarrow \neg\ yellow(x)]$. As an other example, in the area of data bases, one calls "integrity constraint" such a relation that must hold among the values of the descriptors. Besides, as an important feature not insisted upon enough in the literature, the descriptors show an inheritance structure, by which some of them are recognized as being of greater degree of generality than others. It may happen, but this is not compulsory, that this inheritance structure follows the structure of the descriptors. For instance, the descriptor color may be seen has being the parent of its values: beige, red etc. Each de-

---

[1] Since they "take values", the descriptors are called "variables" by people working with numeric techniques. This is possible because they use 0th order logic. Since we are concerned with relationships among these entities, we avoid calling them "variables", we prefer to see them as predicates of 1st order logic, which we call descriptors.

scriptor is usually (in non-trivial cases) part of several of such inheritance structure. For instance, color can be also the parent of "primary color" and secondary color", or of "light color" and dark color" etc. We call BK the set of all descriptors, their values, and of the relations among the descriptors. The existence of such structures may seem innocuous enough at first sight. Actually, we have shown in (Kodratoff, 1990) that some classical paradoxes of induction, namely Hempel's "black crows" and Goodman's "grue emeralds" are nonexistent when the knowledge is so structured. Since we are here concerned with the acquisition of new knowledge which cannot but be an inductive process, it is important for us to define the knowledge we deal with in such a way that induction is not an absurd behavior.

Let us compare BK to other kinds of knowledge by using a characterization of ML algorithms that has been progressively set up in our research group, of which several approximations have already been published (Ganascia and Helft, 1988; Kodratoff, 1989; Bisson and Laublet, 1989; Bratko and Kodratoff, 1989; Morik, Rouveirol and Sims, 1989).

This characterization relies on the assumption that there exist four kinds of knowledge, BK, *strategic knowledge*, examples (or *case-based knowledge*), and *strategic knowledge*. To each of them are associated four kinds of processes that generate and/or control them. BK is generated by the so-called *learning algorithms*, strategic knowledge is generated by a *control and test algorithm*, cases are generated by an *example generator*, and causal knowledge is specific to the *field expert*. Each learning system can then be described by the flow of information between the four kinds of knowledge and the four kinds of processes. Figure one, below, shows the application of this scheme to the description of the functioning of KATE, a ML software developed by the company INTELLISOFT, which combines the power of information compression, as in Quinlan's ID3 (Quinlan, 1983), and the knowledge representation of object-oriented languages. We can now attempt making the definition of BK more precise by singling out its differences with the other kinds of knowledge. Cases are descriptions of instantiated examples illustrating concepts or behaviors of interest to the user, causal knowledge explains the relations between these concepts or behaviors, or attributes a causal label to some of the implications[2]. Therefore, these two kinds of knowledge are very strongly user dependent. This is why we tend to believe that knowledge acquisition from field experts should concentrate on these domains, as we have been doing with our system DISCIPLE (Kodratoff and Tecuci, 1987; Tecuci and Kodratoff, 1990). Strategic knowledge is any kind of knowledge that says how BK must be used in order to optimize a given criterion. In most cases, strategic knowledge consists of an ordering of operators (or of descriptors in the case of symbolic learning), telling which should be used when some given conditions are met. The automation of the acquisition of strategic knowledge is certainly the most common among existing systems. Let us cite here five examples.

ID3 (Quinlan, 1983) optimizes the compression of information in order to generate an ordering on the use of the descriptors. AQ (on the symbolic side, see Michalski (1983, 1984)) and cluster analysis algorithms (on the numeric side, see for instance (Benzecri et al., 1973)) optimize a distance measure in order to select clusters of "closely related" descriptors. Recently, a large emphasis has been given to neural networks that optimize the back-propagation of coefficients in order to attribute coefficients to sites in the network.

---

[2] We are aware that logicians attribute a causal value to any implication. We disagree with this point of view, thus following the now classical Explanation-Based Learning view (Mitchell et al., 1986; DeJong and Mooney, 1986) that an implication has to link *operational predicates* in order to be explanatory.

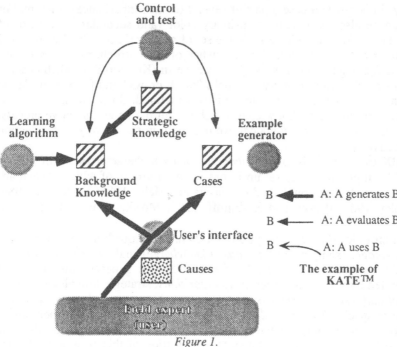

Figure 1.

The characterization of KATE[3] by the flow of information in the system. The expert provides the BK and the cases through a sophisticated interface, the compression information algorithm of the control module generates a decision tree (which is strategic knowledge) by using these two pieces of information. The trees are transformed into rules, thus into BK. The learning module generates an intentional description of the clusters, which is another kind of BK.

Also very important to our advice, are the search algorithms in general, with their last interesting advanced version, genetic algorithms, that use an explicit evaluation function in order to select the next move of the search (or the best genetic operators to be applied, in the case of genetic algorithms). Quite apart form the preceding approaches, let us point at BLIP (Morik, 1989) that uses coherency constraints in order to select the relevant knowledge.

It is quite clear that there are very hard problems linked to the acquisition of causal and case knowledge, and that the acquisition strategic knowledge is still far from being a solved problem. Nevertheless, in this paper we shall focus only on the acquisition of BK. Depending on the way the computation are performed, BK takes two different meanings, as we shall now see.

1.2 Symbolic/numeric knowledge

We must confess our slight dismay at the state-of-the-art relative to the integration of symbolic (mostly AI born) techniques, and more classical numeric and statistical techniques. On the one hand, most people in the application fields are eager to agree that they need such an integration, that pure numeric techniques are unable to solve their problems (nobody from the symbolic side seriously claims that symbolic techniques can solve real-life problems without numeric techniques). On the other hand, except for a very few exceptions, we have met with specialists of numeric techniques that claim that their approach encompasses the symbolic approach, which is useless anyhow, so they

---

[3] KATE is a trademark of the company INTELLISOFT.

claim! This is why we are not going to describe some of the solutions we have been already working on in order to integrate numeric and symbolic techniques (see (Kodratoff, Perdrix and Franova, 1985; Duval and Kodratoff, 1986; Blythe et al., 1987; Kodratoff et al. 1987, 1988; Manago and Kodratoff, 1987; Kodratoff, 1990) but rather come down to the more elementary problem of simply showing that there is indeed a difference between these two approaches, and that none of them includes the other one.

Let us first learn from the classical difference from numeric and symbolic calculus. A computation is said to be numeric when it is performed on numbers, therefore with some approximation. A computation is said to be symbolic when it applied to non instantiated symbols, that have their own combination semantics, often different from the one of the numbers. For instance, the numeric and symbolic computation of the division of X by X, X/X, uses a quite different semantic for /, even if the numeric computation is performed on integers, leading to the same result as the symbolic computation. This gives two consequences. The first is that numeric relationships are hard to express in symbolic form since all the semantic of numbers has to be made again explicit. Conversely, by the second consequence, numeric computation will be unable to perform the sequences of logic reasoning expressing the semantics of the domain under study. Therefore, numeric computation can hardly provide explanations of its behavior, as opposed to the symbolic one, which is more or less aimed at this purpose. This requires for the symbolic computations to take into account at least two different kinds of knowledge, **explicit** BK, as defined above, and the cases to which this knowledge must be applied. In the numeric approach, BK might well exist, but it is then coded **implicitly** and cannot be used to perform logical reasoning. For instance, learning a numeric dependency between the value "crow" and the value "black" does not allow to perform the same kind of inferences as learning the theorem $\forall x$ [crow(x) $\Rightarrow$ black(x)] (even if the theorem is known for being uncertain).

The difference between numeric and symbolic approaches, as we have been presenting it above, is often blurred by other false assertions that we shall now shortly describe. A first error lies in asserting that all symbols can be represented by numbers (which is of course true), while forgetting that all semantics cannot be merged in the semantic of numbers. For instance, representing a color by a string of numbers is quite possible as long as one is concerned by the recognition of the color. As soon as one wishes to perform some reasoning on the colors (e.g., representing that white is a combination of all other colors, that grey, yellow, and white are light colors, etc. and using this knowledge while reasoning about objects), the numeric representation though still achievable, becomes incredibly cumbersome. A second error is to claim that intensional descriptions[4] are reserved to symbolic representations, and that numeric representation can deal only with extensional descriptions. It is only true that numeric representations, when possible, are very efficient and can deal with many more instances than the symbolic ones. It is quite possible that a numeric technique will select the values of the descriptors that characterize a given set of instances, thus providing an intensional description of this set. A third error occurs when zeroth order logic is strictly attributed to numeric approaches,

---

[4] First defined in *La logique ou l'art de penser,* by Arnauld and Nicole (1662), new edition by Froman, Stuttgart 1965, as follows. "I call comprehension of the idea (i.e., intensional description) the attributes it contains and it cannot release without loosing its meaning ... I call extension of the idea, all the instances suitable to the idea". These definitions are the same as the classical ones for which intension contains all the necessary values of descriptors of the concept, while the extension is the set of all instances of the concept.

and first order to symbolic ones. The input of numeric approaches is strictly zeroth order, while the numeric approaches need two kinds of inputs: the cases, that are zeroth order, and the BK that might be possibly first order. The output of numeric approaches is normally of zeroth order, but they can also provide strategic knowledge which, technically, is of higher orders. The output of symbolic techniques is of order zero or one. Notice that most existing symbolic systems work with the "attribute-value" formalism, which is a slight extension of the zeroth order.

It follows that numeric and symbolic approaches view BK in a quite different way. Symbolic approaches, originating from AI, view it as an explicit description of the knowledge of the field expert, in language which as close as possible of the one of the field expert. Numeric approaches, originating from statistics, view it a way of encoding information that will make the semantics of the domain as close as possible of the semantics of numbers. We shall now describe some of the most difficult problems met by the symbolic encoding of KB.

2 - THE DETECTION OF IMPLICIT IMPLICATIONS

We shall say very little on this topic which has already been largely worked upon.
The system AQUINAS is a prototypic example of a system of knowledge acquisition from field experts in which implicit implications are detected and submitted to the expert's appreciation. A general description of AQUINAS is found in (Boose, 1989), and a detailed one in (Boose et al., 1989).
On the side of machine learning, we shall cite two systems. BLIP (Morik, 1989) hypothesizes new implications seemingly present in the data and check them first by using meta-predicates to propagate the consequences of the hypothesized implication, and to see wether it introduces incoherences (in which case, it is rejected), second by asking the field expert's advice. CHARADE (Ganascia, 1988) finds all the possible implications, and proposes them to the field expert together with a belief coefficient depending on the number of times this implication has been found valid in the data.

3 - FIRST ORDER LOGIC KNOWLEDGE REPRESENTATION AND ACQUIRING "SKOLEM" FUNCTIONS

It is necessary to use first order logics when dealing with the relations among a large number of objects. For instance, in order to represent the "to_the_left" relations of n objects, we need n-1 propositions and the theorem $\forall x \ \forall y \ \forall z$ [left(x,y) & left(y,z) => left(y,x)]. In zeroth order logics, we need to write the (n-1)! relations among all the objects.
Another point favoring first order logic representation is that it enables the representation of functional expressions. For instance, let us consider the relation between the speed, the distance and the time. We are actually unable to express it in 0th logic , whereas it is written in first order logic as $\forall x \ \forall t$ distance(x) & time(t) => speed(x/t)], i.e., if the distance is x and the time is t then the speed is x/t.

First order logic allows to express a large variety of knowledge. Nevertheless, it has a well known drawback, namely the undecidability of the proof procedure. Since we want to use a theorem prover that is efficient enough to apply it numerous times on the examples, we have to restrict ourselves to the simple case of Horn clauses. It therefore brings in a new problem: Transforming a theorem into a set of clauses which includes a step known as skolemization, which happens because, in a clause, all variables have to be universally quantified. Therefore, all existentially quantified variables have to be deleted. There are two cases. If the existential quantification is not under the scope of a universal quantifier, as for instance when there are only existentially quantified variables, then they must be replaced by a **new** constant. If the existential quantification is under the scope of one or several universal quantifiers, then the existentially quantified variables must be replaced by a **new** function depending on these universally quantified variables whose $\forall$ occurs ahead of the $\exists$s concerned. In other words, suppose that we have a formula of the form $\forall x \forall y \exists u \forall z \exists v F(x, y, z, u, v)$, then it must be transformed into $\forall x \forall y \forall z F(x, y, z, f(x, y), g(x, y, z))$ where f and g are new symbols of functions. Notice that u has been replaced by a function of x and y because it is under the scope of x and y, while v, which is under the scope of x, y, and z had to be replaced by a function of x, y, and z. That the constant or function introduced are new symbols is essential to the theory. Consider now that when this operation is performed by an expert, as happens in AI, he will not introduce a new symbol which would be meaningless for him. On the contrary, he will insist on finding the "good" symbol that will keep the truth value of his clauses. In other words, the operation performed by a human is a pseudo-skolemisation (hence the quotes we have been using above when speaking of skolemization) in which the pseudo-skolem function is related to the existing knowledge. Let us exemplify the skolemization problem on the clause representation of the sentence: Everybody makes mistakes. In first-order logic this reads: $\forall x \exists y [HUMAN(x) \Rightarrow DOES(x, y) \& MISTAKE(y)]$. The variable y is under the scope of the $\forall$ quantifier that quantifies x, therefore y has to be skolemized as a function of x. We can bring in an arbitrary Skolem function and transform our theorem into $\forall x [HUMAN(x) \Rightarrow DOES(x, g(x)) \& MISTAKE(g(x))]$ where g is a new function symbol. In practice, it is awkward to neglect the information we have about the function "g", which tells us what is done is a misfit action. An expert would even insist on making explicit the kind of actions that are misfit in the considered field of expertise. Suppose that we are in the context of a school class, and the teacher wants to insist on the fact that lack of attention brings mistakes, then he would attribute these errors to unthoughtfulness, and write, instead of g(x), unthoughtful(x) in $\forall x [HUMAN(x) \Rightarrow DOES(x, unthoughtful(x)) \& MISTAKE(unthoughtful(x))]$. To complete the example, let us point out that the expert would also dislike the presence of functions in his predicates, he would then rather give to the theorem the form $\forall x [HUMAN(x) \Rightarrow DOES(x, y) \& MISTAKE(y) \& UNTHOUGHTFUL(x))]$. This last version is no longer equivalent at all to the general theorem we started from. In theory, this is an abomination. In practice, we want the expert happy with the knowledge he has been transmitting into the system. The skolemization process has forced him to make his thought more precise than it was at the beginning, which is a very positive feature of knowledge acquisition.

The choice of an appropriate replacement for a Skolem function is a problem which nobody has envisaged an automatic solution to, as far as we know. However, it is quite alright to convert a sentence expressing a feature into a theorem when its conversion into a clause (or rule) requires a "skolemization" which can only be done well by a domain expert. Techniques for acquiring knowledge to construct expert systems should not fail to get the expert to point out the right supplementary information that allows to avoid the problem of skolemization.

53

5 - UNCERTAIN KNOWLEDGE

When it is confronted to real world problems, the symbolic approach to Artificial Intelligence (AI) needs representing and handling uncertainty. When dealing with uncertain information, three problems occur.

The first problem is the one of the combination of uncertainties during a reasoning phase. There has been many proposals for the solution of this problem, the most famous being the more or less strict Bayesian combinations (Shafer, 1976), belief coefficients (Buchanan and Shortliffe, 1984), and fuzzy sets theory (Zadeh, 1983). We shall not elaborate here on these techniques that simplify the knowledge acquisition work to the point of asking a coefficient to an expert. The second problem comes form the fact that A and $\neg$A being to some extent simultaneously true, the knowledge base contains some kind of contradiction, and the reasoning process must be able to deal with these contradictions. We have been already presenting this problem in great detail in (Kodratoff, Perdrix and Franova, 1985; Duval and Kodratoff, 1986; Kodratoff et al., 1990).

The third problem happens because uncertainty shakes the structure of knowledge obtained in case of certain knowledge. If we are unsure that concepts B and C descend from concept A, how much are we sure that the properties of A are inherited by its descendent? In order to deal with this problem, we shall give a new representation of knowledge, the one of taxonomies of polymorphic concepts. By definition of the word taxonomy, two children of a same parent have no common instances. We propose to extend the concept of taxonomy in order to deal with uncertain concepts by violating this restriction in the definition if a taxonomy.

We shall say that the knowledge is structured by polymorphic taxonomies when
1 - the children contain all the instances of their parents. In particular, supposing that the parent P_1 has some common instances with another concept P_2, then the common elements to P_1 and P_2 are found among the children of P_1.
2 - the children of a same parent may be disjoint. When they are polymorphic, then the intensity of the polymorphy is computed by a demon.
3 - children certainly inherit of their parents properties. There is only one type of uncertainty possible in this matter: it may happen that some instances are children of another parent, of which one is unsure. Therefore, the property inherited from the other parent is uncertain. This effect must die down rapidly in the taxonomy, meaning that a polymorphic grand-parent may still have some influence on the uncertainty of the properties of its grand-children, but that this effect dies out at the next generation.
4 - When the polymorphy is above a given threshold, the two concepts are confused into a unique one. Again, this contradicts the definition of taxonomy which should be a tree. By definition of polymorphic taxonomy, the number of such cases is relatively small, therefore preserving the overall tree structure.

As an example of such taxonomies, let us consider a taxonomy of colors, including the notion of light and dark colors, known for being very polymorphic together. Figure 2, below, illustrates the validity of our hypothesis that properties inherited by polymorphy do not transfer very far. For instance, the polymorphy between yellow and green do not transfer any property to its grand-child dark brown.
The acquisition of polymorphic taxonomies is necessary to a global solution to uncertain knowledge.

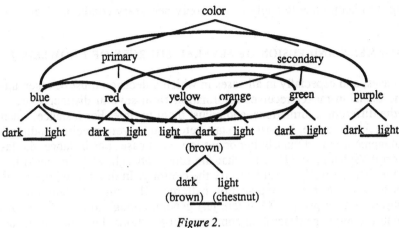

The relation parent-child is shown by a strait thin line, polymorphy relations between colors are shown by curved thick lines, polymorphy relations between light and dark colors are shown by a strait thick horizontal line. Primary is supposed to be non polymorphic with secondary. Blue is polymorphic with red, but not with yellow.

Figure 2.

6 - "WEAK" KNOWLEDGE

We say that the field knowledge is weak whenever it is incomplete and/or incoherent and/or intractable, and that one does not not know in advance which of these properties is showing. We have proposed a solution in order to refine weak knowledge in a system called DISCIPLE which generates examples that reflect the weakness of its knowledge, and which proposes them to the user (Kodratoff and Tecuci, 1987; Tecuci and Kodratoff, 1990) for validation. When the user accepts such a proposal, it is further used as a positive example of the problem solution, while if it is rejected it becomes a negative example. The learning problem of DISCIPLE may be formulated as follows.

Given:
A weak domain theory
The domain theory contains only descriptions of the objects in the world, in terms of their properties and relations.
A problem solving episode
It consists of a problem P to solve and a (partial) solution S.
Determine:
A general problem solving rule.
According to this rule, problems similar to P receive solutions similar to S.

In its first learning step, DISCIPLE tries to find an explanation (within its weak domain theory) of the validity of the solution given by the user. These explanations are then used to build a first set of upper and lower bounds to the validity of the general rule. As in the version spaces, further positive examples generalize the lower bound, and negative examples specialize the upper bound.

DISCIPLE then generates a general solving rule, together with the upper and lower bounds to the preconditions for its application. When the knowledge is really weak, i.e., the weakness is embedded in the field knowledge, not a simple lack of understanding from the field expert, then upper and lower bound will never converge to a necessary and sufficient condition for the application of the rule. In other words, the weakness of the field theory is captured by the existence of distinct upper and lower bounds to the conditions for the application of the rule. This gives an operational representation of the weakness. The main improvement comes from that failures can be understood. For example, a rule may fail to be applied correctly because sufficient conditions have not been met, and an attempt has been done to apply it when only necessary conditions were fulfilled.

8 - TIME MANAGEMENT AND FUSION OF SEVERAL SOURCES OF KNOWLEDGE

In many practical cases, and especially in all cases in which a decision must be taken under constraints, the decision-maker receives information from several distinct sources, and has to merge the different informations, and adjust them in time. For instance, when playing a counter-attack at a game, it must not start before some very precise conditions are met. Time management is particularly important in such a case. For instance, the famous restaurant script (Schank, 1977) states that the bill is brought after the meal has been eaten, while the fastfood script would specify the contrary. In order to work on this problem, we propose to use Schank's explanation patterns (XP, 1987). Schank did the work of determining which scripts and XP where just general enough to be useful to the understanding of natural language describing common sense actions. For each particular application, it will be the work of knowledge engineers to collect the XPs used by the field expert, and to generalize them just enough to make them useful in a system of decision aid. In other words, XPs do not constitute a theoretical advance at all, they are simply a language for setting up good questionnaires that will capture correctly the knowledge of the field expert, and this is all about what knowledge acquisition is. Such schemes can be also used creatively in order to guess parts of the action that are present in the script but that are possibly missing in the case under study. For instance, again using the script restaurant, it may happen that in the case under study there is no information about characters sitting down. Nevertheless, since the restaurant script has been activated, we know that the characters must be sitting at least while they are eating.

XPs allow besides to describe the cause, or the explanation that link some subparts of the XP, or that explain some actions performed in the XP.

An XP contains a list of necessary conditions to the activation of the XP, a list a sufficient conditions, a description of the pattern itself, a list of post-conditions that describe what has been achieved by the XP, and finally a set of explanatory links between the preconditions and the postconditions.

In order to illustrate our ideas, let us develop here the XP "slow down before the traffic lights, and speed up when they turn to green".

XP "slow down before the traffic lights, and speed up when they turn to green"

Figure 3. Descriptive scheme of the XP

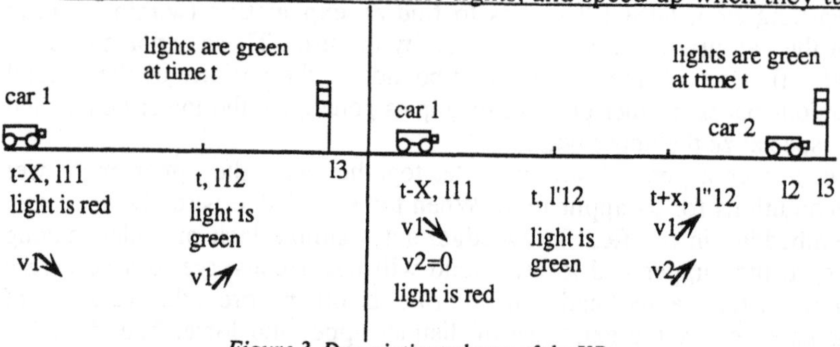

On the left side, the way is free for car1. It will speed up again at time t. On the right side, car1 has to take into account car2 which is already stopped at the traffic light. It cannot speed up before time t+x because car2 does not start at once.

Necessary and sufficient items

car_1 in position between [$<l_{11}, >l_3$] at time [$<t-X, >t$], traffic lights in position l_3

Sufficient items

car_2

Causes

    $Cause_1$. Save gas.

    $Cause_2$. Save time.

    together with a

        metapreconditions on the causes

            IF $cause_1$ activated THEN $cause_2$ inactive

            IF $cause_2$ activated THEN $cause_1$ inactive.

(We have chosen this example because of its simple cause structure)

Preconditions

(Contain in particular the values that must be known to make the XP usable)

    traffic lights are seeable by car_1 in position l_{11}, at time t-X

    traffic lights are red, at position l_3 and will become green at time t.

    Mean time length of lights is d.

(It is important to be able to somewhat evaluate the time the light will stay red)

    Car_1 is aware of the state of the traffic light during the interval $[l_{11}, l_3]$.

    The following values are known: $v_1, l_{11}, l_3, t-X$.

    The following values can approximated as follows. X is approximated by $(l_3-l_{11})/v_1$,

    x is approximated by 15 sec, t is unknown at the beginning of the script. Let us call

    t the exact time at which the light will be turning to green, and t_{aprx} its approxima

    tion before this event happens. Then, t_{aprx} is approximated by (t-X)+X.

(It is the field expert's task to provide correct approximations. The ones given are here simply for illustration)

    IF car_2 is present THEN

        IF car_2 at position l_2 is moving THEN evaluate its speed v'_2 and activate the XP

"follow a moving car before a traffic light" with known values: $l_{11}, l_2, l_3, v_1, v'_2$

        ELSE car_2 is stopped before the lights at position l_2

            IF the speed of car_2 at time t+x cannot be approximated

            THEN activate the XP "stop behind a car at traffic light" with known

            values: l_{11}, l_2, l_3, v_1

            ELSE the speed of car_2 at time t+x can be approximated by v_2

Actions to perform

    Compute dv_1

(this computation depends wether car_2 is present or not, and on the cause of the XP, $cause_1$ or $cause_2$)

    Decrease the speed v_1 of the amount dv_1 at time t-X

    Compute T

(this computation depends wether car_2 is present or not)

        Compute dv'_1 .

(this computation depends wether car_2 is present or not, and on the cause of the XP, $cause_1$ or $cause_2$)

Increase the speed v_1-dv_1 of the amount dv'_1 at time T.

Failure cases

    IF light is still red at time t_{aprx}, then activate the XP "stop at a traffic light" with

parameters $(l_{11} +(v_1-dv_1)* t_{aprx}), l_3, v_1-dv_1$

    IF car_2 is still stopped at time t_{aprx}, then activate the XP "stop behind a car at a

traffic light" with parameters $(l_{11} +(v_1-dv_1)* t_{aprx}), l_2, l_3, v_1-dv_1$

Post-conditions

    - car_1 crosses light at speed $(v_1-dv_1)+dv'_1$.

    - car_1 has been saving gas and time.

(It may happen that one saves gas with the goal of saving time, even though the goals are most often contradictory)

9 - KNOWLEDGE FOR VISION

Even though pattern recognition and artificial intelligence have a long common history, using background knowledge in a systematic way is quite recent, and somewhat isolated in the middle of the mass of work done on "low level". There exist two different implementations of this approach.

The oldest one, illustrated by the system ACRONYM (Brooks, 1981) uses knowledge in the form of semantic networks. Interaction between knowledge and recognition takes place at very high levels of interpretation. For instance, Huertas, Cole, and Nevatia (1989) analyze aerial scenes of airports and use the fact that the "detection of .. a taxiway will increase the confidence of a structure believed to be a passenger terminal (and *vice-versa*)". In this approach, geometrical models are intensively used at the lowest levels of image treatment. Another recent instance is the work of Asada and Shirai (1989). These authors work on the vision system of a mobile robot and, in order to increase the robustness of their geometrical model, they use an object-oriented semantic net (i.e., a semantic net in which inheritance of properties is taken care of) in order to represent semantic constraints among the objects to be recognized.

The newest approach introduces expert systems at various levels of the visual treatment, sometimes including relatively low-levels, such as in (Adorni et al., 1987). The same authors use also an expert system at the interpretation level. The same can be found, for instance, in (Smets, Verbeek, Suetens, and Oosterlinck, 1988; Dawant and Jansen, 1988; Perucca et al., 1988).

Both approaches use knowledge-based systems the rules of which could be also acquired by using ML techniques.

10 - THE CERTIFICATION OF KNOWLEDGE

There is no doubt that ML does help acquiring or refining rules, thus helping to enlarge the "knowledge acquisition bottleneck" (Feigenbaum, 1981). For instance,

- ID3 (Quinlan, 1983; Bratko and Lavrac, 1987) inspired several ML software that have been applied in the medical domain, usually performing better than the the Expert Systems (ES) built by interrogation.

- INDUCE (Michalski, 1984; Michalski et al., 1983; 1986) generated the first ES automatically obtained, the rule of which have been validated by experts

- Structural matching (Kodratoff et al., 1984; Kodratoff, 1988) is applied to air traffic control (Cannat and Vrain, 1988).

- All the deductive methods have been applied to various problem solving. At any rate, this approach will be extremely useful for the refinement of existing ES as we shall briefly describe it now. Given an existing ES, given a set of deep rules expressing the background knowledge of the expert, they will allow improve the ES through casual interaction with expert. The expert uses the ES. Would the expert agree with the ES, then some generalization of the existing rules can be attempted. Would the expert act differently from the ES, then new efficient rules can be learned (Mitchell et al., 1986). Would the expert contradict the ES, new rules will be added to complete the knowledge of the ES.

Existing ES tend to stay in the research and development department of the companies that developed them, instead of moving to application fields as they should. One of the main reason of this lack of large application is that application fields need certified software, and there is presently no way to certify an ES, except some kind of "examination" similar to those students undergo. We claim that ML techniques are the best available tool at present to improve this situation. This can be done in two ways, by helping to specify the knowledge acquisition problem of the ES, and also by providing directly some certification.

10.1 - Specifying the knowledge acquisition problem

ML program themselves need to be characterized by a number of attributes, like the change they do to their initial knowledge, their use of background knowledge etc. Such bench marks for ML programs are also specifications of the task to be performed by the output of the program. For instance, a clear description of the changes performed in the knowledge base specifies the state of the intended output. Similarly, a description of the background knowledge of the ML program specifies the environment in which the ES rules are valid.

10.2 - Validating an ES

A possible solution to the problem of ES validation is the use of machine learning techniques.

Suppose that we have an ES built in a classical way (Human ES), and a ML program the output of which is a program that performs tasks, or at least parts of the tasks, similar to those of the HES. This is an automatically built ES (ML ES).

When analyzing a rule of the Human ES, one can bias the ML system so that it generates a rule as similar as possible to the one under analysis. If one obtains the same rule, then the analysis the way it has been automatically generated will tell which part of the knowledge, and which biasing, it relies on. This part of the knowledge is the validation of the rule, if the knowledge itself has been validated, which brings us back to classical validation techniques. If one obtains a different rule, the same analysis can take place and one asks the human expert to react either by changing the rule or the background knowledge of the ML, or by justifying the rule in the Human ES. If the expert justifies his rule, this is a validation, if he does not, one iterates as long as the rules are not identical.

We had some experience of the latter case when building rules for an ES in aircraft control. The controller would provide rules and examples illustrating their use. The ML system then infers rules from the examples (Cannat and Vrain, 1988). Our current practise was that the automatically generated rules were largely different from those expected by the expert. His explanations of the discrepancies are included in the background knowledge. When convergence has been achieved, the obtained rule is validated by the background knowledge. The whole history of the refinement can be used as an elaborated validating argument.

11 - CONCLUSION

We have been reviewing seven kinds of hard problems for the acquisition, of symbolic background knowledge.

The problem of detecting implicit implications comes from that the experts tend to insist on causal knowledge, and to forget about implications that are "obvious" or do not contain a causal content for the degree of granularity they consider significant.

Experts are also very keen at pointing at relationships that hold in their field, that can be viewed as integrity constraints on the data base made of the field knowledge. Unfortunately, these integrity constraints have to be expressed as first order logic theorems. They must therefore first be put under the form of clauses to be tractable. Transforming theorems into clauses contain a step known as skolemization, necessary to eliminate existentially quantified variables. Normally, this step is performed by adding a totally new symbol to the symbols already existing. This cannot be accepted by an expert who wants to find a "good" skolem function which is related to his prior knowledge of the field. This discrepancy between theory and practise is somewhat disturbing but altogether unescapable.

Uncertain knowledge already received a large amount of attention. We nevertheless suggest that using a new concept, the one of polymorphic taxonomies, can be useful to handle this problem.

Weak knowledge can be also uncertain, but is present when large chunk of knowledge are still missing, and the experts can disagree on the causes of events. In that case, it is essential that the experts see only completely instantiated solutions (on which they are supposed to agree at least). Therefore, the system has to ask the expert's advice on results of the rules it has been building, not on the rules themselves.

In most real life applications, it is essential to be able to manage time, and the coordination of tasks. Unfortunately, the acquisition of temporal information is still in its infancy.

Surprisingly, the situation is as much bad when it comes to visual knowledge. In spite of the high expectations of the AI approach to vision, most researchers still concentrate on "low-level" vision, which uses background knowledge implicitly only, in the way the information is coded. Putting into evidence the visual strategies used by humans faced to ambiguous situations seems to be still an untouched topic for computer science.

The importance of knowledge validation is well established now that a new journal, Applied Expert Systems, is devoted to this topic. Nevertheless, it is still quite open field for research.

REFERENCES

Adorni G., Massone L., Sandini G., Immovilli M., "From early processing to conceptual reasoning: An attempt to fill the gap", in Proc. 10th IJCAI, 1987, pp. 775-778.

Asada M., Shirai Y., "Building a world model for a mobile robot using dynamic semantic constraints", in Proc. 11th IJCAI, 1989, pp.1629-1634.

Benzecri J. P. et alii, *L'analyse des données*, Dunod, Paris, 1973.

Bisson, G., Laublet P., "A Functional Model to Evaluate Learning Systems", in *Proc. 4th EWSL*, Morik K. (Ed), Pitman, London 1989, pp. 37-48.

Blythe J., Needham D, McDowell R., Manago M., Rouveirol C., Kodratoff Y., Lesaffre F.-M., Conruyt N., Corsi P. Knowledge Acquisition by Machine Learning: the INSTIL Project, in *Esprit'88 Putting the Technology to Use*, pp. 769-779, North-Holland, Amsterdam 1988.

Boose, J. H. "A survey of knowledge acquisition techniques and tools", *Knowledge Acquisition 1*, 1989, pp. 3-37.

Boose, J. H., Shema D.B., Bradsi J M. "Recent progress in AQUINAS: a knowledge acquisition workbench", *Knowledge Acquisition 1*, 1989, pp. 139-214..

Bratko I., Lavrac N. (Eds) *Progress in Machine Learning,* Sigma Press, Wilmslow 1987.

Bratko, I., Kodratoff, Y., An analytical report of EWSL-88, *AI Communications 2*, 1989, pp. 24-27.

Brooks R. A., "Symbolic reasoning among 3-D models and 2-D images", *Artificial Intelligence Journal*, 17, 1981, pp. 285-348.

Buchanan B.G., Shortliffe E. H. (Eds.) *Rule-Base Expert Systems*, Addison-Wesley, Reading MA, 1984.

Cannat J. J., Vrain C., "Machine Learning Applied to Air Traffic Control", Proc. Human Machine Interaction, Artificial Intelligence, Aeronautics and Space, Toulouse Sept. 1988, pp. 265-274, CEPAD Toulouse,1988.

Dawant B. M., Jansen B. H., "A coupled expert system for automated signal interpretation", in *Pattern Recognition and Artificial Intelligence*, Gelsema E.S. and Kanal L.N. (Eds), North-Holland, Amsterdam 1988, pp. 471-481.

DeJong G., Mooney R.: "Explanation Based Learning: An Alternative View", *Machine Learning Journal, Vol. 1*, Number 2, 1986, pp. 145-176, Kluwer Academic Publishers.

Duval B., Kodratoff Y. "A Tool for the Management of Incomplete Theories: Reasoning about explanations" in *Machine Learning, Meta-Reasoning and Logics*, P. Brazdil and K. Konolige (Eds.), Kluwer Academic Press, 1990, pp. 135-158.

Feigenbaum E. A. "Expert Systems in the 1980s", in Bond editor, *State of the Art Report on Machine Intelligence*, Maidenhead: Pergamon-Infotech, 1981.

Ganascia J.-G., Helft N., "Evaluation des Systèmes d'Apprentissage", Actes Journées Françaises sur l'Apprentissage, E. Chouraqui editor, Cassis May 1988, CNRS Marseilles 1988, pp. 3-20.

Ganascia, J.-G., "Improvement and Refinement of the Learning Bias Semantic", Proc. ECAI-88, Y. Kodratoff (Ed), Pitman 1988, pp 384-389

Huertas A., Cole W., Nevatia R., "Using generic knowledge in analysis of aerial scenes: A case study", in Proc. 11th IJCAI, 1989, pp. 1642-1648.

Kodratoff Y. "Characterising Machine Learning Programs: A European Compilation", RR 507 LRI, 1989, reproduced in *Artificial Intelligence, Research Directions in Cognitive Science, European Perspectives, Vol. 5*, D. Sleeman and N. O. Bernsen (Eds), Lawrence Erlbaum (to appear)

Kodratoff Y. "Faut-il choisir entre science des explications et science des nombres?", in *Induction symbolique et numérique à partir de données*, Kodratoff Y and Diday E. (Eds), Cepadues Editions, Toulouse 1990 (to appear).

Kodratoff Y. *Introduction to Machine Learning*, Pitman 1988.

Kodratoff Y., Ganascia J.G., Clavieras B., Bollinger T., Tecuci G., "Careful Generalization for Concept Learning", Proc. ECAI-84, Pisa 1984, pp. 483-492. Also in Advances in Artificial Intelligence, T. O'Shea (ed), pp. 229-238, North-Holland Amsterdam 1985.

Kodratoff Y., Rouveirol C., Tecuci G., and Duval B."Symbolic approaches to uncertainty", in Intelligent Systems: Sate of the art and future directions, Ras Z. W. and Zemankova M. (Eds.), Ellis Horwood, 1990 (to appear).

Kodratoff, Y., Manago, M. and Blythe, J., "Generalization and Noise" *Int. J. Man-Machine Studies 27*, 1987, pp. 181-204. Also in *Knowledge Acquisition for Knowledge-Based Systems*, Gaines B. and Boose J. (Eds), Academic Press, London 1988, pp. 301-324

Kodratoff, Y., Manago, M., Blythe, J., Smallman, C. and Andro, Th., : "The Integration of Numeric and Symbolic Techniques in Learning", in *ESPRIT 86 Results and Achievements*, North-Holland, 1987, pp 313-321.

Kodratoff, Y., Perdrix, H. and Franova, M., "Traitement symbolique du raisonnement incertain", Actes Congrès AFCET Matériels et Logiciels pour la 5ème Génération, Paris, March 1985, pp.33-45.

Kodratoff, Y., Tecuci, G., "Techniques of Design and DISCIPLE Learning Apprentice", *International J. of Expert Systems 1*, 1, 1987, pp. 39-66.

Manago M., Kodratoff Y. : "Noise and Knowledge Acquisition", Proc. IJCAI-87, Milan Aug. 87, pp. 348-354.

Michalski R. S. "A Theory and a Methodology of Inductive Learning", in *Machine Learning: An Artificial Intelligence Approach*, R.S. Michalski, J.G. Carbonell, T.M. Mitchell (Eds.), Morgan Kaufmann, Los Altos, 1983, pp 83-134.

Michalski R., "Inductive learning as rule-guided transformation of symbolic descriptions A theory and implementation", in *Automatic Program Construction Techniques*, Biermann, Guiho and Kodratoff editors, Macmillan Publishing Company 1984, pp. 517-552.

Michalski, R.S., Carbonell, J. G., Mitchell, T. M. (Eds.), *Machine Learning: An Artificial Intelligence Approach*, Morgan Kaufmann 1983.

Michalski, R.S., Carbonell, J. G., Mitchell, T. M. (Eds.), *Machine Learning: An Artificial Intelligence Approach, Volume II*, Morgan Kaufmann 1986.

Mitchell T.M., Keller R.M., Kedar-Cabelli S.T. : "Explanation Based Learning: An Unifying View", *Machine Learning Journal, Vol. 1*, Number 1, 1986, pp. 47-80, Kluwer Academic Publishers.

Morik K. "Sloppy Modeling" in *Knowledge Representation and Organization in Machine Learning*, Lecture Note in AI 347, Springer-Verlag, Berlin 1989, pp.107-134.

Morik K., Rouveirol C., Sims P. : "Comparative Study of the representation languages used by the systems of the MLT", rapport ESPRIT D2.1., Nov. 1989.

Perucca G., de Couasnon T., Giorcelli S., Hirsh E., Mangold H., "Advanced algorithms and architecture for speech and image processing", in *Esprit'88, Putting the Technology to Use*, CEC (Ed.), North Holland 1988, pp. 543-561.

Quinlan J.R., "Learning Efficient Classification Procedures and their Application to Chess End Games" in *Machine Learning: An Artificial Intelligence Approach*, R.S. Michalski, J.G. Carbonell, T.M. Mitchell (Eds.), Morgan Kaufmann 1983, pp 463-482

Quinlan, J. R. "Learning efficient classification procedures and their application to chess end games," in *Machine Learning: An Artificial Intelligence Approach*, Michalski R. S., Carbonell J. G., Mitchell T. M. (Eds), Morgan Kaufmann, Los Altos.

Schank R. C. *Explanation Patterns : Understanding mechanically and Creatively*, Ablex Publishing Company, (1987).

Schank R. C., Abelson R. P., *Scripts, Plans, Goals, and Understanding*, Lawrence Erlbaum, Hillsdale, N.J. (1977).

Shafer D. *A mathematical theory of evidence*, Princeton University Press, Princeton NJ, 1976.

Smets C., Verbeek G., Suetens P., Oosterlinck A., "A knowledge-based system for the three-dimensional reconstruction of the cerebral blood vessels from a pair of stereoscopic angiograms", in *Pattern Recognition and Artificial Intelligence*, Gelsema E.S. and Kanal L.N. (Eds), North-Holland, Amsterdam 1988, pp. 425-435.

Tecuci, G., and Kodratoff, Y., "Apprenticeship Learning in Nonhomogeneous Domain Theories", in Kodratoff Y. and Michalski R. S. (Eds.) *Machine Learning: An Artificial Intelligence Approach, Volume 3*, Morgan-Kaufmann 1990 (to appear).

Zadeh L. A. The role of fuzzy logic in the management of uncertainty in expert systems, Fuzzy Sets and Systems, 11, 1983, pp. 199-227.

Subsequential functions: characterizations, minimization, examples

Christophe Reutenauer
Math-info, UQAM
C.P. 8888, Succ. A
Montréal
Canada H3C 3P8

1. Introduction

This is a survey paper on subsequential functions from a free monoid into another. The results presented here are essentially not new, although the presentation and the proofs are different from those found in the litterature.

Subsequential transducers and functions were introduced by Schützenberger [11], as a generalization of the classical sequential transducers and functions [10], [7], [6]. The difference lies in the fact that a subsequential transducer has final states and may add a suffix to the output, once the computation is finished (this suffix depends only on the final state); otherwise, it works as usually, by reading the input string sequentially form left to right, and writing down the output at each stage of the reading process, from left to right.

This new definition has the consequence that many classical functions, such as integer division, integer multiplication, decoding, pattern substitution, which are "sequential" in some intuitive sense, but not in the classical sense, are now subsequentials. Moreover, the classical operations and results on sequential functions are still valid for subsequentical functions. And finally, the theorem of Choffrut characterizing subsequential functions, and extending the theorem of Ginsburg-Rose, justifies a posteriori, from a mathematical point of view, the new definition: a function f is subsequential if and only if f^{-1} preserves regularity of languages, and if f has some property of topological nature.

The paper is divided into 4 sections: in section 2, we give in th.1 the Nerode-like characterization of subsequential functions, and many examples. In section 3, we give the effective construction of the minimal transducer for a given subsequential function. This seems to be written down explicitly for the first time. In section 4, we give general examples and counter examples. In the final section, we state Choffrut's theorem, and give a new proof of it, by introducing the differential of a function, which is similar to Eilenberg's differential of prefix-preserving functions [6].

Some of the results on subsequential functions have been extended to rational functions (these are obtained by composing left right subsequential funcitons, or equivalently, their graph is a rational subset of the product monoid see[6]), in [11].

In the paper, *function* will always mean *partial function* ; if f is a function, its *domain of definition* will be simply called its *domain*, and denoted by dom (f). We write f(x) ≠ Ø to expresss the fact that x ∈ dom (f). We use the convention f(Ø) = Ø, for any function f: this will allow several simplifications (e.g. we always have g o f (x) = g (f(x)). The empty function is denoted by Ø.

2. Characterization of subsequential functions

Subsequential transducers and functions were considered in [12], [3], [4], [5], [1], as a generalization of sequential functions. We modify slightly the definition of a subsequential transducer (by introducing an initial prefix), but the class of functions obtained by these machines will be the subsequential functions as above; the reason of this modification will appear later.

A *subsequential tranducer* is an 8-tuple T = (X, Y, Q, q_, δ, λ, m, ρ) where X, Y are respectively the *input* and *output alphabet*, Q is the finite set of *states*, q_ is the *initial state* , δ : Q × X → Q is the *next state function*, λ : Q × X → Y is the *output funciton* (δ and λ must *have the same domain*), m in Y* is the *initial prefix*, and ρ : Q → Y* is the *terminal function*.. The transducer is *sequential* if m = 1 (= the empty word) and if ρ (q) = 1 for any state q.

As usual, the functions δ and λ are extended to Q × X*, and we denote δ (q, u) = q.u and λ (q,u) = q * u (following [1]). The extension is determined, for any words u and v, by the formulas:

$$\delta (q, uv) = q \cdot uv = (q \cdot u) \cdot v$$
$$\lambda(q,u) = q * uv = (q * u) ((q \cdot u) * v)$$

The function computed by the tranducer is the function

$$X^* \longrightarrow Y^*$$
$$w \longmapsto m \lambda (q_, w) \rho (q \cdot w) = m (q_ * w) \rho(q.w)$$

Such a function will be called a *subsequential function*.

A subsequential transducer admits as usually a graphical representation. An edge p $\xrightarrow{a/u}$ q means that δ (p, a) = q and λ (p, a) = u. A *terminal state* is a state in the domain of ρ. Initial and terminal states are indicated by an arrow pointing in and out, respectively; this arrow will be labelled by m and ρ, respectively; an omitted label means that this label is the empty word.

In the following examples, we denote the empty word by ∈, when 1 serves already as a letter (digit in a given base).

Example 1 (integer division)

The following subsequential transducer associates to each number written in base 2 its integer quotient by 3, also written in base 2

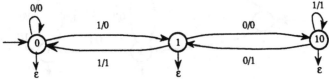

Figure 1

Actually, this transducer is sequential. Moreover it outputs sometimes words beginning with zero's, and it gives sometimes ε as answer, which also unusual. The following subsequential transducer will give the usual outputs (numbers without 0's at the beginning, and 0 in case the quotient is 0).

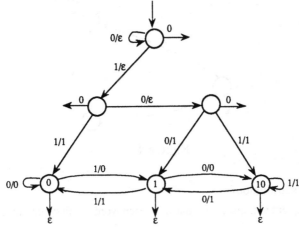

Figure 2

Example 2 (multiplication)

Here, a word on the alphabet {0, 1} will represent a number in base 2, but in the reverse interpretation; for example, 01 will be 2, and 1101 will represent 11.

The following subsequential transducer multiplies by 3 in base 2.

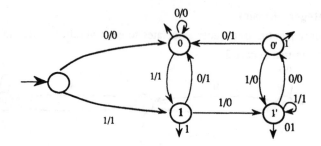

Figure 3

Example 3 (decoder)

The following subsequential transducer computes the inverse of the injective monoid homomorphism $\{x, y\}^* \to \{a, b\}^*$, $x \mapsto a$, $y \mapsto aba$. The empty word is again denoted by 1.

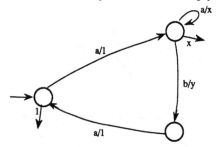

Figure 4

Example 4 (pattern substitution)

The following subsequential transducer replaces in each word the first occurrence of abaa by x.

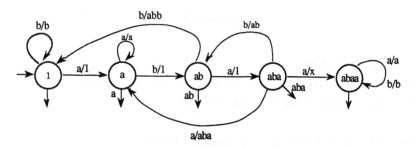

Figure 5

Example 5

Each function $X^* \longrightarrow Y^*$ having a finite domain of definition is subsequential [1] example IV, 2.6. The restriction of each subsequential function to a regular language is subsequential [1] exercise IV.2.3. In particular, if L regular, then the two functions $w \longmapsto w$ and $w \longmapsto 1$, with domain L, are subsequential. With the reverse interpretation, the addition of integers in a given base may be considered as a subsequential function, see [6] XI.4 or [1] Example IV.2.4.

Remark. All these examples will be considered in a more general setting in the sequel of this paper. Concerning example 3, Choffrut [4] has shown that the inverse of an injective morphism $X^* \longrightarrow A^*$ is a subsequential function if and only if $f(X)$ is a code with finite deciphering delay.

If L is a set of words, we denote by $\Lambda\, L$ the longest common left factors of the words in L; if $L = \varnothing$, then $\Lambda\, \varnothing = \varnothing$.

Let $\gamma : X^* \longrightarrow Y^*$ be any function. Then, we define for any word u in X^*, $\lambda(\gamma, u) = \gamma * u$ by

$$(1) \qquad \lambda\,(\gamma,\, u) \ = \Lambda\, \{\gamma(uw) \mid uw \in \mathrm{dom}\,(\gamma)\}$$

In other words, $\lambda(\gamma, u) = \gamma * u$ is the longest common left factor of the words of the form $\gamma(uw)$; $\gamma * u$ is undefined if there is no such word.

Let $u, v \in Y^* \cup \{\varnothing\}$. We define $u^{-1} v$ by

$$u^{-1}v \ = \ \begin{cases} \varnothing \ \text{if } u = \varnothing \text{ or } v = \varnothing \text{ or } v \notin u\, Y^* \\ w \ \text{if } u,\, v \in Y^* \text{and } v = uw \end{cases}$$

With this convention, we may define $\gamma.u$, also denoted $u^{-1}\gamma$ or $\delta(\gamma,u)$, to be the function $X^* \longrightarrow Y^*$ such that

$$(2) \qquad (\gamma.u)\,(w) \ = \ \lambda\,(\gamma,\, u)^{-1}\,\gamma\,(uw)$$

Note that $(\gamma.u)\,(w) \neq \varnothing$ if and only if $\gamma\,(uw) \neq \varnothing$, because $\gamma\,(uw) \neq \varnothing$ implies that $\lambda(\gamma,u) \neq \varnothing$, too. One may view $\gamma.u$ as the function obtained from the function $w \longmapsto \gamma(uw)$ by suppression of the longest common prefix of its image. In particular, $\gamma.1$ is obtained from γ by deleting from each $\gamma(w)$ the longest common prefix of the image of γ.

The following result is the main result of this section. It is implicitly given in [5] (Prop. 4).

Theorem 1 A function $\gamma : X^* \longrightarrow Y^*$ is subsequential if and only if the set $\{\gamma.u \mid u \in X^*\}$ is finite.

Note that this theorem gives the classical Nerode criterion for a language L to be regular, when applied to the function with domain L and image 1. Moreover, it extends also the Nerode-like criterion for sequential functions, as given by Raney [10] and Eilenberg [6] (th.XII.4.2).

Proof. 1. We prove three formulas.

$$(3) \qquad \gamma (uw) = \lambda (\gamma, u) (\gamma.u) (w)$$

$$(4) \qquad \lambda (\gamma, uv) = \lambda (\gamma, u) \lambda (\gamma.u, v)$$

$$(5) \qquad \gamma.uv = (\gamma.u).v$$

Indeed, if $\gamma (uw) = \emptyset$, then by definition, $(\gamma.u) (w) = \emptyset$, so (1) holds in this case; if however $\gamma(uw) \neq \emptyset$, then by definition, (3) holds too.

We have

$$
\begin{aligned}
\lambda (\gamma, uv) &= \wedge \{ \gamma(uvw) \mid uvw \in \mathrm{dom} (\gamma) \} \\
&= \wedge \{ \lambda(\gamma,u) (\gamma.u) (vw) \mid uvw \in \mathrm{dom} (\gamma)\} \\
&= \lambda(\gamma,u) \wedge \{(\gamma.u) (vw) \mid u v w \in \mathrm{dom} (\gamma)\}
\end{aligned}
$$

Note that $us \in \mathrm{dom} (\gamma)$ is equivalent to $s \in \mathrm{dom} (\gamma.u)$, by (2) and (3). Hence

$$
\begin{aligned}
\lambda (\gamma, uv) &= \lambda (\gamma,u) \wedge \{(\gamma.u) (vw) \mid vw \in \mathrm{dom} (\gamma.u)\} \\
&= \lambda(\gamma,u) \ \lambda (\gamma.u, v)
\end{aligned}
$$

For (5), we have by (3) and (4)

$$
\begin{aligned}
\lambda (\gamma,u) \lambda (\gamma.u,v) (\gamma.uv) (w) &= \lambda (\gamma, uv) (\gamma.uv) (w) \\
&= \gamma (uvw) \\
&= \lambda (\gamma,u) (\gamma.u) (v w) \\
&= \lambda (\gamma,u) \lambda (\gamma.u, v) ((\gamma.u) \cdot v) (w)
\end{aligned}
$$

If $\gamma (uvw) \neq \emptyset$, then $\lambda (\gamma,u) \neq \emptyset$ and $(\gamma.u) (vw) \neq \emptyset$, hence $\lambda (\gamma.u,v) \neq \emptyset$, thus one obtains $(\gamma.uv) (w) = ((\gamma.u) \cdot v) (w)$. If $\gamma (uvw) = \emptyset$, then similarly $(\gamma.u v) (w) = \emptyset = ((\gamma.u)\cdot v) (w)$. Hence (5) holds.

2. Now, let $\gamma: X^* \longrightarrow Y^*$ be any function with $\{\gamma.u \mid U \in X^*\}$ finite. We define a subsequential transducer $T_\gamma = (X, Y, Q, q_-, \delta, \lambda, w, \rho)$ with $Q = \{ \gamma.u \mid u \in X^*, \gamma.u \neq \emptyset\}$.

Define $q_- = \gamma.1$. Moreover, let δ, λ be defined by $\delta (q, x) = q \cdot x$ and $\lambda (q,x)$ be as above. Then δ and λ have the same domain $\{(q, x) \in Q \times X \mid x \in X^* \cap \mathrm{dom} (q) \neq \emptyset\}$. Define $m = \lambda(\gamma,1)$ and $\rho (q) = q (1)$.

Then the function computed by this tranducer is $m \lambda(q_-, w) \rho(q_-,w) = \lambda (\gamma,1) \lambda (\gamma.1,w) \rho((\gamma.1).w)$ which is equal by (4) and (5) to $\lambda (\gamma, w) (\gamma.w) (1) = \gamma(w)$ by (3). Hence γ is subsequential.

3. Suppose now that $\gamma(w) = m\,\lambda(q_-,w)\,\rho(q_-\cdot w)$ for some subsequential transducer. We show that $\gamma.u$ depends only on $q_-\cdot u$, which will imply that there are only finitely many functions $\gamma.u$.

Suppose indeed that $q_-\cdot u = q$. Then $\gamma(uw) = m\,\lambda(q_-,uw)\,\rho(q_-\cdot uw) = m\,\lambda(q_-,u)\,\lambda(q,w)\,\rho(q.w)$ which shows that $\gamma.u = \gamma_q.1$ with γ_q the function $w \mapsto \lambda(q,w)\,\rho(q.w)$. □ ■ □

The following result is well-known.

Corollary. If g, f are subsequential functions, then so is $g \circ f$.

Proof. Let $h_{u,v}$ be the funciton $(g.u) \circ (f.v)$. These functions are in finite number. We show that $(g \circ f).u$ is equal to one of the functions $h_{u,v}.1$, which will conclude the proof. We have by (3)

$$(g \circ f)(uw) = g(f(uw))$$
$$= g(\lambda(f,u)(f.u)(w))$$
$$= \lambda(g, \lambda(f,u))(g.\lambda(f,u)) \circ (f.u)(w)$$

This implies that

$$(g \circ f).u = ((g_\cdot \lambda(f,u)) \circ (f.u)) . 1$$

□ ■ □

3. Minimization algorithm

Let T be a a subsequential transducer. It will be called *trim* if it is both *accessible* and *coaccessible*, that is, if for each state q, there is a final state p and a path $q_- \to q \to p$, where q_- is the initial state. Let γ_q be the function computed by the transducer obtained by taking q as initial state, with initial prefix equal to the empty word: this means that $\gamma_q(w) = \lambda(q,w)\,\rho(q.w)$. We say that T is *reduced* if any state q is reduced, that is: the function γ_q statisfies $\gamma_q \cdot 1 = \gamma_q$ (this means that either $\gamma_q = \emptyset$, or $\gamma_q(X^*)$ has no nontrivial common left factor). Moreover, T is called *separated*, if any two distinct states p, q are separated, that is, $\gamma_p \neq \gamma_q$.

Let γ be a subsequential function. We have constructed in the course of the proof theorem 1 a subsequential transducer T_γ: it will be called the *minimal transducer* of γ.

Theorem 2. Let γ be a subsequential function. The only transducer computing γ which is trim, reduced and separated is the minimal transducer T_γ of γ. Moreover, T_γ has the minimal number of states among the transducers computing γ. There is a polynomial algorithm to construct T_γ, if γ is given by a subsequential transducer.

The theorem does not say that T_γ is the only transducer computing γ with the minimal number of states (see example 6). However, T_γ is obtained from such a transducer by reducing it, as the proof will show.

Example 6. The function $x^{2n}y \to (xy)^n x$ $(n \geq 0)$ is computed by the minimal transducer

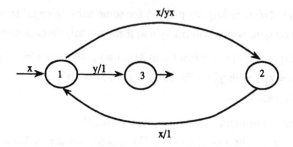

Figure 6

But it is also computed by several other transducers with 3 states, as the followings:

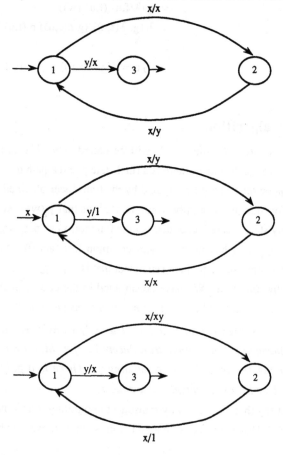

Figure 7

For the first and last, each word γ_1 (w) begins by x, so 1 is not reduced. For the first also, each word γ_2 (w) begins by y, so 2 is not reduced. For the second, each word γ_2(w) begins by x, so 2 is not reduced.

Proof 1. Let $T = (X, Y, Q, q\text{-}, \delta, \lambda, m, \rho)$ be a trim, reduced and separated transducer computing γ. Let $Q_\gamma = \{ \gamma.u \mid u \in X^*, \gamma.u \neq \varnothing \}$ be the set of states of the minimal automaton T_γ of γ. We define a bijective map h: $Q \longrightarrow Q_\gamma$ which commutes with λ and δ; further, we show that $h(q\_) = \gamma.1$, $m = \lambda(\gamma, 1)$ and $\rho(q) = (h(q))$ (1) for any state q, which will imply that T and T_γ are isomorphic.

Let q be in Q. Then, T being accessible, there exists $u \in X^*$ such that $q = q\_.u$. Then $\gamma_q = \gamma.u$: indeed, $\gamma(uw)$ $= m \lambda (q\_, u) \lambda(q,w) \rho (q.w) = m \lambda(q\_,u) \gamma_q (w)$; as γ_q is reduced, we obtain $\lambda(\gamma,u) = m \lambda(q\_,u)$ by (1), and $\gamma.u = \gamma_q$ by (2).

Moreover, $\gamma_q \neq \varnothing$, q being coaccessible. Hence, we may define h by $h(q) = \gamma_q$. The previous argument shows that h is surjective; moreover, it is injective, T being separated. It commutes with δ (i.e $h(\delta(q,x)) = h(q.x) = h(q) \cdot x$) by construction. Moreover, it commutes with λ, that is $\lambda(q,x) = \lambda(\gamma_q, x)$: indeed $\lambda (\gamma_q, x) = \Lambda \{\gamma_q(xw) \mid w \in X^*\} = \Lambda \{ \lambda(q,x) \lambda(q.x, w) \mid w \in X^*\}$; if $\delta(q,x) = q.x = \varnothing$, then also $\lambda(q,x) = \varnothing$ (δ and λ have the same domain), and $\lambda(\gamma_q,x) = \varnothing$. If $q.x = p \neq \varnothing$ then $\lambda (\gamma_q,x) = \lambda (q,x) \Lambda \{\gamma_p(w) \mid w \in X^*\}$ and as γ_p is reduced, $\lambda(\gamma_q,x) = \lambda(q,x)$. It is clear that $h(q\_) = \gamma.1$. Moreover, $m = \lambda (\gamma,1)$ because $\gamma(w) = m \gamma_{q\_} (w)$ and $\gamma_{q\_}$ is reduced. Finally, $\rho(q) = \gamma_q (1) = (\gamma.u) (1)$.

2. The minimality of the number of states of T_γ will be implied by the minimization algorithm. This algorithm has three steps:

a. Remove unnecessary states in order to obtain a trim transducer.

b. Reduce the transducer (this changes only m, λ and ρ; in particular, the number of states is the same).

c. Take the quotient of Q by the inseparability equivalence

a. This is trivial.

b. For each state q, define $m_q = \lambda(\gamma_q, 1)$: in other words, m_q is the longest common left factor of the language recognized by the non deterministic generalized (= with labels in Y^*) automaton, which is obtained from T by replacing each edge $p \xrightarrow{x/u} q$ by $p \xrightarrow{u} q$. It is clear that computing all the m_q' s may me done in polynomial time. Now, define new functions λ' and ρ' and a new m' by: $m' = mm_{q\text{-}}$; $\lambda' (q,x) = m_q^{-1} \lambda (q,x) m_{q.x} \in Y^*$ (note that $\gamma_q (xw) = \lambda(q,x) \gamma_{q.x}$ (w) hence m_q is a left factor of all the $\lambda(q,x) \gamma_{q.x}$ (w), hence also of $\lambda(q,x) m_{q.x}$); $\rho'(q) = m_q^{-1}$ $\rho(q) \in Y^*$ (note that $\gamma_q(1) = \rho(q)$, hence m_q is a left factor of $\rho(q)$).

Let T' denote the new transducer and γ'_q the function $w \mapsto \lambda'(q,w)\,\rho'(q)$. We show that γ'_q = $\gamma_q \cdot 1$: this will imply that T' is reduced; moreover, the function computed by T' is then $m'\,\gamma'_q$. $(w) = m\,m_{q_-}\,(\gamma_{q_-}.1)\,(w) = m\,m_{q_-}\,m_q^{-1}\,\gamma_{q_-}\,(w) = m\,\gamma_{q_-}\,(w) = \gamma(w)$ (with computations in the free group $Y^{(*)}$ over Y). Hence T' computes γ.

Let $w = x_1 \ldots x_n$ and $q_i = q.x_1 \ldots x_i$. Then

$$\gamma'_q(w) \;=\; \lambda'(q,w)\,\rho'(q.w)$$

$$=\; (\prod_{i=0}^{n-1} \lambda'(q_i, x_{i+1}))\,\rho'(q_n)$$

$$=\; (\prod_{i=0}^{n-1} m_{q_i}^{-1}\,\lambda(q_i, x_{i+1})\,m_{q_{i+1}})\,m_{q_n}^{-1}\,\rho(q_n)$$

$$=\; m_q^{-1}\,(\prod_{i=0}^{n-1} \lambda(q_i, x_{i+1}))\,\rho(q_n)$$

$$=\; m_q^{-1}\,\lambda_q(w)$$

$$=\; \lambda(\gamma_q, 1)^{-1}\gamma_q(w)$$

$$=\; (\gamma_q.1)(w)$$

what was to be shown.

It is clear that T' is trim too.

c. We have now a trim and reduced transducer T computing γ. Define the inseparability equivalence relation on Q: $p \sim q$ iff $\gamma_p = \gamma_q$.

We extend $\sim$ to $Q \cup \{\varnothing\}$ by putting $\varnothing$ in a one-element class mod. $\sim$. Moreover, we define $\gamma_\varnothing = \varnothing$. observe that we have

$$\lambda(p,x)\;\gamma_{p.x}(w) \;=\; \lambda(p,x)\,\lambda(p.x, w)\,\rho(p.x.w) \quad \text{(by definition of } \gamma_p)$$

$$=\; \lambda(p, xw)\,\rho(p.xw)$$

$$=\; \gamma_p(xw)$$

We show that $p \sim q$ implies that $\rho(p) = \rho(q)$, and that for any letter x, $\lambda(p,x) = \lambda(q,x)$ and $p.x \sim q.x$. This will show that the transducer obtained by merging inseparable states is trim, reduced, separable and computes γ.

So let $p \sim q$. We deduce $\rho(p) = \gamma_p(1) = \gamma_q(1) = \rho(q)$. Moreover the above computations show that $\lambda(p,x)\,\gamma_{p.x}(w) = \lambda(q,x)\,\gamma(q,x)(w)$.

Suppose that $p.x \neq \varnothing$. Then, as λ and δ have the same domain (by definition of the subsequential transducers), we have $\lambda(p,x) \neq \varnothing$. Moreover, as T is coaccessible, $\gamma_{p.x}$ is not the empty function.

By the above equality, we deduce that $q.x \neq \emptyset$, $\lambda(q,x) \neq \emptyset$, $\gamma_{q.x} \neq \emptyset$. We cannot have $|\lambda(p,x)| < |\lambda(q,x)|$, otherwise $\gamma_{p.x}$ is not reduced. Hence, by symmetry, $|\lambda(p,x)| = |\lambda(q,x)| \Rightarrow \lambda(p,x) = \lambda(q,x)$ and finally $\gamma_{p.x} = \gamma_{q.x}$, i.e. $p.x \sim q.x$.

d. It remains to compute $\sim$. This is similar to the algorithm for the minimization of a deterministic automaton. We begin with an equivalence relation $\sim_o$ defined by: $p \sim_o q$ iff $\rho(p) = \rho(q)$ and $\lambda(p,x) = \lambda(q,x)$ for any letter x. If $\sim_n$ is defined, then:

- If there is a letter x and two states p_o, q_o such that $p_o \sim_n q_o$ and no $(p_o.x \sim_n q_o.x)$, then define $\sim_{n+1}$ by: $p \sim_{n+1} q$ iff $p \sim_n q$ and $p.x \sim_n q.x$ (it is clear that in this case $\sim_{n+1}$ is strictly finer than $\sim_n$ that is, $p \sim_{n+1} q \Rightarrow p \sim_n q$ and $\sim_{n+1} \neq \sim_n$).
- Otherwise stop, and put $N := n$.

This algorithm is classically polynomial. We show that $\sim_N = \sim$.

We first show by induction on n that $p \sim q$ implies $p \sim_n q$. This is true for n = 0, as we have seen in c. Suppose it is true for n: then $p \sim q \Rightarrow p \sim_n q$; moreover $p \sim q \Rightarrow p.x \sim q.x \Rightarrow p.x \sim_n q \cdot x$ (induction). Thus $p \sim_{n+1} q$. We may thus conclude that $p \sim q \Rightarrow p \sim_n q \Rightarrow p \sim_N q$.

Conversely, we show that $p \sim_n q \Rightarrow p \sim q$ that is, $\gamma_p(w) = \gamma_q(w)$ for any word w, by induction on |w|. If w = 1, it is clear because $\gamma_p(w) = \rho(p) = \rho(q) = \gamma_q(w)$, because $p \sim_n q \Rightarrow p \sim_o q \Rightarrow \rho(p) = \rho(q)$. Let w = xu. Then $\gamma_p(w) = \lambda(p,x) \gamma_{p.x}(u)$ and $\gamma_q(w) = \lambda(q,x) \gamma_{q.x}(u)$. By construction, $p \sim_N q \Rightarrow p \sim_o q \Rightarrow \lambda(p,x) = \lambda(q,x)$, and $p \sim_N q \Rightarrow p.x \sim_N q.x \Rightarrow \gamma_{p.x}(u) = \gamma_{q.x}(u)$ by induction. Hence $\gamma_p(w) = \gamma_q(w)$.

The proof is complete. ◻◼◻

Example 7 The minimization algorithm is illustrated on the following transducer.

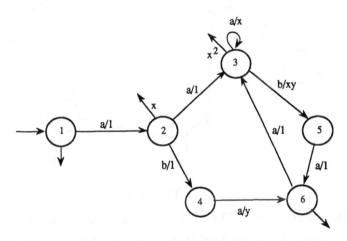

Figure 8

It is trim. In order to reduce it, we compute the words m_q: for this, consider the generalized automaton obtained by forgetting the inputs:

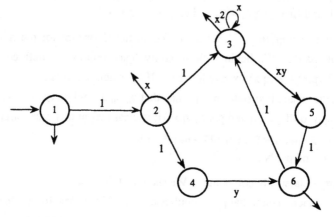

Figure 9

Recall that m_q is the longest prefix to all the words in the language recognized when one takes q as initial state; hence $m_1 = 1$, $m_2 = 1$, $m_3 = x$, $m_4 = y$, $m_5 = 1$, $m_6 = 1$.

The reduced transducer is:

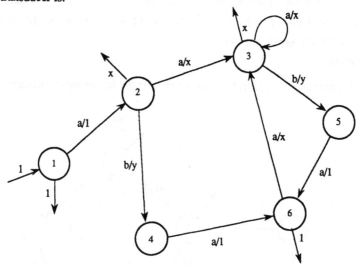

Figure 10

The equivalence relation $\sim_0$ is $1 / 23 / 45 / 6$. The transitions a and b, when applied to this relation, give respectively $2 / 33 / 66 / 3$ and $\varnothing / 45 / \varnothing\varnothing / \varnothing$, hence $\sim_0$ is already equal to $\sim_N$. The minimal transducer is

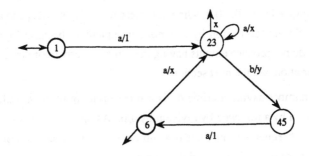

Figure 11

4.   Examples and counter examples

1.   Consider the general case of the *pattern substitution transducer* (cf. example 4): let u in A^* and let $\gamma: A^* \longrightarrow (A \cup x)^*$ be the function which replaces in a word w the first occurrence of u by x, and leaves w unchanged if w is not in $A^* u A^*$. To construct its minimal transducer, one constructs first the minimal outomaton of $A^* u A^*$: the set of state Q is the set of left factors of u, and for $p \in Q\backslash u$, $a \in A$, p.a is equal to pa if pa is a left factor of u, and otherwise p.a is the longest proper left factor of pa which is also right factor of pa ("longest border"); for $p = u$, one defines u.a = u.   By [2] or [9], this automaton may be constructed in linear time. The minimal transducer of γ is deduced from this automaton by adding outputs: let $u = u'b$ ($b \in A$). If $p \in Q\backslash\{u,u'\}$ and p.a = pa, let $\lambda(p,a) = 1$; if $p = u'$, put $\lambda(u',b) = x$, and if $p = u$, put $\lambda(u,a) = a$ for any letter a. Otherwise, p.a is the longest border v of pa: then pa = tv and let $\lambda(p,a) = t$.   The initial prefix is empty, and the terminal function is $\rho(p) = p$, except for $p = u$, where $\rho(u) = 1$.

It is clear that this automaton is minimal (it is reduced if $x \notin A$ and could not have fewer states than $|u| + 1$), and may be constructed in linear time.   We leave the reader verify that it computes γ.

2.   It is well-known that the euclidean division by a given number in a given basis b is a subsequential function (cf. example 1).   We show here that the multiplication by a given number a in base b is subsequential if and   only if a and b have the same prime divisors (however multiplication is subsequential from right to left, see the sequel of this paper).

First, suppose that a is a prime number not dividing b.   Let p be such that $b^p \equiv 1$ mod. a and $b^p > a^2$.   Let $x_n = (b^{pn} - n)/a$.   Suppose by contractiction that x_1 in base b is written $(b-1)^r$.   Then $x_1 = (b^p - 1)/a = b^r - 1 \Rightarrow p \geq r$ and $b^p - 1 = a(b^r - 1) \Rightarrow a \equiv 1$ mod. $b^r \Rightarrow a > b^r$.   Hence $a^2 > ab^r > a(b^r - 1) = b^p - 1$, a contradiction.   Thus x_1, in base b, is written u_1 dv, for some digit $d \neq b - 1$.   We deduce that $x_n = (p^{pn} - b^p)/a + (b^p - 1)/a = b^p x_{n-1} + x_1$ is written u_n dv.   With $|dv| = \ell$, we see that x_n and $x_n + 1$ differ only in the last ℓ digits.   However, a x_n is represented in base b by the word $(b-1)^{pn}$ and a $(x_n + 1)$ by $10...0$ u, where u represents a - 1: thus ax_n and $a(x_n + 1)$ differ by the second digit. So, multiplication by a is not subsequential, because inputs having a long common left factor do not produce outputs having the same property (more precisely, this function has not bounded variation, see the next section).

Now, let a be any number having a prime divisor p not dividing b: then multiplication by p is equal to multiplication by a followed by division by a/p. As this division is subsequential and as the composition of subsequential functions is a subsequential function, multiplication by a is not subsequential (otherwise so would be multiplication by p).

Now, let a be a prime number dividing b: then multiplication by a is equal to multiplication by b followed by the division by b/a; as multiplication by b is subsequential (you have just to add a 0 at the end of the word), multiplication by a is subsequential. The general case follows by composition.

3. We now consider words on A = {0, 1, 2,..., b - 1}, but read from right to left. In other words, we will consider functions which are subsquential from right to left. We show that multiplication in base b by a given number a is such a function. For this, let $\gamma : A^* \longrightarrow A^*$ represent multiplication by a. We use the dual form of theorem 1. Let a be represented by α_k ... α_o, that is, $a = \alpha_{k-1} b^{k-1} + ... + \alpha_1 b + \alpha_o$ $(0 \leq \alpha_i \leq b - 1)$. Consider the function γ_t which represents in base b the function: $x \mapsto ax + t$. We show that for any word u, $u.\gamma$ is among the functions $1.\gamma_t$ for $0 \leq t < b^k$: this will imply by theorem 1 that γ is subsequential from right to left. Let $u = \beta_{\ell-1} ... \beta_1 \beta_0$ with $\beta_i \in A$, represent the number s. Then, if w represents the number x, $\gamma(wu)$ represents the number $a (x b^\ell + s) = (ax + as/b^\ell) b^\ell + (as \bmod. b^\ell)$, where i /j is the quotient of the euclidean division of i by j. This shows that $u.\gamma = 1.\gamma_t$ for $t = as/b^\ell$. But $t = as / b^\ell < b^k b^\ell / b^\ell = b^k$, which shows the claim.

A simple arithmetical argument shows also that division by a is not subsequential from right to left, except when a and b have the same prime factors : in this case, the division is subsequential from right to left, as one shows easily.

4. Let A be a finite field. Then each word in A^* represents a polynomial over A written in decreasing powers of the variables. With this representation, the euclidean quotient by a fixed polynomial is a subsequential function, and the multiplication by a given polynomial is subsequential from right to left. When this operations are done in the reverse direction, then they are no more subsequential, except when the fixed polynomial is a monomial. We leave the details to the reader.

5.   Choffrut's theorem

The *prefix distance* between two words u and v is the number

$$\| u, v \| = |u| + |v| - 2|u \wedge v|$$

where u $\wedge$ v is the longest common left factor of u and v. In other words, if u = pu', v = pv' where u' and v' have no left factor in common, then $\| u, v \| = |u'| + |v'|$. A function γ: $X^* \longrightarrow Y^*$ has *bounded variation* if for any integer k, there exists and integer K such that

$$u, v \in dom\ (\gamma),\ \| u, v \| \le k \Rightarrow \| \gamma\ (u), \gamma\ (v) \| \le K.$$

It is easily seen that a subsequential funciton has bounded variation.

For a given function γ: $X^* \longrightarrow Y^*$, its *differential* (as a generalization of [6] X1.6) is the function ϕ: $X^+ \longrightarrow Y^{(*)}$ (where $Y^{(*)}$ is the free group over Y) defined by: $\phi(w) = \gamma(w)$ if w has no proper left factor in dom (γ); otherwise, let u be the longest proper left factor of w which is in dom (γ): then $\phi\ (w) = \gamma\ (u)^{-1}\ \gamma(w)$. The differential allows to reconstruct γ: indeed, let w $\in$ dom (γ); then w may be written $u_1...u_p$ where $u_1, u_1 u_2, ..., u_1...u_p$ are all the left factors of w which are in dom (γ). Then

$$(6) \qquad\qquad \gamma\ (w)\ =\ \gamma(u_1)\ \gamma(u_1\ u_2)\ ...\ \gamma(u_1...u_p)$$

Note also that dom (γ) = dom $(\gamma) \setminus 1$.

The following result characterizes completely subsequential functions.

Theorem 3 *(Choffrut [4], [5]) Let γ: $X^* \longrightarrow Y^*$ be a function. The following conditions are equivalent:*

(i) γ *is a subsequential function.*

(ii) γ *has bounded variation and $\gamma^1(L)$ is a regular for any regular language L.*

(iii)   *The differential has finite codomain and γ^1 (g) is a regular language for any g in $Y^{(*)}$.*

It is worth to note that an easy consequence of this result is the theorem of Ginsburg - Rose [8], as proved by Choffrut (see [1] IV.2 for details).

We shall decompose the nontrivial part of the proof into two lemmas.

Lemma 1. *Let γ: $X^* \longrightarrow Y^*$ be a function, p and integer and u a word such that*

(i)   *For any word w, the words $\gamma(w)$ and $\gamma(u)$, if defined, differ only by a right factor of length < p.*

(ii)   *For any regular language L in Y^*, $\gamma^1(L)$ is regular.*

Let g_1, g_2 in Y^* of length < p and without common left factor. Then the language

$$\{w \in X^* | \exists\ s \in Y^*, \gamma(w) = sg_1\ and\ \gamma\ (wu) = sg_2\}$$

is regular.

Proof. We show that for w in X^* with $| \gamma(w) |, | \gamma(wu) | \ge 2$ p, the condition

(7) $\exists\, s \in Y^*,\ \gamma(w) = sg_1,$ and $\gamma(wu) = sg_2$

is equivalent to the condition

(8) $\exists\, i \in \{0, ..., 2p-1\}, \exists\, h \in Y^p$ such that $\gamma(w) \in Y^i\,(Y^{2p})^*\, h\, g_1$ and $\gamma(wu) \in Y^i\,(Y^{2p})^*\, hg_2$

Suppose this is proved. Then, if L is the language of the lemma, then there is a partition $L = L_1 \cup L_2$ where

$$L_1 = \{w \in X^* \mid w \text{ satisfies to (8)}\} \text{ and } L_2 = \{w \in X^* \mid w \in L \text{ and } |\gamma(w)| \text{ or } |\gamma(wu)| < 2p\}.$$

Now L_1 is regular by (ii) and the fact that (8) is a regular condition. Moreover, if $\gamma(w)$ is short, then $\gamma(wu)$ is short too, by (i), and conversely. Hence L_2 is a finite union of languages of the form

$$L_s = \{\, w \in X^* \mid \gamma(w) = sg_1 \text{ and } \gamma(wu) = sg_2\}$$

These languages are regular by (ii), so finally L is regular.

Now, it is clear that (7) implies (8). Suppose that (8) holds, that is, $\gamma(w) = s_1hg_1$, $\gamma(wu) = s_2hg_2$ with $|s_1|, |s_2| \equiv i \bmod. 2p$. We must show that $s_1 = s_2$. We know from (i) that for some words t, h_1, h_2 with $|h_1|, |h_2| < p$, one has $\gamma(w) = t\, h_1,\ \gamma(wu) = t\, h_2$. Hence, $|s_1h|$ and $|t|$ differ by at most p, and similarly for $|s_2\,h|$ and $|t|$. This shows that $||s_1\,h| - |s_2\,h|| < 2\ p \Rightarrow |s_1\,h| = |s_2\,h| \Rightarrow |s_1| = |s_2|$. We have $th_1 = s_1\,h\,g_1$ and $th_2 = s_2\,h\,g_2$. Thus it suffices to show that s_1, s_2 are shorter than t. Suppose that $|t| < |s_1|$; then $|h_1| > |hg_1| \geq p$ (because $h \in Y^p$), which is impossible. Hence $|t| \geq |s_1|$ and similarly $|t| \geq |s_2|$, which concludes the proof. □ ■ □

Lemma 2. *Let* γ_1, γ_2 *be functions* $X^* \longrightarrow Y^*$, *h be a function* $X^* \longrightarrow Y^{(*)}$ *(the free group over Y) and* g_1, g_2 *in* $Y^{(*)}$ *such that for any word w in* X^*, *one has* $\gamma_i(w) = g_i\, h(w)$ $(i = 1, 2)$. *Then* $\gamma_1 . 1 = \gamma_2.1$.

Proof. Each element in $Y^{(*)}$ will be represented as a word over $Y \cup Y^{-1}$, in reduced form (i.e without occurence of $y\, y^{-1}$ or $y^{-1}y$). Let us write $g_i = u_i\, g_i'$ with $u_i \in Y^*$ and $g_i' \in Y^{(*)}$ beginning by an inversed variable, or equal to 1. Then for any word w in X^*, as $u_i\, g_i'\, h\,(w) \in Y^*$, $h\,(w)$ must begin by $g_i'^{-1}$; this is true for $i = 1$ and 2, which implies that one of $g_1'^{-1}$, $g_2'^{-1}$ is a left factor of the other, hence one of g_1', g_2' is a right factor of the other: thus for instance $g_1' = g\, g_2'$, h begins with $g_2'^{-1}\, g^{-1}$ and we may write $h(w) = g_2'^{-1}\, g^{-1}\, k(w)$, with no cancellation between g^{-1} and $k(w)$. As $\gamma_2(w) = u_2\, g^{-1}\, k(w) \in Y^*$, this implies that $k(w) \in Y^*$ and $u_2\, g^{-1} = u_2' \in Y^*$. Hence $\gamma_2\,(w) = u_2'\, k(w)$ and $\gamma_2.1 = k.1$. Moreover, $\gamma_1(w) = u_1\, k(w) \Rightarrow \gamma_1.1 = k.\, 1$, what was to be shown. □ ■ □

Proof of theorem 3

(i) $\Rightarrow$ (ii) is trivial.

(ii) $\Rightarrow$ (iii)   That ϕ has finite codomain is clear, by bounded variation and the fact that dom (γ) is regular. Let us show that $\gamma^{-1}(g)$ is regular for any g in $Y^{(*)}$.   If $\phi^{-1}(g) \neq \emptyset$, then $g = g_1^{-1} g_2$ for some words g_1, g_2 in Y^* without common left factor. Let n be the number of states of a finite automaton recognizing dom (γ). Let p be such that w, wu $\in$ dom (γ), $| u | < n \Rightarrow \gamma (w), \gamma(wu)$ differ only by a suffix of length $< p$ (it exists because γ has bounded variation). If t is in dom (γ), then either t has no proper left factor in dom (γ) and $\phi(t) = \gamma(t)$, or $t = wu$ with $w \in$ dom (γ), $u \neq 1$ and $\forall$ $u = u_1 u_2$ $(u_i \neq 1)$, $wu_1 \notin$ dom (γ), with $| u | < n$ and $\phi(t) = \gamma (w)^{-1} \gamma(u)$.   This shows that $\phi^{-1}(g)$ is equal to the union of $\{t \in X^* \mid \gamma(t) = g \} \cap {}^c(\text{dom } (\gamma)X^+)$ (which is regular) and of $\bigcup_{0<|u|<n} (L \cap L_u) u$ where L is the language of lemma 1 (hence regular) and

$$L_u = \bigcap_{\substack{u=u_1u_2\\u_1u_2 \neq 1}} \{ w \in X^* \mid wu_1 \notin \text{dom } (\gamma)\}.$$

This shows that $\phi^{-1}(g)$ is regular. $\square$

(iii) $\Rightarrow$ (i)   By hypothesis, dom (ϕ) is regular, hence so is dom (γ). Let n be the number of states of a finite automaton for dom (γ). By theorem 1, we have to show that the set $\{\gamma.u \mid u \in X^*\}$ is finite. We show that $\{\gamma.u \mid u \in$ dom $(\gamma)\}$ is finite: this is enough, because if $|u| \geq n$, then $u = u's$ with $u' \in$ dom (γ) and $|s| < n$ and $\gamma.u = (\gamma.u')$. s.   In fact, we show that for u, v $\in$ dom (γ), if for any g in $Y^{(*)}$, $u^{-1} \gamma^{-1}(g) = v^{-1} \gamma^{-1}(g)$, then $\gamma.u = \gamma.v$. This will imply the theorem, because there are only finitely many languages $\gamma^{-1}(g)$, that they are regular, hence that the languages of the form $u^{-1} \gamma^{-1}(g)$ are finitely many by Nerode's criterion.

Hence, let us suppose that for any g in $Y^{(*)}$ and any word r:

(9) $u r \in \phi^{-1}(g) \Leftrightarrow v r \in \phi^{-1}(g).$

Define $h_u: X^* \longrightarrow Y^{(*)}$ by: $h_u(w) = \emptyset$ if $uw \notin$ dom (γ); otherwise, let $w = s_1...s_p$ such that u, $us_1,...,u s_1...s_p$ are the elements of the set $\{us \mid s \in$ dom (γ) and $\exists$ t, $w = st\}$, and put $h_u(w) = \phi(u s_1)... \phi(u s_1...s_p)$ (if $w = 1$, then $h_u (w) = 1$). Note that u^{-1} dom$(\phi) = v^{-1}$ dom (γ) (because dom $(\gamma) \setminus 1 =$ dom $(\phi) = \bigcup \gamma^{-1}(g)$). Hence $h_v (w) = \phi(vs_1)... \phi(vs_1...s_p)$.   By (9), $us_1...s_i \in \phi^{-1}(g) \Leftrightarrow vs_1...s_i \in \phi^{-1} (g)$. This shows that $h_u = h_v = h$.

Now, by (6), one has $\gamma(uw) = \gamma(u) h(w)$ and $\gamma(vw) = \gamma(v) h(w)$. Hence by lemma 2, $\gamma.u = \gamma.v$. $\square \blacksquare \square$

REFERENCES

[1]   J. Berstel, Transductions and context-free languages, Teubner (1979).

[2]   R. Boyer, J.S. Moore, A fast string searching algorithm, Comm. Assoc. Comput. Machin. 20, 10 (1977) 762-772.

[3]   C. Choffrut, Une caractérisation des fonctions séquentielles et des fonctions sous-séquentielles en tant que relations rationnelles, Theor. Comput. Sci. 5 (1977) 325-337.

[4]   C. Choffrut, Contribution à l'étude de quelques familles remarquables de fonctions rationnelles, Thèse Sci. Math. Université Paris VII (1978).

[5]   C. Choffrut, A generalization of Ginsburg and Rose's characterization of g-s-m mappings, Proc. of the 6th Intern. Congress on Automata, Languages and Programming, Graz (1979), Lecture Notes Comput. Sci. 71, 88-103.

[6]   S. Eilenberg, Automata, languages and machines, vol. A, Acad. Press (1974).

[7]   S.Ginsburg, An introduction to mathematical machine theory, Addison- Wesley, Reading, Massachussets (1962).

[8]   S. Ginsburg, G.F. Rose, A characterization of machine mappings, Can. J. Math. 18 (1966) 381-388.

[9]   D.E. Knuth, J.H. Morris, V.R. Pratt, Fast pattern-matching in strings, S.I.A.M. J. Comput. 6(1977) 323-350.

[10] G. Raney, Sequential functions, J.Assoc. Comput. Mach. 5 (1958) 177-180.

[11] C. Reutenauer, M.-P. Schützenberger, Minimization of rational word functions, to appear in Siam J. of Computing.

[12] M.P. Schützenberger, Sur une variante des fonctions séquentielles, Theor. Comput. Sci. 4 (1977) 47-57.

PAST PROVES MORE INVARIANCE PROPERTIES BUT NOT PCA'S

Ildikó Sain

Mathematical Institute of the Hungarian Academy of Sciences

Budapest, Pf. 127, H-1364, Hungary

The sentence in the title refers to the proof theoretic consequences of adding the modality *"Sometime-in-the-past"* to temporal logics of programs. Here we investigate the proof theoretic powers of first order temporal logics (FTL's) from the point of view of provability of program properties. (We also investigate completeness issues of FTL's in general.)

FTL as introduced in Manna-Pnueli [18] contains the modality *Sometime-in-the-future* $\langle F \rangle$ but not *Sometime-in-the-past* $\langle P \rangle$. Later Lichtenstein–Pnueli–Zuck [17] argued that adding $\langle P \rangle$ to FTL in [18] is useful. In Sain [22, 23, 24] we proved that

(1) adding $\langle P \rangle$ to the FTL in [18] does not increase its power for proving partial correctness assertions (pca's) for deterministic programs.

Pca's are special invariance properties. Below we prove that (1) does not generalize from pca's to invariance properties in general, not even in the deterministic case.

We will look into the *nondeterministic* and *concurrent* cases at the end of this paper, and will state some open problems most of which were already raised (explicitly or implicitly) in Abadi-Manna [4], Abadi [1], Andréka-Németi-Sain [9], Sain [25]. An extended abstract of the first part of this paper is [26].

§1. SYNTAX AND SEMANTICS OF FIRST ORDER TEMPORAL LOGICS

Throughout, ω denotes the set of all natural numbers. We start out from a first order multimodal (actually temporal) logic with five modalities $\odot$, $\bigcirc$, $\Box$, $[F]$, and $[P]$. We call them *"First"*, *"Next"*, *"Always"*, *"Always-in-the-future"*, and *"Always-in-the-past"* respectively. The duals of $\Box$, $[F]$, $[P]$ are denoted by $\Diamond$, $\langle F \rangle$, $\langle P \rangle$, and called *"Sometime"*, *"Sometime-in-the-future"*, and *"Sometime-in-the-past"* respectively.[1] Given a first order similarity type or language L, the usual predicate etc. symbols of L are considered to be *rigid*, i.e. their meanings do not change in time (cf. [11], p.255). A nonlogical symbol is called *flexible* as opposed to *rigid* if it is allowed to change in time.[2] Similarly, individual variables x_i ($i \in \omega$) are rigid. To this we add an infinity c_i ($i \in \omega$) of *flexible constants*. That is, the meaning of c_i is allowed to change in time. Formulas of FTL are built up the usual way from the nonlogical symbols in $L + \{c_i : i \in \omega\}$ using the standard first order logical connectives and quantifiers, together with our five modalities mentioned above. $Fm(\text{FTL}) = Fm_L(\text{FTL})$ denotes the set of all FTL-formulas (of similarity type L) just described. For any $\varphi \in Fm(\text{FTL})$, φ is called a *rigid formula* if it contains no flexible constants. Otherwise we call φ a *flexible formula*.

---

[1] We use here Goldblatt's notation for *Always*, *Always-in-the-future*, and *Always-in-the-past*, see §6 pp.39–40 of [14].

[2] The terminology *rigid — flexible* comes from philosophical logic (cf. e.g. the Handbook [11], pp.254–317, and the above quoted papers of Abadi and Manna on computer science temporal logics). Some computer science works (e.g. Kröger [16]) use the words "global" and "local" for "rigid" and "flexible" respectively.

For semantic purposes, we use classical two-sorted models $\mathfrak{M} = \langle \mathbf{T}, \mathbf{D}, f_0, \cdots, f_i, \cdots \rangle_{i\in\omega}$ where $\mathbf{D}$ is a classical first order structure of similarity type L, $\mathbf{T} = \langle T, 0, succ, \leq \rangle$ is a structure similar to (of the same language as) the standard structure $\mathbf{N} = \langle \omega, 0, succ, \leq \rangle$ of the natural numbers, and for $i \in \omega$, $f_i \in {}^T D$ (i.e. $f_i : T \longrightarrow D$ is a function from T into D) serves to interpret the flexible constant c_i. $\mathbf{T}$ is called the time-frame of $\mathfrak{M}$, and, except for its language, is arbitrary. For simplicity, we often write c_i for f_i. Mod denotes the class of all models $\mathfrak{M}$ of the above kind. (To be precise, we should write Mod_L.) The members of Mod are the same as Kripke models known from the traditional literature of FTL, cf. [11]. The next definition also agrees with the tradition of philosophical logic [11].

To associate meanings to FTL-formulas in models from Mod, we follow the standard procedure of correspondence theory (cf. [11] §II.4.2.5 pp.214–217), and define a translation function

$$P : Fm(\text{FTL}) \longrightarrow Fmcl(\text{Mod}),$$

where $Fmcl(\text{Mod})$ is the set of all *classical* (two-sorted) first order formulas in the language of Mod. In $Fmcl(\text{Mod})$, x_i ($i \in \omega$) are the variables of sort D (data), and t_i ($i \in \omega$) are variables of sort T (time). We will consider $\Box\varphi$ as an *abbreviation* for $\odot[F]\varphi$, therefore in our definitions $\Box$ will not occur explicitly. We may assume that all occurrences of the flexible constants c_i are of the form $c_i = x_j$ in the FTL-formulas (every formula is easily seen to be equivalent with one of this form as it is well known, cf. [10]). For any $\varphi \in Fm(\text{FTL})$, we let

$$P(\varphi) \stackrel{\text{def}}{=} P^*(\varphi, t_0),$$

where $P^* : Fm(\text{FTL}) \times \{t_i : i \in \omega\} \longrightarrow Fmcl(\text{Mod})$ is defined as follows (intuitively, $P^*(\varphi, t)$ means that φ is true at time t):

For every $t \in \{t_i : i \in \omega\}$, $i, j \in \omega$, and $\varphi, \psi \in Fm(\text{FTL})$, we let $t_i \neq t$, and

$P^*(c_i = x_j, t) \stackrel{\text{def}}{=} (f_i(t) = x_j)$,

$P^*(\psi, t) \stackrel{\text{def}}{=} \psi$ whenever ψ is atomic and rigid (i.e. contains none of the c_i's),

P^* preserves classical connectives and quantifiers (i.e.: $P^*(\varphi \wedge \psi, t) \stackrel{\text{def}}{=}$ $P^*(\varphi, t) \wedge P^*(\psi, t)$, $P^*(\neg\varphi, t) \stackrel{\text{def}}{=} \neg P^*(\varphi, t)$, $P^*(\exists x_i \varphi, t) \stackrel{\text{def}}{=} \exists x_i P^*(\varphi, t)$), and

$P^*(\odot\varphi, t) \stackrel{\text{def}}{=} \exists t_0 (t_0 = 0 \wedge P^*(\varphi, t_0))$,

$P^*(\bigcirc\varphi, t) \stackrel{\text{def}}{=} \exists t_i (t_i = succ(t) \wedge P^*(\varphi, t_i))$,

$P^*([F]\varphi, t) \stackrel{\text{def}}{=} (\forall t_i \geq t) P^*(\varphi, t_i)$,

$P^*([P]\varphi, t) \stackrel{\text{def}}{=} (\forall t_i \leq t) P^*(\varphi, t_i)$.

This completes the definition (by recursion) of the translation functions P and P^*. We let

$$\mathfrak{M} \models \varphi \quad \stackrel{\text{def}}{\Longleftrightarrow} \quad \mathfrak{M} \models P(\varphi), \qquad \text{for any } \varphi \in Fm(\text{FTL}).$$

Here $\mathfrak{M} \models P(\varphi)$ is understood in the usual classical sense.

For any $K \subseteq \text{Mod}$, we let

$$K \models \varphi \quad \stackrel{\text{def}}{\Longleftrightarrow} \quad (\forall \mathfrak{M} \in K)\mathfrak{M} \models \varphi.$$

Note that $\mathfrak{M} \models \varphi$ iff $\mathfrak{M} \models \Box\varphi$ iff $\mathfrak{M} \models \forall t_0 P(\varphi)$.

A model $\mathfrak{M} = \langle \mathbf{T}, \cdots \rangle$ is called a *standard-time model* iff $\mathbf{T} = \mathbf{N}$, i.e. iff $\mathbf{T}$ is the standard model of arithmetic.

For any $\varphi \in Fm(\text{FTL})$, $\models^\omega \varphi$ is defined to hold iff φ is valid in every standard-time model.

The semantics $\models^\omega \varphi$ is too restrictive, while $\text{Mod} \models \varphi$ is too general. Therefore, as usual in modal– and temporal logic, we introduce first order axiomatizable sub-classes of Mod, and will use *these* for semantic purposes. To this end, we recall two sets Ind, $Tord \subseteq Fmcl(\text{Mod})$ of postulates called *"induction"*, and *"ordering of time"* respectively. These are used in the literature for singling out workable model classes (i.e. semantics) for FTL.[3] Throughout this paper, we use the convention thet "$\wedge$" binds stronger than "$\rightarrow$", hence e.g. $\varphi \wedge \psi \rightarrow \gamma$ means $(\varphi \wedge \psi) \rightarrow \gamma$.

$$Ind \overset{\text{def}}{=} \{\varphi(0) \wedge \forall t(\varphi(t) \rightarrow \varphi(succ(t))) \rightarrow \forall t\varphi(t) : \varphi \in Fmcl(\text{Mod})\},$$

where $\varphi(0)$ is obtained from φ by replacing the free occurrences of t in φ with 0, and similarly for $\varphi(succ(t))$. Since $\varphi(t)$ may contain free variables other than t, this induction allows the use of parameters (of both sorts time and data).

Tord is the full first order theory of the *standard* structure $\mathbf{N} = \langle \omega, 0, succ, \leq \rangle$. (Note that *Tord* is finitely axiomatizable.) See the 1977 version of [7] or [6] for more detail, where the present approach (including P and P^*) to FTL was first introduced (adapting the standard methodology of philosophical logic to Computer Science Temporal Logics). Later Abadi [1–3] adopted the same definitions from [6] etc.

For any $Th \subseteq Fmcl(\text{Mod})$ and $\varphi \in Fm(\text{FTL})$, we let

$$\text{Mod}(Th) \overset{\text{def}}{=} \{\mathfrak{M} \in \text{Mod} : \mathfrak{M} \models Th\} , \quad \text{and}$$

$$Th \models \varphi \quad \overset{\text{def}}{\Longleftrightarrow} \quad \text{Mod}(Th) \models \varphi.$$

Now, the most frequently used semantics for FTL-formulas φ is $(Ind + Tord) \models \varphi$. Abadi [1–3] writes $\vdash_0 P(\varphi)$ for $(Ind + Tord) \models \varphi$.

The notation $Ind \models \varphi$ might seem confusing, since Ind is in one language, $Fmcl(\text{Mod})$, while φ is in another, namely in $Fm(\text{FTL})$. However, these two languages have the same class Mod of models, thus our notation makes sense.

§2. INFERENCE SYSTEMS FOR FIRST ORDER TEMPORAL LOGICS

Next we will consider *inference systems* for FTL. Let $\vdash$ be an inference system for FTL. Let $K \subseteq \text{Mod}$. Following the tradition, we say that

$\vdash$ is *complete* w.r.t. the semantics $(K \models)$ iff $(\forall \varphi \in Fm(\text{FTL}))(K \models \varphi \Longrightarrow \vdash \varphi)$;

$\vdash$ is *sound* w.r.t. the semantics $(K \models)$ iff $(\forall \varphi \in Fm(\text{FTL}))(K \models \varphi \Longleftarrow \vdash \varphi)$.

---

[3] These postulate systems were first proposed for the present purpose by the "Nonstandard Logics of Programs school", see e.g. Sain [21], Németi [19], [6–7].

Axiomatization of temporal logic:

Consider axioms $(A1, 2)$ and rules $(R1 - 3)$ below.

(A1) *Propositional axioms:*

    (1) (BOOL) :   All Boolean tautologies

    (2) K($\square$) : $\square(\varphi \to \psi) \to (\square\varphi \to \square\psi)$ where $\square \in \{\odot, \bigcirc, \square, [F], [P]\}$

    (3) (fun$_\square$) : $\square\neg\varphi \leftrightarrow \neg\square\varphi$ where $\square \in \{\odot, \bigcirc\}$

    (4) (mix) : $[F]\varphi \to (\varphi \wedge \bigcirc[F]\varphi)$

    (5) (ind$_{[F]}$) : $[F](\varphi \to \bigcirc\varphi) \to (\varphi \to [F]\varphi)$

    (6) (first) : $\varphi \to \odot\langle F\rangle\varphi$

    (7) (const) : $\odot\varphi \to [F]\odot\varphi$

    (8) (Grz$_{[P]}$) : $[P]([P](\varphi \to [P]\varphi) \to \varphi) \to \varphi$

    (9) ($\bigcirc[P]$) : $[P]\varphi \wedge \bigcirc\varphi \to \bigcirc[P]\varphi$

    (10) ($\odot[P]$) : $\odot\varphi \leftrightarrow \langle P\rangle[P]\varphi$

    (11) K$_t$($[F], [P]$): $\varphi \to [F]\langle P\rangle\varphi \wedge [P]\langle F\rangle\varphi$

    (12) (con) : $\square\varphi \to [F][P]\varphi \wedge [P][F]\varphi$

(A2) *First order (i.e. quantifier) axioms:*

    For every temporal formula φ, if φ is valid in every model $\mathfrak{M} \in \text{Mod}$ then φ is in (A2).

    Remark: (A2) can be replaced with the Hilbert-style axioms:

    $\{(\varphi \leftrightarrow \square\,\varphi)$ for every modality $\square$ (i.e. $\square \in \{\odot, \bigcirc, \square, [F], [P]\}$) if φ is rigid (contains no flexible symbols);

    $(\forall x \square\varphi \leftrightarrow \square\forall x\varphi)$ for every modality $\square$;

    $\varphi \to \forall x\varphi$ if x is not a free variable of φ;

    all the usual equality axioms of first order logic;

    $\exists x(\neg\varphi \leftrightarrow \neg\forall x\varphi)$;

    $\forall x\varphi \to \varphi(x/\tau)$ for any term τ such that the substitution $x \mapsto \tau$ does not create new bound occurrences of variables or new occurrences of flexible symbols in the scope of modalities in φ.$\}$

    For the proof methods for showing that the listed axioms together with (A1)+ (R1-3) have the desired completeness property stated as the first sentence of (A2), see e.g. [13] or Abadi [1] Thm.4.1 on p.48.

(R1) $\{\varphi, \varphi \to \psi\} \vdash \psi$,   (*modus ponens*)

(R2) $\varphi \vdash \square\varphi$ ($\square$-*generalization*)

    for every $\square \in \{\odot, \bigcirc, \square, [F], [P], \forall x : x$ is any individual variable$\}$,

(R3) $\{\odot\varphi, \varphi \to \bigcirc\varphi\} \vdash \varphi$ (*induction*).

We note the following about (A1):

(2.1) For any propositional temporal schema ψ valid in the standard-time models $\langle\omega, \ldots\rangle$, all (first order) instances of ψ are provable from (A1)+(R1-3).

    (2.1) was proved by V. Goranko [15], [5]. Actually (A1) was designed by V. Goranko.

Remark 2.1. *As axiom (A1)(10) shows, we could eliminate the modality $\odot$ and use it as an abbreviation of $\langle P\rangle[P]$. The problem with this is that we need $\odot$ in the fragments not containing $\langle P\rangle$.*

Derivability by (A1,2)+(R1-3) is denoted by $\vdash_{SFP}$, derivability by $(A1,2)+(R1-3)$ in the fragment not containing $[P]$ is $\vdash_{SF}$. By derivability in the fragment not containing $[P]$ (i.e. by $\vdash_{SF}$) we mean that we restrict ourselves to formulas which do not contain $[P]$ (or $\langle P\rangle$), and accordingly we delete those axioms and rules from (A1,2)+(R1-3) which refer to $[P]$ (or $\langle P\rangle$). So, $\vdash_{SF}$ is axiomatized by (A1)(1-7), (R1,R3), and the natural restrictions of (A2), (R2). Restricting (R2) is particularly easy: we simply write $\square \in \{\odot, \bigcirc, [F], \forall x : \ldots\}$ in place of the similar condition there. Derivability by (A1-R3) in the fragment not containing either $[P]$ or $[F]$ but containing $\square$ is denoted by $\vdash_S$ (recall that $\square$ abbreviates $\odot[F]$ in $\vdash_{SF}$ or $\vdash_{SFP}$). Defining $\vdash_S$ is more difficult because one of its basic modalities, $\square$, does not occur in the original system $\vdash_{SFP}$ (it is only an abbreviation in $\vdash_{SFP}$). Therefore we cannot simply restrict the axiomatization of $\vdash_{SFP}$ to the language of $\vdash_S$ (without risking making it terribly incomplete). To avoid the problem, we simply list the axiomatization of $\vdash_S$ from scratch, below the following remark.

Remark 2.2. *Despite of the presence of the induction rule (R3), the induction axiom $(\mathrm{ind}_{[F]})$ (i.e. (A1)(5)) cannot be omitted from (A1) since it cannot be derived from the rest of the $\vdash_{SF}$-fragment of $\vdash_{SFP}$. So dropping $(\mathrm{ind}_{[F]})$ would make (2.1) false for $\vdash_{SF}$.*

On the other hand: Let $\vdash_{SFP}^0$ be $\vdash_{SFP}$ without $(\mathrm{ind}_{[F]})$. Then $\vdash_{SFP}^0$ and $\vdash_{SFP}$ are equivalent, i.e. $(\mathrm{ind}_{[F]})$ is provable in $\vdash_{SFP}^0$.

Sketch of the proof of $\vdash_{SFP}^0$ $(\mathrm{ind}_{[F]})$: Let ψ be $\langle P\rangle(\varphi \wedge [F](\varphi \rightarrow \bigcirc\varphi)) \rightarrow \varphi$, φ is arbitrary. We would like to apply the induction rule (R3) to prove ψ. To this end, it is enough to derive $\odot\psi$ and $(\psi \rightarrow \bigcirc\psi)$.

$\odot\psi$ is immediate from $\odot(\langle P\rangle\varphi \rightarrow \varphi)$, which in turn follows from $(\mathrm{Grz}_{[P]})$ (which implies $[P]\langle P\rangle\varphi \rightarrow \langle P\rangle[P]\varphi$) as follows. $\odot\langle P\rangle\varphi \rightarrow \langle P\rangle[P]\langle P\rangle\varphi \rightarrow \langle P\rangle\langle P\rangle[P]\varphi \rightarrow \langle P\rangle[P]\varphi \rightarrow \odot\varphi$.

One proves $\psi \rightarrow \bigcirc\psi$ by observing that $\bigcirc\psi$ is equivalent with $\bigcirc\langle P\rangle\chi \rightarrow \bigcirc\varphi$ where χ is $\varphi \wedge [F](\varphi \rightarrow \bigcirc\varphi)$; and that $\bigcirc\langle P\rangle\chi \rightarrow (\bigcirc\chi \vee \langle P\rangle\chi)$ (roughly, we proceed by case distinction: if $\bigcirc\chi$ holds, we are done; else $\langle P\rangle\chi$ enables us to apply the inductive assumption ψ which is $\langle P\rangle\chi \rightarrow \varphi$, together with the fact $\vdash_{SFP}^0 \langle P\rangle\chi \rightarrow (\varphi \rightarrow \bigcirc\varphi)$).

We have seen $\vdash_{SFP}^0 \odot\psi$ and $\vdash_{SFP}^0 (\psi \rightarrow \bigcirc\psi)$. From these (R3) yields $\vdash_{SFP}^0 \psi$. That is,

$$(2.2) \qquad \vdash_{SFP}^0 \langle P\rangle(\varphi \wedge [F](\varphi \rightarrow \bigcirc\varphi)) \rightarrow \varphi.$$

We want to prove $\vdash_{SFP}^0 (\varphi \wedge [F](\varphi \rightarrow \bigcirc\varphi)) \rightarrow [F]\varphi$ i.e. $\vdash_{SFP}^0 \chi \rightarrow [F]\varphi$.
$\vdash_{SFP}^0 \chi \rightarrow [F]\langle P\rangle\chi$ by (A1)(12) (con),
$\vdash_{SFP}^0 [F](\langle P\rangle\chi \rightarrow \varphi)$ by (2.2) and $[F]$-generalization,
$\vdash_{SFP}^0 [F]\langle P\rangle\chi \rightarrow [F]\varphi$ by K($[F]$),
$\vdash_{SFP}^0 \chi \rightarrow [F]\varphi$ by two of the previous steps.
We have proved $\vdash_{SFP}^0 (\mathrm{ind}_{[F]})$.

(Further it seems possible that $(\mathrm{Grz}_{[P]})$ and $(\odot[P])$ together can be replaced with the simpler $\odot = \langle P\rangle[P] = [P]\langle P\rangle$.) ∎

The axioms and rules of $\vdash_S$ **are the following:**

(A3) *Propositional axioms:* (V. Goranko [15], [5])

(1) (BOOL)

(2) K($\Box$)   for $\Box \in \{\odot, \bigcirc, \Box\}$

(3) (fun$_\Box$)   for $\Box \in \{\odot, \bigcirc\}$

(4) S5($\Box$)   that is

  (ref): $\Box\varphi \to \varphi$

  (tran): $\Box\varphi \to \Box\Box\varphi$

  (sym): $\Box\neg\Box\varphi \leftrightarrow \neg\Box\varphi$

(5) (incl): $\Box\varphi \to \odot\varphi \wedge \bigcirc\varphi$

(6) (con$_\odot$) $\odot\varphi \to \Box\odot\varphi$

(A2)

(R1-3)

Note that $\vdash_S$, $\vdash_{SF}$, $\vdash_{SFP}$ are frequently used established temporal logics.

Statement (2.1) remains true for $\vdash_{SF}$ and $\vdash_S$. That is:

Theorem 2.3 (V. GORANKO). *The* propositional *versions of* $\vdash_S$, $\vdash_{SF}$, $\vdash_{SFP}$ *are complete for standard time models, in the sense that they prove all propositional formulas valid in the standard models.*

In the direction of proving Theorem 2.3 we will fully prove here only Lemma 2.4 below. Lemma 2.4 says that though the induction axiom

(ind$_{\Box,\odot}$): $$\Box(\varphi \to \bigcirc\varphi) \to (\odot\varphi \to \Box\varphi)$$

(which is analogous to (ind$_{[F]}$)) is not listed among the axioms of $\vdash_S$, it is provable in $\vdash_S$. The main device for deriving (ind$_{\Box,\odot}$) is the induction rule (R3). The rest of the proof of Theorem 2.3 is in Andréka-Goranko-Németi-Sain [5]; we do not recall it here. It seems to us that the proof of Theorem 4.1 in our §4 does not use the full power of Theorem 2.3 but it does rely heavily on Lemma 2.4. (In passing we note that (ind$_{\Box,\odot}$) is provable in $\vdash_{SF}$ and $\vdash_{SFP}$ too, as it is fairly easy to see because of the availability of (ind$_{[F]}$) in these systems. This claim also follows directly from Lemma 2.4 and Corollary 2.5 below.)

Lemma 2.4.

(i) $\vdash_S \odot\varphi \wedge \Box(\varphi \to \bigcirc\varphi) \to \Box\varphi$.

(ii) $\vdash_S \bigcirc\Box\varphi \to \Box\varphi$ for $\Box \in \{\odot, \Box\}$.

Proof: *(ii)(a)* $\vdash_S \Box\psi \to \bigcirc\psi$ ((A3)(5)). $\Box\psi \to \bigcirc\psi$ is equivalent to $\bigcirc\psi \to \Diamond\psi$, thus $\vdash_S \bigcirc\psi \to \Diamond\psi$. Let us choose ψ to be $\Box\varphi$. Then $\vdash_S \bigcirc\Box\varphi \to \Diamond\Box\varphi$. By (A3)(4)(sym), $\vdash_S \bigcirc\Box\varphi \to \Box\varphi$.

(ii)(b) An $\vdash_S$-derivation of $\bigcirc\odot\varphi \to \odot\varphi$ is the following:

$\vdash_S \odot\varphi \to \Box\odot\varphi$ by (A3)(6),

$\vdash_S \bigcirc(\odot\varphi \to \Box\odot\varphi)$ by (R2),

$\vdash_S \bigcirc\odot\varphi \to \bigcirc\Box\odot\varphi$ by (A3)(2) and (R1),

$\vdash_S \bigcirc\odot\varphi \to \Box\odot\varphi$ by (ii)(a) above,

$\vdash_S \bigcirc\odot\varphi \to \odot\varphi$ by (A3)(4)(ref).

(i) Let χ be the formula $\odot\varphi \wedge \Box(\varphi \to \bigcirc\varphi) \to \varphi$. We will prove

(2.3)
$$\vdash_S \odot\chi$$

and

(2.4)
$$\vdash_S \chi \to \bigcirc\chi.$$

From (2.3) and (2.4), using rule (R3), we get $\vdash_S \chi$. Then using (R2) we get $\vdash_S \Box\chi$, that is

$\vdash_S \Box(\odot\varphi \wedge \Box(\varphi \to \bigcirc\varphi) \to \varphi)$.   Now using (A3)(2), we get

$\vdash_S \Box(\odot\varphi \wedge \Box(\varphi \to \bigcirc\varphi)) \to \Box\varphi$,   and from this

$\vdash_S \odot\varphi \wedge \Box(\varphi \to \bigcirc\varphi) \to \Box\varphi$ by (ii) and (A3)(4)(ref).

It remains to prove (2.3) and (2.4).

Proof of (2.3): By (A3)(2,3), $\odot\chi$ is equivalent to $\odot\varphi \wedge \odot\Box(\varphi \to \bigcirc\varphi) \to \odot\varphi$. Since this is a propositional tautology, $\vdash_S \odot\chi$.

Proof of (2.4): Let

χ_1 be $\odot\varphi \wedge \Box(\varphi \to \bigcirc\varphi)$ (hypothesis part of χ), and

χ_2 be $\bigcirc\odot\varphi \wedge \bigcirc\Box(\varphi \to \bigcirc\varphi)$.

$\chi \to \bigcirc\chi$ is $\chi \to \bigcirc(\chi_1 \to \varphi)$ which is (provably) equivalent to $\chi \to (\bigcirc\chi_1 \to \bigcirc\varphi)$. The latter is equivalent to $\chi \wedge \bigcirc\chi_1 \to \bigcirc\varphi$ by (BOOL).

$\vdash_S \bigcirc\chi_1 \to \chi_1$ because $\bigcirc\chi_1$ is equivalent to χ_2 and because $\vdash_S \bigcirc\odot\varphi \to \varphi$ and $\vdash_S \bigcirc\Box\psi \to \Box\psi$ by (ii) above. Therefore

$\vdash_S (\chi \wedge \bigcirc\chi_1) \to (\chi \wedge \chi_1)$. But $\chi \wedge \chi_1$ is $(\chi_1 \to \varphi) \wedge \chi_1$ which is equivalent to $\chi_1 \wedge \varphi$ by (BOOL). Hence

$\vdash_S (\chi \wedge \bigcirc\chi_1) \to (\chi_1 \wedge \varphi)$. Thus, for proving $\vdash_S \chi \wedge \bigcirc\chi_1 \to \bigcirc\varphi$, it is enough to prove that

$\vdash_S (\chi_1 \wedge \varphi) \to \bigcirc\varphi$ that is

$\vdash_S \odot\varphi \wedge \Box(\varphi \to \bigcirc\varphi) \wedge \varphi \to \bigcirc\varphi$.

The latter holds because

$\vdash_S \odot\varphi \wedge \Box(\varphi \to \bigcirc\varphi) \wedge \varphi \to \Box(\varphi \to \bigcirc\varphi) \wedge \varphi$ and

$\vdash_S \Box(\varphi \to \bigcirc\varphi) \wedge \varphi \to (\varphi \wedge \bigcirc\varphi) \wedge \varphi$ follow immediately from the axioms. ∎

Corollary 2.5. $\vdash_S$, $\vdash_{SF}$, and $\vdash_{SFP}$ *are conservative extensions of each other. More precisely:*

$\vdash_S \quad\quad \Longrightarrow \vdash_{SF} \varphi$ *for every φ in the language of $\vdash_S$, and*

$\vdash_{SF} \varphi \Longrightarrow \vdash_{SFP} \varphi$ *for every φ in the language of $\vdash_{SF}$.* ∎

Remark 2.6. *The fragment FTL_0 of FTL containing no other modalities than $\bigcirc$ and $\odot$ is important because it corresponds to Floyd-Hoare logic ([9], Prop.1). $\vdash_0$ denotes derivability by an inference system designed for FTL_0, such that $\vdash_0$ is axiomatized by an $(A1_0)$ enjoying property (2.1) together with the restriction of (A2-R3) to FTL_0. We will not use $\vdash_0$ here too much, therefore we do not go into further detail. (For completeness: Mechanical restriction of (A1-R3) to FTL_0 does not enjoy property (2.1) because e.g. $\bigcirc\odot\varphi \leftrightarrow \odot\varphi$ is not derivable in it. Adding the postulate "$\bigcirc\odot = \odot\odot = \odot$" seems to be sufficient for propositional completeness i.e. for ensuring (2.1), but we did not check the details very carefully. What we checked is that for any $(A1_0')$, if $(A1_0') + (R1-R3)$ is complete for the class of all those Kripke models in which $\bigcirc$ is interpreted by a function* and $\odot$ by a *constant [constant valued function]* then $(A1_0') + (R1\text{-}3)$ *is actually complete for the standard models too [on the propositional level of course].*)

§3. First order Temporal Logics of Programs; Invariance Properties

If p is a program then $Ax(p)$ is the temporal logic formula expressing that c is an execution sequence of p (i.e. c is a time sequence of values of the variable or "register" of the program p; if p contains more variables then the formula becomes more complicated the obvious way). For example if $\ell_1 \xrightarrow{\ x:=x+2\ } \ell_2$ is an edge (or command) of p then $Ax(p)$ contains the subformula $(\text{"at } \ell_1\text{"}) \to \exists x \big(x = c \land \bigcirc(c = x + 2 \land \text{"at } \ell_2\text{"})\big)$.

Now,

(3.1) a *temporal proof* of a partial correctness assertion $\{\varphi\}p\{\psi\}$ is a proof of the temporal formula γ expressing

$$\big(\text{"}c \text{ is at the halt label of } p\text{"} \to \psi(c)\big),$$

from $Ax(p)$ and $\odot \varphi(c)$, using one of the inference systems $\vdash_S$, $\vdash_{SF}$, and $\vdash_{SFP}$. The formulas γ, $Ax(p)$, and $\odot \varphi(c)$ belong to the fragment $\vdash_S$, cf. e.g. Pnueli [20]). We write $\vdash_S \{\varphi\}p\{\psi\}$ for $\{Ax(p), \odot \varphi(c)\} \vdash_S \gamma$ and similarly for the other inference systems $\vdash_{SF}$ etc.

We note that this definition of $\vdash_S \{\varphi\}p\{\psi\}$ is equivalent with $\vdash_S \Box Ax(p) \land \odot\varphi(c) \to \Box\gamma$. The advantage of our original definition is that it is applicable to the fragment FTL_0 where $\Box$ is not available. (For more about $Ax(p)$ and temporal provability of a pca see §5.)

An *invariance property* of the same program p discussed above is a statement of the kind $\Box Ax(p) \to \Box(\text{"}at(\ell_i)\text{"} \to \psi(c))$ for some arbitrary but fixed classical first order formula $\psi(x)$ and arbitrary but fixed label ℓ_i. It is an obvious generalization of the pca discussed above. Its temporal provability is defined completely analogously.

§4. The Theorem

The following theorem states that $\vdash_{SFP}$ is stronger than $\vdash_{SF}$ already from the point of view of provability of invariance properties of *deterministic* programs. To be able to appreciate this, we note that (i) such properties are expressible already in $\vdash_S$ (therefore the difference is *not* in expressive power)[4], and that (ii) from the point of view of provability of pca's (special invariance properties) $\vdash_{SF}$ and $\vdash_{SFP}$ are equivalent. (The latter is a relatively old result from [22], cf. also e.g. [9] Coroll.4.) So, while adding Sometime–in–the–past ($\langle P\rangle$) to the temporal logic $\vdash_{SF}$ suggested in Manna-Pnueli [18] does not increase its pca-proving power, it does increase $\vdash_{SF}$'s invariance property proving power (for the same kind of programs).

---

[4] Actually, they are expressible in FTL_0!

THEOREM 4.1. *There is a deterministic program p and an invariance property φ of p such that*

$$\vdash_{SFP} \varphi \qquad \text{but} \qquad \nvdash_{SF} \varphi.$$

Proof: Consider the data domain $\mathbf{D} = \langle \mathbf{Z}, 0, succ, R \rangle$ where $\langle \mathbf{Z}, 0, succ \rangle$ is the standard structure of the integers, and $R = \{\langle z, -z \rangle : z \in \mathbf{Z}\}$.

D:

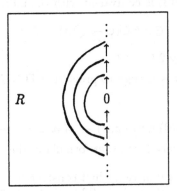

Let the program p start with $c := 0$ and then increase the value of c with 1 in each step. (So, in particular, p never terminates.)

p:

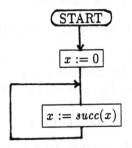

The invariance property ψ of p states that during any execution of p, c (i.e. the program register x) will never have the value -1. This is expressible e.g. by the temporal formula "$\Box Ax(p) \rightarrow \Box(succ(c) \neq 0)$". Let $Th \overset{\text{def}}{=} Th(\mathbf{D})$ be the full first order (nontemporal!) theory of $\mathbf{D}$. It is enough to show that

(4.1) $Th \vdash_{SFP} \psi$, and
(4.2) $Th \nvdash_{SF} \psi$

because of the following. By (4.1) and compactness, there is a sentence $\gamma \in Th$ such that $\gamma \vdash_{SFP} \psi$. Since γ is a rigid sentence, $\vdash_{SFP} (\gamma \rightarrow \psi)$. Let φ be $(\gamma \rightarrow \psi)$. Then φ is an invariance property, since $\gamma \rightarrow (\Box Ax(p) \rightarrow \Box(succ(c) \neq 0))$ is equivalent to $\gamma \wedge \Box Ax(p) \rightarrow \Box(succ(c) \neq 0)$ i.e. $\Box Ax(p) \rightarrow (\gamma \rightarrow \Box(succ(c) \neq 0))$ which is equivalent to $\Box Ax(p) \rightarrow \Box(\gamma \rightarrow succ(c) \neq 0)$ since γ is rigid. Now we have $\vdash_{SFP} \varphi$ and $\nvdash_{SF} \varphi$, proving the theorem.

To prove (4.2), consider the Kripke model $\mathfrak{M} = \langle \langle \mathbf{Z}, 0, succ, \mathbf{Z} \times \mathbf{Z} \rangle, \mathbf{D}, Id \rangle$ where Id is the identity function. The point here is that the relation $\leq^{\mathfrak{M}}$ interpreting $[F]$ in $\mathfrak{M}$ is the "nihilistic" relation $\mathbf{Z} \times \mathbf{Z}$. Clearly

$$(4.3) \qquad\qquad \mathfrak{M} \models Th \cup \{\neg\psi\}.$$

It is not hard to check that all the axioms (and rules) of $\vdash_{SF}$ are true in $\mathfrak{M}$ except for induction (which appears both in (A1) and in (R3)).

In the language of $\vdash_{SF}$, (R3) is equivalent with the induction formula

$$(\text{ind}_{\square,\odot}) \qquad\qquad \odot\varphi \wedge \square(\varphi \to \bigcirc\varphi) \to \square\varphi,$$

see Lemma 2.4 and Corollary 2.5 in §2.

To prove $\mathfrak{M} \models (\text{ind}_{\square,\odot})$, it is enough to prove that $\mathbf{D} \models Indcl$ where $Indcl$ is classical first order induction

$$Indcl = \{\varphi(0) \wedge \forall x\, (\varphi(x) \to \varphi(succ(x))) \to \forall x \varphi(x) :$$
$$\varphi(x) \text{ is an arbitrary first order formula in the language of } \mathbf{D}\}.$$

This can be proved by the usual ultraproduct constructions in e.g. [7], [19], [23–24]. We omit the details of the latter. So we have $\mathfrak{M} \models (\text{ind}_{\square,\odot})$. This in turn implies that *all* axioms and rules of $\vdash_{SF}$ are true in $\mathfrak{M}$. So by induction on the length of proofs, for any formula ρ we have $\vdash_{SF} \rho \Rightarrow \mathfrak{M} \models \rho$. Therefore, by (4.3), we have $\mathfrak{M} \not\models \varphi$ hence $\not\vdash_{SF} \varphi$ proving (4.2).

To prove (4.1), one proves by temporal induction

$$(4.4) \qquad\qquad \exists x\, (c = x \wedge [P]c \neq succ(x) \to [P]\neg(cRx)).$$

Now we assume $\neg\psi$ that is $\lozenge c = -1$. Then $\lozenge(c = -1 \wedge \langle F \rangle c = 1)$ which implies $\lozenge(c = 1 \wedge \langle P \rangle c = -1)$ which, by $-1R1$, contradicts (4.4). It is very easy to formalize this informal argument in $\vdash_{SFP}$. This proves (4.1). ∎

§5. Concurrency

Recall that $Ax(p)$ was our set of temporal axioms expressing that the vector $\bar{c}$ of flexible constants $c_0, c_1, \ldots$ constitutes an execution sequence of our program p. $Ax(p)$ was expressed according to the following ideas:

Let p be a program with $\bar{x} = \langle x_0, \ldots, x_k \rangle$ its data variables (or its registers) and control variable. I.e. a state of p in a data domain $\mathbf{D} = \langle D, \ldots \rangle$ is an evaluation $f : \{x_0, \ldots, x_k\} \longrightarrow D$ of $\bar{x}$ into $\mathbf{D}$. Then there is a classical first order formula $\pi(\bar{x}, \bar{x}')$ describing the state transition relation of p (π contains no modalities and no flexible symbols). Intuitively, $\pi(\bar{x}, \bar{x}')$ means that $\bar{x}$ is a possible state of p, and $\bar{x}'$ is a *possible successor* state of $\bar{x}$ in some execution of p. Further $\pi(\bar{x}, \bar{x})$ means that $\bar{x}$ is a halting state of p. Now, $Ax(p)$ was defined to be $\forall \bar{x}\, (\pi(\bar{c}, \bar{x}) \to \bigcirc(\bar{c} = \bar{x}))$.

Clearly $Ax(p)$ is a temporal formula, and for any Kripke model $\mathfrak{M}$, if $\mathfrak{M} \models Ax(p)$ then $\mathfrak{M} \models \square Ax(p)$. Actually the intended meaning of $Ax(p)$ is $\square Ax(p)$. The only reason for dropping $\square$ was that this way we were expressing the same thing by using fewer modalities, permitting this way greater flexibility in applications.

Let now $\vdash^*$ be a temporal logic (e.g. $\vdash^*$ can be $\vdash_S$, $\vdash_{SF}$ etc. introduced at the beginning of this paper). Let $\{\varphi\}p\{\psi\}$ be a pca where $\pi\left(\bar{x}, \bar{x}'\right)$ defines the state transition relation of p (as above). (Here φ and ψ are $\varphi(\bar{x})$ and $\psi(\bar{x})$, and they contain no modalities or flexible symbols.)

We say that $\{\varphi\}p\{\psi\}$ is $\vdash^*$-provable, in symbols $\vdash^* \{\varphi\}p\{\psi\}$, iff

$$(5.1) \qquad \{Ax(p), \odot\varphi(\bar{c})\} \vdash^* \pi(\bar{c}, \bar{c}) \to \psi(\bar{c}).$$

In (5.1), $\varphi(\bar{c})$, $\psi(\bar{c})$, and $\pi(\bar{c}, \bar{c})$ can be formalized more carefully as $\exists x\,(\bar{x} = \bar{c} \wedge \varphi(\bar{x}))$ and the same for ψ or π. Note that (5.1) is a more detailed (but otherwise equivalent) version of the definition of $\vdash_S \{\varphi\}p\{\psi\}$ given in item (3.1) in §3.

Temporal provability of other program properties (e.g. invariance properties, termination etc.) are defined analogously to (5.1).[5] In passing we note the following. An important feature of (5.1) is that it uses no modality other than $\bigcirc$ and $\odot$. Therefore $\vdash^*$-provability of pca's makes sense in any fragment $\vdash^*$ of temporal logic containing $\bigcirc$ and $\odot$, even in $\vdash_0$ not containing any other modality (not even "plain sometime" $\lozenge$). This fragment $\vdash_0$ is interesting because it is equivalent with Floyd-Hoare logic w.r.t. provability of pca's ([9] Prop.1). Availability of (5.1) in all fragments makes it possible to compare the pca-proving powers of these fragments.

Let us turn to _concurrency_. For certain reasonings about concurrent situations, $\Box Ax(p)$ is too strong a description: If we are executing several processes $p_1, \ldots, p_\ell$ in a concurrent fashion which are _not_ synchronized then the use of "$\bigcirc$" in $\Box Ax(p_1)$ introduces an artificial synchronization. For this and related reasons we have to revise $Ax(p)$ and replace it with more subtle formalizations (of basically the same idea). Let p and π be as above. Then $Axinv(p)$ is the formula

$$\left(\forall \bar{x}, \bar{x}'\right)\left(\bar{c} = \bar{x} \wedge \pi\left(\bar{x}, \bar{x}'\right) \to \bigcirc\left(\bar{c} = \bar{x}' \vee \bar{c} = \bar{x}\right)\right).$$

Now, $Axinv(p)$ differs from $Ax(p)$ in that it expresses that we do not know how long it takes to execute a transition step $\pi\left(\bar{x}, \bar{x}'\right)$ of the program p, but as far as the step is not finished, we remain in the old state $\bar{x}$, and when it is finished we get into the new state $\bar{x}'$. The only thing that can go wrong with this formula is that it does not express that executing a step takes only a finite amount of time. (Actually if the process p has to wait for something then this finiteness condition may not even be true, but let us come back to this later.) Already $Axinv(p)$ is strong enough to prove all invariance properties (in FTL) that were provable from $Ax(p)$. That is, let $\vdash$ be a temporal logic containing at least $\odot$ and $\bigcirc$ and the induction rule ((R3) in §2). (Actually we assume that $\vdash$ restricted to $\odot$ and $\bigcirc$ satisfies (2.1) and (A2), where the latter is conceived as a condition. In other words, we are assuming that $\vdash$ contains $\vdash_0$ discussed at the end of §2.) Let φ be an invariance property of p (see in §3). Then

$$Ax(p) \vdash \varphi \qquad \text{iff} \qquad Axinv(p) \vdash \varphi.$$

This is what the "inv" part refers to in the abbreviation $Axinv$. In particular, we can prove the same pca's from $Axinv(p)$ as from $Ax(p)$. But we cannot prove eventualities

---

[5]In particular, for invariance properties the definition given in (5.1) becomes $\{Ax(p), \odot\varphi(\bar{c})\} \vdash^* \psi(\bar{c})$ (with exactly the same restrictions on φ, ψ as above, i.e. as in the pca case).

like total correctness, termination, fairness etc. from $Axinv(p)$. To this end let $Axfair(p)$ be the formula

$$\forall \bar{x} \left(\pi(\bar{c}, \bar{x}) \to \langle F \rangle \bar{c} = \bar{x} \right).$$

Now, from $Axinv(p) \wedge Axfair(p)$, the same program properties (both invariance, eventualities etc.) can be proved in FTL as from $Ax(p)$. The advantage is that the new axioms do not imply any undesired synchronization and hence can be applied to concurrent situations more realistically. At the same time we can use the same axiomatizations of FTL as before (cf. the beginning of this paper and/or Abadi [1], Abadi-Manna [4], Andréka-Goranko-Németi-Sain [5]) and they will have basically the same proof theoretic powers for deriving the same program properties as they had with $Ax(p)$.

For some concurrent situations $Axfair(p)$ might be too strong. (E.g. because it might be $Axfair(p)$ itself what we want to *prove* from some more basic assumptions. Or we might want to prove deadlock freedom [and then assuming $Axfair$ to start with is not quite fair].) We might have a temporal formula $Enabled(p_i)$ associated to each program p_i which expresses that the execution of p_i *can* proceed whenever $Enabled(p_i)$ is true. Then $Axfair^+(p)$ is the formula

$$\forall \bar{x} \left((\pi(\bar{c}, \bar{x}) \wedge [F]\langle F \rangle Enabled(p)) \to \langle F \rangle \bar{c} = \bar{x} \right).$$

Using the new $Axinv(p) \wedge Axfair^+(p)$, we can reason about concurrent situations quite realistically, without having to change our basic temporal logic $\vdash_{SF}$ (or $\vdash_{SFP}$).

Remark 5.1. *If we do not need $Axfair^+$ but only $Axfair$ then the necessity of using all modalities of $\vdash_{SF}$ to express $Axinv(p) \wedge Axfair(p)$ might seem a high price. Do we really need $\langle F \rangle$ here? Let $Axfair^0$ be $\forall \bar{x} \left(\pi(\bar{c}, \bar{x}) \to \Diamond \bar{c} = \bar{x} \right)$. If $Ax^0(p)$ is $Axinv(p) \wedge Axfair^0(p)$, then we can write up $Ax^0(p)$ in $\vdash_S$ already. For many purposes $Ax^0(p)$ might be just as good as $Ax(p)$ or $Axinv + Axfair$. Clearly the same invariance properties can be proved from $Ax^0(p)$ as from the rest (as was observed earlier), and it seems likely that this extends to total correctness and termination properties (we did not check this, though). We do not know how suitable $Ax^0(p)$ is (in comparison with $Ax(p)$ and $Axinv + Axfair$) for proving temporal properties of programs in general.*

§6. Open Problems

PROBLEM 6.1. *Is $\vdash_{SFP}$ complete w.r.t. the semantics $Mod(Ind + Tord)$?*

PROBLEM 6.2. *Is $\vdash_{SFP}$ complete for proving invariance properties of deterministic programs w.r.t. $Mod(Ind + Tord)$?*

CONJECTURE 6.3. *$\vdash_{SFP}$ is complete for proving pca's of nondeterministic programs w.r.t. $Mod(Ind + Tord)$.*

PROBLEM 6.4. *Is $\vdash_{SF}$ complete for pca's of nondeterministic programs w.r.t. $Mod(Ind + Tord)$?*

PROBLEM 6.5. *Find an elegant Hilbert-style inference system in the language of $\vdash_{SF}$ which is complete for $Mod(Ind + Tord)$.*

92

REFERENCES

1. M.Abadi, *The power of temporal proofs*, Theoretical Computer Science Vol **64** (1989), 35–84.
2. M.Abadi, *corrections to "The power of temporal proofs"*, Theoretical Computer Science (to appear).
3. M.Abadi, *The power of temporal proofs*, Proceedings of the Second Annual IEEE Symposium on Logic in Computer Science, Ithaca, NY, USA; (1987), 123-130.
4. M.Abadi and Z.Manna, *A timely resolution*, First Annual Symposium on Logic in Computer Science (1986), 176–189.
5. H.Andréka, V. Goranko, I.Németi, and I.Sain, *Effective first order temporal logics*, In preparation.
6. H.Andréka, I.Németi and I.Sain, *Henkin-type semantics for program schemes to turn negative results to positive*, In: Fundamentals of Computation Theory'79, ed.: L.Budach (Proc. Conf. Berlin 1979) Akademie Verlag, Berlin Band **2** (1979), 18–24.
7. H.Andréka, I.Németi and I.Sain, *A complete logic for reasoning about programs via nonstandard model theory, Parts I–II*, Theoretical Computer Science Vol **17** Nos **2, 3** (1982), 193–212 and 259–278.
8. H.Andréka, I.Németi, and I.Sain, *On the strength of temporal proofs (extended abstract)*, In: Mathematical Foundations of Computer Science 1989 (eds: A.Kreczmar and G.Mirkowska), Springer Lecture Notes in Comp. Sci. Vol **379** (1989), 135–144.
9. H.Andréka, I.Németi, and I.Sain, *On the strength of temporal proofs*, Theoretical Computer Science (an extended abstract of this is [8]) (to appear).
10. J.Barwise (ed.), *Handbook of Mathematical Logic*, North–Holland (1977).
11. D.Gabbay and F.Guenthner (eds), *Handbook of philosophical logic*, D.Reidel Publ. Co. Vol **II** (1984).
12. D.Gabbay, A.Pnueli, S.Shelah and J.Stavi, *On the temporal analysis of fairness*, Preprint Weizman Institute of Science, Dept. of Applied Math. (1981).
13. J.Garson, *Quantification in modal logic*, in: D.Gabbay and F.Guenthner (eds.), Handbook of philosophical logic, D.Reidel Publ. Co. (1984).
14. R.Goldblatt, *Logics of time and computation*, Center for the Study of Language and Information, Lecture Notes Number **7** (1987).
15. V.Goranko, *Letter to I.Németi*, July 9, 1990.
16. F.Kröger, *Temporal logic of programs*, EATCS Monographs on Theoretical Computer Science (1988).
17. O.Lichtenstein, A.Pnueli, and L.Zuck, *The glory of the past*, Proc. Coll. Logics of Programs, Brooklyn, USA, Springer Lecture Notes in Comp. Sci. (ed.: R.Parikh) Vol **193** (1985), 196–218.
18. Z.Manna and A.Pnueli, *The modal logic of programs*, International Colloquium on Automata, Languages and Programming'79, Graz, Springer Lecture Notes in Computer Science Vol **71** (1979), 385-409.
19. I.Németi, *Nonstandard Dynamic Logic*, In: Logics of Programs, Proc. Conf. New York 1981 (ed.: D.Kozen), Springer Lecture Notes in Computer Science Vol **131** (1982), 311–348.
20. A.Pnueli, *Specification and development of reactive systems*, Information Processing (IFIP'86), H.-J. Kugler (ed.) North–Holland Vol **86** (1986), 845–858.
21. I.Sain, *There are general rules for specifying semantics: Observations on Abstract Model Theory*, CL&CL (Computational Linguistics and Computer Languages) Vol **XIII** (1979), 195–250.
22. I.Sain, *The reasoning powers of Burstall's (modal logic) and Pnueli's (temporal logic) program verification methods*, In: Logics of Programs, Proc. Conf. Brooklyn USA 1985 (Ed.: R.Parikh), Springer Lecture Notes in Computer Science Vol **193** (1985), 302–319.
23. I.Sain, *Nonstandard Logics of Programs*, Dissertation, Hungarian Academy of Sciences, Budapest (in Hungarian) (1986).
24. I.Sain, *Comparing and characterizing the power of established program verification methods*, In: Many Sorted Logic and its Applications (Ed.: J.Tucker), Proc. Conf. Leeds, Great Britain 1988 (to appear).
25. I.Sain, *Temporal logics need their clocks*, Theoretical Computer Science (to appear).
26. I.Sain, *Results on the glory of the past*, Proc. Mathematical Foundations of Computer Science'90, Springer Lecture Notes in Computer Science (to appear).

Complexity Issues in Discrete Neurocomputing

Juraj Wiedermann *

VUSEI-AR, Dúbravská 3, 842 21 Bratislava
Czechoslovakia

Abstract: An overview of the basic results in complexity theory of discrete neural computations is presented. Especially, the computational power and efficiency of single neurons, neural circuits, symmetric neural networks (Hopfield model), and of Boltzmann machines is investigated and characterized. Corresponding intractability results are mentioned as well. The evidence is presented why discrete neural networks (inclusively Boltzmann machines) are not to be expected to solve intractable problems more efficiently than other conventional models of computing.

1. Introduction

1.1. *Motivation.* The recent renewed interest in neurocomputing is undoubtedly motivated by our ever increasing quest for exploiting new, non-traditional ways of computing. Along these lines at the border between computational physics and neurobiology a new computational paradigm is emerging saying that certain collective spontaneous properties of a mass of some simple computational devices can be used to immediately realize the computations. This gives rise to a brand-new class of computational machines in which the physics of the machine is intimately related to the algorithm of computations.

The prominent representatives of simple computational devices from which the resulting machines are assembled, are (artificial) neurons. These neurons are connected into a neural network and depending on the way in which the neurons work and cooperate, and on the topology of the resulting network, various types of neural nets can be distinguished: neural circuits, symmetric neural networks (so-called Hopfield neural networks), Boltzmann machines, etc.

So far these machines have been experimentally used for solving various isolated problems, like associative memory realizations [12, 13], solving some combinatorial problems [2,15,18], simple models of learning [2], or speech recognition [14].

Despite some promising experimental evidence of these machines no sufficient attention from the side of computer science has been paid to these machines and therefore the corresponding complexity theory that would answer the general questions concerning their computational power and efficiency has emerged only slowly and in fact only recently [25, 31].

One reason for this unfortunate state of the matters could be that until recently the corresponding devices have developed themselves mostly outside the framework of complexity theory — viz. within the framework of artificial intelligence, computational physics, or neurobiology.

---

* This work was finished while the author was visiting the Department of Computer Science, University of Saarland, West Germany (Spring 1990). During this stay the research was partially supported by the ESPRIT II Basic Research Action Program of the EC under contract No. 3075 (Project Alcom).

As a result, the main emphasis was put mostly on the learning abilities of these devices, too often without bothering explicitly about their computational power and efficiency. The second reason could have been that the results were scattered throughout non-computer science journals, the respective models varied from author to author, the used terminology ranged from that of mechanics through electricity up to biology, both discrete as well as analog devices were used, and therefore it was difficult for an 'outsider' to arrive at a reasonable computational model, from the viewpoint of complexity theory.

But, slowly, as the field has matured and certain devices have established themselves as more or less fundamental ones, the attention of computer science has been caught, especially when the neurocomputing researchers reported unusual efficiency of their devices in solving some intractable problems [15, 17, 19].

Nowadays, at least as far as discrete neurocomputing is concerned, the complexity theory disposes of quite a solid body of knowledge about these devices that places them into the proper perspective among the other known models of computations and thus explains some of experimentally observed phenomena [32].

Nevertheless, the analog neurocomputing remains still outside the reach of today's complexity theory, as it is regrettably the case with analog computations per se.

1.2. *The aims.* The goal of the paper presented is to give a contemporary state-of-the art survey on the basic complexity results concerning the fundamental classes of discrete neural machine models. We shall not be concerned in neural learning although this topic traditionally ranks among prime 'practical' motivations in studying neurocomputing. Notwithstanding, our results will shed some light on a problem what, at least in principle, can be learned by neural nets, and therefore they can be seen as a prelude to more advanced studies in neural learning. As a preliminary or companion reading an excellent introduction by Parberry [25] is recommended. The present paper tries to complement the Parberry's paper by new results or by results not covered in details in his paper. However, in striving for selfconsistency of our paper the overlapping of some topics could not have been avoided.

1.3. *Contents.* First, in Section 2, we shall introduce the notion of an abstract neuron and we shall characterize its computational power. We shall also present a new result that such an apparently simple problem as deciding whether a given boolean function can be realized by a single neuron, presents a Σ_2-complete problem (where Σ_2 denotes the complexity class in Stockmeyer's polynomial time hierarchy — see e.g. [5] or [11]). This result explains the exponential complexity of all known neural learning algorithms, most notably of that by Rosenblatt (which is known as perceptron learning procedure [23]).

In Section 3 we shall introduce the notion of neural networks and describe the way they compute, and the corresponding complexity measures.

In Section 4 the notion of neural circuits will be introduced and we shall briefly investigate their computational power and efficiency. We shall show that neural circuits can simulate efficiently any neural network. Moreover we shall also show that in the case of bounded fan-in these circuits are equivalent to standard combinatorial circuits, while in the case of unbounded fan-in they can compute any boolean function in constant parallel time, however, using an exponential number of neurons. Therefore in the rest of this Section we shall focus our attention on an interesting intermediate case of neural circuits of polynomial size and constant depth.

In Section 5 we shall continue our excursion with investigation of symmetric neural nets (so-called Hopfield model [13]). We shall show that the computational power and efficiency of these networks is equivalent to that of neural circuits [31, 32]. Further we shall introduce the notion of energy function for symmetric neural networks which exemplifies the close connection between computations of these networks and energy states of certain physical systems. We shall state here the fundamental Hopfield's result that any computation of symmetric neural networks can be seen as the minimization process of the corresponding energy function [13]. We will also study the relation between nondeterministic computations and energy function minimization problem and we show that the process of minimizing the energy function of a symmetric neural network presents an NP–complete problem. As a consequence we obtain the main result of this Section stating that any nondeterministic Turing machine computation can be realized by a symmetric neural network that ends its computation in a state that presents the global minimum of the corresponding energy function [32]. We shall close this section by investigating briefly the terminating problem for parallel symmetric neural networks.

Finally, in Section 6 we shall further enrich the computational capabilities of neural networks by introducing the probability into the computations of the respective neurons. As a result we obtain a discrete Boltzmann machine, studied intensively in the connection with so-called simulated annealing [18]. We will sketch here the recent surprising result by Parberry and Schnitger [27] that from computational complexity point of view these machines are equivalent to neural circuits introduced in Section 4.

In Conclusions we shall briefly summarize the importance and the contribution of neurocomputing to complexity theory.

2. Neurons

2.1. *Basic definitions.* A 'neuron' is a catchy name, inspired by the analogy with real neurons (in biology), of an abstract device that is capable to compute the values of so-called linearly separable, or weighted threshold functions in one computational step.

Definition 2.1. *A boolean function f of n variables $\vec{x} = (x_1, x_2, \ldots, x_n)$ is called a linearly separable function if and only if there is an integer vector $\vec{w} = (w_1, w_2, \ldots, w_n)$ and an integer constant t such that the set $f^{-1}(1) \stackrel{def}{=} \{\vec{x} \mid f(\vec{x}) = 1\}$ equals the set $\{\vec{x} \mid (\vec{w}, \vec{x}) \geq t\}$ and $f^{-1}(0) \stackrel{def}{=} \{\vec{y} \mid f(\vec{y}) = 0\}$ equals the set $\{\vec{y} \mid (\vec{w}, \vec{y}) < t\}$, where $(\vec{w}, \vec{x}) = \sum_{i=1}^{n} w_i x_i$ denotes the usual operation of scalar product of vectors $\vec{w}$ and $\vec{x}$.* ∎

Following the geometrical interpretation we say that the sets $f^{-1}(1)$ and $f^{-1}(0)$ are *linearly separable* by a *separating hyperplane* whose equation in an n-dimensional Euclidean space is given by $(\vec{w}, \vec{x}) = t$.

Such a separable function can be formally represented by a so-called *weighted boolean threshold function* $f[\vec{w}, t]$ defined as follows: $f[\vec{w}, t](\vec{x}) = 1$ iff $(\vec{w}, \vec{x}) \geq t$.

Definition 2.2. *An n-input neuron with weights $(w_1, \ldots, w_n)$ and the threshold t is an abstract device capable to compute the values of a weighted threshold function $f[\vec{w}, t](\vec{x})$ in one computational step, for any $\vec{x}$.* ∎

Schematically, a neuron computing the function $f[\vec{w}, t]$ is depicted in Fig. 1.

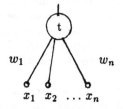

The values of $\vec{x}$ are called *the inputs* of a neuron. When for a given input $\vec{x}$ $f[\vec{w}, t](\vec{x}) = 1$ we say that the corresponding neuron is *active*, or is in an *active state*; its *output* is then defined to be 1; otherwise it is in a *passive state* and its output is then 0.

Fig. 1 A neuron

2.2. *Size of neural representation.* Clearly, by changing the weights or the threshold of a neuron we obtain another neuron that may compute another weighted boolean threshold function. We may now ask what is the number $N(n)$ of different n-input neurons (i.e., those computing different functions)?

Although $N(n)$ is not known to be determined exactly, except for small values of $n \leq 8$ [24], its asymptotic behavior is known: from [22] it follows that $N(n) = 2^{\Theta(n^2)}$, i.e., there exist approximatively 2^{n^2} different n-input neurons.

This means that to be able to describe an arbitrary n-input neuron in general $\Theta(n^2)$ bits are necessary and enough. It follows that in the worst case there must exist weights of size at least $\Omega(n)$ bits. Further, it is known [22] that it is enough for weights to be of size $O(n \log n)$, and as Parberry [25] noticed it is an open problem whether $O(n)$ bits would be always sufficient.

2.3. *The complexity of finding neural representation.* Given a boolean function f, e.g. by the help of a formula in a conjunctive normal form, it seems that it is not an easy task to find the corresponding neural representation (i.e., its representation as a weighted boolean threshold function), providing that f is a linearly separable function. In fact, the next theorem shows that the corresponding decision problem of asking whether a given boolean function is linearly separable presents an intractable problem.

Theorem 2.1. *The SEPARABILITY problem of deciding whether a given boolean function f is linearly separable is a Σ_2-complete problem.*

Proof (Sketch): First we shall show that the above problem is in Σ_2, i.e., in the class of polynomially time–bounded alternating Turing machine computations that use at most 2 alternations on each computational path, starting in an existential state (see [5] and [11] for the definition of the complexity class Σ_2).

Consider therefore an alternating Turing machine M that works in the following manner. The machine M starts in existential mode guessing the neural representation f_N of f — which is of size $O(n^2 \log n)$ bits (see 2.2), and therefore can be guessed in polynomial time. Then, in parallel, M verifies for each input $\vec{x}$ of size n whether $f_N(\vec{x}) = f(\vec{x})$. This takes again a polynomial time.

Secondly, we show that the problem of testing the validity of a given quantified boolean formula F in a conjunctive normal form with m variables, starting with existential quantifiers followed by universal ones, is polynomial-time reducible to SEPARABILITY. Since it is known that the validity problem of such formulae presents a Σ_2-complete problem [11], this will be enough to prove the Σ_2-completeness of SEPARABILITY.

Hence our goal will be to construct a boolean function $f \not\equiv 0$ which will be separable iff F is valid.

W.l.o.g. suppose that F is of form $(\exists x_1) \ldots (\exists x_k)(\forall x_{k+1}) \ldots (\forall x_m) g(x_1, \ldots, x_m)$ of length n, where g is a boolean formula, and suppose that F is valid. This means that there exist $z_1, \ldots, z_k \in \{0, 1\}$ such that $g(z_1, \ldots, z_k, x_{k+1}, \ldots, x_m) = 1$ irrespective of the values of x_i's. W.l.o.g. suppose further that $z_1 = \ldots = z_p = 1$ and $z_{p+1} = \ldots = z_k = 0$, for some p, $0 \leq p \leq k$, and put $w_1 = \ldots = w_p = 1$, $w_{p+1} = \ldots = w_k = -(p+1)$, $w_{k+1} = \ldots = w_m = 0$, and $t = p$, and define f as $f(\vec{x}) := $ if $(\vec{w}, \vec{x}) \geq t$ then $g(\vec{x})$ else 0 fi.

We shall show that f is separable. For that purpose consider the values of $(\vec{w}, \vec{x})$ for all $\vec{x}$. If the vector $\vec{x} = (z_1, \ldots, z_k, x_{k+1}, \ldots, x_m)$, then $(\vec{w}, \vec{x}) \geq t$, $g(\vec{x}) = 1$, and therefore also $f(\vec{x}) = 1$. On the other hand, when the first k components of $\vec{x}$ are different from $z_1, \ldots, z_k$, the scalar product $(\vec{w}, \vec{x}) < t$, and due to the definition of f, $f(\vec{x}) = 0$. This means that $h : (\vec{w}, \vec{x}) = t$ is a separating hyperplane of f indeed, and therefore f is a separable function.

Let f be a separable function — i.e., there is a hyperplane $h : (\vec{w}, \vec{x}) = t$ such that $f(\vec{x}) = 1$ iff $(\vec{w}, \vec{x}) \geq t$. W.l.o.g. suppose that $w_i \neq 0$ for $i = 1, \ldots, k$, and $w_j = 0$ for $j = k + 1, \ldots, m$, for some k, $1 \leq k \leq m$. Then, clearly, the formula $F : (\exists x_1) \ldots (\exists x_k)(\forall x_{k+1}) \ldots$

$(\forall x_m) f(x_1, \ldots, x_m)$ is valid: namely, to achieve $f(\vec{x}) = 1$ it is enough to choose such an $\vec{x} : (\vec{w}, \vec{x}) \geq t$. —

The previous Theorem thus explains the exponential time complexity of all known neuron learning algorithms, among them most notably of that by Rosenblatt (see e.g. in [23], a so-called perceptron learning procedure).

3. Neural networks

3.1. *Basic definition.* Informally, neural networks are obtained from individual neurons by connecting the outputs of some neurons to inputs of some neurons and by declaring certain neurons as input ones, others as output ones.

Definition 3.1. *A neural network is a 7-tuple* $M = (N, C, I, O, A, w, h)$ *, where*
— N *is a finite set of neurons*
— $C \subseteq N \times N$ *is a set of oriented interconnections among neurons*
— $I \subseteq N$ *is a set of input neurons*
— $O \subseteq N$ *is a set of output neurons*
— $A \subseteq N$ *is a set of initially active neurons,* $A \cap T = \emptyset$
— $w : C \rightarrow Z$ *is a weight function; Z is the set of all integers*
— $h : N \rightarrow Z$ *is a threshold function*

The ordered pair (N, C) *forms an oriented graph that is called an interconnection graph of* M. ∎

Each neuron $u_i \in N$ can enter two different *states*: 0 (inactive) or 1 (active) as characterized by its *output* x_i. There is a so-called *threshold value* $t_i \in Z$ assigned by the function h to each neuron u_i. Each neuron has an arbitrary number of input and output *connections* that are labeled by *weights*. The *total input* to each neuron u_i at any moment is given by the sum $h_i = \sum_{j=1}^{n} a_{i,j} x_j$, where $a_{i,j} \in Z$ is the weight (assigned by the function w) of the u_i's input connection leading from u_j to u_i, x_j is the state of u_j at a given moment and n is the total number of neurons in the network.

3.2. *Neural network computation.* The *computation* of such a system on a given input starts by initializing the states of input neurons in the set I to corresponding *input values* (0 or 1), the states of neurons (if any) in the set A of initialized neurons to 1's, and the remaining neurons are left in a passive state.

The description of states of all neurons in the network at any moment is called a *configuration* of that network at that moment. Further the network can compute in two different ways: in a parallel, and in a sequential mode. In a *parallel (sequential)* mode each neuron u_i samples its inputs synchronously in parallel with other neurons (sequentially, in any order in each step) and if $h_i \geq t_i$ the output x_i is set to 1, otherwise to 0.

The time interval within which the actions of all neurons are accomplished is called a *computational cycle*. Note that in a parallel computational mode the number of computational cycles performed during a computation corresponds to parallel computational time.

The network then works as described above and the computation on a given input is *finished* when a *stable state* is achieved which is the situation in which the state of each neuron remains unchanged during one computational cycle. In that case we say that the computation was *convergent*.

The *result* of the convergent computation on a given input is given by the states of some selected *output neurons*. When the stable state is not reached the output of the computation is not defined.

Note that due to the fact that the neurons in a sequential computation mode can sample their inputs in any order even from the same initial configuration each sequential computation can lead to different results or some (in any mode) can lead to no results at all. It will be our concern to design the network in such a way that the computations will be convergent and the results will be unique if necessary. However, the satisfaction of the latter two conditions can be guaranteed only for certain special classes of neural networks that we shall deal with in a sequel.

3.3. *Complexity measures.* The *time complexity* of a convergent computation on an input of length n will be given as the maximum number of computational cycles needed for achieving a stable state taken over all inputs of length n.

The *size* of the network will be given by the number of its neurons.

4. Neural circuits

4.1. *Basic definition.* Neural circuits are special instances of neural networks:

Definition 4.1. *A neural circuit is a neural network with a directed acyclic interconnection pattern; its input neurons are those having no predecessors and its output neurons those having no successors in its interconnection graph.*

The depth of a neural circuit is the length of the longest path between some input and some output neuron. ∎

From this definition it follows that neural circuits possess some desirable properties which cannot be guaranteed in the general case of neural networks: it is clear that starting from a given initial configuration any computation of a neural circuit must terminate always in the same stable final configuration, in parallel mode in a time that is proportional to the depth of the circuit, and in sequential mode in a time that is proportional to its size.

4.2. *Neural networks and neural circuits.* Neural circuits, being a special case of neural networks, cannot be computationally more powerful than neural networks. Nevertheless the following adaptation of a standard simulation technique from complexity theory (see e.g. [26, 27]) shows that everything what can be computed by neural networks can be computed by neural circuits as well, even in the same parallel time.

Theorem 4.1. *Any neural network N of size $S(n)$ and of parallel time complexity $T(n)$ can be simulated by a neural circuit C of size $O(S(n)T(n))$ in parallel time $O(T(n))$.*

Proof (Sketch). We shall construct a circuit C in which the computation proceeds through a sequence of 'layers', i—th layer corresponding to i-th configuration c_i of N.

In the first layer of C there is exactly $S(n)$ input neurons. At the beginning of the computation the state of each of them corresponds to that in the initial configuration c_0 of the respective neurons in N. In the next layers inputs to any neuron u in the $(i+1)$—st layer are connected by oriented edges with the same weights as in N to those neurons in the i—th layer whose outputs are sampled by u in N, for $i = 0, 1, \ldots, T(n) - 1$. This construction guarantees that there are no cycles in C and when the computation of C terminates the states of neurons in its $T(n)$—th layer correspond to those in the final configuration of N. ∎

4.3. *The computational power of neural circuits.* The previous result states that the computational power of neural circuits equals to that of neural networks. But what is the computational power of these devices when compared to more traditional models of computation? It appears that in this respect there is no difference between neural circuits and boolean combinatorial circuits.

It is not difficult to verify that neurons from Fig. 2 realize the basic logical operations AND, OR and NOT; it follows that every combinatorial circuit can be simulated by a neural

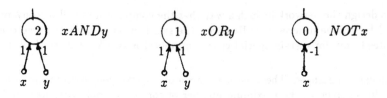

Fig. 2 Neural realization of basic boolean operations

circuit of the same topology, i.e., of the same size and depth (see also [21] for the proof that any deterministic Turing machine can be build out of neurons!).

However, using the 'full capacity' of neural circuits, i.e., the unbounded fan-in, it is possible to compute any boolean function f by a neural circuit of constant depth, simply by constructing a circuit that mimics the representation of f in its disjunctive normal form (Fig. 3).

It follows that in a parallel computation mode the value of any boolean function can be computed by a neural circuit in constant time! It is not known whether in general the size of such circuit can be substantially less than as in the above example while maintaining the constant depth of a circuit.

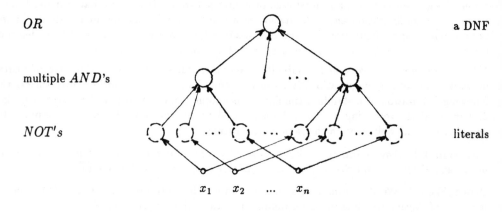

Fig. 3 A circuit computing a boolean function in DNF

4.4. Neural circuits of constant depth and polynomial size. The circuit from the last example has the size exponential w.r.t. the number of its inputs. Circuits of exponential size have to be considered as unrealistic ones from the same reasons as exponential time is considered as an intractable one. Therefore the attraction of researchers has focused to an interesting intermediate case — namely that of neural circuits of simultaneously polynomial size and constant depth.

Such circuits can be also very powerful — e.g. in Fig. 4 there is a so-called binary sorting circuit , of linear size, that rearranges the 0's and 1's appearing on its input so that 1's precede the 0's on its output, in a constant parallel time.

4.5. Threshold circuits. In the complexity theory a somewhat special case of neural circuits hidden under the disguise of so called *threshold circuits* has been extensively studied.

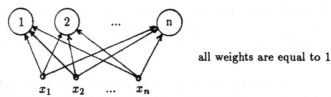

all weights are equal to 1

Fig. 4 A neural binary sorter

A threshold circuit (TC) is just a neural circuit with unit weights. In fact, both neural circuits from Fig. 3 and 4 are threshold circuits.

The full characterization of the class of functions that can be computed by TC's of polynomial size and constant depth in terms of some standard complexity classes is not known. Nevertheless, it is known that some very important classes are computed by such circuits. Along these lines the important recent result is that by Reif and Tate [28], who found the surprising relationship between TC's and so-called *finite field* $Z_{P(n)}$ *circuits* (FFC's). In the latter circuits each node computes either multiple sums or products of integers modulo a prime $P(n)$. FFC's are especially suitable for the realization of various basic numerical algorithms like simple and iterated addition and multiplication, computing integer reciprocal, etc.

The main result of Reif and Tate is that all functions computed by TC's of size $S(n) \geq n$ and depth $D(n)$ can also be computed by FFC's of size $O(S(n) \log S(n) + nP(n) \log P(n))$ and depth $O(D(n))$, and vice versa, all functions computed by FFC's of size $S(n)$ and depth $D(n)$ can be computed by TC's of size $O((S(n) \log P(n)^{1+\epsilon}/\epsilon^2)$ and depth $O(D(n)/\epsilon^5)$.

They got many useful and quite surprising consequences of this result. For example, integer reciprocal can be computed in size $n^{O(1)}$ and depth $O(1)$. More generally, any analytic function (such a sine, cosine, exponentiation, square root, and logarithm) can be computed within accuracy 2^{-n^c}, for any constant c, by TC's of polynomial size and constant depth. In addition, integer and polynomial quotient and remainder, FFT, polynomial interpolation, Chinese Remaindering, all the elementary symmetric functions, banded matrix inverse, and triangular Toeplitz matrix inverse can be exactly computed by such TC's. For details see the original paper [28].

5. Symmetric neural networks

5.1. *Basic definition.* Symmetric neural networks are neural networks with an undirected interconnection graph containing no loop-edges:

Definition 5.1. *A symmetric neural network M is a neural network for which $a_{i,j} = a_{j,i}$ and $a_{i,i} = 0$, where $a_{i,j}$ is the weight of an edge connecting an i-th neuron with a j-th neuron in M.*

Symmetric neural networks are often termed *Hopfield neural networks* since it was apparently Hopfield who as the first recognized that these special instances of neural networks are of particular interest. Namely, for any Hopfield network the termination of any computation in the sequential mode can always be guaranteed (see Section 5.3.)! Moreover, there exist some natural physical realizations just of this type of neural networks — viz. Ising spin glasses [3], or certain models of so-called 'optical computers' [8].

It is therefore quite surprising that until recently the computational power of symmetric neural networks has not been known [7, 10] as it was conjectured that perhaps these networks need not be as powerful as asymmetric ones since the former are but a special case of the latter ones.

5.2. *The computational power of symmetric neural networks.* We shall show now the result by Wiedermann [31, 32] that the computational power and efficiency of symmetric neural networks is no less as that of neural circuits (the independent proof is given also in [25]). To prove this claim we shall need the following definition.

Definition 5.2. *We shall say that a given neuron u (with symmetric weights) has the insensitivity range $\langle a, b \rangle$, with $a \leq 0$, $b > 0$, if the addition of a further input with weight $w \in \langle a, b \rangle$ will not affect the activity of u (i.e., its behavior will further depend only on the original inputs).* ∎

In the proof of the following lemma we shall see that the definition of insensitivity range is correct, i.e., that the insensitivity range of any neuron always comprises an interval of form $\langle a, b \rangle$, with $a \leq 0$ and $b > 0$. The lemma actually says more:

Lemma 5.1. *For any neuron u and any $\alpha \leq 0$ and $\beta > 0$ there is an equivalent neuron v that computes the same function as u does, and with insensitivity range $\langle \alpha, \beta \rangle$.*

Proof (Sketch). Let $w_1, w_2, ..., w_k$ be the input weights of u and t its threshold. Define $a = max\{\sum_{i=1}^{k} w_i x_i \mid \sum_{i=1}^{k} w_i x_i < t, x_i \in \{0, 1\}\}$ and $b = min\{\sum_{i=1}^{k} w_i x_i \mid \sum_{i=1}^{k} w_i x_i \geq t, x_i \in \{0, 1\}\}$.

Clearly $a < t \leq b$ and $\langle t - b, t - a \rangle$ is the insensitivity range of u, for any $t \in (a, b)$. Select now such a $t_0 \in (a, b)$ that splits the interval (a, b) in the same ratio in which 0 splits the interval $\langle \alpha, \beta \rangle$ — i.e., $t_0 = (\alpha a - \beta b)/(\alpha - \beta)$. To obtain the weights and the threshold of v multiply all weights of u and t_0 by $(\beta - \alpha)/(b - a)$. ∎

Now we are ready to formulate the main result of this subsection.

Theorem 5.1. *Any neural circuit C of size $S(n)$ and depth $D(n)$ can be simulated by a symmetric neural network N of size $S(n)$ in parallel time $O(D(n))$.*

Proof (Sketch). The main idea in the construction of N is to adjust the weights and the thresholds of each neuron in C with the help of Lemma 5.1 so as the total minimal and maximal sum of its output weights would lie in the insensitivity range of each neuron. This will enable then to introduce to each output connection the symmetric connection with the same weight — i.e., the transformation of C to N. To do so start with the set of neurons of C that have no successors in C and leave their weights and thresholds as they are and consider these neurons as being already adjusted. Now proceed recursively as follows : for each neuron v whose weights have already been adjusted compute the minimal sum α and the maximal sum β of its output weights. Then adjust the input weights and the threshold of v with help of Lemma 5.1 so that the insensitivity range of v would be $\langle \alpha, \beta \rangle$. The process will stop at input neurons that have no predecessors.

As a result we obtain a circuit C' equivalent to C. To obtain N introduce the backward connections to existing ones in C' with the same weights and note that these connections can by no means affect the behavior of the corresponding target neurons since their contribution lies always in the insensitivity range of target neurons.

Thus the neurons that are farther from the input neurons cannot affect those that are closer to them; hence in a sense the computation is directed from input neurons towards the output ones. Therefore the computation time will be $O(D(n))$. ∎

Thus, recalling also the result of Theorem 4.1 it follows that from a computational point of view there is no difference between the computational power of neural circuits and that of symmetric neural networks. The transformation from the previous theorem can be of practical significance e.g. in a case when the technological constraints allow only for realization of Hopfield networks.

5.3. The termination of sequential symmetric network computations. Hopfield [13] has shown that the computation of any symmetric neural network can be thought of as a process of a minimization of a certain energy function. This energy function takes the form $E = -\frac{1}{2} \sum_{i=1}^{n} \sum_{j=1}^{n} a_{i,j} x_i x_j + \sum_{i=1}^{n} t_i x_i$, with $a_{i,j} = a_{j,i}$, $a_{i,i} = 0$, and the meaning of individual symbols as described in Section 3.2. Hopfield proved in fact the following theorem that makes symmetric neural networks so attractive:

Theorem 5.2. *Starting from any initial configuration any symmetric neural network with energy function E computing in a sequential mode will achieve a stable state after at most $O(p)$ computational cycles, where $p = \frac{1}{2}\sum_{i=1}^{n}\sum_{j=1}^{n}|a_{i,j}| + \sum_{i=1}^{n}|t_i|$; moreover this stable state represents a local minimum of E.*

Proof (Sketch). The change ΔE in E due to changing the state of i–th neuron by Δx_i is $\Delta E = -\sum_{j=1}^{n}[a_{i,j}x_j - t_j]\Delta x_i$. According to the mechanism of neural network computation the change of x_i is positive if and only if the expression in the bracket is positive and similarly for the negative case. Thus any action of any neuron cannot cause the increase of the value of E and whenever some neuron changes its state the value of E will decrease. Since $|E|$ is bounded by p after at most p computational cycles the network must reach a stable state which is a local minimum of E. ∎

5.4. *Nondeterministic computations and energy function minimization.* From Theorem 5.2 it follows that the computation of any symmetric neural network in sequential mode will always terminate in some final configuration in which the corresponding energy function achieves its minimum. Which minimum will be achieved — whether a local or a global one — depends, of course, on the initial configuration and in the sequential computational mode also on the order in which neurons sample their inputs during each computational cycle.

Later on we shall see that certain computations of symmetric neural networks are of special interest — namely those for which the corresponding energy function achieves its global minimum at the end of computation. Such computations correspond to successful nondeterministic computations (see Corollary 5.3.1). Therefore it is worth to study the minimization problem of energy functions of such networks. Unfortunately, the following theorem by Wiedermann [32] shows that the above minimization problem is a difficult one.

Theorem 5.3. *Let N be a symmetric neural network with weights of at most polynomial size in the size of N. Then for any integer k the problem of deciding whether there exists an initial configuration of N for which a stable state with energy not greater than k will be achieved is an NP–complete problem.*

Proof (Sketch). First we shall show that the above problem is in NP. Consider therefore a nondeterministic Turing machine M that simulates N. M first guesses the initial configuration of N. This takes time polynomial in the size of N since the size of each configuration is linear. Then for this configuration M simulates the computation of N. According to Theorem 5.2. this simulation will end in polynomial time due to our assumption concerning the size of weights of N.

The computation of M ends successfully if and only if for our initial configuration a stable state with energy $\leq k$ is achieved.

Thus the total running time of M's simulation is polynomial and hence our problem belongs to NP.

Next we shall construct a special symmetric network N with energy function E that tests the satisfiability of a given boolean formula f in a conjunctive normal form with n variables. It is known that the satisfiability problem of such formulae presents an NP–complete problem [11]. Then we will show that there is a constant k such that f is satisfiable if and only if there is an initial configuration for which a local minimum of E with a value $\leq k$ is achieved.

The schema of N is depicted in Fig. 5.

In this figure the thresholds of only some neurons that will be important in the following explanation are given in circles representing the corresponding neurons; similarly important edges are labeled by their weights.

The states of neurons $i_1, i_2, ..., i_n$ play the role of boolean variables in f; neurons $n_1, n_2, ..., n_q$ are negating neurons that compute literals (they are present only when the respective variable has to be negated in the corresponding clause of f). Neurons $a_1, a_2, ..., a_r$ compute

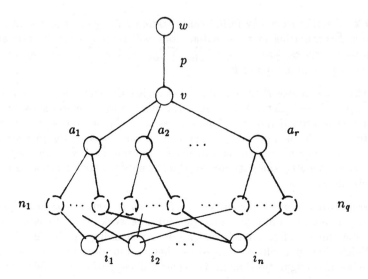

Fig. 5 A schema of a symmetric network for satisfiability testing

multiple OR's — i.e., individual clauses of f and the neuron v computes the multiple AND of all clauses — i.e., the value of f on the input represented by states of $i_1, i_2, ..., i_n$.

The purpose of w is to decrease the value of E as low as we wish in the case that v is active; this is achieved by choosing p large enough. Note that when neurons v and w are both active they contribute with a value of $\Theta(p)$ to the energy function.

In the initial configuration of N the neurons i_j's corresponding to variables in f represent the input neurons . The states of all other neurons are initialized to 0.

Under this arrangement it follows that for some initial configuration the neuron v could be active in some stable state if and only if f is a satisfiable formula.

Consider now the corresponding energy function E. It is clear by now that by a suitable choice of p we can achieve that the value of E is $\leq k$ for any computation that starts in any initial configuration that satisfies f.

Finally note that the value of p need not be greater than the one used in Theorem 5.1. and that all weights in N, and the size of N, is polynomial in the length of f. Therefore the reduction from f to N (and hence to E) takes polynomial time. ∎

Corollary 5.3.1. *Let M be an arbitrary single–tape nondeterministic Turing machine of time complexity $T(n) \geq n \log n$. Then there is a symmetric neural network N of size $O(T(n))$ with energy function E and a constant k such that M accepts its input if and only if there is such an initial configuration of N for which a stable state with energy $\leq k$ is achieved.*

Proof (Sketch). There is a reduction [29] from a single–tape nondeterministic Turing machine with time complexity $T(n) \geq n \log n$ to a boolean formula f in conjunctive normal form of length $T(n)$ which is satisfiable if and only if the machine accepts its input. For this formula use the construction from the previous theorem. ∎

Observe the 'cautious' formulation of the last corollary: it is not claimed here that N will always find a solution of the original problem. No doubt that the network will converge to some stable state but not necessarily to that in which the value of E is $\leq k$. The network will converge to that local minimum that is a so–called *attractor* of the initial configuration of the network. Hence the convergence can be 'directed' by a suitable choice of initial states of certain neurons — but Theorem 5.3. and its proof show that exactly this presents an NP–complete problem by itself! This also seems to be the bottleneck of analog Hopfield networks when used for solving NP–complete problems (see e.g. [16]) where in order to obtain a correct or a good approximate solution, it was necessary to set the initial values of analog variables so as they lie in the region of attraction of sufficiently low local minimum of the corresponding energy function.

Note also that if there were a uniform family of symmetric neural networks of polynomial size, with weights also of polynomial size that would always find a solution of some NP–complete problem, it would imply that $P = NP = co - NP$!

5.5 *The terminating problem of parallel symmetric neural networks.* Providing the sequential computational mode Theorem 5.2 guarantees the termination of any symmetric neural network computations. Surprisingly the result does not hold for parallel computational mode as seen from the simple example of a symmetric neural network consisting of two zero–threshold neurons connected by an edge with weight equal to -1. Starting from an initial configuration in which both neurons are in the same state the network will flip–flop for ever between two configurations. However, the computation of the same network will terminate when started in a configuration with different states of both neurons. This observation can be generalized to the case of arbitrary symmetric neural networks [4,25].

Theorem 5.4. *Starting from any initial configuration after at most $O(p)$ parallel computational steps any symmetric neural network N will alternate between two configurations or will achieve a stable state (where p is the same as in Theorem 5.2).*

Proof (Sketch). We shall construct a symmetric neural network M that will simulate N in a sequential mode. M will consist of two sets of neurons — M_0 and M_1, respectively. There is one-to-one correspondence between neurons of N and M_0, and N and M_1 (and therefore M_0 and M_1 are of equal cardinality). There are no connections among the neurons in M_0 and the same holds for M_1. However, if in N there is a neuron u that is connected with neurons $u_1, \ldots, u_k$ for some $k \geq 1$, then the corresponding neuron in M_0 is connected with the corresponding neurons in M_1, and vice versa. Doing so, the respective weights and thresholds remain the same as in N.

At the beginning of the simulation of N by M the neurons in M_0 are initialized similarly as the neurons in N; neurons in M_1 are set into passive states. Then the sequential simulation can start. First, the states of all neurons in M_1 are updated sequentially, then again the states of all neurons in M_0, etc.

It is clear that during the simulation the following invariant holds: for i even (odd), after updating the states of all neurons in M_0 (M_1), the configuration of neurons in M_0 (M_1) corresponds to the configuration of neurons in N after i–th parallel step of N.

Since our simulation is sequential due to Theorem 5.2 it must terminate in some stable configuration after at most $O(p)$ computational cycles (note that the energy function of M differs from that of N only by the multiplicative factor of 2). When in this stable configuration of M the configuration of neurons in M_0 is different from those in M_1 the original parallel network N will alternate between these two configurations; otherwise it will stop as well. ∎

6. Boltzmann Machines

6.1. *Escaping from local minima.* In the last section we have demonstrated a close connection between nondeterministic computations and the minimization of energy function that corresponds to some symmetric neural network. We have seen that in order to get the correct result of the original nondeterministic computation it was necessary to ensure somehow, by a choice of a suitable initial configuration, the convergence of the computation to some 'sufficiently low' local minimum — of course, the best of all, to a global minimum.

However, since the finding of such a suitable initial configuration presents an NP-complete problem by itself, as we have proved, even without knowing the theoretical reason physicists devised other, in fact heuristics techniques how to increase the probability of arriving into some acceptable local minimum of energy function.

Roughly, the idea is as follows. We start from any initial configuration and wait until the network converges by repeatedly transiting from a given configuration to a configuration with a lower energy, in accordance with Theorem 5.2., into some stable state. Now, if the value of the corresponding energy function is not sufficiently low, we try to 'escape' from the local minimum we are in by changing temporarily the mode of neuron computations! This is achieved by allowing also transitions from configurations to other configurations with higher energy.

6.2. *Simulated annealing.* The mechanism that allows for escaping from local minima of energy functions is the probabilism. Namely, we arrange the things so that the neurons are not necessarily obliged to change their states as dictated by the deterministic rule described in Section 3, i.e., depending on whether the total input exceeds the corresponding threshold value or not. Rather, this change becomes now a subject of a probabilistic decision — the neurons will change their state only with a certain probability that can be controlled, so to speak, from outside.

From historical reasons in analogy with statistical mechanics (the behavior of systems with many degree of freedom in thermal equilibrium at a finite temperature) the process of probability approaching 1 in the behavior of neurons is termed 'temperature lowering' or 'cooling'.

Thus, to escape from a local minimum (which, in physical terms, corresponds to a complete 'freezing' of a system) we start to increase the temperature slowly in order to come temporarily into higher energy states, and than again we start with cooling, in hoping that we arrive into another local minimum, with lower energy than before.

The whole process is appropriately termed *simulated annealing* and its history goes back to Metropolis et al. [20], and Kirpatrick et al. [18]. The corresponding device is called a *Boltzmann machine,* and the above physical motivation explains how Boltzmann's name came into the play.

6.3. *The Boltzmann machine definition.* Formally, a discrete Boltzmann machine is modeled by a symmetric neural network with neurons enhanced by a probabilistic mechanism.

Definition 6.1. *A discrete Boltzmann machine is a symmetric neural network enhanced by a so-called temperature function* $\tau : N \times Z \to Z$ *which assigns a 'temperature' to each neuron and time.* ∎

The state of each neuron is updated as follows. The total input to the i−th neuron u_i in time $m > 0$ is given similarly as in Section 4 by the sum $h_i(m) = \sum_{i=0}^{n} a_{i,j} x_j(m-1)$, where $a_{i,j} \in Z$ is the weight of an edge connecting u_i with u_j, and $x_j(m)$ is the state of u_j in time m. Then u_i is active in time m with some probability $p(h_i(m) - t_i, m) = p(\Delta_i(m), m)$, where t_i is the threshold of u_i. Typically, in the literature the activation probability function $p(\Delta_i(m), m) = 1/(1 + e^{-\Delta_i(m)/\tau(i,m)})$ is recommended.

Note that as τ approaches ∞, the above probability approaches $1/2$, and thus the network behaves more or less unpredictably, and as τ approaches 0, the neurons start to act deterministically, as in an ordinary neural network.

The machine usually operates in a parallel mode.

6.4. *The art of simulated annealing.* There is a lot of interesting and successful experiments with simulated annealing used in solving various problems (like traveling salesman problem and wire routing [18], independent set, max cut, graph coloring [19]) described in the literature.

Most of the results were obtained with the help of an *analog Boltzmann machine*, i.e., such where the 'state' of neurons can take continuous values between 0 and 1.

Computational experiments with these machines seem to indicate that the convergence to sufficiently minimal energy states need not occur if the temperature is lowered too fast through many different levels. Thus various annealing schedules that could guarantee the convergence to the global optimum have been investigated. Numerical experience of most researchers recommends the following procedures to yield the best results: iterate at a fixed temperature 'long enough' before lowering the temperature to the next level. Then usually few different temperatures were sufficient.

Theoretical explanation why the latter procedure should be preferred over the first one is given in [9]. However, it must be noted that in general the convergence to a global minimum could not be guaranteed and that the above methods can give acceptable results only when good, not necessarily optimal solutions are sufficient to obtain.

6.5. *Boltzmann machines and neural circuits.* Bellow we shall sketch a recent and a quite surprising result by Parberry and Schnitger [26, 27] that Boltzmann machines are not much more powerful than neural circuits introduced in Section 4.

More precisely these authors have shown that any Boltzmann machine of polynomial time complexity as defined in Section 6.3 can be simulated by a neural circuit with running time greater by a constant factor and size greater by a polynomial. It means that probabilism and the related ability to perform simulated annealing are unimportant from the complexity point of view!

The proofs of the above claim are based on known techniques from theory of iterative arrays and combinatorial circuits. First, the cycles are removed from the interconnection graph of a Boltzmann machine B at hand using the method of 'unwrapping' the computation in time, i.e., a circuit is build in which i–th layer corresponds to a configuration of B immediately after performing its i–th computational cycle (similarly as in the proof of Theorem 4.1). Then, the probabilism is removed from neurons firstly by replacing each neuron by a small number of deterministic neurons with random inputs, and then by using the well-known technique by Adlemann [1] that transforms the above circuit with random inputs to a completely deterministic one. As a result a neural circuit equivalent to B with complexity characteristics as above is obtained.

6.6. *The computational limits of Boltzmann machines.* Although occasionally some experimental researchers report that Boltzmann machines are surprisingly good in solving some NP–complete problems where only exact rather than approximate solutions make sense (like in the 3-satisfiability problem — see e.g. [17]), and thus seem to indicate that it might be the case that $P = NP$, we will further give a strong evidence why such claims should be regarded with the greatest possible care.

Our reasoning will be based on some of our earlier results mentioned here and, for the sake of correctness, it must be stressed that it holds only for discrete Boltzmann machines.

Imagine therefore that we wish to solve some NP–complete problem $\mathcal{P}$ with the help of a Boltzmann machine B as described in Section 6.2. Due to the last result from Section 6.5 there is a neural circuit C of polynomial size that is equivalent to B. In turn, according to Theorem 4.1, C is further equivalent to a symmetric neural circuit N. To solve $\mathcal{P}$ on N we have to initialize N so as its computation ends in a stable state with sufficiently low energy. According to Theorem 5.3 this presents an NP–complete problem by itself!

Thus we see that unless $P = NP$ even discrete Boltzmann machines do not present a way to go round the intractability of NP–complete problems.

7. Conclusions

7.1. *Summary.* In the previous review we have presented basic models of abstract discrete neural devices: single neurons, neural circuits, symmetric neural networks, and Boltzmann machines. We have seen that except single neurons, whose computational power is restricted to linearly separable boolean functions, all the other devices are equivalent in the sense that they can compute any recursive function. For a given boolean function we have shown that the problem of deciding whether there exists an equivalent neural representation presents an intractable problem. Moreover, we have seen that all the above neural networks can simulate each other with at most polynomial increase in size and a constant increase in time — whether in a parallel or in a sequential computational mode.

The link to traditional models of computations was provided via combinatorial circuits. It is well-known that combinatorial circuits with bounded fan-in belong to a so-called *second machine class* [30] that embodies machines allowing for unrestricted parallelism. For instance, this class includes alternating Turing machines, vector machines, array processing machines, various versions of parallel RAM's, etc. It follows that neural circuits with bounded fan-in belong also to the second machine class, while these with unbounded fan-in are outside of this class, since they can compute any boolean function in a constant depth.

For symmetric neural networks it was shown that there is a close connection between nondeterministic computations and minimization of corresponding energy functions.

Finally, the evidence was presented that even discrete Boltzmann machines, with their added ability to perform simulated annealing, are not much more powerful than simple models of neural nets.

7.2. *The significance of neurocomputing* . From the complexity point of view the previous results demonstrate that models of discrete neurocomputing just enrich the classic repertoire of computational models by devices that are inspired by biological or physical motivations — depending on which framework is preferred. The computational power and efficiency of these models have been studied already for years and our review shows in fact that most of results and open problems achieved in neural formalism can be translated into other formalisms, and vice versa. Nevertheless, there are also results specific to neurocomputing — most notably those concerning the relation between nondeterministic computations and energy function minimization – that have brought new insights into general mechanisms of computations.

Last but not least, the significance of discrete neurocomputing should be seen also on a methodological level, where these models provide new natural conceptual tools for modeling some problems that we believe can be related to brain activities.

References

[1] Adlemann, L.: Two Theorems on Random Polynomial Time, *Proc. 19-th FOCS*, Washington D. C., 1978, pp. 75–83

[2] Ackley, D. N. — Hinton, G. E. — Sejnowski, T. I.: A Learning Algorithm for Boltzmann Machines. *Cognitive Science* 9, 1985, pp. 147–169

[3] Barahona, F.: On the Computational Complexity of Ising Spin Glass Models. *J. Phys. A.* 15, 1982, pp. 3241–3253

[4] Bruck, J. — Goodman, J. W.: A Generalized Convergence Theorem for Neural Networks and Its Application in Combinatorial Optimization. *Proc. IEEE First International Conf. on Neural Networks*, Vol. 3, 1987, pp.649–656

[5] Chandra, A. K. — Kozen, D. C. — Stockmeyer, L. I.: Alternation. *JACM* 28, 1981, pp. 114–133

[6] Chandra, A. K. — Stockmeyer, L. I. — Vishkin, U.: Constant Depth Reducibility. *SIAM J. Comput. Vol.* 15, No. 3, 1984, pp. 423–432

[7] Egecioglu, O. — Smith, T. R. — Moody, I.: Computable Functions and Complexity in neural networks. *Tech. Rep. ITP–124*, University of California, Santa Barbara, 1986

[8] Farhat, N. H. — Psaltis, D. — Prata, A. — Paek, E.: Optical Implementation of the Hopfield Model. *Applied Optics,* **24**, 1985, pp. 1469–1475

[9] Faigle, U. — Schrader, R.: On the Convergence Of Stationary Distributions in Simulated Annealing Algorithms. *Inf. Proc. Letters,* **27**, 1988, pp. 189–194

[10] Feldman, J. A.: Energy and the Behavior of Connectionist Models. *Tech. Rep. TR–155,* University of Rochester, Nov. 1985

[11] Garey, M. R. — Johnson, D. S.: Computers and Intractability. A Guide to the Theory of NP–Completeness. *Freeman and Co.,* San Francisco, 1979

[12] Hopfield, J. J.: Neural Networks and Physical Systems with Emergent Collective Computational Abilities. *Proc. Natl. Acad. Sci. USA* **79**, 1982, pp. 2554–2558

[13] Hopfield, J. J.: Neurons with Graded Response Have Collective Computational Properties Like Those of Two–state Neurons. *Proc. Natl. Acad. Sci. USA,* 1984, pp. 3088–3092

[14] Hopfield, J. J.: The Effectiveness of Neural Computing. *Proc. IFIP'89,* North-Holland, l989, pp. 503–507

[15] Hopfield, J. J. — Tank, D. W.: 'Neural' Computations of Decisions in Optimization Problems. *Biol. Cybern.* **52**, 1985, pp. 141–152

[16] Hopfield, J. J. — Tank, D. W.: Computing with Neural Circuits: A Model. *Science* **233**, 1986, pp.625–633

[17] Johnson, J. l.: A Neural Network Approach to the 3-Satisfiability Problem. *J. of Parall. and Distrib. Comput.* **6**, 1989, pp. 435–449

[18] Kirkpatrick, S. — Gellat, C. D., Jr. — Vecchi, M. P.: Optimization by Simulated Annealing. *Science,* **220**, No. 4598, 1983

[19] Korst,. J. H. M. — Aarts, E. H. L.: Combinatorial Optimization on a Boltzmann Machine. *J. of Parall. and Distrib. Comput.* **6**, 1989, pp. 331–357

[20] Metropolis, N. — Rosenbluth, A. — Rosenbluth, M. — Teller, A. — Teller, E.: *J. Chem. Phys.,* **21**, 1087, 1953

[21] Minsky, M.: Computation. Finite and Infinite Machines. *Prentice Hall,* Englewood Cliffs, NJ, 1967

[22] Muroga, S.: Threshold Logic and Its Applications. *Wiley–Interscience,* New York, 1971

[23] Minsky, M.— Papert, S.: Perceptrons. An Introduction to Computational Geometry. *The MIT Press,* Cambridge, Mass., 1969

[24] Muroga, S. — Tsubi, T. — Baugh, Ch. R.: Enumeration of Threshold Functions of Eight Variables. *IEEE Trans. on Comp.,* C-19, No. 9, 1970, pp. 818–825

[25] Parberry, I.: A Primer on the Complexity Theory of Neural Networks. *Research Report CS-88-38,* Dept. of Comp. Sci., The Pennsylvania state university, October 1988

[26] Parberry, I. — Schnitger, G.: Parallel Computation with Threshold Functions. *JCSS* **36**, 1988, pp. 278–302

[27] Parberry, I. — Schnitger, G.: Relating Boltzmann Machines to Conventional models of Computations. *Neural Networks,* **2**, 1989

[28] Reif, J. H. — Tate, S. R.: On Threshold Circuits and Polynomial Computation. *Technical Report,* Dept. of Comp. Sci., Duke University, 1988

[29] Robson, J. M.: Linear Size Formulas for Non–deterministic Single Tape Computations. *Proc. 11–th Australian Comp. Sci. Conference,* Brisbane, Feb. 3–5, l988

[30] van Emde Boas, P.: Machine Models and Simulations. *ITLI Prepublication Series of Computation and Complexity Theory CT–88–95,* University of Amsterdam, 1988

[31] Wiedermann, J.: On the Computational Power of Neural Networks and Related Computational Systems. *Technical Report OPS-9/1988,* Department of Programming Systems, VUSEI-AR, Bratislava, June 1988 (in Slovak), also in *Proc. SOFSEM'88,* VUSEI-AR Bratislava, November 1988, pp. 73–78

[32] Wiedermann, J.: On the Computational Efficiency of Symmetric Neural Networks. *Proc. 14-th Symp. on Math. Found. of Comp. Sci., MFCS'89,* LNCS Vol. **379**, Springer Verlag, Berlin, 1989, pp. 545–552

Part III
Communications

Two-way Reading on Words

M. Anselmo

L.I.T.P. - Université Paris 7
2, place Jussieu
F-75251 PARIS Cedex 05
France

Dip. Mat. ed appl. - Univ. di Palermo
Via Archirafi, 34
I-90100 PALERMO
Italy

Abstract. We study the phenomena produced when inversion of direction is allowed when reading a word. Two-way reading on a given language x can be reduced to left-to-right reading on a language containing x, which is regular whenever x is so. We present two characterizations of "zig-zag languages". We then consider and compare two possible ways of counting two-way reading on a regular language, and thus, of defining the behaviour of two-way automata. For each one definition, we show the construction of a one-way automaton equivalent in multiplicity to a given two-way automaton, this generalizing Rabin, Scott and Shepherdson's Theorem.

1. Introduction

Two-way reading on words is formalized by the zig-zag operation "$\uparrow$", introduced in [1] for formal languages and extended here to every formal power-series. Two-way reading can be reduced to one-way reading. This is shown here by producing a generator system of the zig-zag language over a (not necessarily regular) language. This generator system is rational and constructable when the starting language is.

Two characterizations of zig-zag languages emphasize their importance: one is in terms of the dominion of a semigroup; the other one relates $x^\uparrow$ to $(x \cup \overline{x})*$.

The problem of counting two-way reading of a word on a regular language brings us to the problem of counting the computations of a word in a $2FA$ with multiplicity. We present two possible approaches and compare them.

Following a first definition, we count all the paths computing a word and obtain a power-series having also "∞" as value. We present a construction of a

1FA with multiplicity in $\mathcal{N} = \mathbf{N} \cup \infty$ recognizing the same power-series as a 2FA with multiplicity in $\mathbf{N}$. This shows in particular that the behaviour of a 2FA with multiplicity in $\mathbf{N}$, is always a rational power-series with values in $\mathcal{N}$.

A second definition, introduced in [5], considers only a finite number of representative paths and gives some not always rational power-series. Also in this case, if some necessary conditions are satisfied, we can construct a K-1FA recognizing the same power-series as a given K-2FA [5].

These results extend Rabin, Scott and Shepherdson's Theorem to the case of automata with multiplicity. We recall that Rabin, Scott and Shepherdson's Theorem [11, 12, 16, 21, 22] states the equivalence between 2FA and 1FA as far as recognition of formal languages is concerned. A care is necessary with respect to the model of 2FA used by each author. The model of 2FA used here is the one of [9, 10, 11, 14].

Definitions about formal power-series can be found in [8, 17]. We recall that rationality of a power-series is equivalent to its recognizability by one-way automata with multiplicity, following Schützenberger's Theorem. For the definitions about one-way automata with multiplicity and Schützenberger's fundamental Theorem, see [8, 15, 18, 19, 20].

2. Operation †

The concatenation of words is expressed by the operation * (star) over formal languages and power-series. We recall that, for every language X over a finite alphabet A, we have $X^* = \{x_1 x_2 \ldots x_n \in A^* \ / \ x_i \in X \text{ for every } i = 1, 2, \ldots, n\}$, and for every power-series $S : A^* \to K$ with coefficients in a semiring K, such that $(S, \varepsilon) = 0$, we have $S^* = \sum S^n$. In other words, for every $w \in A^*$, S^*: $w \to \sum (S, x_1)(S, x_2) \ldots (S, x_n)$, where the sum can be taken over all the factorizations of $w = x_1 x_2 \ldots x_n$ as a concatenation of words in the support of S.

Two-way reading of a word on a language can be expressed as an operation over languages and power-series, in the following way.

Let X be a language over a finite alphabet A and τ be the equivalence relation in $A^* \times A^*$ generated by $Z = \{ ((w', xw''), (w'x, w'')) \ / \ w', w'' \in A^*, x \in X \}$. We write $(w', w'') \to (v', v'')$ and we call it a *step* over X iff $((w', w''), (v', v'')) \in Z$ or $((v', v''), (w', w'')) \in Z$. The *zig-zag language* over X is the set

$$X^† = \{ w \in A^* \ / \ \varepsilon \odot w = w \odot \varepsilon \}$$

where the symbol $w' \odot w''$ denotes the class of τ-equivalence of the pair (w', w''). This means that a word w of A^* belongs to $X^†$ if there exists a finite sequence of steps linking (ε, w) to (w, ε), like in the following picture.

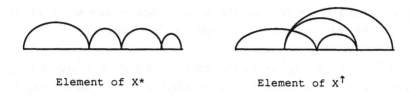

Element of X*   Element of X$^\uparrow$

Fig. 1

For a word $w \in X^\uparrow$, a *zig-zag factorization* over X is a sequence of steps over X

$$(\varepsilon, w) = (w'_1, w''_1) \to \dots \to (w'_j, w''_j) \to (w'_{j+1}, w''_{j+1}) \to \dots \to (w'_n, w''_n) = (w, \varepsilon)$$

such that for every $i \neq j$ we have $(w'_i, w''_i) \neq (w'_j, w''_j)$.

This condition forbids the presence of "loops" over one and the same position.

Example. Let X be the language X=a+aba over the alphabet A=a+b.

The word w=ababa belongs to X* and not to X*. A zig-zag factorization of w over X is: $(\varepsilon, w) = (\varepsilon, ababa) \to (aba, ba) \to (ab, aba) \to (ababa, \varepsilon)$, represented like in Fig. 2. One can show [1] that X$^\uparrow$ =a(a+ba)* + ε.

Fig. 2

The operation $^\uparrow$ (*arrow*) over power-series can be defined as follows. Let S be a power-series $S : A^* \to K$ such that $(S, \varepsilon) = 0$ and w be a word in $X^\uparrow$. Consider every zig-zag factorization $f = p_1 p_2 \dots p_n$ of w over the support of S, where p_i is a step $p_i = (u, x_i v) \to (u x_i, v)$ or $p_i = (u x_i, v) \to (u, x_i v)$, and define $S(f) = (S, x_1)(S, x_2) \dots (S, x_n)$. The power-series $S^\uparrow$ is defined for every $w \in A^*$ as

$$S^\uparrow : \quad w \to \sum S(f)$$

where the sum is taken over all the zig-zag factorizations f of w over the support of S.

The *zig-zag power-series* over a regular language X is the power-series $(\underline{X})^\uparrow$, where $\underline{X}$ is the characteristic series of X. It thus associates to a word the number of its different zig-zag factorizations over X.

The arrow operation is a generalization of the star operation, given that every concatenation of words in a language X is a special zig-zag factorization over X. We are going to show how two-way reading on a given language can be reduced to left-to-right reading. For this, observe that for every language X, the language

$x^\dagger$ is a submonoid of $A*$, because the concatenation of two words of $x^\dagger$ is still a word of $x^\dagger$. We will construct a significant generator system of $x^\dagger$.

DEFINITION 1. A zig-zag factorization f of a word w over a language x is *decomposable* if we can split w in $w=w_1w_2$ and f in $f=f_1f_2$ such a way f_1 is a zig-zag factorization of w_1 over x and f_2 is a zig-zag factorization of w_1 over x.

A word w is an *elementary* word of $x^\dagger$ if it has a zig-zag factorization over x which is not decomposable.

PROPOSITION 1. *Let x be a language over a finite alphabet A. The language E of all elementary words of $x^\dagger$ is a generator system of $x^\dagger$, i.e. $x^\dagger=E*$.*

Proof. Every word in $x^\dagger$ can be splitted in a concatenation of elementary words. Conversely, every word of $E*$ also belongs to $x^\dagger$.□

Let us now examine the case of regular languages.

The sets of "zig-zags" over regular languages are well represented by two-way automata (2FA). These are machines halfway between Turing machines and finite automata: they are able to read on an input word moving the reading head in both directions. Right-to-left moving of a 2FA over an alphabet A is represented here by edges labelled by a "barred" letter, i.e. a letter of $\overline{A}=\{ \ \overline{a} \ / \ a \in A\}$ [1-6, 9, 10, 14]. For a path u in a 2FA computing a word $w=v'w'=v"w"$, writing $(v',w')|u|=(v",w")$ means that u brings us from position (v',w') to position $(v",w")$ of w.

For every regular language x, we can construct a family $\mathcal{Z}(x)$ of 2FA recognizing $x^\dagger$ [1, 2, 6]. The "star" of a given automaton [7] is a new automaton recognizing the language $\mathcal{L}(\mathcal{A})*$ and constructed by identifying all initial and final states in a unique state. For every regular language x, let $\mathcal{E}(x)$ be the family of all 1FA that are the "star" of a 1FA whose behaviour is the characteristic series of x. The family $\mathcal{Z}(x)$ consists of all 2FA obtained from each automaton in $\mathcal{E}(x)$ by adding in the initial state a "barred and reversed" copy of it, like in Fig. 3.

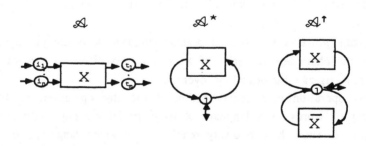

Fig.3

REMARK 1. In [1] it is shown that every automaton of $\mathscr{Z}$ (X) recognizes the zig-zag language over X, which is thus rational by Rabin, Scott and Shepherdson's Theorem and Kleene's Theorem. The arrow operator thus preserves rationality of languages; this is not the case anymore for rationality of power-series ([4]).

PROPOSITION 2. *Let* X *be a regular language. The language of all elementary words of* $X^\uparrow$ *is rational and constructable.*

Proof. It is sufficient to consider a 2FA of $\mathscr{Z}$ (X) and construct the equivalent one-way automaton $\mathscr{B}$ following Rabin and Scott's construction [6, 12, 16]. One finds that $\mathscr{B}$ has a unique initial state, state 1, that is also the unique final state. The set of all elementary words of $X^\uparrow$ is then represented by the set of all succesful paths in $\mathscr{B}$ which do not go through state 1. And this is a regular language.□

3. Two characterizations of zig-zag languages

Let X be a sub-set of the free monoid A* over a finite alphabet A.

The *dominion* of X in A* [13] is the set $\mathrm{Dom}_{A*}(X)$ of elements $d \in A*$ such that for every semigroup S and for every pair of morphisms of semigroups $\beta, \gamma : A* \to S$, then β and γ coincide on X iff they coincide on d. The proof of the following proposition follows from Isbell's zig-zag theorem [13].

PROPOSITION 3. *Let* X *be a language over a finite alphabet* A. *Then* $X^\uparrow = \mathrm{Dom}_{A*}(X) \cup \varepsilon$.

For a word $u = a_1 a_2 \ldots a_n \in A^+$ let $\overline{u}$ denote its barred copy in $\overline{A}^+$, i.e. $\overline{u} = \overline{a}_n \ldots \overline{a}_2 \overline{a}_1$. Let us define for a word $w \in A*$, $\underline{\mathrm{red}}(w)$ as the reduced word of w with respect to the rules $u\overline{u}u \to u$ and $\overline{u}u\overline{u} \to \overline{u}$, with $u \in A^+$ (this word is well-defined, cf. [14]). By applying to a two-way automaton $\mathscr{A}$ belonging to $\mathscr{Z}$ (X), Pécuchet's formula [14] relating the language recognized by $\mathscr{A}$ (that is $X^\uparrow$) to its control language we obtain the following characterization.

PROPOSITION 4. *Let* X *be a regular language over a finite alphabet* A. *Then* $X^\uparrow = A* \cap \underline{\mathrm{red}}(X\overline{U}\overline{X})*$.

4. Counting two-way computations on words

The representation of two-way reading over a regular language by 2FA reduces the problem of counting two-way reading on a regular language to the one of defining the behaviour of two-way automata. More generally, we will consider two-way automata with multiplicity, that is 2FA where a multiplicity, i.e. an element of a semiring, is assigned to each edge.

We consider two possible ways of counting paths in a two-way automaton. A first approach is to count all the paths computing a given word, which can be in infinite number. Some limits of such a definition lead to state a second definition considering only a finite number of representative paths, like introduced in [5]. The rationality of the introduced power-series is studied here. For more details of proofs, see [6].

DEFINITION 2. A *two-way automaton with multiplicity in a semiring* K (K-2FA) over a finite alphabet A, is a quadruple $\mathscr{A} = (Q, f, l, c)$ composed of:
- a finite set Q of *states*;
- a *transition function* $f: Q \times (A \cup \overline{A}) \times Q \to K$;
- an *input function* $l: Q \to K$;
- an *output function* $c: Q \to K$.

The *multiplicity* with respect to $\mathscr{A}$ of a path $u = e_1 e_2 \dots e_n$, where $e_i = (p_i, a_i, p_{i+1}) \in Q \times (A \cup \overline{A}) \times Q$ are consecutive edges, is the element $m_{\mathscr{A}}(u) = l(p_1) f(e_1) f(e_2) \dots f(e_n) c(p_{n+1})$ in K.

4.1 First definition of behaviour

DEFINITION 3a. The *behaviour* of a K-2FA, $\mathscr{A}$, is the power-series $\mathscr{S}(\mathscr{A}): A^* \to K \cup \infty$ associating to a word the sum of the multiplicities of all paths in $\mathscr{A}$ computing it.

THEOREM 1. *Let $\mathscr{A}$ be a two-way automaton with multiplicity in the semiring* $\mathbb{N}$ *of positive integers. There exists a one-way automaton $\mathscr{B}$ with multiplicity in* $\mathscr{N} = \mathbb{N} \cup \infty$, *such that $\mathscr{S}(\mathscr{B}) = \mathscr{S}(\mathscr{A})$.*

In order to prove this result, we need to introduce some definitions [5].
Let $\mathscr{A} = (Q, f, l, c)$ be a K-2FA and u be a path computing a word $w = w'w''$.
The *local configuration* of u under position (w', w'') is the couple

$$LC_u(w', w'') = (cs, I_u(cs)) \in Q^n \times \{r, t\}^n$$

where $cs = (q_1, q_2, \dots, q_n) = cs_u(w', w'')$ is the crossing sequence of u under position (w', w'') (that is the sequence of the states of $\mathscr{A}$ when u crosses the position, [1-6, 12]) and $I_u(cs) = (i_u(q_1), i_u(q_2), \dots, i_u(q_n))$ is such that for every $j = 1, 2, \dots, n$, we have $i_u(q_j) = r$ iff u inverts its direction in q_j under position (w', w''). It is *initial* if $w' = \varepsilon$, and *final* if $w'' = \varepsilon$.

We say that a local configuration $(cs_1, I(cs_1))$ *matches* with another local configuration $(cs_2, I(cs_2))$ on a letter a, if there exists a path u of $\mathcal{A}$ computing a word $w = w'aw''$ such that $LC_u(w', aw'') = (cs_1, I(cs_1))$ and $LC_u(w'a, w'') = (cs_2, I(cs_2))$.

For a path $u = e_1e_2...e_n$ in $\mathcal{A}$ computing a word $w'aw''$, the *section of the computation* u under the letter a is the sequence $s_u(a) = (e_{i_1}, e_{i_2}, ..., e_{i_k})$ with $i_1 < i_2 < ... < i_k$, of all edges such that for $j = 1, ..., k$, we have $(w', aw'')|e_{i_j}| = (w'a, w'')$ or $(w'a, w'')|e_{i_j}| = (w', aw'')$.

In [5] it is shown that if $(cs_1, I(cs_1))$ and $(cs_2, I(cs_2))$ are two local configurations matching on a letter a, then the section of a computation under a is the same for every words w', w'' and for every path u computing $w'aw''$ such that $LC_u(w', aw'') = (cs_1, I(cs_1))$ and $LC_u(w'a, w'') = (cs_2, I(cs_2))$.

The symbol CS_i will denote the set of all crossing sequences of paths computing some words, which contain at most i occurrences of a same state.

Sketch of proof of Theorem 1. Let $\mathcal{A} = (Q, f, 1, c)$ be a two-way automaton with multiplicity in $\mathbb{N}$. The value $(\mathcal{S}(\mathcal{A}), w)$ is infinite for a word w iff there exists a path in $\mathcal{A}$ computing w such that all its crossing sequences contain at most two occurrences of a same state and one at least contains twice a same state. On the other hand, for a word of finite multiplicity there is a bijection between the paths computing it in $\mathcal{A}$ and the sequence of their local configurations in the following positions. A one-way automaton $\mathcal{B} = (Q', f', 1', c')$ with multiplicity in $\mathcal{N}$ recognizing the power-series $\mathcal{S}(\mathcal{A})$ can be constructed as follows.

- $Q' = \{(cs, I(cs)) / cs \in CS_2\}$;

- $f'(((cs_1, I(cs_1)), a, (cs_2, I(cs_2)))) = \infty$ if $cs_1 \notin CS_1$ or $cs_2 \notin CS_1$

                         $= f(e_1)...f(e_m)$

     if $cs_1, cs_2 \in CS_1$, $(cs_1, I(cs_1))$ matches with $(cs_2, I(cs_2))$ over a and $(e_1, ..., e_m)$ is the computation's section under a

                       $= 0$ otherwise;

for $cs = (q_1, q_2, ..., q_n)$:

- $1'((cs, I(cs))) = \infty$ if $cs \notin CS_1$

                $= 1(q_1)$ if $(cs, I(cs))$ is an initial local configuration

                $= 0$ otherwise;

- $c'((cs, I(cs))) = \infty$ if $cs \notin CS_1$

                $= c(q_n)$ if $(cs, I(cs))$ is a final local configuration

                $= 0$ otherwise. $\square$

4.2 Limits of the first definition

We give some examples showing some limits of Definition 3a. The value "∞" sometimes hides other suitable information on the number of paths computing a word; often only a finite number of paths is significant.

Example 1a: family $\mathscr{X}(X)$. For every regular language X and for every two-way automaton $\mathscr{A}$ belonging to $\mathscr{X}(X)$, we have $(\mathscr{S}(\mathscr{A}),w)=\infty$ if $w \in X^{\uparrow}$ and $(\mathscr{S}(\mathscr{A}),w)=0$ otherwise. Words belonging to $X^{\uparrow}$ are thus indistinguishable.

Example 2a. Consider the following two-way automaton $\mathscr{A}$.

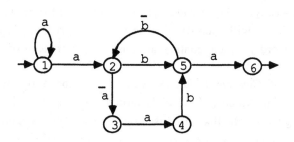

Fig. 4

It recognizes the language $\mathscr{L}(\mathscr{A})$ = a*aba. By Definition 3a, this automaton recognizes the power-series having always ∞ as value on its support. But, among all the paths computing $a^n aba$, except for two, the others repeat the following two loops over position $(a^n a, ba)$. For every word $a^n aba$, only two paths computing it can be considered significant.

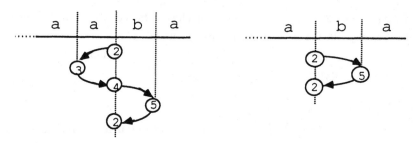

Fig. 5

4.3 Second definition of behaviour [5]

Let $\mathscr{A}=(Q,f,1,c)$ be a K-2FA. We say that a state in $\mathscr{A}$ is an *inversion state* if there exists a path computing a word and inverting direction in it. For a path u computing a word w, a *loop* of u over the section (w',w'') of w, is a sub-path

$b : q \to q$ such that q is an inversion state and $(w', w'') \, |b| = (w', w'')$. A path is *successful* if it has no loops.

DEFINITION 3b. The *(zig-zag) behaviour* of a $K-2FA$, $\mathscr{A}$, is the power-series $\mathscr{S}_z(\mathscr{A}) : A^* \to K$ associating to a word the sum of the multiplicities of all the successful paths in $\mathscr{A}$ computing it.

By an analoguous construction of the proof of Theorem 1, we can find the following result.

THEOREM 2 ([5]). *Let $\mathscr{A}$ be a two-way finite automaton with multiplicity in a commutative semiring K and CS be the set of all crossing sequences of successful paths in $\mathscr{A}$ computing some words.*

If the set CS is finite, then we can construct a one-way finite automaton $\mathscr{B}$ with multiplicity in K such that $\mathscr{S}(\mathscr{B}) = \mathscr{S}_z(\mathscr{A})$.

REMARK 2. The condition "CS finite" is also necessary for two-way automata in $\mathscr{Z}(X)$ [5, 6].

Let us reconsider the examples studied in section 4.2.

Example 1b: family $\mathscr{Z}(X)$. Following Definition 3b, the behaviour of an automaton $\mathscr{A}$ in $\mathscr{Z}(X)$ is exactly [4] the zig-zag power series over X: $\mathscr{S}_z(\mathscr{A}) = (\underline{X})^{\uparrow}$.

Example 2b. For every word $a^n aba$, the paths repeating the loops shown in Fig. 5, are considered "not-successful" following Definition3b. We thus have that $\mathscr{S}_z(\mathscr{A}) = 2\underline{a^* aba}$.

5. Acknowledgements

I wish to thank Prof. D. Perrin for his guidance and continuous encouragements.

REFERENCES AND BIBLIOGRAPHY

[1] M.Anselmo, Automates et codes ZigZag, to appear in RAIRO *Inform. Théor* and tech. report LITP n° 88-74, Nov. 1988.

[2] M. Anselmo, Sur les codes zig-zag et leur décidabilité, to appear in *Theoret. Comput. Sci.*; and tech. report LITP n° 89-36, Mai 1989

[3] M. Anselmo, Sur la rationalité de la série des zig-zag et des séries reconnues par les automates bilatères, tech. report LITP n° 89-61, July 1989

[4] M. Anselmo, The zig-zag power-series: a two-way version of the star operator, to appear in *Theoret. Comput. Sci.*, special issue

[5] M. Anselmo, Two-way automata with multiplicity, *Proceed.* ICALP 90

[6] M. Anselmo, Automates bilatères et codes zig-zag, *Ph. D. thesis*, Univ. Paris 7 (1990); and tech. report LITP n° 90-27, Mars 1990

[7] J. Berstel - D.Perrin, *Theory of codes*, (Academic Press, New York, 1985).

[8] J.Berstel - C.Reutenauer, *Les séries rationnelles et leur languages*, (Masson, Paris, 1984)

[9] J.C. Birget, Concatenations of Inputs in a Two-way Automaton, *Theoret. Comput. Sci.* 63 (1989) 141-156; and tech. report n°46, Dept. of Computer Science, Univ. of Nebraska, Lincoln, April 1987.

[10] J.C. Birget, Two-way Automaton Computations, to appear in RAIRO *Inform. Théor.* and tech. report n° 60, Dept. of Computer Science, Univ. of Nebraska, Lincoln, July 1987.

[11] S. Eilenberg, *Automata, Languages and Machines, Vol. A* (Academic Press, New York, 1974).

[12] J.E. Hopcroft - J.D. Ullman, *Introduction to Automata Theory, Languages and Computation*, (Addison-Wesley, Reading MA, 1979)

[13] J.M. Howie, *An introduction to Semigroup Theory*, (Academic Press, New York, 1976)

[14] J.P. Pécuchet, Automates boustrophédons, semi-groupe de Birget et monoïde inversif libre, RAIRO *Inform. Théor.* 19 (1985) 17-100 and Automates boustrophédons, langages reconnaissables de mots infinis et variétés de semigroupes, Thèse d'Etat, LITP Mai 1986.

[15] D. Perrin, Automates avec multiplicités, tech. report LITP n° 88-42, Mai 1988

[16] M. O. Rabin - D. Scott, Finite Automata and their Decision Problems, *IBM J. Res. Dev.* 3, (1959) 114-125; and in E.F. Moore, *Sequential Machines: Selected Papers*, (Addison-Wesley, Reading, MA, 1964).

[17] A. Saloma - M. Soittola, *Automata-theoretic Aspects of Formal Power Series*, (Springer Verlag, 1978)

[18] M.P. Schützenberger, On the definition of a family of automata, *Information and Control* 4, (1961) 245-270

[19] M.P. Schützenberger, On a theorem of R. Jungen, *Proc. Amer. Math. Soc.*, 13, (1962) 885-889

[20] M.P. Schützenberger, Certain elementary families of automata, *Proc. Symposium on Math. th. of Automata*, Polytechnic Institute of Brooklyn, (1962) 139-153

[21] J.C. Shepherdson, The Reduction of Two-way Automata to One-way Automata, *IBM J. Res.* 3 (1959), 198-200; and in E.F. Moore, *Sequential Machines: Selected Papers*, (Addison-Wesley, Reading, MA, 1964).

[22] M. Y. Vardi, A Note on the Reduction of Two-way Automata to One-way Automata, *Information Processing Letters* 30, (1989) 261-264.

Proofs and reachability problem
for ground rewrite systems [1]

Coquidé J.L.(*)   Gilleron R.(**)
(*)L.I.F.L(CNRS URA 369), University of Lille-Flandres-Artois
UFR IEEA, 59655 Villeneuve d'Ascq cedex, France
(**)L.I.F.L(CNRS URA 369), IUT A, departement informatique, BP 179
59653 Villeneuve d'Ascq cedex, France

abstract: The different reachability problems for ground rewrite systems are decidable[OY86], [DEGI89]. We prove these results using ground tree transducers of [DATI85] and wellknown algorithms on recognizable tree languages in order to obtain efficient algorithms. We introduce and study derivation proofs to describe the sequences of rules used to reduce a term t in a term t' for a given ground rewrite system S and sketch how compute a derivation proof in linear time. Moreover, we study the same problem for recognizable tree languages.

1 INTRODUCTION

The reachability problem for rewrite system is to decide whether, given a rewrite system S and two ground terms t and t', t can be reduced in t' with S. It is well-known that this problem is undecidable for general rewrite systems. We study this problem for ground rewrite systems, that is to say finite rewrite systems for which the left-hand sides and right-hand sides of rules in S are ground terms(without variables). The reachability problem for ground rewrite systems was proved decidable by Oyamaguchi in [OY86] and by Dauchet and Tison in [DATI85] as a consequence of decidability of confluence for ground rewrite systems. In [DEGI89], we also study this problem and give a real time decision algorithm, this after the compilation of the ground rewrite system in a ground tree transducer(a software Valeriann is an implementation of these algorithms[DADE89]). More recently, Dauchet and Tison have proved that the theory of ground rewrite systems is decidable, see [DATI90]. In this paper, we consider some other reachability problems. Given two recognizable tree languages F and F', different reachability problems are: Is the set of reductions of terms in F with S included in F'?, is there some term in F which reduces in a term in F'?... We prove these problems decidable using algebraical tools of tree automata(these algorithms are now implemented in Valeriann). As the reachability problems are decidable, a natural question is: If t can be reduced to t' with S, how can we reduce t to t' with S? We introduce the notion of derivation proofs as terms over a new ranked alphabet in order to obtain the "history" of a reduction of t in t' with S. The frontier of a derivation proof gives the sequence of rules used to reduce t in t',

---

[1]This work was in part supported by the "PRC Mathématiques et Informatique" et ESPRIT2 Working Group ASMICS.

moreover, we can find at which occurence a rule is applied. We prove that the set of derivation proofs is a recognizable tree language and give a linear time algorithm for a derivation proof for the reachability problem.

2 PRELIMINARIES

Let Σ be a finite ranked alphabet and T_Σ be the set of terms over Σ.
Let X be a denumerable set of variables, $X_m = \{x_1, \ldots, x_m\}$, $T_\Sigma(X)$ and $T_\Sigma(X_m)$ the set of terms over $\Sigma \cup X$ and $\Sigma \cup X_m$. A context c is a term in $T_\Sigma(X_m)$ such that each variable occurs exactly once in c and we denote $c(t_1, \ldots, t_m)$ the result of the substitution of each x_i by a term t_i.

2.1 Rewrite systems

A rewrite system $S = \{l_i \rightarrow r_i \ / \ l_i, r_i \in T_\Sigma(X), i \in I\}$ on T_Σ is a set of pairs of terms in $T_\Sigma(X)$. We only consider the case I finite. $\rightarrow_S$ is the rewrite relation induced by S and $\stackrel{*}{\rightarrow}_S$ the reflexive and transitive closure of $\rightarrow_S$. A ground rewrite system is such that l_i and r_i are ground terms (without variables). For more developments see [HUOP80] and [DEJO89].

2.2 Tree automata and recognizable tree languages

A bottom-up automaton (or frontier to root) is a quadruple $A = (\Sigma, Q, Q_f, R)$ where Σ is a finite ranked alphabet, Q a finite set of states of arity 0, Q_f a subset of Q, R a finite set of rules of the next configuration:
(i) $f(q_1, \ldots, q_n) \rightarrow q$ with $n \geq 0$, $q_1, \ldots, q_n$ in Q or (ii) $q \rightarrow q'$ with q, q' in Q (ϵ-rules).
Note we can consider R as a ground rewrite system on $T_{\Sigma \cup Q}$, $\rightarrow_A$ is the rewrite relation $\rightarrow_R$.
The tree language recognized by A is $L(A) = \{t \in T_\Sigma \ / \ t \stackrel{*}{\rightarrow}_A q, q \in Q_f\}$.
Let A be a bottom-up automaton, there exists a bottom-up automaton without ϵ-rules such that $L(B) = L(A)$ and there exists a deterministic(i.e no ϵ-rules and no two rules with the same left-hand side) bottom-up automaton C such that $L(C) = L(A)$.
A tree language F is recognizable if there exists a bottom-up automaton A such that $L(A) = F$.
The class of recognizable tree languages is closed under union, intersection and complementation. We can decide if a recognizable tree language is empty, inclusion, equality of recognizable tree languages.
A regular grammar is a quadruple $G = (A, V, \Sigma, R)$ where V is a set of variables of arity 0, V and Σ are disjoint, A belongs to V and R is a finite set of rules, $R = \{l \rightarrow r \ / \ l \in V, r \in T_{\Sigma \cup V}\}$. G generates the tree language $L(G) = \{t \in T_\Sigma \ / \ A \stackrel{*}{\rightarrow}_R t\}$. $L(G)$ is a recognizable tree language. For more developments see [GEST84]

2.3 Reachability problems

Let S be a rewrite system, the first order reachability problem is: Given two terms t and t', can we reduce t to t' by S. Different second order reachability problems are: Given two recognizable tree languages F and F', is the set of reductions of terms in F by S included in F' or is there some term in F which reduces to a term in F' by S,...

2.4 Ground tree transducers

A ground tree transducer (gtt) is a pair $V=(A,B)$ of bottom-up automata. Let $A=(\Sigma,Q_A,Q_{Af},R_A)$ and $B=(\Sigma,Q_B,Q_{Bf},R_B)$. The tree transformation induced by V is the set $r(V)=\{(t,t') \ / \ t\in T_\Sigma, \ t'\in T_\Sigma, \ \exists s\in T_{\Sigma\cup(Q_A\cap Q_B)}$ such that $t\xrightarrow{*}_A s \ _B\xleftarrow{\neq} t'\}$ or $r(V)=\{(t,t') \ / \ t=c(t_1,...,t_n)\xrightarrow{*}_A s=c(i_1,...,i_n) \ _B\xleftarrow{\neq} t'=c(t'_1,...,t'_n),$ $t_j,t'_j\in T_\Sigma, \ i_j\in Q_A\cap Q_B\}$.

Note that we can choose $Q_{Af} = Q_{Bf} =\varnothing$. The states in $Q_A\cap Q_B$ are called interface states.

The class of the tree transformations induced by ground tree transducers is closed by inverse, composition and iteration. For union, the next property holds: Let $V_1=(A_1,B_1)$ and $V_2=(A_2,B_2)$ be two ground tree transducers with disjoint sets of states, V be the ground tree transducer obtained by union of states and union of rules, we have $r(V)^*=(r(V_1)\cup r(V_2))^*$. The proofs can be found in [DATI85] and [DHLT87], see also[FUVA90].

3 REACHABILITY PROBLEM FOR GROUND REWRITE SYSTEMS

3.1 Ground rewrite systems and ground tree transducers

Proposition. For each ground rewrite system S, there exists a ground tree transducer V such that $\xrightarrow{*}_S = r(V)$.

A first proof of this proposition is in [DATI85], a polynomial time algorithm to compute V from S is in [DEGI89].We first compute a ground tree transducer U such that $\to_S = r(U)$ and then compute a ground tree transducer V such that $r(V) = (r(U))^* = \xrightarrow{*}_S$. An example is in figure 1.

3.2 Ground rewrite systems and recognizable tree languages

Proposition. Let S be a ground rewrite system and F a recognizable tree language, the set [F]S of reductions of terms in F by S is recognizable.

Proof. Let $V=(A,B)$ be the ground tree transducer such that $r(V)= \xrightarrow{*}_S$. So we have $[F]_S =\{(t,t') \ / \ t \xrightarrow{*}_S t'$ and $t\in F\}=\{(t,t') \ / \ (t,t')\in r(V)$ and $t\in F\}$ and so $[F]_S=\{(t,t')/F\ni t=c(t_1,...,t_n)\xrightarrow{*}_A s=c(i_1,..,i_n) \ _B\xleftarrow{\neq} t'=c(t'_1,...,t'_n), \ t_j,t'_j\in T_\Sigma, \ i_j\in Q_A\cap Q_B\}$

Let $A=(\Sigma,Q_A,\varnothing,R_A)$, $B=(\Sigma,Q_B,\varnothing,R_B)$ and $M=(\Sigma,Q_M,Q_{Mf},R_M)$ a deterministic bottom-up automaton such that $L(M)=F$. We suppose Q_B and Q_M are disjoint set of states.

We define a bottom-up automaton $C=(\Sigma,Q_C,Q_{Cf},R_C)$ with $Q_C=Q_B\cup Q_M$, $Q_{Cf}=Q_{Mf}$, $R_C=R_B\cup R_M\cup R'$ where $R'=\{i\rightarrow q/\ i\in Q_A\cap Q_B,\ q\in Q_M,\ \exists u\in T_\Sigma\ \text{s.t}\ u\overset{*}{\rightarrow}_A i$ and $u\overset{*}{\rightarrow}_M q\}$. As the sets $\{s\ /\ s\overset{*}{\rightarrow}_A i\}$ and $\{s\ /\ s\overset{*}{\rightarrow}_M q\}$ are recognizable, we can construct R'. We have $L(C)=[F]_S$. The complete proof is with a double inclusion. We just point out how we can recognize a term t' in $[F]_S$ with C. We first use rules of B so $t'=c(t'_1,..,t'_n)\overset{*}{\rightarrow}_B c(i_1,..,i_n)$, then we use rules in R' then we have $c(i_1,..,i_n)\overset{*}{\rightarrow}_{R'} c(q_1,...,q_n)$ and using rules of M, $c(q_1,...,q_n)\overset{*}{\rightarrow}_M q\in Q_{Mf}=Q_{Cf}$.

3.3 Reachability problem for ground rewrite systems

Proposition. The first-order reachability problem for ground rewrite systems is decidable.
Proof. Let t be a term of T_Σ, the set $[t]_S$ of reductions of t by S is recognizable, so we can decide if t' is in $[t]_S$.
Proposition. The different second-order reachability problems for ground rewrite systems are decidable
Proof. Let F and F' two recognizable tree languages, the set $[F]_S$ of reductions of terms in F by S is recognizable so the different second order reachability problems for ground rewrite systems are decidable, for example, we can decide if $[F]_S$ is included in F', if the intersection of $[F]_S$ and F' is not empty,..., this, using classical algorithms for recognizable tree languages.

---

figure 1

Exemple : Let $\Sigma=\{a,b,c,f,g\}$ avec a,b,c,f,g with arity 0,0,0,1,1
Let R={1: a $\rightarrow$ f(b); 2: b$\rightarrow$ g(c); 3: f(g(c)) $\rightarrow$ g(a) } ground rewrite system
G_1: a $\rightarrow$ i_1 D_1: b $\rightarrow$ q'$_1$, f(q'$_1$)$\rightarrow$ i_1
G_2: b $\rightarrow$ i_2 D_2: c $\rightarrow$ q'$_2$, g(q'$_2$)$\rightarrow$$i_2$
G_3: c $\rightarrow$$q_1$, g(q_1)$\rightarrow$ q_2 , f(q_2)$\rightarrow$ i_3 D_3: a $\rightarrow$ q'$_3$, g(q'$_3$)$\rightarrow$$i_3$
We first construct U=(G,D) with $R_G=R_{G_1}\cup R_{G_2}\cup R_{G_3}$ and $R_D=R_{D_1}\cup R_{D_2}\cup R_{D_3}$
In order to have the ground tree transducer V such that $r(V)=(r(U))^*=\overset{*}{\rightarrow}_R$, we add new rules to the bottom-up automaton G and D.
We obtain E={ q'$_3\rightarrow$ i_1 (a$\rightarrow$$_G$ i_1 , a$\rightarrow$$_D$ q'$_3$)
                    q'$_1\rightarrow$ i_2 (b$\rightarrow$$_G$ i_2 , b$\rightarrow$$_D$ q'$_1$)
                    q'$_2\rightarrow$ q_1 (c$\rightarrow$$_G$ q_1 , c$\rightarrow$$_D$ q'$_2$)
                    $i_2\rightarrow$ q_2 (g(q_1)$\rightarrow$$_G$ q_2 , g(q'$_2$)$\rightarrow$$_D$ i_2 , q'$_2$ $\rightarrow$$_E$ q_1)
                    $i_1\rightarrow$ i_3 (f(q_2)$\rightarrow$$_G$ i_3 , f(q'$_1$)$\rightarrow$$_D$ i_1 , q'$_1\rightarrow$$_E$ i_2 $\rightarrow$$_E$ q_2) }
Let V=(A,B) with $R_A=R_G\cup\{i_2\rightarrow$ q_2 , $i_1\rightarrow$ $i_3\}$ and $R_B=R_D\cup\{i_1\rightarrow$ q'$_3$, $i_2\rightarrow$ q'$_1$, $i_3\rightarrow$ $i_1\}$
With R , a $\overset{*}{\rightarrow}_R$ g(a)
With U, a$\overset{*}{\rightarrow}_G$ i_1 D$\overset{*}{\leftarrow}$ f(b) $\overset{*}{\rightarrow}_G$ f(i_2) D$\overset{*}{\leftarrow}$ f(g(c)) $\overset{*}{\rightarrow}_G$ i_3 D$\overset{*}{\leftarrow}$ g(a)
With V , a $\overset{*}{\rightarrow}_A$ i_3 B$\overset{*}{\leftarrow}$ g(a).
Note that the new rules suppress the generation-erasing steps for U

Note that the proposition in the section 3.2 is a consequence of results in [DATI85], but, here we have a direct proof and construct a bottom-up automaton to recognize [F]$_S$ in order to obtain more efficient algorithms. Note also that in [DEGI89], we study the reachability problem for ground rewrite systems modulo some sets of equations (commutativity, associativity, commutativity and associativity). We have got some new results for ground rewrite systems modulo ACI(associativity, commutativity and idempotency), that is to say: with restriction on the configuration of terms, the first order reachability problem is decidable and if we can apply the rules ACI on a finite set of terms, then, recognizability is preserved. See [GI90].

4 DERIVATION PROOFS FOR THE REACHABILITY PROBLEM

4.1 Introduction and notations

Let S be a ground rewrite system, t and t' two ground terms, we can decide if t reduces to t' with S, our aim is now to find a or all the possible derivations of t in t' with S. We define derivation proofs as terms in T_Δ where Δ is a new ranked alphabet such that the frontier of a term gives the sequence of rules used to reduce t in t' with S. See the figure 2 and figure 3 for examples. We only consider standard ground rewrite systems as defined further. In Section 4.2, we define the recognizable tree language of derivation proofs for the first order reachability problem for (t,t',S), in Section 4.3, we sketch the construction for the second order reachability problem for (F,F',S) and in Section 4.4, the construction of a derivation proof for (t,t',S) in linear time. In Section 4.5, we consider the case of general ground rewrite systems. We denote r(b) the arity of a symbol b in Σ, hg(t) the height of a term t and $\Phi(t)$ the frontier of a term t.

$S=\{l_i \rightarrow r_i /i\in I\}$ is a ground rewrite system of standard rules, that is to say we have three kind of rules:

$\quad$ (i) Erasing rules: $f(a_1,...,a_n)\rightarrow a$, $f\in \Sigma_n, a_1,...,a_n, a\in \Sigma_0$

$\quad$ (ii) Generating rules: $a\rightarrow f(a_1,...,a_n)$, $f\in \Sigma_n, a_1,...,a_n, a\in \Sigma_0$

$\quad$ (iii) ϵ-rules: $a\rightarrow b$, $a,b\in \Sigma_0$

Δ is a finite ranked alphabet, $\Delta=\Sigma\cup I\cup\{\beta_c/c\in \Sigma, c\notin \Sigma_0, r(\beta_c)=r(c)+2\}\cup\{\alpha/ r(\alpha)=2\}$.

4.2 Derivation proofs for the first-order reachability problem

Theorem. Let t, t' be terms in T_Σ and S a standard ground rewrite system, the set of all the derivation proofs for (t,t',S) is a recognizable tree language.

Proof. We define in the sections 4.2.1 to 4.2.5 a regular grammar in order to generate this tree language.

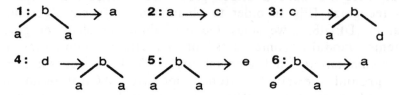

Figure2

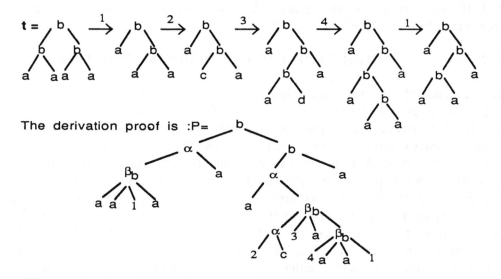

Let S={1,2,3,4,5,6} and let us consider the derivation

The derivation proof is :P=

The projection of the frontier of P in I* is 12341
Note: α is for height preserving reductions
Note: β is for height decreasing or increasing reductions

4.2.1: First we study the derivation proofs for (a,b,S) with a, b symbols of Σ_0 with a sequence of reductions such that all reductions with generating rules preceed the reductions with erasing rules. Let G_1 be the regular grammar $\mathcal{G}_{a,b} = (G_{a,b}, V_1, \Delta, R_1)$ with $V_1 = \{G_{a',b'} / (a',b') \in \Sigma_0 * \Sigma_0\}$ and R_1 is defined as follow:

$$G_{a,a} \to a + \sum_{i:a \to a'} \alpha(i, G_{a',a}) + \sum_{i:b' \to a} \alpha(G_{a,b'}, i) + \sum_{\substack{j:a \to c(a_1,...,a_n) \\ k:c(a'_1,...,a'_n) \to a}} \beta_c(j, G_{a_1,a'_1}, ..., G_{a_n,a'_n}, k)$$

$$a \neq b: \quad G_{a,b} \to \sum_{i:a \to a'} \alpha(i, G_{a',b}) + \sum_{i:b' \to b} \alpha(G_{a,b'}, i) + \sum_{\substack{j:a \to c(a_1,...,a_n) \\ k:c(a'_1,...,a'_n) \to b}} \beta_c(j, G_{a_1,a'_1}, ..., G_{a_n,a'_n}, k)$$

Lemma. $\mathcal{F}(\mathcal{G}_{a,b})= \{$derivation proofs for (a,b,S) with a, b symbols of Σ_0 using all the generating rules before the erasing one$\}$

sketch of proof. We first apply ε-rules, then, if we apply a generation rule,the root of the rule will not be erased during the generation part and when this node will be erased,we could only use ε-rules or erasing rules. The reduction terminates with ε-rules. We prove the lemma by induction on the length of the derivation and the height of the tree.

4.2.2: We study the derivation proofs for (a,b,S). We define a regular grammar $\mathcal{H}_{a,b} = (H_{a,b}, V_2, \Delta, R_2)$: $V_2 = V_1 \cup \{H_{a',b'} \, / \, (a',b') \in \Sigma_0^* \Sigma_0\}$

$R_2 = R_1 \cup \{$ rules defined as follow:

$$H_{a',b'} \rightarrow G_{a',b'} + \sum_{c \in \Sigma_0} \alpha(\, H_{a',c}\, ,\, H_{c,b'}\,) + \sum_{\substack{j:a' \rightarrow c(a_1,...,a_n) \\ k:c(a'_1,...,a'_n) \rightarrow b'}} \beta_c(\, j\, ,\, G_{a_1,a'_1}\, ,...,\, G_{a_n,a'_n}\, ,\, k\,)$$

Lemma. $\mathcal{F}(\mathcal{H}_{a,b}) = \{$derivation proofs for (a,b,S) with a, b symbols of $\Sigma_0\}$

sketch of proof. If in the derivation there is several sequences generation-erasing , we separate them, then we use the rules of R_1. We prove the lemma by induction on the length of the derivation and the height of the tree.

4.2.3: We study the derivation proofs for (t,a,S) where t is a term and a a symbol in Σ_0. We define a regular grammar $\mathcal{H}_{t,a} = (H_{t,a}, V_3, \Delta, R_3)$:

$V_3 = V_2 \cup \{H_{u,a'} \, / \, a' \in \Sigma_0$, u is a ground subtree of $t\}$

$R_3 = R_2 \cup \{$ rules defined as follows:

$$H_{t,a} \rightarrow \sum_{\substack{t \notin \Sigma_0 \\ k:c(a'_1,...,a'_n) \rightarrow a'}} \beta_c(\, H_{t_1,a'_1}\, ,...,\, H_{t_n,a'_n}\, ,\, k\, ,\, H_{a',a}\,)$$

Lemma. $\mathcal{F}(\mathcal{H}_{t,a}) = \{$derivation proofs for (t,a,S) / $t \in T_\Sigma$, $a \in \Sigma_0\}$.

sketch of proof. If the root of t is c , we must erase it during the derivation; so we apply an erasing rule the root of which is c; we iterate that process. When we have only an element of Σ_0, we use the rules of the previous part. We prove the lemma by induction on the length of the derivation and the height of the tree.

4.2.4: We study the derivation proofs for (a,t,S) where t is a term of T_Σ, a is a symbol of Σ_0. We define a regular grammar $\mathcal{H}_{a,t} = (H_{a,t}, V_4, \Delta, R_4)$:

$V_4 = V_2 \cup \{H_{a',u} \, / \, a' \in \Sigma_0$, u is a ground subtree of $t\}$

$R_4 = R_2 \cup \{$ rules defined as follows:

$$H_{a,t} \rightarrow \sum_{\substack{t \notin \Sigma_0 \\ k:a' \rightarrow c(a'_1,...,a'_n)}} \beta_c(\, H_{a,a'}\, ,\, k\, ,\, H_{a'_1,t_1}\, ,...,\, H_{a'_n,t_n})$$

Lemma. $\mathcal{F}(\mathcal{H}_{a,t}) = \{$derivation proofs for (a,t,S) / $a \in \Sigma_0$, $t \in T_\Sigma\}$.

sketch of proof. Similar to the previous one.

4.2.5: We study the derivation proofs for (t,t',S), t and t' terms of T_Σ. We define a regular grammar $\mathcal{H}_{t,t'} = (H_{t,t'}, V_5, \Delta, R_5)$:

$V_5 = V_3 \cup V_4$

$R_5 = R_4 \cup R_3 \cup \{$ rules defined as follows:

C is the set of common contexts of t and t'

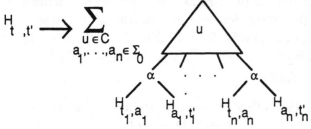

Lemma. $\mathcal{F}(\mathcal{H}_{t,t'})= \{$derivation proofs for (t,t',S) / $t, t' \in \Sigma\}$

sketch of proof. We first prove

$(t \overset{*}{\to}_S t') \Leftrightarrow (\ \exists\, u \in T_\Sigma(X_n), \exists\, t_1,...,t_n,t'_1,...,t'_n \in T_\Sigma, \exists\, a_1,...,a_n \in \Sigma_0$

$$t = u(t_1,...,t_n) \overset{*}{\to}_S u(a_1,...,a_n) \overset{*}{\to}_S u(t'_1,...,t'_n) = t' \qquad)$$

using this decomposition, the previous lemmas and the definition of $\mathcal{H}_{t,t'}$, we can prove the result. Moreover, the proof of the theorem is achieved as $\mathcal{F}(\mathcal{H}_{t,t'})$ is a recognizable tree language.

---

figure 3

1: $a \to f$
     |
     a

2: $a \to c$

3: $f \to c$
   |
   c

Let S={1,2,3}.The recognizable tree language of derivation proofs

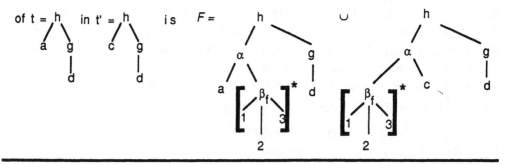

of $t = \overset{h}{\diagup\diagdown}$ in $t' = \overset{h}{\diagup\diagdown}$ is $F =$

4.3 Derivation proofs for the second-order reachability problem

Let F,F' recognizable tree languages and S a standard ground rewrite system. We consider the following second order reachability problem: Is $[F]_{S} \cap F' \neq \emptyset$, that is to say is there some term t in F which reduces in a term t' in F'.

Theorem. Let F, F' be recognizable tree languages and S a standard ground rewrite system, the set of derivation proofs for (F,F',S) is a recognizable tree language.
sketch of proof. As for the previous theorem, we define a regular grammar to generate this recognizable tree language. The construction is similar, we use the bottom-up automata M and M' such that $L(M)=F$ and $L(M')=F'$. The derivation proofs for (F,F',S) is the set of all derivation proofs for (t,t',S) such that $t \in F$, $t' \in F'$ and $t \xrightarrow{*}_S t'$.

4.4 A derivation proof for the first order reachability problem
The method used in Sections 4.3 and 4.4 is only interesting from a theoretical point of view, our aim is now to find an algorithm which computes a derivation proof for (t,t',S) in linear time in order to realize an implementation of this algorithm in our software Valeriann.
Proposition. Let S be a standard ground rewrite system, For every data t and t', we can, in linear time, decide if t reduces in t' with S and build a derivation proof for (t,t',S).
Sketch of proof. (a complete proof is in [CO90])
Let us remember that it is well-known that for a non deterministic bottom-up-automaton, it is possible to recognize a term t in linear time. The idea is to associate to each node the set of states which can reach this node with M(we reduce the non-determinism along the branches of the term t).

first step: During the compilation of the ground rewrite system S in a ground tree transducer $V=(A,B)$, we associate to each ε-rule a derivation proof. The compilation is in polynomial time (see [DEGI89]).

second step: Let c be the greatest common context of t and t'. Let us consider $T=c(\#(t_1,t'_1),...,\#(t_n,t'_n))$ with # new symbol of arity 2, $t=c(t_1,...,t_n)$ and $t'=c(t'_1,...,t'_n)$. We define a deterministic bottom-up tree transducer U in order to associate to each node of T the sets of states which can reach this node with A and B. We obtain U(T).

Third step: $t \xrightarrow{*}_S t'$ if and only if, for every branch starting from the top of U(T) to a symbol #, there exists a node such that the corresponding sets of states for A and B contain a same interface state. So, we have $t=u(u_1,...,u_n) \xrightarrow{*}_A s=u(i_1,...,i_n) \ _B\xleftarrow{*} t'=u(u'_1,...,u'_n)$ and then $t \xrightarrow{*}_S t'$ and then we can decide in linear time if $t \xrightarrow{*}_S t'$. Further more, we build in linear time a derivation proof. We use the previous decomposition and the table which associate to each ε-rule a derivation proof. This last construction can be implemented with a top-down tree transducer starting from U(T). A complete algorithm is in [CO90].

4.5 General case for ground rewrite systems

If we do not suppose S standard, that is to say S is a ground rewrite system, using new symbols, we can decompose each rule of S in standard rules, then we can associate to S a standard ground rewrite system S'. We can define a regular grammar for S' to obtain the derivation proofs for S' and then with a tree transducer, we can obtain the derivation proofs for S.

5 CONCLUSION

We are now working to extend the algorithm for a derivation proof in linear time to general ground rewrite systems and have to implement this algorithm in Valeriann.

Bibliography

[BR69] Brainerd, W.S, Tree generating regular systems, *Inf. and control*, 14 (1969), pp217-231.

[CO90] Coquidé, J.L. , *Ph.D*, Lille, to appear. (1990).

[COU89] Courcelle, B.,On recognizable sets and tree automata, *Resolution of Equations in Algebraic Structures*, Academic Press, M.Nivat & H. Ait-Kaci edts, (1989).

[DADE89] Dauchet, M., Deruyver, A., "VALERIANN":Compilation of Ground Term Rewriting Systems and Applications, Rewriting Technics and Applications, (1989), *Lec. Notes Comp. Sci.*, 355(Dershowitz ed.).

[DHTL87] Dauchet, M., Heuillard, P., Lescanne, P., Tison, S., Decidability of the Confluence of Ground Term Rewriting Systems, *2nd Symposium on Logic in Computer Science*, New-York, IEEE Computer Society Press (1987)

[DATI85] Dauchet, M., Tison, S., Decidability of Confluence in Ground Term Rewriting Systems, Fondations of Computation Theory, Cottbus, *Lec. Notes Comp. Sci.*, 199, (1985)

[DATI90] Dauchet, M., Tison, S., The theory of Ground Rewrite System is Decidable, IEEE Symposium on Logic in Computer Science, to appear, (1990)

[DEGI89] Deruyver, A., Gilleron, R., Compilation of Term Rewriting Systems, CAAP 89, *Lec. Notes. Comp. Sci.*, (Diaz ed), 354, (1989)

[DEJO89] Dershowitz, N., Jouannaud, J.P., Rewrite systems, *Handbook of Theoretical Computer Science*, J.V.Leeuwen editor, North-Holland, to appear.(1989).

[EN75] Engelfriet, J., Bottom-up and Top-down Tree Transformations, a Comparison, *Math. Systems Theory*, 9, (1975)

[FUVA89] Fülöp, Z., Vàgvölgyi, S., Ground Term Rewriting rules for the Word Problem of Ground Term Equations, submitted paper, (1989).

[GEST84] Gecseg, F., Steinby, M., Tree automata, *Akademiai Kiado*, (1984).

[GI90] Gilleron, R., *Ph.D*, Lille, to appear (1990).

[HUOP80] Huet, G., Oppen, D.C., Equations and Rewrite Rules: A survey, in R.V.Book, ed., New York, *Academic Press*, Formal Language Theory: Perspectives and Open Problems, (1980).

[NEOP80] Nelson, G., Oppen, D.C., Fast Decision Procedures Based on Congruence Closure, *JACM*, 27, (1980).

[OY86] Oyamaguchi, M., The reachability Problem for Quasi-ground Term Rewriting Systems, *Journal of Information Processing*, 9-4, (1986).

[TI89] Tison, S., The Fair Termination is decidable for Ground Systems, Rewriting Technics and Applications, Chapel Hill, *Lec. Notes Comp. Sci.*, 355 (Dershowitz ed.), (1989).

Problems complete for $\oplus L$

Carsten Damm

Sektion Mathematik
Humboldt-Universität zu Berlin
DDR-1086 Berlin, PO-Box 1297

Abstract

$\oplus L$ is the class of languages acceptable by logarithmic space bounded Turing machines that work nondeterministically and are equipped with parity-acceptance, i.e. an input word is accepted if and only if the number of possible correct computation paths on this input is odd. Several natural problems are shown to be complete for $\oplus L$ under NC^1-reductions. A consequence is that $\oplus L$ is the $\mathbf{F}_2$-analogon of Cook's class DET, the class of problems NC^1-reducible to the computation of determinants over $\mathbf{Z}$.

1. Introduction

In [Me88] Meinel introduced the notion of Ω-branching programs. These are branching programs some of whose nodes may perform Boolean operations from a finite set Ω of two-variable Boolean functions. $\mathcal{P}_{\Omega-BP}$ is the class of problems computable by polynomial size Ω-branching programs. Considering logspace-uniform sequences of Ω-branching programs the corresponding class is denoted $\mathcal{P}_{\Omega-BP}(logspace)$. In [Me88] it is shown that at most four different complexity classes can arise from this approach. In the uniform setting these classes are $\mathcal{P}_{\emptyset-BP}(logspace) = L$, $\mathcal{P}_{\{\wedge\}-BP}(logspace) = \mathcal{P}_{\{\vee\}-BP}(logspace) = NL$, $\mathcal{P}_{\{\wedge,\vee\}-BP}(logspace) = P$ and $\mathcal{P}_{\{\oplus\}-BP}(logspace)$. $\mathcal{P}_{\{\oplus\}-BP}(logspace)$ equals $\oplus L$ the class of languages accepted by logspace-bounded parity Turing machines ([Me87]). Clearly any separation result between two of these classes would be a breakthrough in complexity theory. The feeling that there are striking differences in the powers of the various computational concepts has been substantiated in several papers regarding restricted versions of the Ω-branching program model : [KMW88, KMW89, Kr89, DM89]. Concerning the general model we can at least try to understand the nature of the various computational concepts. One widely accepted approach for doing this, is to present natural problems that are complete in the complexity classes in consideration w.r.t. an appropriate reducibility notion. We proceed along this line.

Starting from a problem which is known to be complete for $\oplus L$ we derive a variety of problems of the same complexity. These problems include all standard problems of linear algebra over the field $\mathbf{F}_2$.

It is easily seen that all the results could be formulated and proved in a nonuniform setting too.

2. Definitions

A $\oplus$-branching program over $X^n = \{x_1, x_2, \ldots, x_n\}$ is a finite, directed, acyclic graph $P = (V,E,v,e)$ together with a vertex labelling $v : V \longrightarrow X^n \cup \{\oplus\} \cup \{0,1\}$ and an edge labelling $e : E \longrightarrow \{0,1\}$ with the following properties : If $q \in V$ is a *sink* (i.e. $outdeg(q) = 0$) then $v(q) \in \{0,1\}$. If q is a *non-sink* then $outdeg(q) = 2$, $v(q) \in X^n \cup \{\oplus\}$ and one edge leaving q is labelled 0 the other one is labelled 1. The vertices $q \in V$ of P are also called *nodes*. We denote the endpoints of the edges starting in a non-sink q of P labelled 0 and 1, respectively by $q0$ and $q1$, respectively. For $q \in V$ and $\mathbf{a} \in \{0,1\}^n$ define $f_q : \{0,1\}^n \longrightarrow \{0,1\}$ recursively as follows : If $v(q) \in \{0,1\}$ then $f_q(\mathbf{a}) = v(q)$. If $v(q) = x_i \in X^n$ then $f_q(\mathbf{a}) = (\neg a_i \wedge f_{q0}(\mathbf{a})) \vee (a_i \wedge f_{q1}(\mathbf{a}))$ and if $v(q) = \oplus$ then $f_q(\mathbf{a}) = f_{q0}(\mathbf{a}) \oplus f_{q1}(\mathbf{a})$. In other words : $f_q(\mathbf{a}) = 1$ iff the number of computation paths consistent with $\mathbf{a}$ that lead from q to sinks labelled 1 is odd. Here a computation path is a path from q to a sink of the underlying graph, such that the edge labels along this path correspond to the actual variable settings.

Since $\oplus$ is associative and commutative we allow $\oplus$-nodes v of arbitrary fan-out in the $\oplus$-branching program and forget the labelling of the outgoing edges of such nodes. It is clear how to adapt the definition of the computation process to these cases. These nodes can easily be simulated by $O(outdeg(v))$ $\oplus$-nodes of outdegree 2. If P has a single *source node* q_0 $(indeg(q_0) = 0)$ then f_{q_0} is called the function *computed by P*. Please note that we do not require $\oplus$-branching programs to have exactly one source. If exactly m sources are present P computes a function $\{0,1\}^n \longrightarrow \{0,1\}^m$ (defined according to a fixed numeration of the sources). It is clear that any function $\{0,1\}^n \longrightarrow \{0,1\}^m$ can be computed by a certain $\oplus$-branching program. The *size* of a $\oplus$-branching program is the number of non-sinks.

Formally a *problem* is an infinite sequence of functions $f_1, f_2, \ldots, f_n, \ldots$ with $f_n : \{0,1\}^n \longrightarrow \{0,1\}^{m_n}$. But we will describe problems in a rather informal way. The reformulation into a sequence of functions is easy. A problem is said to be *computable by polynomial-size $\oplus$-branching programs* if there is a polynomial p and a sequence $P_1, P_2, \ldots, P_n, \ldots$ of $\oplus$-branching programs such that for all n program P_n computes f_n and $size(P_n) \leq p(n)$. A sequence of branching programs P_n (or of circuits C_n, cf [Co85]) is said to be *logspace uniform* if there is a deterministic Turingmachine which when started on input 1^n produces a standard coding of the n-th program P_n (circuit C_n) in that sequence using no more than $O(log(size\ P_n))$ $(O(log(size\ C_n)))$ cells on the work tapes. We define

$$\mathcal{F}_{\{\oplus\}-BP}(logspace) = \{\mathcal{F}\mid\mathcal{F}\ is\ a\ problem\ computable\ by\ logspace\ uniform$$
$$polynomial\text{-}size\ \{\oplus\}\text{-}branching\ programs\}.$$

As already mentioned

$$\mathcal{F}_{\{\oplus\}-BP}(logspace) = \oplus L\ (\text{see [Me87]}).$$

We use the following reducibility notion : *a problem* $\mathcal{F}$ *is* NC^1- *reducible to a problem* $\mathcal{G}$ $(\mathcal{F} \leq \mathcal{G})$ if there is a logspace uniform sequence $C_1, C_2, \ldots , C_n, \ldots$ of circuits computing $\mathcal{F}$ such that $depth(C_n) = O(log\ n)$ and each C_n is allowed to have oracle gates for $\mathcal{G}$. An *oracle gate for* $\mathcal{G}$ is a node with r input edges and s output edges that computes $g_r : \{0,1\}^r \longrightarrow \{0,1\}^s$ if $\mathcal{G} = g_1, g_2, \ldots , g_n, \ldots$ This node counts as depth $\lceil log(r+s)\rceil$. For the original definition and for standard definitions concerning Boolean circuits cf. [Co85]. In fact Cook's notion of reducibility is slightly more stringent but it is not hard to see that our constructions fulfil also the stronger conditions. $\oplus L$ is easily seen to be closed under NC^1-reducibility. This is because the circuits in question can be simulated by circuits consisting of AND-, NOT- and oracle gates only. Negation can be modelled with the help of the parity-acceptance and conjunctions can be simulated by an corresponding serial arrangement. $\mathcal{F}$ is said to be $\oplus L$-*complete w.r.t.* NC^1-*reductions* if $\mathcal{F} \in \oplus L$ and for all $\mathcal{G} \in \oplus L$ holds $\mathcal{G} \leq \mathcal{F}$. In the sequel we will shortly say $\mathcal{F}$ *is* NC^1-*complete for* $\oplus L$.

3. The results

Consider the ring $\mathbf{M}(R,n)$ of $n \times n$-matrices over a certain ring R. Throughout the paper R denotes either the two element field $\mathbf{F}_2$ or the ring $\mathbf{F}_2[x]$ of univariate polynomials over $\mathbf{F}_2$. We consider the following problems :

MATPOW(R) : Given $A \in \mathbf{M}(R,n)$, *compute the powers* $A^1, A^2, \ldots , A^n$ *(I.e. if* $R = \mathbf{F}_2$ *then, for* $i,j,k \leq n$ *output* a^k_{ij}, *the* i,j-*th entry of* A^k. *If* $R = \mathbf{F}_2[x]$ *we suppose that the degrees of the entries of* A *are bounded say by* n. *In this case , for* $i,j,k \leq n$ *and* $l \leq n^2$ *output* a^k_{ijl}, *the coefficient of* x^l *in the* i,j-*th entry of* A^k.)

We prove that both problems are NC^1-complete for $\oplus L$. Beforehand we describe a problem which is trivially complete for $\oplus L$ ([Me87]).

$\oplus$-GAP : Given $A \in M(F_2, n)$, decide whether A is the adjacency matrix of a monotone graph G on $\{1, 2, \dots , n\}$ with an odd number of paths in G
leading from vertex 1 to vertex n .

Here a directed graph on $\{1, 2, \dots , n\}$ is said to be *monotone* if it contains
no edge (i,j) with $i \geq j$.

<u>Proposition 3.1</u>   MATPOW(F_2) and MATPOW($F_2[x]$) are NC^1-complete for $\oplus L$.

<u>Proof</u> : $\oplus - GAP \leq MATPOW(F_2)$ by the following observation :If A is the adjacency
matrix of a directed monotone graph G on $\{1, 2, \dots , n\}$ then $(A^k)_{i,j} = 1$ iff
the number of paths of length k leading from i to j is odd.
MATPOW(F_2) $\leq$ MATPOW($F_2[x]$) is obvious. It suffices now to prove   MATPOW($F_2[x]$) $\in$
$\oplus L = \mathcal{P}_{\{\oplus\}-BP}(logspace)$. First we prove MATPOW($F_2$) $\in \mathcal{P}_{\{\oplus\}-BP}(logspace)$ by an inductive construction and explain then how the idea carries over to the more general
case.
For fixed n let i, j, r be any integers with $1 \leq i, j, r \leq n$. In the following
let P^r denote a $\{\oplus\}$-branching program that computes the entries of A^r if the
entries of A are given as inputs. Each P^r will contain $P^1, P^2, \dots , P^{r-1}$ as
subprogramms. Let $q^r_{i,j}$ denote that source of P^r at which the (i,j)-th entry of
A^r is computed. Further let $P^r_{i,j}$ be the subprogram of P^r induced (as a graph)
by the set of nodes of P^r reachable from $q^r_{i,j}$. For variables $z_1, z_2, \dots , z_l$
let

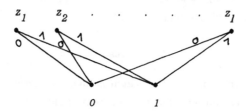

be symbolized by

(here the t-th $\bullet$ at the upper edge symbolizes the source labelled z_t). Now we
can start the construction. Clearly

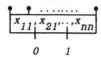

can serve as P^1. Suppose P^r has already been defined. Let

symbolize the branching program P^r_{ij} embedded in P^r. The following picture shows how P^{r+1} is constructed.

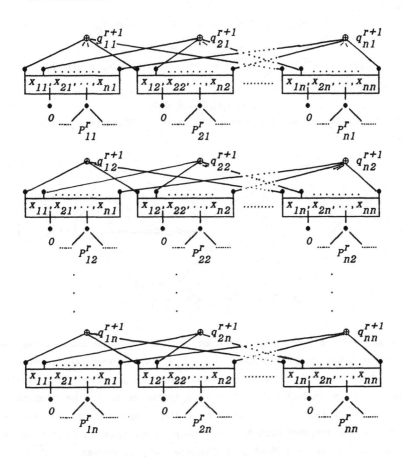

It is obvious that $(A^{r+1})_{ij}$ is computed at q^{r+1}_{ij}. Further $size(P^{r+1}) = size(P^r)$ $+ n^2 + n^3$. Hence $size(P^n) = O(n^4)$. From P^n one easily constructs a $\{\theta\}$-branching program that computes $MATPOW(\mathbb{F}_2)$. Just create $n^2(n - 1)$ additional sources and pipeline the intermediate results of $P^1, P^2, \ldots, P^{n-1}$ to them. Thus $MATPOW(\mathbb{F}_2)$ $\in \mathcal{F}_{\{\theta\}-BP}(logspace)$. Observe that the entries of the j-th column of A^{r+1} are computed in the j-th layer of the program making use of accesses to the inputs and of the entries of only the j-th column of A^r . Thus intermediate results are computed once but accessed several times from different points of the programm. This is achieved by arranging nodes at which intermediate results are computed deeper in the program than those at which only input variables are accessed, since access to them is cheap.

How can A^n be computed if $A \in M(F_2[x], n)$?

First we show how the coefficients of the product of two polynomials over F_2 can be computed.

$$\text{Let} \quad a(x) = a_r x^r \oplus a_{r-1} x^{r-1} \oplus \ldots \oplus a_0,$$

$$a(x) = b_r x^r \oplus b_{r-1} x^{r-1} \oplus \ldots \oplus b_0, \text{ and}$$

$$c(x) = c_{2r} x^{2r} \oplus c_{2r-1} x^{2r-1} \oplus \ldots \oplus c_0 \text{ with } c(x) = a(x) \cdot b(x).$$

Obviously for any i holds

$$c_i = a_i b_0 \oplus \ldots \oplus a_0 b_i.$$

The following picture shows how two consecutive coefficients c_i and c_{i+1} are computed.

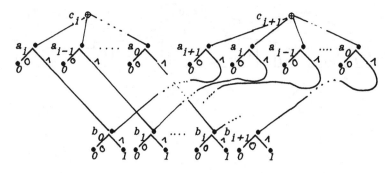

Observe that each b_j appears only once as label of some node, while the a_j's appear several times. Now interpret the b_j's as intermediate results, i.e. the test nodes with labels b_j stand for whole branching programs. This situation does not change if inner products of vectors of polynomials are to be computed. It can always be achieved that the coefficients of the components of the second factor appear later in the program (and therefore only once). Thus we can follow the same strategy as above : Let $A \in M(n, F_2[x])$. Compute the j-th column of A^{r+1} by multiplying A with the j-th column of A^r in that way that accesses to entries of A^r appear after accesses to entries of A. Followingly $MATPOW(F_2[x]) \in \mathcal{F}_{\varnothing|-BP}(logspace)$. This completes the proof.∎

In [Co85] Cook introduces DET the class of problems NC^1-reducible to the computation of determinants of integer matrices. DET characterizes the complexity of linear algebra in vector spaces over the rationals as all standard problems of linear algebra (over the rationals) can be solved in DET and most of them are NC^1-complete for DET (see [Co85]). The same role plays $\oplus L$ for linear algebra over $\mathbf{F}_2$. To show this, we consider a number of problems which all turn out to be complete for $\oplus L$. We define these problems in an informal way. They all can be coded similarly to those defined above.

ITMATPROD(R) : *Given* $A_1, A_2, \dots, A_n \in M(R,n)$, *compute the product* $A_1 \cdot A_2 \cdot \dots \cdot A_n$.

DET(R) : *Given* $A \in M(R,n)$, *compute the determinant* $det(A)$.

MATINV($\mathbf{F}_2$) : *Given* $A \in M(\mathbf{F}_2,n)$, *compute* A^{-1} *if it exists, the zero matrix otherwise.*

CHARPOL(R) : *Given* $A \in M(R,n)$, *compute* $charpol(A) = (c_0, c_1, \dots, c_n)$ *where* $\sum_{i=0}^{n} c_i \lambda^i = det(\lambda I - A)$.

RANK($\mathbf{F}_2$) : *compute the rank of* $A \in M(n,\mathbf{F}_2)$,

BASIS($\mathbf{F}_2$) : *given a set* $M = \{v_1, v_2, \dots, v_m\}$ *of vectors from* $\mathbf{F}_2^n$, *output a bit representation of a maximal independent set* $A \subseteq M$,

EQUATIONS($\mathbf{F}_2$) : *given a system of linear equations with coefficients from* $\mathbf{F}_2$, *output a solution if there exists one and an error message otherwise,*

NULLSPACE($\mathbf{F}_2$) : *output a basis of the kernel of a linear map* $\mathbf{F}_2^n \longrightarrow \mathbf{F}_2^m$ *which is given by a matrix.*

All the problems mentioned above are NC^1-reducible to each other and each of them is reducible to $MATPOW(\mathbf{F}_2[x])$. This is shown in [Be84, BvzGH82, Mu86]. The original proofs in fact work over the ring of integers but it is not hard to see that they work over $\mathbf{F}_2$ too. Since $MATPOW(\mathbf{F}_2[x]) \in \oplus L$, all these problems are complete for $\oplus L$ as well. Further problems in $\oplus L$ can be derived from problems mentioned in [Co85, BvzGH82].

4.Conclusions

In [IL89] the authors study the complexity of iterated multiplication in various semigroups. Among others they conjecture that $ITMATPROD(bool)$ (iterated matrix multiplication over the Boolean semiring $(\{0,1\},\wedge,\vee))$) is reducible to $ITMATPROD(\mathbf{F}_2)$. A consequence would be $NL \subseteq \oplus L$ (since $ITMATPROD(bool)$ is NC^1-complete for NL) which seems to be unlikely. We believe instead that both complexity classes are not comparable at all. For restricted versions of Ω-branching programs (for trees and for input oblivious linear depth programs) at least this has already been shown ([DM89,Kr89]).

5.Acknowledgements

I would like to thank an unknown referee for some valuable hints. Thanks also to Ch.Meinel, M.Krause and T.Zeugmann for helpfull discussions.

References

[Be84] S.J.Berkowitz: On computing the determinant in small parallel time using a small number of processors, Information Processing Letters 18(1984), 147-150

[BvzGH82] A.Borodin,J.v.z.Gathen,J.Hopcroft: Fast parallel matrix and GCD computations, Information and Control 52(1982),241-256

[Co85] S.A.Cook: A taxonomy of problems with fast parallel algorithms, Information and Control 64(1985), 2-22

[DM89] C.Damm,Ch.Meinel: Separating completely complexity classes related to polynomial size $\oplus$/-decision trees, Proc. FCT'89, LNCS 380, 127-136

[IL89] N.Immermann,D.Landau: The complexity of iterated multiplication, Proc. 4th Structure in Complexity Theory Conference (1989),104-111

[KMW88] M.Krause,Ch.Meinel,S.Waack: Separating the eraser Turing machine classes $\mathcal{L}_e$, $\mathcal{NL}_e$, co-$\mathcal{NL}_e$ and $\mathcal{P}_e$, Proc. MFCS'88, LNCS 324, 405-413

[KMW89] M.Krause,Ch.Meinel,S.Waack: Separating complexity classes related to certain input oblivious logarithmic space bounded Turing machines, Proc. 4th IEEE Structure in Complexity Theory Symposium, 1989

[Kr89] M.Krause: Separating $\oplus$L from L, NL, co-NL and AL = P for oblivious Turing machines of linear acces time, to appear in Proc. MFCS'90, Springer Verlag, LNCS??

[Me87] Ch.Meinel: Polynomial size Ω-branching programs and their computational power, to appear in Information and Computation

[Mu86] K.Mulmuley: A fast parallel algorithm to compute the rank of a matrix over an arbitrary field, Proc. 18th ACM STOC(1986), 338-339

CONSTRUCTIVE MATCHING · EXPLANATION BASED METHODOLOGY FOR INDUCTIVE THEOREM PROVING

Marta Fraňová
CNRS & Université Paris Sud
LRI, Bât. 490
91405 Orsay, France

ABSTRACT

Given formula F and axioms, theorem proving methods try to prove F. If F is provable, the proof obtained provides an explanation of the fact that F is a theorem. It may happen that F is **FALSE** or, for some reason, that we fail to prove F. Several theorem proving methods provide different kinds of the so-called "failure formulae". The failure formulae explain why the proof of F failed.

This paper illustrates the kind of failure formulae generated by the methodology we have developed for inductive theorem proving of theorems containing existential quantifiers. We reveal the importance of the failure formula vocabulary for generating of the so called missing lemmas.

The paper uses the vocabulary presented in [7].

1. INTRODUCTION

The concept of explicability, so much advocated by the work of DeJong [19], Mitchell [15], Kodratoff [11], is now recognized as one of the main characteristics of Artificial Intelligence (AI). An AI approach to automated (inductive) theorem proving requires explanations understandable for the user and suitable for the system.

In this paper we try to illustrate on a non-trivial example how our *Constructive Matching* (*CM*) methodology satisfies this requirement.

CM is a methodology for proving by induction Specification Theorems, i.e. theorems of the form $\forall x \exists z (P(x) \Rightarrow Q(x,z))$. This kind of theorems formalizes the program synthesis problem: for a given input vector x verifying the input condition $P(x)$, find an output vector z such that the input-output relation $Q(x,z)$ holds.

In its generality, the *CM* methodology is a way of solving problems[1] occurring in inductive theorem proving and program synthesis from formal specifications. As we explain in detail in [7], the main difference of *CM* with other approaches lies very deep in a basic step of any theorem proving methodology, viz. in the way atomic formulae are proven[2].

Classical methods for proving atomic formula can be classified as simplification methods, i.e., they attempt transform the atomic formula into simpler and simpler form, until the formula TRUE is reached. As we show later in this paper, this effort to obtain very simple formula leads to failure formulae that are very far from the vocabulary of a given problem. Therefore, when a classical theorem prover fails to prove a theorem, it simply signals this failure.

1/   These problems are: choice of the induction variable, generating and applying the induction hypotheses, solving equations, generalization, generating missing lemmas, analysis of failures, strategy for guiding deductions.
2/   In [7] we have shown the consequences of the choices done at such a low level on the way subproblems are generated during the course of a complete proof.

Our method for proving atomic formulae can rather be qualified as a "complication" method, stressing so that we rather progressively build more and more large sets of constraints describing the condition at which the formula is TRUE. The proof is completed when these conditions are proven to be implied by those of the problem. Since our method has been developed as a generalization of explanatory reasoning (see section 3 and [7]), it tends to "explain" its failure by proposing to the user other theorems to prove in order to get out of the failure case.

In this paper we show that suitable explanations may make the explanation process tied up with the process of invention. The process of invention in program synthesis through inductive theorem proving means invention of new concepts, which are programs or predicates. In this paper we present how, during a program synthesis process, we may realize the necessity of missing concepts in a given theory.

In **section 2** we recall what is understood by Program Synthesis (PS) from formal specifications and we lay stress upon the problem of the strategy in inductive theorem proving of existentially quantified theorems. **Section 3** recalls briefly our *Constructive Matching* methodology, compares it to the classical "simplification" way of proving theorems by induction. In **section 4** we solve a program synthesis problem: find a program for sorting lists of natural numbers. We show that we fail to prove the corresponding specification theorem using definitions given in appendix. We show that the failure formula leads to generating of a lemma, which expresses a concept that is not given explicitly in the theory.

2. PROGRAM SYNTHESIS FROM SPECIFICATIONS

Given an input vector x, an input condition P, and an input-output relation Q describing relational links between the input and the output, the goal of PS is to find a program, Prog such that

(1) $z = Prog(x)$

(2) if $P(x)$ then $Q(x,z)$.

Let us consider now the theorem $\forall x \, (P(x) \Rightarrow \exists z \, Q(x,z))$, called Specification Theorem (ST). This theorem comes simply from the specification "for x satisfying $P(x)$ find z verifying $Q(x,z)$" where we quantify universally the input vector x and existentially the output vector z. Let us denote by $F(x)$ the formula $P(x) \Rightarrow \exists z \, Q(x,z)$, i.e. $\forall x \, F(x)$ is exactly ST. An inductive proof of ST provides a recursive definition of the Skolem function ϕ verifying $Q(x,\phi(x))$, i.e., ϕ is Prog we seek for.

In [7] we make clear the main problems to be dealt with when synthesizing programs through inductive theorem proving: how to **decompose** into inductive subproblems; how to **solve** the generated inductive subproblems; how to **extract** programs from the proof obtained.

It is now widely recognized that the question of strategic aspects of inductive theorem proving for theorems containing existential quantifiers is a very difficult problem. Even if the problem cannot be solved in its generality, already partial results are interesting. The pioneer work in this field has been done by Z. Manna and R. Waldinger. We have presented the main difference of our method with the existing ones (W. Bibel [1], S. Biundo [3], N. Dershowitz [5], Z. Manna & R. Waldinger [13], Y. Kodratoff & H. Perdrix [10], [16], D. Smith [17]) in [6], and in detail in [7].

Our Constructive Matching methodology can be considered as a general strategy for specifications (i.e. specification theorems) satisfying the requirements given in [7]. It relies on the five following basic principles.

[1] Inductive theorem proving (ITP) is considered as a very powerful tool. It can provide a remedy for failures of a less powerful symbolic evaluator (Instead of a simplification of a formula F with a symbolic evaluator, a theorem prover will provide either a proof for F or a condition for the validity of F.) It can provide a remedy for failures of a less powerful equation solving tool (An equation E to be solved can be considered as a theorem where unknowns from E are existentially quantified.)

Note that this principle requires a method which recognizes when a formula is not evaluated enough, and which recognizes that there should be more solutions than those obtained by simpler equation-solving tools.

[2] Our method for ITP directs the deductions performed and thus it requires almost no help from the outside (at least, in principle).

[3] Our method for ITP recognizes when, in the course of a proof, a given theory does not contain explicitly all the knowledge necessary for the success, it is able to formulate this missing knowledge and to prove it.

[4] Our method for ITP provides clear failure formulas (explanations) pointing out the main problems in the course of a proof.

[5] We do not require the efficiency of synthesized programs (those, in fact, can be improved later on using program transformation techniques). The primary goal is to obtain[3] an algorithm proven equivalent to its specification.

More about the practical consequences of these principles for our method can be found in [7].

In the following section we present our $\mathcal{CM}$ methodology applied for solving a particular problem: strategy for proving an atomic formula.

3. CONSTRUCTIVE MATCHING METHODOLOGY - A GENERALIZATION OF EXPLANATORY REASONING

In [7] we explain that $\mathcal{CM}$ is a result of a generalization of our way of proving theorems $\forall x\, F(x)$ using the structural induction scheme

$$F(0)$$
$$\frac{F(a) \Rightarrow F(\text{suc}(a))}{\forall x\, F(x)}$$

When using this scheme, we have realized that we <u>know what we want to obtain</u>, i.e., analogously to a student knowing the result of a given integral and seeking for an explanation of this result, we know our result, and this is:

❑ in the base case: for a "concrete element" (here 0) the formula $F(0)$ from the axioms of our theory

❑ in the general case: for a "concrete element" (here suc(a)) the formula $F(\text{suc}(a))$ from the axioms of our theory and the induction hypothesis $F(a)$.

In order to find an <u>explanation</u> of our result, which, in this case, is a proof of the base and general cases, we can proceed as follows.

3/ In our opinion, a general method cannot incarnate all ingenious heuristics used by humans to construct an algorithm from its specification.

Looking at the form of F(0) or F(suc(a)), we try to find, what allows us to obtain such formulae, i.e., we look at the axioms available. Using the result of our observation (suitable axioms, here, provide conditions of validity for a formula of the form F(.)), we try then to put 0 or suc(a) as the argument of F(.), in order to compose F(0) or F(suc(a)). The formalization of this procedure resulted in the so called CM-formula construction.

3.1. CM-FORMULA CONSTRUCTION

When proving an atomic formula $F(t_1,t_2)$, created from a predicate F and two terms t_1 and t_2, we start by building an abstract formula $F(t_1,\xi)$ with an abstract argument ξ. The definition of F provides conditions for the validity of the formula $F(t_1,\xi)$. Let us denote by C the set of all ξ for which $F(t_1,\xi)$ is true, i.e.

$$C = \{\xi \mid F(t_1,\xi) \text{ is true}\}.$$

We are then left with checking if the replacement of ξ by t_2 preserves the validity of $F(t_1,\xi)$, i.e. we have to check whether $t_2 \in C$.

In this paper we give only the general scheme of our algorithm for the CM-formula construction. We shall denote here by σ_x the representation of the induction variable and by $\sigma_{smal(x)}$ the representation of elements smaller than x. [7] refines this general procedure.

$$\sigma_x F(t_1,\xi)$$

STEP 1
evaluate term $\sigma_x t_1$

$\downarrow$

STEP 2
use definition of F in order to find cond. for validity

$\downarrow$

$\sigma_x F(t_1,\xi)$ if   comp(G,$\sigma_{smal(x)}F(t_1,\xi)$)

STEP 3
apply induction hypothesis in order to concretize ξ
$\alpha := $ concretized(ξ)

$\downarrow$

$\sigma_x F(t_1,\alpha)$ if   comp(G',$\sigma_{smal(x)}F(t_1,\alpha)$)

simplify
eliminate recursion formula
$\sigma_{smal(x)}F(t_1,\alpha))$

$\downarrow$

$\sigma_x F(t_1,\alpha)$ if   G"

STEP 4
replace α by $\sigma_x t_2$
problem generated:
$\alpha =? \sigma_x t_2$

$\downarrow$

$\sigma_x F(t_1,t_2)$ if   (G" & H)

STEP 5
simplify

$\downarrow$

$\sigma_x F(t_1,t_2)$ if   H'

The formula H' obtained in step 5 is a condition. If it evaluates to TRUE then it can be viewed as an **explanation** of success. If H' evaluates to FALSE then it can be viewed as an explanation of failure. As an example of failure, the CM-construction fails for the formula 4<2 in NAT. H' for this example is the formula

2=suc(suc(suc(suc(suc(z))))),

which says that 4<2 is FALSE, since the generic form of all elements t satisfying the formula 4<t is suc(suc(suc(suc(suc(z))))), and 2 is not of this form. If H' is not TRUE in general but may be TRUE for particular values of x, then H' expresses a condition necessary for a success.

In the case of universally quantified theorems we thus obtain a missing precondition. In the case of theorems with existential quantifiers, a proof of a specification theorem leads to a sequence H_1, ..., H_k of conditions. For each of them a particular value of Skolem function sf_i is found. H_i is evaluated to TRUE for a particular value of the input variable x only. From this we obtain then programs in the form

$$\text{if } H_i(x) \text{ then } sf_i.$$

Note that in all cases the vocabulary used in H' is very near to the one used by the user when he has been stating his problem.

Note also that at any step of our formula construction we know what <u>we want to obtain</u> and **how to obtain it**.

❑ Clearly, in order to <u>find conditions for the validity</u> of $\sigma_x F(t_1, \xi)$ we **expand** $\sigma_x F(t_1, \xi)$ using the definition of F.

❑ We know then that we have to <u>apply induction hypotheses</u>, so we **generate equations comparing IH and the previously obtained expansion**.

❑ The success of the last equation solving problem allows to replace the abstract argument ξ by a more concrete α (i.e. the <u>concretization</u> of ξ) and allows at least the most trivial <u>simplification</u>, which is here **eliminating recursion formulae from the obtained expansion**.

❑ We have then to <u>replace α by $\sigma_x t_2$</u>, so we **generate an equation between α and $\sigma_x t_2$**.

3.2. CLASSICAL FORMULA SIMPLIFICATION

We speak about a classical way of proving theorems, when, in the first step, one applies transformations to the formula one wants to prove with the aim of giving to it the form of a composition of the induction hypothesis and of a formula G. In the second step, one then simplifies G to put it into the form trivially TRUE, thus proving the formula ([4]).

The formula G or its simplifications may also be considered as explanations. The difference with explanations provided by our method is that the effort to simplify G to TRUE makes the vocabulary, in which G is expressed, be further away from the vocabulary in which the original problem is stated. For instance, dealing with $\mathcal{NAT}$, attempting to prove in classical way the formula 4<2, the formula G is suc(z)<0, which explains that 4<2 is FALSE, since there is no z for which suc(z)<0 is TRUE. As we mention above, using our method, the explanation of the failure is the formula 2=suc(suc(suc(suc(suc(z))))), which says that 4<2 is FALSE, since the form of all elements t satisfying the formula 4<t is suc(suc(suc(suc(suc(z))))), and 2 is not of this form.

Our "constructive" way makes the proof more complicated, when dealing with universally quantified theorems only [7]. It is important, however, that its complexity remains the same when existential quantifiers are involved.

4. CONSTRUCTIVE MATCHING AND EXPLANATIONS

In this section we give a rather difficult example, which speaks for "good" explanations in program synthesis, and illustrates also the present implementation of our method, i.e. the system $\mathcal{PRECOMAS}$ (see [8]). We present the problem of finding a sorted permutation of a given list, as it is done by our method. A synthesis of a sorting algorithm is a test through which each program synthesis system has to "pass". And it happens that this example is not at all trivial. It is easy enough to synthesize a sort program, when "good" definitions and lemmas are given, but, in the most cases, a user has to point out the steps in which these lemmas are used. For instance, in [20] this way of interacting with the user is adopted and one can find there synthesized "select sort", "merge sort", etc.

At present, our system $\mathcal{PRECOMAS}$ also needs the help of a user. The difference is only that the system works on a simple knowledge base, i.e. no lemmas are given in advance, thus the user does not interfere with the strategy of the system. For implementation reasons, however, the most difficult problem, for which the user's help is necessary, is quantifying a formula provided by our system, thus formulating a lemma. In the present implementation, an other kind of interaction is that the system formulates equations and the user has to use our equation solving tool to solve them, but this is not at all difficult, and does not mean that the user interferes with the strategy of the system.

The specification theorem corresponding to the specification for sorting a list of elements is $\forall x_1 \exists z \; permut(x_1,z) \; \& \; ordered(z)$.

We will use the definitions given in Appendix. Let us denote by ϕ the Skolem function corresponding to this theorem.

In order to illustrate the interactivity of $\mathcal{PRECOMAS}$ ($\mathcal{P}$ for short), we give here a commented script of the session. We stress upon the operations that the user ($\mathcal{U}$ for short) has to perform.

Base Step

In the base step the system tries to find values for z which will validate the formula $permut(x_1,z)$ for the representation of the induction variable x_1 by nil.

The system finds the solution $z \leftarrow nil$. With the obtained substitution the system then validates the formula $ordered(z)$. The system then extracts the following partial program
$$if \; x_1 = nil \; then \; z \leftarrow nil.$$

Induction step

The system tries to find values for z which will validate the formula $permut(x_1,z)$ for the representation of the induction variable x_1 by $cons(a,w)$.

Before pursuing the execution of the system, let us consider the induction hypotheses generated by the system:
$$\exists e_1 \; permut(w,e_1) \; \& \; ordered(e_1) \tag{H1}$$
and
$$\forall p \; smaller(delete(p,cons(a,w)),cons(a,w))$$
$$\Rightarrow \exists e_2 \; permut(delete(p,cons(a,w)),e_2) \; \& \; ordered(e_2). \tag{H2}$$

Consider the induction hypothesis H1. In this hypothesis, there are two "variables". The first one, called w is our notation for $cdr(x_1)$. x_1 is the input variable. Thus, for a given input x_1 we know compute the value of $cdr(x_1)$, i.e. w is an **explicit**, or equivalently, a **concrete** or a **computable** value.

The variable e_1 in our induction hypothesis is then the value of $\phi(cdr(x_1))$, which, by this induction hypothesis, we know how to compute, i.e. e_1 is an explicit value.

In H2, the element called p is a **parameter** which represents any element for which $delete(p,cons(a,w))$ is smaller than $cons(a,w)$. This induction hypothesis provides no algorithm to compute p. This is why, we say that p is **not explicit enough to be computed**.

In consequence, any founded substitution which will contain p will not give evaluable expressions. This is why we say that such a substitution is not explicit enough to be computed. However, our program synthesis tool recognizes and allows us to **make explicit** (or **concretize**) such substitutions, as we show later.

Presently, let us pursue the execution of the system.

$\boxed{P}$ **The problem is finding values for z with respect to which the formula**
$$\text{permut(delete(car(z),cons(a,w)),cdr(z))}$$
may become valid.
Here, it should be done by the application of the induction hypothesis H1.

$\boxed{U}$ **Propose solutions!**

$\boxed{P}$ **Create equations putting into correspondence arguments in** **permut(w,e_1) and**
$$\text{permut(delete(car(z),cons(a,w)),cdr(z)).}$$

Here, the user creates the equations
$$w = \text{delete(car(z),cons(a,w))}$$
$$e_1 = \text{cdr(z)}$$
with the unknown z and solves them using theorem proving tools of $\mathcal{PRECOMAS}$.

$\boxed{U}$ z $\leftarrow$ cons(a,e_1)) is the solution for the problem (1).

With this substitution, when verifying the formula ordered(z), the system will find out that this substitution is correct provided the condition ltl(a,e_1)) holds.

Now, the system generates the following problem.

$\boxed{P}$ **The problem is finding values for z with respect to which the formula**
$$\text{permut(delete(car(z),cons(a,w)),cdr(z))}$$
may become valid. Here, it should be done by the application of the induction hypothesis H2.

$\boxed{U}$ **Propose solutions!**

$\boxed{P}$ **Create equations putting into correspondence arguments in**
$$\text{permut(delete(p,cons(a,w)),e_2)}$$
and
$$\text{permut(delete(car(z),cons(a,w)),cdr(z)).}$$

Here, the user creates the equations

$$\text{delete(p,cons(a,w))} = \text{delete(car(z),cons(a,w))} \tag{E1}$$
$$e_2 = \text{cdr(z)} \tag{E2}$$

with the unknown z and solves them using theorem proving tools of $\mathcal{PRECOMAS}$. The user obtains a conditional substitution

$\boxed{U}$ z $\leftarrow$ cons(p,e_2) is the solution for the problem provided the condition member(p,w) is verified.

This conditional substitution is obtained through evaluation of the term delete(p,cons(a,w)), the value of which is

$$= \begin{cases} w, & \text{if equal(p,a)} \\ \text{cons(a,delete(p,w)),} & \text{if member(p,w) \& not(equal(p,a))} \end{cases}$$

The equation E1 is therefore divided to two equations

$$w = \text{delete(car(z),cons(a,w)), if equal(p,a)} \tag{E11}$$
$$\text{cons(a,delete(p,w))} = \text{delete(car(z),cons(a,w)), if member(p,w) \&} \tag{E12}$$
$$\text{not(equal(p,a))}$$

The solution of E11 and E2 leads to the substitution z $\leftarrow$ cons(a,e_2) equivalent to the previously obtained substitution z $\leftarrow$ cons(a,e_1). This is why the user considers only the conditional substitution z $\leftarrow$ cons(p,e_2) as the solution of E12 and E2.

This substitution is recognized by the system as a value which is **not evaluable**, since the induction hypothesis does not specify p in a unique way.

In the present implementation, the system asks therefore the user to replace the last substitution by something "explicit". The user is aware that p depends on x_1 and he can therefore replace p by aux(x_1), where aux is a not yet defined auxiliary function.

$\boxed{P}$ **For the obtained substitution $z_1 \leftarrow$ cons(p,e_2), can you find a new substitution which is explicit under the validity of the condition**
$$\text{member}(p,w)\&\text{not}(\text{equal}(p,a))\&\text{ltl}(p,e_2)? \qquad (C)$$

$\boxed{u}$ $z \leftarrow$ cons(aux(x_1),e_2) is the solution for the problem.

Now the system extracts the partial program synthesized in the induction step.

> **if**   equal(x_1,cons(car(x_1),cdr(x_1))) & ltl(car(x_1),ϕ(cdr(x_1)))
>
> > **then** $z \leftarrow$ cons(car(x_1),ϕ(cdr(x_1)))
> >
> > **else** $z \leftarrow$ cons(aux(x_1),ϕ(delete(aux(x_1),x_1)))

The condition (C) is an explanation of the failure of the system to provide completely executable program for generating ordered permutations. The user has therefore modify the obtained code as it is described below in order to obtain a recursive definition for the program **aux**.

ANALYSIS OF THE SYSTEM EXPLANATION

It is clear that (C) becomes a basis for a new lemma which has to provide a way of computing p. From the semantic point of view, we can realize that the element p should be the minimum of x_1. But, *PRECOMAS* is not (and we suppose that no automated system is) able to recognize semantics of problems. What it can do, however, is to recognize that e_2 depends on p. This is why, whenever we succeed in specifying the concrete value of p, we will at once know the value of e_2.

Our aim is to make explicit the value of p. Consequently, in our generated theorem p will be existentially quantified. Let us denote by z_1 this variable. Taking into account the above condition C, we know that the formula member(p,w) has to be verified. This means that the formula
$$\text{member}(z_1,w)$$
will be a component of the generated theorem. Further condition imposed upon p is ltl(p,e_2). Since e_2 depends on p and this dependency is determined within the formula permut(cons(a,w),cons(p, e_2)), i.e.
$$\text{permut}(\text{cons}(a,w),\text{cons}(z_1,e_2)),$$
we will look also for an element z_2 (i.e. e_2) such that
$$\text{ltl}(z_1,z_2) \& \text{permut}(\text{cons}(a,w),\text{cons}(z_1,z_2)). \qquad (*)$$
Since the formula ltl(z_1,z_2) does not contain parts of the induction variable, we reverse the order of the formulae in (*) and we obtain
$$\text{permut}(\text{cons}(a,w),\text{cons}(z_1,z_2)) \& \text{ltl}(z_1,z_2).$$
By the hypothesis ordered(e_2) holds. This is why, in our new problem the formula ordered(z_2) will have to be valid. Finally, we have the problem

> find z_1, find z_2 such that
>
> member(z_1,w) & permut(cons(a,w),cons(z_1,z_2)) & ltl(z_1,z_2) & ordered(z_2).

This can be generalized to

$$\forall x \; (x \neq nil) \Rightarrow \exists z_1 \; \exists z_2 \; \{member(z_1,x) \; \& \; permut(x,cons(z_1,z_2)) \; \& \; ltl(z_1,z_2) \; \&$$
$$ordered(z_2) \; \}$$

This theorem can be proved by our method. (The proof is not a simple one, since it requires multiple application of induction hypotheses).

Let us call φ the Skolem function corresponding to the variable z_1, i.e. $\varphi(x) = z_1$. Analogously, let us call ψ the Skolem function corresponding to the variable z_2.

Proving the last theorem we have obtained the concretization of p and e_2 in $z \leftarrow cons(p,e_2)$. The required concretization of p is by $\varphi(cons(a,w))$ and the concretization of e_2 is by $\psi(cons(a,w))$. Then, the substitution

$$z \leftarrow cons(\varphi(cons(a,w)),\psi(cons(a,w)))$$

is explicit.(This substitution has to replace the substitution $cons(aux(x_1),e_2)$).

Therefore, the above partial program is replaced by

if $\quad equal(x_1,cons(car(x_1),cdr(x_1))) \; \& \; ltl(car(x_1),\phi(cdr(x_1)))$

$\qquad$ **then** $z \leftarrow cons(car(x_1),\phi(cdr(x_1)))$

$\qquad$ **else** $z \leftarrow cons(\varphi(x_1),\psi(x_1))$

Presently, our system is not able to perform analysis of its failure formulae, but our *CM* methodology allows to perform this analysis in a systematic (and therefore implementable) way.

CONCLUSION

In [18] we have explained what we mean by an explanation in inductive theorem proving and we reveal the importance of explanations in program synthesis. We show there that the interest for suitable explanations in inductive theorem proving is motivated by their application to predicate synthesis, and by their use as (missing) lemmas in program synthesis and theorem proving.

In this paper we illustrate the explanatory character of our method. In particular, we show that a failure formula (obtained for the problem of finding a sorted permutation of a given list) generates a new existentially quantified lemma, the proof of which provides an explicit definition of a concept which has not been known to our system *PRECOMAS* in advance. During the analysis of the explanation provided by the system we have found a rather particular specification for this concept. This particularity shows that a kind of invention is possible even within a deductive system. Naturally, our method is not always able to find specifications that are the "best" from the human point of view. On the contrary, we think that specifications for missing concepts will always be particular cases depending on the problem and given definitions. Nevertheless, it is already one step toward the complete automation of the program synthesis process.

While *CM* is a quite powerful methodology, the actual implementation does not match it completely yet (and there is much implementation work still to be done, see [8]).

ACKNOWLEDGMENTS

I would like to express my warmest thanks to Yves Kodratoff for all his support of the research behind this paper. His constructive critics improved in very important way the final form of this paper.

This work has been partially supported by the ESPRIT (ALPES P373 and P973) projects and PRC-IA of French *Ministère de la Recherche et de la Technologie*.

APPENDIX

Definition of permut: $LIST\text{-}of\text{-}NAT \times LIST\text{-}of\text{-}NAT \rightarrow BOOL$
al34: permut(nil,u), if equal(u,nil).
al35: permut(u,nil), if equal(u,nil).
al38: permut(cons(u,v),w), if permut(delete(car(w),cons(u,v)),cdr(w)).
al39: permut(w,cons(u,v)), if permut(cdr(w),delete(car(w),cons(u,v))).

Definition of member: $NAT \times LIST\text{-}of\text{-}NAT \rightarrow BOOL$
al23: member(x,nil), if false.
al24: member(x,cons(y,l)), if x = y.
al25: member(x,cons(y,l)), if not(x=y)& member(x,l).

Definition of delete: $NAT \times LIST\text{-}of\text{-}NAT \rightarrow LIST\text{-}of\text{-}NAT$
al31: delete(x,nil) = nil.
al32: delete(x,cons(y,l)) = l, if x = y.
al33: delete(x,cons(y,l)) = cons(y,delete(x,l)), if not(x = y) & member(x,l).

Definition of ordered: $LIST\text{-}of\text{-}NAT \rightarrow BOOL$
al29: ordered(nil).
al30: ordered(cons(x,l)), if ltl(x,l) & ordered(l).

Definition of ltl: $NAT \times LIST\text{-}of\text{-}NAT \rightarrow BOOL$
al26: ltl(x,nil).
al27: ltl(x,cons(y,l)), if x = y & ltl(x,l).
al28: ltl(x,cons(y,l)), if x<y & ltl(x,l).

Definition of <: $NAT \times NAT \rightarrow BOOL$
ai40: 0<u, if not(0 = u).
ai41: suc(u)<suc(v), if u<v.

REFERENCES

[1] W. Bibel, K. M. Hoernig: LOPS - A System Based on a Strategical Approach to Program Synthesis; in [2], 69-91.
[2] A. Biermann, G. Guiho,Y. Kodratoff (ed): Automatic Program Construction Techniques; Macmillan Publishing Company, London, 1984.
[3] S. Biundo: A synthesis system mechanizing proofs by induction; in: ECAI' 86 Proceedings, Vol. 1, 1986, 69-78.
[4] R. S. Boyer, J S. Moore: A Computational Logic; Academic Press, 1979.
[5] N. Dershowitz: Synthesis by Completion; in [9], 208-214.
[6] M. Franova: Fundamentals for a new methodology for inductive theorem proving: *CM*-construction of atomic formulae; in [12], 137-141.
[7] M. Franova: Fundamentals of a new methodology for Program Synthesis from Formal Specifications: *CM*-construction of atomic formulae; Thesis, Université Paris-Sud, November, Orsay, France, 1988.
[8] M. Franova: Precomas 0.3 User Guide; Rapport de Recherche No.524, L.R.I., Université de Paris-Sud, Orsay, France, October, 1989.
[9] A. K. Joshi, (ed): Proceedings of the Ninth International Joint Conference on Artificial Intelligence; August, Los Angeles, 1985.
[10] Y. Kodratoff, M.Picard: Complétion de systèmes de réécriture et synthèse de programmes à partir de leurs spécifications; Bigre No.35, October, 1983.
[11] Y. Kodratoff: An Introduction to Machine Learning; Pitman, London, 1988.
[12] Y. Kodratoff: Proceedings of the 8th European Conference on Artificial Intelligence; August 1-5, Pitman, London, United Kingdom, 1988.
[13] Z. Manna, R.Waldinger: A Deductive Approach to Program Synthesis; ACM Transactions on Programming Languages and Systems, Vol. 2., No.1, January, 1980, 90-121.
[14] R. Michalski, J. G. Carbonell, T. M. Mitchell (eds): Machine Learning: An Artificial Intelligence Approach; Tioga, Palo Alto, California, 1983.
[15] T. M. Mitchell: Learning by experimentation, acquiring and refining problem-solving heuristics; in [14], 163-190.
[16] H. Perdrix: Program synthesis from specifications; ESPRIT'85, Status Report of Continuing Work, North-Holland, 1986, 371-385.
[17] D. R. Smith: Top-Down Synthesis of Simple Divide and Conquer Algorithm; Artificial Intelligence, vol. 27, no. 1, 1985, 43-96.
[18] M. Franova: Explanations in inductive theorem proving; to appear in Proceedings of the AAAI 90 Workshop on Learning.
[19] G. DeJong, R. Mooney: Explanation-Based Learning: An Alternative View; Machine Learning 1, 1986, 145-176.
[20] K. L. Clark, J. Darlington: Algorithm classification through synthesis; The Computer Journal, Vol. 23, No 1, 61-65.

Characterizing Complexity Classes by Higher Type

Primitive Recursive Definitions, Part II

Andreas Goerdt

Universität -GH- Duisburg
Fachbereich Mathematik
Fachgebiet Praktische Informatik
Lotharstrasse 65
D-4100 Duisburg 1
West-Germany

Helmut Seidl

Fachbereich Informatik
Universität des Saarlandes
Im Stadtwald
D-6600 Saarbrücken 11
West-Germany

ABSTRACT

Higher type primitive recursive definitions (also known as Gödel's system T) defining first-order functions (i.e. functions of type $ind \to ... \to ind \to ind$, ind for individuals, higher types occur in between) can be classified into an infinite syntactic hierarchy: A definition is in the n'th stage of this hierarchy, a so called rank-n-definition, iff n is an upper bound on the levels of the types occurring in it.

We interpret these definitions over finite structures and show for $n \geq 1$: Rank-$(2n+2)$-definitions characterize (in the sense of [Gu83], say) the complexity class $DTIME(exp_n(poly))$ whereas rank-$(2n+3)$-definitions characterize $DSPACE(exp_n(poly))$ (here $exp_0(x) = x$, $exp_{n+1}(x) = 2^{exp_n(x)}$). This extends the results that rank-1-definitions characterize LOGSPACE [Gu83], rank-2-definitions characterize PTIME, rank-3-definitions characterize PSPACE, rank-4-definitions characterize EXPTIME [Go89a].

0. Introduction

The characterization of complexity classes by considering definitional devices (logical formulas, programming languages, automata computing in an interpretation) in finite structures is a topic well known in the literature [Sa80, TiUr83, Gu83, Gu84, Ti86, Im87, Lei87, Go89a, Go89b]. In notation and results we build on [Gu83, Gu84, Go89a, Go89b]. Higher type primitive recursive definitions were introduced by Gödel in 1958 (see [Ba84], p. 568 ff for history and introduction). Their expressive strength when interpreted over **N** was studied (with a proof theoretical motivation in mind) in [Schw75, Te82].

The idea to interpret definitional devices using higher order objects in finite structures occurs several times in the literature. In [Im87] it is shown that second order logic plus transitive closure characterizes PSPACE, Leivant [Lei87] introduces Turing machines with pointers to higher order objects computing in finite structures, Tiuryn [Ti86] characterizes iterated exponential space complexity classes by higher order arrays and iterated exponential time complexity classes by higher order stacks. We interpret higher type primitive recursive definitions in finite structures and get the unexpected alternation of time and space complexity classes as mentioned above. The results here should be contrasted with those in [Go89b] where we show for $n \geq 0$: *general* recursive definitions in higher types of rank $n+1$ characterize DTIME($\exp_n$(poly)).

The results of the present paper are not obtained by a straight forward extension of the proof techniques from [Go89a]. Instead, we have to combine the methods of [Go89a] with the concept of "infinite terms" used in proof theoretical contexts. We learned it from [Schw75]. "Infinite terms" in the context of finite structures have the appearance of families of related terms: Instead of one term we consider one term for each structure. Moreover, we use an observation relating size and depth of terms before and after some (essentially β-) reduction steps.

In section 1 we introduce basic definitions and results. The results in section 2 are prerequisites to showing that primitive recursive definitions can be evaluated in the required time and space bounds. In section 3 we give our characterization of time complexity classes, in section 4 of space complexity classes. We recommend to read the first halfs of the proofs of the main theorems 3.1 and 4.1 before the rest of the paper. In the conclusion we point out the new ideas of the present proofs when compared to the proofs in [Go89a].

1 Basics

The family of *types*, Type = (Type^n | n $\in$ $\mathbb{N}$) is given by: ind $\in$ Type^0; if $\tau \in$ Type^m and $\sigma \in$ Type^n then $\tau \to \sigma \in$ Type^k where k=max$\{m+1,n\}$. $\to$ associates to the right. level τ = n iff $\tau \in$ Type^n. Var = (Var$^\tau$ | $\tau \in$ Type) denotes a typed family of *variables*, Opsym = (Opsym^n | n $\in$ $\mathbb{N}$) a finite signature of *operation symbols*. The family of *terms* or *primitive recursive definitions* Term = (Term$^\tau$ | $\tau \in$ Type) is given by: Var$^\tau \subseteq$ Term$^\tau$, NEXT $\in$ Term$^{\text{ind} \to \text{ind}}$, MIN, MAX $\in$ Term^{ind}, Opsym$^m \in$ Term$^{\text{ind} \to .. \to \text{ind}}$. These are the atomic terms. If t:$\tau \to \sigma$ and s:τ (meaning: t $\in$ Term$^{\tau \to \sigma}$ and s $\in$ Term$^\tau$) then t(s):σ. If t:σ and y:τ then λy.t : $\tau \to \sigma$. If t:$\tau \to$ ind $\to \tau$ then R(t):$\tau \to$ ind $\to \tau$ (primitive recursion). A term is of level n iff iff its type is of level n, *first-order terms* are terms of level ≤ 1. A term is of rank n iff all its subterms are of level $\leq n$. fr t is the set of *free variables* of t. Writing t($\overline{x}$) or t($\overline{x},\overline{y}$) we mean that the free variables of t are contained in $\overline{x}$ or $\overline{x},\overline{y}$. *Closed terms* are terms without free variables. For t:$\tau_1 \to .. \to \tau_n \to$ ind (each type can be uniquely decomposed like this), it is t$\downarrow$ = t(x_1)..(x_n):ind , x_k new and pairwise different. We always assume that bound variables are different, and variables bound at different places are different. For s, y of the same type t[s/y] denotes the *substitution* as usual.

<u>Semantics:</u> We only consider finite interpretations I with: Set of individuals I = $\{0,...,n\}$, and interpretation I(op) of operation symbols op. D_I = (D_I^τ | $\tau \in$ Type) denotes the full type structure over I, i.e. D_I^{ind} = $\{0,...,n\}$, $D_I^{\tau \to \sigma}$ = $\{f:D_I^\tau \to D_I^\sigma\}$. Usually C (for cardinality) stands both for the last element of an interpretation and for an interpretation with last element C. We tend to omit indices indicating the interpretation. Let ρ be a fixed representation of D_C as follows: For i $\leq$ C, ρ(i) is i in binary, for d $\in$ D$^{\tau \to \sigma}$, ρ(d) = ($\rho(e_1),\rho(d(e_1))$) ... ($\rho(e_n),\rho(d(e_n))$) if D$^\tau$ = $\{e_1,...,e_n\}$. If $\tau \to \sigma$ is of level $\leq n$ then the length of ρ(d) for d $\in$ D$^{\tau \to \sigma}$ is bounded by $\exp_{n-1}(p(C))$, p a polynomial depending on $\tau \to \sigma$. In algorithmic

contexts we implicitly refer to this representation and will only distinguish between $\rho(d)$ and d itself if necessary. The semantics of a term t in C w.r.t. to the type respecting assignment of variables in D, μ is given by:

$$C[\![y]\!]\mu = \mu(y) \ , \ C[\![\text{NEXT}]\!]\mu(m) = \begin{cases} m+1 & \text{if } m<C \\ C & \text{otherwise} \end{cases}$$

$$C[\![\text{MIN}]\!]\mu = 0 \ , \ C[\![\text{MAX}]\!]\mu = C \ , \ C[\![\text{op}]\!]\mu = C(\text{op}) \text{ for op} \in \text{Opsym}$$

$$C[\![t(s)]\!]\mu = C[\![t]\!]\mu(C[\![s]\!]\mu) \ , \ C[\![\lambda y.t]\!]\mu(d) = C[\![t]\!]\mu[d/y]$$

($\mu[d/y]$ the variant of μ by assigning d to y)

$$C[\![R(t)]\!]\mu(d)(m) = \begin{cases} C[\![t]\!]\mu(C[\![R(t)]\!]\mu(d)(m-1))(m-1) & \text{if } m>0 \\ d & \text{if } m=0 \end{cases}$$

A *global function* [Gu83] G is a function which takes an interpretation C and individuals $i_1,...,i_n$ from C as arguments and maps these to the individual $C(G)(i_1)...(i_n)$ - the value of G in C (therefore "C(G)" instead of "G(C)" as perhaps expected). We represent the interpretation C as input of a Turing machine in a natural way (see [Gu83] for some details). The length of the representation of C is polynomially related to the number C at least if there is a non-nullary operation symbol. A Turing machine TM computes G iff TM with input C and $i_1,...,i_n$ gives $C(G)(i_1)...(i_n)$ as output. G is computable in DTIME($\exp_n$(poly)) or SPACE($\exp_n$(poly)) if there is a Turing machine for G which computes G in time or space $\exp_n(p(C))$ respectively for some polynomial p. Conversely w.r.t. a fixed number n and a fixed signature Opsym containing at least one non-nullary operation symbol, the input of an arbitrary Turing machine TM may be interpreted as (a coding of) C, $i_1,...,i_n$. Thus, TM can be viewed as a realization of some global function G. This allows us to consider complexity classes of global functions as usual complexity classes. Closed primitive recursive first-order definitions t define global functions in a natural way by: $C(G)(i_1)...(i_n) = C[\![t]\!](i_1)...(i_n)$.

The following notion of terms over C is crucial for showing that terms can be evaluated within certain bounds. We use terms over C in a similar way as infinite terms are used in [Schw75]: to eliminate recursion which in turn allows us to lower the rank of a primitive recursive definition in a controlled way (section 2).

1.1 Terms over C

The family of *terms over C*, $\text{Term}_C = (\text{Term}_C^\tau | \tau \in \text{Type})$ is defined by (we omit the C):

$\text{Var}^\tau \subseteq \text{Term}^\tau$, $D_C^\tau \subseteq \text{Term}^\tau$,

$\text{NEXT} \in \text{Term}^{\text{ind} \to \text{ind}}$, MIN, MAX $\in \text{Term}^{\text{ind}}$, $\text{Opsym}^m \in \text{Term}^{\text{ind} \to .. \to \text{ind}}$.

These are the atomic terms from Term_C.

If $t \in \text{Term}^\sigma$, $y \in \text{Var}^\tau$, then $\lambda y.t \in \text{Term}^{\tau \to \sigma}$.

If $t_0,...,t_C \in \text{Term}^{\text{ind}}$, then $<t_0,...,t_C> \in \text{Term}^{\text{ind} \to \text{ind}}$ (sequence).

We have no primitive recursion. W.r.t. an interpretation C primitive recursion can be represented by a sequence (unwinding the recursion). Term and Term_C are to be carefully distinguished. All notions defined for Term are naturally transferred to Term_C. For $t_0,...,t_C : \tau$, $\tau = \sigma_1 \to .. \to \sigma_n \to \text{ind}$, $<t_0,...,t_C>$

abbreviates $\lambda y_0, y_1, \ldots, y_n . <t_0(y_1) .. (y_n), \ldots, t_C(y_1) .. (y_n) > (y_0)$.

For $t \in Term_C$ the semantics of t, $C[[t]]\mu$ is given by $C[[<t_0, \ldots, t_C>]]\mu(j) = C[[t_j]]\mu$. The rest is as for ordinary terms.

The denotational semantics induces an obvious reduction relation on terms over C: NEXT(m)$\rightarrow$m+1 if m<C, NEXT(C)$\rightarrow$C, MIN$\rightarrow$0, MAX$\rightarrow$C, $(\lambda y.t)(s) \rightarrow t[s/y]$ (β-reduction), $<t_0, \ldots, t_C>(j) \rightarrow t_j$, $\rho(d)(\rho(e)) \rightarrow \rho(d(e))$. Standard λ-calculus techniques prove that for t closed of type ind, $C[[t]] = d$ iff t reduces to d.

1.2 Depth and Length

One may represent terms as trees as follows: Abstraction becomes a node with one son, application a node with two sons, sequence a node with C+1 sons. Then the depth corresponds to the length of the longest branch. Thus, the depth of $t \in Term_C$, Dp t, is defined by: Dp t = 1 if t is atomic; Dp r(s) = 1+max{Dp r, Dp s}; Dp $(\lambda y.t)$ = 1+Dp s; Dp $<t_0, \ldots, t_C>$ = 1+max{Dp t_j}.

The length counts the number of internal nodes and adds the sum of the lengths of the leafs. Therefore, the length of $t \in Term_C$, Lg t, is defined by: Lg t = 1 if t is atomic and $t \notin D$; Lg d is the length of the encoding $\rho(d)$; Lg r(s) = Lg r +Lg s; Lg $(\lambda y.t)$ = 1+Lg t; Lg $<t_0, \ldots, t_C>$ = $1+\sum_j$ Lg t_j.

An easy induction on the structure of terms shows:

Fact

Dp $t \le$ Lg t

Dp t[s/y] $\le$ Dp t +Dp s

Lg t[s/y] $\le$ Lg t $\cdot$ Lg s $\square$

2 Lowering the Rank

The first transformation of this section shows how to use the sequencing operator to eliminate recursion from a given primitive recursive definition w.r.t. an interpretation C. The transformation is inspired by 2.4 in [Schw75]. The second transformation shows how to lower the rank of a given term over C without recursion, such that length and depth increase in a controlled way (cf. 2.10 of [Schw75]).

2.1 Elimination of Recursion

Recursion elimination w.r.t. C is the transformation RE_C:Term$\rightarrow$Term$_C$ given by the following induction on the syntax of terms (we omit the index C):

RE t = t if t is atomic; **RE** t(s) = **RE** t (**RE** s); **RE** $(\lambda y.t)$ = $\lambda y.(\textbf{RE} \ t)$; **RE** R(t) = $\lambda x.<t_0, \ldots, t_C>$ with t_0 = x:τ, t_{j+1} = (**RE** t)(t_j)(j):τ where t:$\tau\rightarrow$ind$\rightarrow\tau$.

Fact

(1) $C[[t]]\mu = C[[\textbf{RE}_Ct]]\mu$

(2)   Lg $(\textbf{RE}_Ct) \le$ p(C) for some polynomial p depending on t. $\square$

2.2 Lowering the Rank

For $n \geq 1$ and an interpretation C the transformation to lower the rank $\mathbf{LR}^{n+1} : \mathrm{Term}_C \to \mathrm{Term}_C$ is defined inductively on the syntax of terms by (omitting the n+1):

$\mathbf{LR}\ t = t$ if t is atomic; $\mathbf{LR}\ r(s) = r'[\mathbf{LR}\ s\ /y]$ provided level $r \geq n+1$ and $\mathbf{LR}\ r = \lambda y.r'$ and $\mathbf{LR}\ r(s) = (\mathbf{LR}\ r)(\mathbf{LR}\ s)$ otherwise; $\mathbf{LR}\ \lambda y.s = \lambda y.(\mathbf{LR}\ s)$; $\mathbf{LR}\ \langle t_0,...,t_C \rangle = \langle \mathbf{LR}\ t_0,...,\mathbf{LR}\ t_C \rangle$.

An induction on the structure of t shows:

Fact

Assume t is of rank n+1 without atomic subterms of level n+1. Then

(1) $C[\![t]\!]\mu = C[\![\mathbf{LR}\ t]\!]\mu$.

(2) $\mathbf{LR}^{n+1}\ t$ contains no subterms of the form r(s) where r is of level n+1.

(3)   If level $t \leq n$, then $\mathbf{LR}^{n+1}\ t$ has rank n.

(4) $\mathrm{Lg}\ (\mathbf{LR}^{n+1}\ t) \leq 2^{\mathrm{Lg}\ t}$,
      $\mathrm{Dp}\ (\mathbf{LR}^{n+1}\ t) \leq \mathrm{Lg}\ t.$ □

3 TIME

3.1 Theorem

Let $N \geq 1$. A global function G is computable in time $\exp_N(p(C))$ for a polynomial p iff there is a primitive recursive rank-(2N+2)-definition which defines G.

Proof: Let G be computed by the Turing machine TM in time $\exp_N(p(x))$. A primitive recursive definition of rank 2N+2 to simulate TM: The configurations of TM with input C are bounded in their length by $\exp_N(p(x))$. Hence, their contents can be represented by a level-(N+1)-variable conf:τ over C. As the single step function of TM involves only simple syntactic manipulations, we can define a primitive recursive definition SING:$\tau \to \tau$ (of level N+2) to simulate this function. Nesting primitive recursion and using N-fold iterated copying made possible by the term $\mathrm{COPY} \equiv \lambda y,z.y(y(z))$ for the levels 2N+2 through N+3, we can generate SING(...(SING(INIT))...) where INIT represents the initial configuration of TM and SING is applied $\exp_N(p(C))$ times. This term simulates TM.

The proof of the opposite direction makes up 3.2 to 3.4 .

3.2 The Evaluation Algorithm

From now on, $N \geq 1$ is fixed, T is a fixed closed primitive recursive definition of first-order type and rank 2N+2. The evaluation algorithm $\mathbf{EVAL}_T$ takes an interpretation C and a vector of individuals $\bar{i}$ as arguments and computes

$$\mathbf{EVAL}_T[C,\bar{i}] = (N+2)\text{–}\mathbf{CBV}\text{–}(N+1)\ [S_C] \text{ where}$$

$$S_C = \mathbf{LR}^{N+3}[...[\mathbf{LR}^{2N+2}[\mathbf{RE}_C\ T]]...]$$

The function procedure **RE** eliminates the recursions in one bottom-up left-to-right pass over the term T using the definitional equations of 2.1. Since the final term and all intermediate terms are of length polynomial in C, **RE** uses time q(C) for some polynomial q.

The function procedure $\mathbf{LR}^j$ applied to a term t reduces redices $(\lambda y.r)(s)$ where $\lambda y.r$ is of level j also in one bottom-up left-to-right pass (this is possible since no new such redices are generated). Therefore, at most Lg t substitutions have to be performed where the length of occurring terms is bounded by $2^{\text{Lg } t}$. Therefore, $\mathbf{LR}^j[t]$ can be computed in time $\exp_1(q(\text{Lg } t))$ for some polynomial q.

From this we conclude: S_C is computed in time $\exp_N(r(C))$ for some polynomial r depending only on T where Lg $S_C \leq \exp_N(r(C))$ and Dp $S_C \leq \exp_{N-1}(r(C))$ (see proposition of 2.2). This difference of one exponentiation between length and depth is crucial for our analysis.

CBV or (N+2)-**CBV**-(N+1), evaluates rank-(N+2)-terms call-by-value for arguments of level $\leq$ N+1, i.e. **CBV** reduces the head redex in $(\lambda y.r)(t_1)..(t_n)$ only if $t_1 \in D$. If $t_1 \notin D$, the value of t_1, $d = C[\![t_1]\!] \in D$ is computed first; then **CBV** proceeds to evaluate $t[d/y](t_2)..(t_n)$. Clearly, $\mathbf{EVAL}_T[C,\bar{i}] = C[\![T]\!](\bar{i})$.

A straight forward application of the reduction rules from 1.1 would give us another evaluation strategy. But, in this strategy there can occur an $\exp_{2N+1}(q(C))$-fold growth due to iterated copying. This growth is avoided by our call-by-value strategy. Note that an evaluation strategy where arguments of level $\geq$ N+2 are evaluated call-by-value also does not stay within the required time bounds.

We show that $\mathbf{EVAL}_T[C,\bar{i}]$ takes time $\leq \exp_N(p(C))$ for some polynomial p depending on T. **CBV** is only applied to particular terms of Term_C: To closed terms of type ind which do not contain elements from D_C of level $\geq$ N+2. The types occurring in these terms are only those which occur as subtypes in S_C. In fact, the set of occurring types is contained even in the set of subtypes occurring in T which is independent of C.

If we talk of terms in relation with **CBV**, we mean terms occurring as subterms (to allow for inductive arguments) of the terms as described above, in particular they only contain free variables and elements from D of level $\leq$ N+1.

The maximal number of argument tuples (w.r.t. C) is given by

$\text{Maxarg}_C = \max\{\text{Card } D_C^{\tau_1} \cdot ... \cdot \text{Card } D_C^{\tau_n} \mid \tau_1 \to ... \to \tau_n \to \text{ind is of level } \leq \text{N+1 and occurs in } S_C\}$.

The maximal length of an element is

$\text{Maxel}_C = \max\{\text{Lg } d \mid d \in D_C^\tau \text{ for a type } \tau \text{ of level } \leq \text{N+1 in } S_C\}$.

We have $\text{Maxarg}_C \leq \exp_N(q(C))$ and $\text{Maxel}_C \leq \exp_N(q(C))$ for a suitable polynomial q.

To estimate the time complexity of **CBV** we prove upper bounds on the total number of recursive calls recursive calls of **CBV** when evaluating some term t.

For a closed term $t \in \text{Term}_C^{\text{ind}}$, Calls t denotes the total number of calls of **CBV** necessary to compute $C[\![t]\!]$. For t not closed and/or of type $\neq$ ind, we define

Calls $t = \max\{\text{calls } t\!\downarrow\!(\bar{d}) \mid \bar{d} \text{ a suitable vector from } D_C \text{ for } \bar{x}\}$.

3.3 Theorem

Calls $t \leq \text{Lg } t \cdot \text{Maxarg}_C^{\text{Dp } t}$ for every term t over C.

As the claim is defined for terms of any type with free variables, it is amenable to an inductive argument on the syntax of terms. It reflects the **CBV**-strategy in that argument terms (being of level $\leq$ N+1) are evaluated for all of their arguments. The remarks on length and depth of S_C imply an $\exp_N(p(C))$ bound on the number of calls of **CBV**.

Proof: Let C be fixed, we sometimes omit the index C.

Induction step:

Assume t is a non-atomic term where $t\downarrow = t\downarrow(\overline{x}) = t(u_1)..(u_n)$, i.e. $\overline{x}$ contains the free variables of t plus the new $u_1,..,u_n$. Let $\overline{d}$ be a vector of elements from D corresponding to $\overline{x}$. Let $t\downarrow(\overline{d}) = t(\overline{d})(d_1)...(d_n)$. We distinguish three cases according to the syntactical structure of t.

Application: Let $t = r(s)$. Then $t\downarrow(\overline{x}) = r(\overline{x})(s(\overline{x}))(u_1)..(u_n)$.

If $s(\overline{d}) = e \in D$, we have Calls $t\downarrow(\overline{d}) =$ Calls $r\downarrow(\overline{d})(e)(d_1)..(d_n)$ which implies the claim by induction hypothesis.

If $s(\overline{d}) \notin D$, we have

$$\text{Calls } t\downarrow(\overline{d}) \leq \text{Calls } s(\overline{d})\cdot\text{Maxarg}_C + \text{Calls } r(\overline{d}) \quad \{\text{The value of } C[\![s(\overline{d})]\!] \text{ is computed first}\}$$

$$\leq \text{Lg } r(s)\cdot\text{Maxarg}_C^{Dp\ r(s)} \quad \text{by ind. hyp.}$$

The remaining cases sequence and abstraction follow easily with the induction hypothesis. $\square$

3.4 Corollary

$EVAL_T[C,\overline{i}]$ takes $exp_N(p(C))$ time for a polynomial p.

Proof: According to 3.3 the computation of $S_C = LR^{N+3}[...[LR^{2N+2}[RE\ T]]...]$ takes $exp_N(r(C))$ time for some polynomial r depending on T where $Lg\ S_C \leq exp_N(r(C))$ and $Dp\ S_C \leq exp_{N-1}(r(C))$.

By 3.4 the computation of $CBV[S_C(\overline{i})]$ uses $exp_N(q(C))$ recursive calls of CBV for some polynomial q. Since during the computation every variable is substituted only by some value of D, it follows that all terms to which CBV is applied are bounded in length by $Lg\ S_C \cdot Maxel_C \leq exp_N(q'(C))$ for some polynomial q'. Thus, a Turing machine using the standard pushdown implementation of CBV returns the result in time $exp_N(p(C))$ for some polynomial p. $\square$

4 SPACE

4.1 Theorem

Let $N \geq 1$. A global function G is computable in space $exp_N(p(C))$ for a polynomial p iff there is a primitive recursive rank-(2N+3)-definition which defines G.

Proof: Let G be computed by the Turing machine TM in space $exp_N(p(C))$. A primitive recursive definition of rank 2N+3 to simulate TM: There is a polynomial q such that TM makes at most $exp_{N+1}(q(C))$ steps on inputs $(C,\overline{i})$ without looping. We proceed as in the time-case. Configurations are represented by the variable conf:τ of level N+1. SING:$\tau \to \tau$ simulates the single step function of TM. To generate SING(...(SING(INIT))...) with $exp_{N+1}(q(C))$ many SINGs we make use of the (N+1)-fold iterated copying ability by using the term COPY (cf. proof of 3.1) for levels 2N+3 through N+3 and nested primitive recursion to generate sufficiently many initial COPYs (of level 2N+3). Note, we have here one level more than in 3.1 for iterated copying.

The proof of the opposite direction makes up the rest of the paper.

4.2 The Evaluation Algorithm

From now on, $N \geq 1$ is fixed, T is a fixed closed primitive recursive definition of first-order type and rank $2N+3$. As in the time-case we define the evaluation algorithm $\mathbf{EVAL_T}$ and show that $\mathbf{EVAL_T}[C,\bar{i}]$ as described below takes space $\leq \exp_N(p(C))$ for some polynomial p depending on T. The evaluation algorithm $\mathbf{EVAL_T}$ takes an interpretation C and a vector of individuals $\bar{i}$ as arguments and computes

$$\mathbf{EVAL_T}[C,\bar{i}] = (N+3)-\mathbf{CBV}-(N+1) \; [S_C] \text{ where}$$

$$S_C = \mathbf{LR}^{N+4}[...[\mathbf{LR}^{2N+3}[\mathbf{RE}_C \; T]]...]$$

The definition of $\mathbf{RE}$ and $\mathbf{LR}^j$ is as in the time case. The analysis in 3.2 shows that S_C is computed in space $\exp_N(q(C))$ for some polynomial q where $\text{Lg } S_C \leq \exp_N(q(C))$ and $\text{Dp } S_C \leq \exp_{N-1}(q(C))$.

After execution of $\mathbf{RE}$ and the $\mathbf{LR}$s $(N+3)$-$\mathbf{CBV}$-$(N+1)$ evaluates terms of rank $N+3$ "call-by-value for arguments of level $\leq N+1$". Hence, arguments of level $N+2$ are not evaluated call-by-value. Note that elements from D of level $N+2$ cannot be represented within the required space bounds.

Let t be a closed term from $\text{Term}_C^{\text{ind}}$. $(N+3)$-$\mathbf{CBV}$-$(N+1)$ (again $\mathbf{CBV}$ for short) differs from $(N+2)$-$\mathbf{CBV}$-$(N+1)$ only in the case where t is an application $t = s(t_1)..(t_n)$ with s not an application i.e. $s = \lambda y.r$. In this case $(N+3)$-$\mathbf{CBV}$-$(N+1)$ behaves as follows:

> If: level $t_1 = N+2$
>> Then: $\mathbf{CBV}[r[t_1/y](t_2)..(t_n)]$; {i.e. t_1 is *not* evaluated in advance}
>> Else: as in the time-case; {i.e. t_1 is evaluated in advance}
> Fi;

Again, $\mathbf{CBV}$ is only applied to particular terms of Term_C: To closed terms of type ind which do not contain elements from D_C of level $\geq N+1$. The types occurring in these terms are only those which occur as subtypes in S_C. In fact, the set of occurring types is contained even in the set of subtypes occurring in T which is independent of C.

If we talk of terms in relation with $\mathbf{CBV}$, we mean terms occurring as subterms (to allow for inductive arguments) of the terms as described above, in particular they only contain free variables of level $\leq N+2$ and elements from D of level $\leq N+1$.

The maximal length of an element (w.r.t. C) is given by

$\text{Maxel}_C = \max\{\text{Lg d} \mid d \in D_C^\tau \text{ for a type } \tau \text{ of level } \leq N+1 \text{ in } S_C\}$.

We have $\text{Maxel}_C \leq \exp_N(q(C))$ for a suitable polynomial q.

For $t \in \text{Term}_C^{\text{ind}}$, t closed, Ncalls t is the maximal number of pending calls to $\mathbf{CBV}$ (i.e. the depth of the recursion stack) when evaluating $\mathbf{CBV}[t]$; Parl t is the maximal length of terms (including t) occurring as actual parameters of $\mathbf{CBV}$ when evaluating $\mathbf{CBV}[t]$.

For arbitrary $t \in \text{Term}_C$ with $t\downarrow = t\downarrow(\bar{y})$ where $\bar{y}$ only contains variables of level at most $N+1$, we define

Ncalls $t = \max\{\text{Ncalls } t\downarrow(\bar{d}) \mid \bar{d} \text{ suitable vector for } \bar{y}\}$

Parl $t = \max\{\text{Parl } t\downarrow(\bar{d}) \mid \bar{d} \text{ suitable vector for } \bar{y}\}$.

Clearly, the space needed for computing $\mathbf{CBV}[t]$ is polynomially related to the product Ncalls t $\cdot$(Parl t $+\text{Maxel}_C$).

4.3 Theorem

Let $t \in \mathrm{Term}_C$, $t{\downarrow} = t{\downarrow}(\overline{x},\overline{y})$ (cf. 4.2) where $\overline{x}$ contains the variables of level N+2 , $\overline{y}$ contains the variables of level $\leq$ N+1. Let $\overline{U} = U_1,..,U_k$ be a vector of closed terms over C corresponding to $\overline{x}$. Let $M \geq$ Ncalls U_j , $K \geq$ Parl U_j, $L \geq$ Lg U_j, Maxel_C . Then

Ncalls $t{\downarrow}(\overline{U},\overline{y}) \leq$ Lg $t^{Dp\,t} + M$,

Parl $t{\downarrow}(\overline{U},\overline{y}) \leq \max\{$Lg $t^{Dp\,t}{\cdot}L$, K$\}$.

These formulas reflect our evaluation strategy in that the U_j are evaluated only after their arguments, being of level $\leq$ N+1, are already evaluated. The evaluation of the U_j takes place independent of the evaluation of t. That implies that the numbers of pending calls and the parameter lengthes occurring in evaluating U_j mix in a controlled and simple way with the numbers of pending calls and parameter lengthes inside of t. The remarks in 4.2 imply an $\exp_N(p(C))$ bound both on the number of pending calls of **CBV** in **EVAL**$_T[C,\overline{i}]$ and on the lengthes of actual parameters of these calls.

Proof: If t is atomic the assertion trivially is true.

Induction step:

Let t be a non-atomic term with $t{\downarrow}(\overline{x},\overline{y}) = (t(\overline{x},\overline{y}))(u_1)..(u_n)$. Let $\overline{d}$ a vector of elements from D_C corresponding to $\overline{y}$ and $t{\downarrow}(\overline{U},\overline{d}) = (t(\overline{U},\overline{d}))(d_1)..(d_n)$. We distinguish three cases.

Application: Let $t = r(s)$. Let $r{\downarrow} = r{\downarrow}(u_0,\overline{x},\overline{y}) = r(u_0)(u_1)..(u_n)$.

Let level $s \leq$ N+1 . If $s(\overline{U},\overline{d}) = e \in D$, then

Ncalls $t{\downarrow}(\overline{U},\overline{d}) =$ Ncalls $r{\downarrow}(e,\overline{U},\overline{d})$

Parl $t{\downarrow}(\overline{U},\overline{d}) =$ Parl $r{\downarrow}(e,\overline{U},\overline{d})$

which implies the claim by the induction hypothesis.

If $s(\overline{U},\overline{d}) \notin D$ then

      Ncalls $t{\downarrow}(\overline{U},\overline{d}) =$ Ncalls $r{\downarrow}(s(\overline{U},\overline{d}),\overline{U},\overline{d})$

                 $\leq \max\{1+$Ncalls $s(\overline{U},\overline{d})$, Ncalls $r{\downarrow}(u_0,\overline{U},\overline{d})\}$ by definition of **CBV**

                 $\leq$ Lg $t^{Dp\,t}+M$ by ind. hyp.

      Parl $t{\downarrow}(\overline{U},\overline{d}) =$ Parl $r{\downarrow}(s(\overline{U},\overline{d}),\overline{U},\overline{d})$

                 $\leq \max\{$Lg $t{\downarrow}(\overline{U},\overline{d})$, Parl $s(\overline{U},\overline{d})$, Parl $r(u_0,\overline{U},\overline{d})\}$ by definition of **CBV**

                 $\leq \max\{$Lg $t^{Dp\,t}{\cdot}L$, K$\}$ by ind. hyp.

Now, assume level $s = $ N+2. Then

      Ncalls $t{\downarrow}(\overline{U},\overline{d}) =$ Ncalls $r{\downarrow}(s(\overline{U},\overline{d}),\overline{U},\overline{d})$

                 $\leq$ Lg $r^{Dp\,r}+\max\{M,$ Ncalls $s(\overline{U},\overline{d})\}$ by ind. hyp.

                 $\leq$ Lg $r^{Dp\,r}+$Lg $s^{Dp\,s}+M \leq$ Lg $t^{Dp\,t}+M$

      Parl $t{\downarrow}(\overline{U},\overline{d}) =$ Parl $r{\downarrow}(s(\overline{U},\overline{d}),\overline{U},\overline{d})$

                 $\leq \max\{$Lg $t{\downarrow}(\overline{U},\overline{d})$, Lg $r^{Dp\,r}{\cdot}$Lg $s{\cdot}L$, Lg $s^{Dp\,s}{\cdot}L$, K$\}$ by ind. hyp.

$$\leq \max\{ \text{Lg } r(s)^{Dp\ r(s)}\cdot L,\ K\}$$

The other cases are easier and follow with the definition of CBV and the induction hypothesis. □

Analogously to 3.4 we derive:

4.4 Corollary

$EVAL_T[C,\bar{i}]$ takes $\exp_N(p(C))$ space for a polynomial p. □

Conclusion

The time case compared to [Go89a]: In [Go89a] we have shown that rank-2-definitions characterize PTIME. To show that rank-2-definitions can be evaluated in polynomial time, we used the strategy **2-CBV-1**. In the present paper we showed for N≥1 that rank-(2N+2)-definitions are in DTIME($\exp_N$(poly)). We could *not* generalize the methods of [Go89a] in an obvious way to higher ranks and use **(2N+2)-CBV-(N+1)**: for this, one somehow has to keep track of all the reductions occurring at levels ≥ N+2. Instead, we first eliminate primitive recursion and lower the rank to N+2. Then we apply **(N+2)-CBV-(N+1)**. The price to be paid is, that one rank-(2N+2)-definition induces a different rank-(N+2)-term for each C. This means that our inductive analysis must be uniform in some features (here length and depth) of the term. In [Go89a] this was not necessary. Similar arguments apply to the space case.

Conversely note, that the method used here to show that primitive recursive definitions can be evaluated within certain bounds: Eliminate recursion first, lower rank, then evaluate,- does *not* yield the results of [Go89a] for rank 2 and rank 3 either. The reason is that in eliminating primitive recursion, the depth of the resulting term becomes polynomial in C. Since in our inductive arguments of 3.3 and 4.3 the depth occurs in the exponent, no polynomial resource bound can be derived.

Literature

[Ba84]   Barendregt, H., The lambda calculus. North Holland 1984.

[Go89a]   Goerdt, A., Characterizing complexity classes by higher type primitive recursive definitions, LICS (1989), 364-374.

[Go89b]   Goerdt, A., Characterizing complexity classes by finitely typed λ-terms, Workshop Computer Science Logic 1988, LNCS, to appear.

[Gu83]   Gurevich, Y., Algebras of feasible functions, 24th FOCS (1983), 210-214.

[Gu84]   Gurevich, Y., Toward logic taylored for computational complexity, computation and proof theory, LNM 1104 (1984), 175-216.

[Im87]   Immerman, N., Expressibility as a complexity measure: results and directions, 2nd Conf. Structure in Complexity Theory (1987), 194-202.

[KfTiUr87] Kfoury, A., Tiuryn, J.,Urzyczyn, P., The hierarchy of finitely typed functional programs, LICS (1987), 225-235.

[Lei87]   Leivant, D., Characterization of complexity classes in higher order logic, 2nd conf. Structure in Complexity Theory (1987), 203-218.

[Pl77]   Plotkin, G., LCF considered as a programming language, TCS 5 (1977), 223-257.

[Schw75]   Schwichtenberg, H., Elimination of higher type levels in definitions of primitive recursive functions by means of transfinite recursion, Logic Colloquium 1973, North Holland.

[Sa80]   Sazonov, V., Polynomial computability and recursivity in finite domains, EIK 16 (1980), 319-323.

[Te82]   Terlouw, J., On the definition trees of ordinal recursive functionals: reduction of recursion orders by means of type level raising, J. Symbolic Logic 47 (1982), 395-403.

[Ti86]   Tiuryn, J., Higher order arrays and stacks in programming: An application of complexity theory to logics of programs, 12th MFCS (1986), LNCS 233, 177-198.

[TiUr83]   Tiuryn, J.,Urzyczyn, P., Some connections between logic of programs and complexity theory. 24th FOCS (1983), 180-184.

The Distributed Termination Problem : Formal Solution and Correctness Based on Petri Nets [1]

Dominik Gomm   Rolf Walter

Technische Universität München, Institut für Informatik, Arcisstraße 21, D-8000 München 2

1 Introduction

A network of processes exchanging information by message passing is called a distributed system. Each process has computing and storage facilities and is connected to some other processes via bidirectional communication channels. Termination detection in such a distributed system is one of the classical theoretical problems dealing with local protocols to achieve global knowledge about the system state.

In the literature various solutions are proposed. They differ in their algorithmic idea and in their level of formal representation. Our work is based on [9] which generalizes the restrictive but interesting concept of [3] to consider a distributed computation as a *Diffusing Computation* towards *Multi Diffusing Computations*. The solution proposed in [9] was the first that fulfills the quality criteria of genericity, symmetry and indulgence. This was done by computing monotonous local states, thereby achieving consistent global system states without the need of synchronization mechanisms like interruption of the message exchange during a global state check. (i.e. [5]).

To verify a solution correctly a formal model for the description of nonsequential behaviour must be chosen for both the problem specification and the modelling of the algorithm. The solution presented in this paper is based on Petri nets with structured tokens introduced in [8]. Besides the powerful modelling facilities adequate for dealing with distributed systems and the clarity of their graphical representations, Petri nets supply a lot of analysis techniques for formal verification. In this paper we will use particularly *place invariants*, and we will integrate graphtheoretical concepts into the calculus by regarding some predicates in the set of reachable markings.

Chapter 2 gives some basic definitions. In chapter 3 the problem is specified as a property of a Petri net for an arbitrary distributed computation. A solution is given by two net extensions in chapter 4. We begin with a protocol for computing a stable meaningful condition. Then a diffusion protocol is specified to visit all processes. Thereby the stable condition is used as a delay. Both protocols together are verified to detect distributed termination always and correctly.

2 Basic definitions

Definition 2.1 *A net is a triple* $N = (P, T, F)$ *with* $P \cap T = \emptyset$ *and* $F \subseteq ((P \times T) \cup (T \times P))$. *P and T are sets of places resp. transitions; F is the set of arcs between them.* ∎

Nets are used as models of concurrent systems in the following way: places (O) represent local states, transitions (□) represent action schemes. A *high level net system* is an annotated net [7]. Annotations are *terms* generated by a *multiset* specification $\widehat{SPEC} = (\widehat{S}, \widehat{OP}, \widehat{E})$ and a set of variables X. $\widehat{SPEC}$ is a canonical extension of a given specification $SPEC = (S, OP, E)$ [4, 8] (see figure 1). Figure 2 shows the specification for an (multiset) algebra which will be used for the

---

[1]partly supported by DFG-SFB 342, W.G. A3: SEMAFOR and Esprit Basic Research Action No. 3148: DEMON

modelling of the distributed termination problem and its canonical multiset extension.

sorts: m_s

opns: $\check{O} :\longrightarrow m_s$

$MAKE_s^+ : s \longrightarrow m_s$

$MAKE_s^- : s \longrightarrow m_s$

$+_s : m_s\, m_s \longrightarrow m_s$

eqns: $a \in s,\ p,q,r \in m_s$

$+_s(p,\check{O}) = p$

$+_s(p,q) = +_s(q,p)$

$+_s(p,+_s(q,r)) = +_s(+_s(p,q),r)$

$+_s(MAKE_s^+, MAKE_s^-) = \check{O}$

sorts: processes, messtypes, channels, messages

opns: $p_1...p_n :\longrightarrow$ processes

$w_1...w_n, e, c :\longrightarrow$ messtypes

$COMM$: processes processes $\longrightarrow$ channels

$MESS$: channels messtypes $\longrightarrow$ message

$SEND$: channels $\longrightarrow$ processes

REC: channels $\longrightarrow$ processes

OWN: messages $\longrightarrow$ processes

eqns: $p,q \in$ processes, $z \in$ messtypes

$SEND(COMM(p,q)) = p$

$REC(COMM(p,q)) = q$

$OWN(MESS(COMM(p,q)),c) = p$

$OWN(MESS(COMM(p,q)),e) = q$

Fig.1 : *Multiset specification $\widehat{SPEC}$ for SPEC*   Fig.2 : Specification for the solution

We denote with T(X) the set of $\widehat{SPEC}$-terms, with $GT \subset T(X)$ the set of *ground*-terms, i.e. terms without variables. The set of *positive*-terms $T^+(X)(orGT^+)$ comprises all terms which are equal to terms which do not use the '-' operation. We call t_1 *less-equal* t_2 $(t_1 \leq t_2)$ iff $t_1 - t_2 \in T^+(X)$.

Definition 2.2 *A SPEC-inscribed high level system $\Sigma = (N, X, \tau, M^0)$ consists of*
(i) a net $N = (P,T,F)$ and a set of variables X,
(ii) a mapping $M^0 : P \rightarrow GT^+$, called initial marking of Σ, and
(iii) a mapping $\tau : F \rightarrow T^+(X)$, called arc inscription of Σ. ∎

Often it is useful to use an extended arc inscription $\overset{p,t}{\rightarrow}: (P \times T) \cup (T \times P) \rightarrow T^+(X)$ defined by

$$\overset{x,y}{\rightarrow}= \begin{cases} \tau(x,y) & \text{iff } (x,y) \in F \\ \check{O} & \text{otherwise (with } \check{O} \text{ denoting the empty multiset)} \end{cases}$$

For each $t \in T$ the *transition vector* $\underline{t} : P \rightarrow T_{\widehat{OP}}(X)$ is defined by $\underline{t} =\overset{t,p}{\rightarrow} - \overset{p,t}{\rightarrow}$.
System dynamics is described by the following definition:

Definition 2.3 *Let Σ be a SPEC-inscribed high level system.*
(i) Markings of N are mappings $M : P \rightarrow GT^+$. We call these ground-terms tokens.
(ii) An occurrence mode on N is an assignment $\beta : X \rightarrow GT^+$.
(iii) A transition $t \in T$ is enabled in mode β at a marking M iff for all $p \in P$: $\bar{\beta}(\overset{p,t}{\rightarrow}) \leq M(p)$
$(\bar{\beta} : T(X) \rightarrow GT$ denotes the canonical extension of β to terms).
(iv) If t is β-enabled at M, t may occur in mode β. The occurence of t in mode β (we write $M \overset{t,\beta}{\rightarrow} M'$)
leads to a follower marking M' which is defined for each $p \in P$ by $M'(p) = M(p) - \bar{\beta}(\overset{p,t}{\rightarrow}) + \bar{\beta}(\overset{t,p}{\rightarrow})$.
(v) For a marking M of N, the set $[M\rangle$ of reachable markings from M is the smallest set of markings
such that $M \in [M\rangle$ and if $M' \in [M\rangle$ and $M' \overset{t,\beta}{\rightarrow} M''$ then $M'' \in [M\rangle$. ∎

The most important analysis tool for Petri nets are place invariants, that is an invariant vector specified by a weight-mapping W.

Definition 2.4 *Let $SIG =< S, OP >$ be a signature, X and Y sets of pairwise disjoint variables.*
For $t, t_1, t_2 \in T(X), u \in T(Y)$ and m_d a one-elementary multiset $MAKE(d)$ we define:
$m_d \cdot u = u_Y^{m_d}$ (see below), $(t_1 + t_2) \cdot u = t_1 \cdot u + t_2 \cdot u$, $(-t_1) \cdot u = -(t_1 \cdot u)$.
$u_Y^{m_d}$ denotes the term u with all variables occuring in u substituted by m_d. ∎

Using the above product place invariants can be defined such that the weighted markings $M' \cdot W$ are constant for each reachable marking $M' \in [M\rangle$. markings. Furthermore they can be characterized as solutions of an equational system derived from N.

Definition 2.5 *Let Σ be a SPEC-inscribed high level system and Y a set of variables disjoint from X. A vector $i : P \to T_{\widehat{OP}}(Y)$ is a place invariant of sort s of N iff for all markings M, M' of N with $M' \in [M]$: $M \cdot i = M' \cdot i$.* ∎

Theorem 2.6 *Let Σ be a SPEC-inscribed high level system and Y a set of variables disjoint from X, and $i : P \to T(Y)$ a place invariant. If $\underline{t} \cdot i = \check{O}$ for all $t \in T$, then i is a place invariant.*

Proof: see [8] ∎

Clearly all definitions have to be made sound considering the different sorts of terms. We skipped this in favour of simplicity, for details we refer to [4, 8].

3 Specification of the distributed termination problem

Instead of talking intuitively about the problem we will model the behaviour of the processes in a distributed system as a Petri net. This will lead us to a formal specification of the problem, particularly to the definition of a global system state meeting *distributed termination*, thereby leaving no formal gap between the problem and its solution.

Figure 3 specifies the behaviour of a process p in the distributed system. Initially the process p is *active* and may compute locally (E), send messages to neighbours (A), or receive arriving messages (B). The forwarding of messages is controlled by the neighbourhood place *nb1*. For each reachable marking, *nb1* holds the set of p's outgoing channels represented by the term ν_p. This guarantees $\beta(y)$ being a neighbour of p for every transition occurence of A in mode $\beta(x) = p$. p doesn't know anything about channels between two other processes.

Whenever p finishes its local computation, p may become *passive* (C). A passive process can only receive messages. After that it is active. We abstract from the concrete task of each process and the content of each message. With the distributed termination problem in mind we are only interested in the change of the local states active and passive.

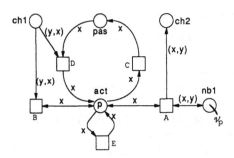

Fig.3 : Behaviour of a process p   Fig.4 : Behaviour of all processes

All processes behave similarly. Therefore, their behaviour is folded into one net in figure 4 (transition E is omitted). For each process the incoming and outgoing channels *ch1* and *ch2*, respectively, are folded into one single place *cha*, too. The initial marking yields the sum of the initial markings of figure 3 for each process : All processes are active and place *nb1* is marked with all the channels $\nu = \sum_{i=1}^{n} \nu_{p_i}$. Each transition occurence in mode β is a local event of process $\beta(x)$.

Regarding the set of reachable markings there exists exactly one reachable marking M^{Term} under which no further event can happen. It holds: $M_{cha}^{Term} = M_{act}^{Term} = \check{O}$. If no process is active, and no message is in transit the distributed system is terminated.

4 Formal solution to the distributed termination problem

The task is now to find a protocol such that every process can detect M^{Term} always and correctly. M^{Term} is a global system state consisting of the local states of all processes and channels. Each process can only determine its own local state. Even a passive process p cannot be sure about being passive forever.

The desired protocol should give each process a global view of the system relevant to the problem. It has to be realized distributedly and without the assumption of global time. There are two main problems to be solved:

- A global view of the system must consist of some local conditions of all processes.
- The global view must be *consistent*: All these local conditions must be valid concurrently:

The first problem can be solved by a general *Diffusion Algorithm* flooding the whole system with control messages. Thereby a set of communication channels is chosen nondeterministically upon local decisions spanning up a tree on the communcation graph. The tree structure is used for visiting all processes. This permits the root process to collect informations about all processes.

To solve the consistency problem a protocol for computing local *traffic lights* is modelled as a net extension of figure 4. Initially all traffic lights are *red*. Upon local decisions they can change to *green*. Green traffic lights never swap to red again. We will verify that all processes having green traffic lights is equivalent to no process being active and no message in transit. In a last step the two protocols are linked together efficiently: Each process delays the diffusion until its traffic light is green. Doing so, there is no need for additional synchronization mechanisms in the diffusion protocol, and a root process detects distributed termination iff the tree traversal is finished. Consistency of the information that all processes have green traffic lights is gained due to the *stability* of green.

4.1 Protocol for computing a meaningful stable condition

A condition is said to be meaningful if all processes satisfying this condition is equivalent to no process being active and no message in transit. Such a condition cannot be the local states passive, because all processes being passive gives no information about the number of messages in transit.

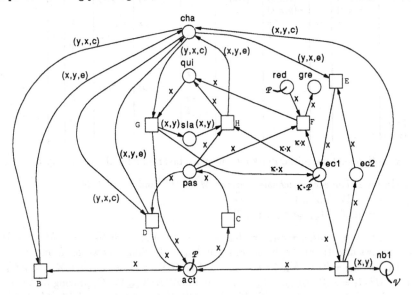

Fig.5 : Protocol for computing conditions *quiet* and *green*

All channels must be empty, too. In the case of asynchronous communication, messages are physically on the way, and no time limit for their run time can be given.

Figure 5 shows the protocol that enables the processes to compute a meaningful condition *quiet*. Every receipt of a message is immediately acknowledged by sending back an echo (B or D). Analogously a process receives echos (E). For every message forwarded by a process p, p waits for an echo (*ec2*). Only in the case of all echos received (κ tokens p on *ec1*), p can be sure about having empty outgoing channels. If p is passive, too, then p may become quiet (F). By that, quiet is a meaningful local condition, but can be destroyed locally upon message receipt (G), i.e. is not stable.

Instead of having a protocol that checks if all processes are quiet (and which indeed would require synchronization mechanisms to guarantee their consistency) we refine the reply mechanism to compute a *stable* meaningful condition. This is specified in figure 5, too. Whenever a process becomes quiet the first time (F), its traffic light swaps from *red* to *green*. A green process p changes its protocol behaviour: When p gets reactivated (G), p does not reply this message receipt immediately, but stores the sender q of this message on place *sla*. We speak of p being enslaved by master q if $M_{sla} \geq (p,q)$. The acknowledgement of messages is now controlled *very first in/very last out*. An enslaved process sends back the echo to its master upon becoming quiet again (H). This guarantees this echo to be the last one forwarded during slavery. Transition F is not enabled any more because of the condition red in its preset.

4.1.1 Safety and liveness properties

Obviously, the condition green is stable. This supports an easy collection in a diffusion protocol. But to ensure that this collection makes any sense at all we first have to verify that green is a meaningful condition. In the case of a *safety* argument we have to show that the distributed computation is terminated if all processes are green. Using one of the place invariants given in figure 6 we first show that quiet is a meaningful condition. Furthermore we can ensure that there are no more echos in transit if all processes are quiet, and that no process is enslaved by a quiet process.

	A	B	C	D	E	F	G	H	M_0	i_4	i_5	i_6
cha	(x,y,c)	(x,y,e) $-(y,x,c)$		(x,y,e) $-(y,x,c)$	$-(y,x,e)$		$-(y,x,c)$	(x,y,e)				$OWN(z)$
act	$x-x$	$x-x$	$-x$	x			x		$\mathcal{P}$	s		
pas			x	$-x$		$-x$		$-x$		s		
ec1	$-x$				x	$-\kappa \cdot x$	$\kappa \cdot x$	$-\kappa \cdot x$	$\kappa \cdot \mathcal{P}$			s
ec2	x				$-x$							
qui					x		$-x$	x		s	s	$\kappa \cdot s$
sla							$-(x,y)$	(x,y)			$SEND(z)$	$REC(z)$
red						$-x$			$\mathcal{P}$		s	
gre						x						
nbl	(x,y) $-(x,y)$								$\mathcal{V}$			

Fig.6 : Transition vectors, initial marking and place invariants for the net in fig. 5

Proposition 4.1 *For each reachable marking $M \in [M^0\rangle$ and $p \in \mathcal{P}$ holds:*
(a) $M_{qui} = \mathcal{P} \Rightarrow OWN(M_{cha}) + M_{act} = \breve{O}$
(b) $M_{qui} \geq p \Rightarrow REC(M_{sla}) \not\geq p$ for $p \in \mathcal{P}$

Proof: We get from i_4: $M_{act} + M_{pas} + M_{qui} = M_{act} \cdot s + M_{pas} \cdot s + M_{qui} \cdot s = M \cdot i_4 = M^0 \cdot i_4 = \mathcal{P}$. $M_{act} = \breve{O}$ follows directly under the assumption $M_{qui} = \mathcal{P}$. Similarly we get from i_7:
$OWN(M_{cha}) + M_{ec1} + REC(M_{sla}) + \kappa \cdot M_{qui} = M_{cha} \cdot OWN(t) + M_{ec1} \cdot s + \kappa \cdot M_{qui} \cdot s + M_{sla} \cdot REC(z)$
$= M \cdot i_7 = M^0 \cdot i_7 = \kappa \cdot \mathcal{P}$. Again, $M_{qui} = \mathcal{P}$ implies $OWN(M_{cha}) = \breve{O}$, proving part (a).
(b) follows from i_7 for any $p \in \mathcal{P}$ with $M_{qui} \geq p$: $OWN(M_{cha}) + M_{ec1} + REC(M_{sla}) \not\geq p$. ∎

Furthermore we can prove that quiet processes are not enslaved. More generally holds: Each process is either red, quiet or enslaved.

Proposition 4.2 *For each reachable marking $M \in [M^0\rangle$ holds: $M_{qui} + M_{red} + SEND(M_{sla}) = \mathcal{P}$.*

Proof: $M_{red} + M_{qui} + SEND(M_{sla}) = M_{red} \cdot s + M_{qui} \cdot s + M_{sla} \cdot SEND(z) = M \cdot i_5 = M^0 \cdot i_5 = \mathcal{P}$. ∎

By the very first in/very last out echo control, *trees* underlying the communication graph are constructed dynamically. Using Petri nets there is no need for arguing informally about such invariant properties of graphtheoretical means. They can be stated formally and elegantly if we integrate such constructions in the calculus of Petri nets.

Definition 4.3 *For each reachable markings $M \in [M^0\rangle$ the marking graph $W_M = (N_M, E_M)$ is defined by $N_M = \{p \in P \mid SEND(M_{sla}) + REC(M_{sla}) \geq p\}$ and $E_M = \{(p,q) \mid M_{sla} \geq (q,p)\}$* ∎

A process r, being enslaved by neighbour q, defines an edge in the graph leading from the master to the slave. Nodes are all masters and slaves. As an invariant property we can show that this graph forms a set (or wood) of trees.

Proposition 4.4 *For each reachable marking $M \in [M^0\rangle$: W_M is a set of disjoint trees.*

Proof: We apply structural induction over $[M^0\rangle$: $W_{M^0} = (\emptyset, \emptyset)$ is the empty set of disjoint trees. Let W_M be a set of disjoint trees and $\xrightarrow{t,\beta}$ a step. If $t \notin \{G, H\}$ then $W_{M'} = W_M$. For $t = H$ we yield $W_{M'} \subset W_M$, implying that $W_{M'}$ is a set of disjoint trees, too.
Let $t = G$ and $\beta(x) = p, \beta(y) = q$. Then $M_{qui} \geq p$ holds because G is M-enabled. This implies $SEND(M_{sla}) + REC(M_{sla}) \not\geq p$ (4.1b and 4.2). This yields $p \notin W_M$ by definition. By that, no cycle exists in $E_{M'} = E_M \cup \{(q,p)\}$, and $W_{M'}$ is a set of disjoint trees. ∎

Enslaved processes and their masters are nodes in the tree by definition. More relations between the state of a process and its appearance in the marking graph can be stated, e.g. quiet ones are not represented in the tree, and root nodes have to be red.

Proposition 4.5 *For each reachable marking $M \in [M^0\rangle$ holds:*
(a) $M_{qui} \geq p \Rightarrow p \notin N_M$
(b) p is root-node in $W_m \Rightarrow M_{red} \geq p$

Proof: (a) is shown as part of proof for 4.4. From $p \in N_M \wedge SEND(M_{sla}) \not\geq p$ we get with (a): $M_{qui} \not\geq p \wedge SEND(M_{sla}) \not\geq p$ and with proposition 4.2 : $M_{red} \geq p$. ∎

A process, which is a root node in W_M, may only become green if all enslaved processes in its tree became quiet causally before. We can speak roughly of root processes taking care of all processes in its tree, realized by missing some echos of particularly these processes. Conversely we conclude, that as long as one process is active, there will always be at least one red process, maybe itself, taking care of the active one. Such intuitive operational reasoning often leads to errors, but to ensure that the protocol is safe we can prove the following proposition formally:

Proposition 4.6 *For all $M \in [M^0\rangle$ holds: $M_{gre} = \mathcal{P} \Rightarrow M_{cha} + M_{act} = \breve{O}$*

Proof: We have $M_{red} = \breve{O}$ if and only if $M_{gre} = \mathcal{P}$. From $M_{red} = \breve{O}$ we get: $M_{qui} + SEND(M_{sla}) = \mathcal{P}$ (proposition 4.2)   and $W_M = (\emptyset, \emptyset)$ (proposition 4.5b). Because empty trees have no inner nodes, $SEND(M_{sla}) = \breve{O}$ holds, ensuring $M_{qui} = \mathcal{P}$: All processes are quiet. The proposition follows directly from proposition 4.1a. ∎

Reversely the protocol of figure 4 can be shown to be *live (deadlock free)*, i.e. after termination of the distributed computation all processes eventually become green. Only transitions E,F and H may still be enabled. The only events which can happen are the receipt of echoes and the change from passive to quiet until all processes have green traffic lights. A simple progress assumption for permanently enabled transitions is sufficient for a more formal proof.

4.2 Protocol for visiting all processes

The stable condition green can now be used as a delay in a general *diffusion algorithm* [1]. Figure 7 shows the first part of this protocol using the same communication graph. Initially only one process p can start a *wave* by sending exactly one wave-message to each of its neighbours (J). The tokens on place *nb2* are converted into wave-messages on p's outgoing channels.

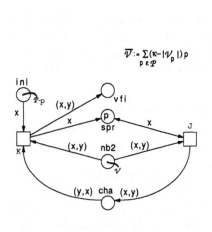

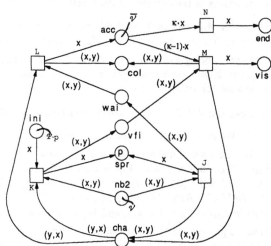

Fig.7 : Spreading a wave to each process   Fig.8 : Protocol to visit each process in a wave

Each process q different to p can receive only one wave-message chosen nondeterministically from one of its neighbours. The sender r of that message is stored on place *vfi*. Causally after receipt q spreads wave-messages to all its neighbours but r: the corresponding token was removed from place *nb2* upon receipt. Thereby (analogously to 4.3,4.4) a tree with root p is induced dynamically.

Proposition 4.7 *For each reachable marking* $M \in [M^0)$, *the graph* $T_M = (N_M, E_M)$ *with* $N_M = \{q \mid M_{vfi} \geq (q,r) + (r,q)\}$ *and* $E_M = \{(q,r) \mid M_{vfi} \geq (r,q)\}$ *is a tree.* ∎

In a maximal protocol execution every process will be reached by a wave-message such that the tree is spanning, i.e. all processes are nodes. Figure 8 shows the remaining part of the protocol. Every process may receive all other wave-messages (L) only after the receipt of a first message (K) and the spreading of the wave (J). Each process stores all received messages but the first on place *col* and counts them on place *acc*. A process q can send back the wave-message received very first (M) only if q has received wave-messages from all its other neighbours, too. This guarantees that the message received very first is dispatched very last. This is q's last action in the protocol: A token q on place *vis* indicates that process q has been visited. By this local very first in/very last out message control a global causality order is obtained : Each path of the spanning tree gets reduced deterministically bottom up until p receives wave-messages from all its neighbours and finishes the tree traversal (N).

4.2.1 Safety and liveness properties of the diffusion protocol

We show that all processes have been visited in p's wave if p receives messages from all its neighbours. The main argument is that the spanning tree can be reduced only bottom up: Processes are visited only from the leafs to the root. To prove this, some invariant properties are explained.
i_1 states that the weighted sum of tokens on the places $nb2, vfi, wai, acc, vis$, and end is κ for each process. In particular:

1. *If a process q waits for a message, q neither has been visited nor can be visited.*

For each $M \in [M^0\rangle$ we get from i_1: $SEND(M_{nb2} + M_{vfi} + M_{wai}) + M_{acc} + \kappa \cdot (M_{vis} + M_{end}) = M_{nb2} \cdot SEND(z) + M_{vfi} \cdot SEND(z) + M_{wai} \cdot SEND(z) + M_{acc} \cdot s + M_{vis} \cdot \kappa \cdot s + M_{end} \cdot \kappa \cdot s = M \cdot i_1 = M_0 \cdot i_1 = \nu \cdot SEND(z) + \bar{\nu} \cdot s = \kappa \cdot \mathcal{P}$. For each process q there are exactly κ tokens (with first component q) on the specified places. We assume that $SEND(M_{wai}) \geq q$ holds.
If $M_{vis} + M_{end} \geq q$, the left side of the equation would yield more than κ tokens for process q. Therefore the transitions M and N in the preset of vis and end have not occured so far. Analogously, $SEND(M_{vfi} + M_{acc}) \not\geq \kappa \cdot q$ holds : The transitions M and N are not enabled for process q. ∎

	J	K	L	M	N	M_0	i_1	i_2	i_3
cha	(x,y)	$-(y,x)$	$-(y,x)$	(x,y)					$z+\hat{z}$
spr	$x-x$	x				p			
nb2	$-(x,y)$	$-(x,y)$				ν	$SEND(z)$	z	
vfi		(x,y)		$-(x,y)$			$SEND(z)$	z	$z+\hat{z}$
ini		$-x$				$\mathcal{P}-p$			
wai	(x,y)		$-(x,y)$				$SEND(z)$	z	$-z-\hat{z}$
acc		x	$-(\kappa-1)\cdot x$	$-\kappa \cdot x$		$\bar{\nu}$	s		
end					x		$-\kappa \cdot s$		
vis					x		$-\kappa \cdot s$		
col			(x,y)	(x,y)				z	

$\hat{z}$ is a shortcut for: $COMM(REC(z), SEND(z))$

Fig.9 : Transition vectors, initial marking and place invariants for the net in fig.8

Information about the message exchange between two neighbouring processes is exhibited by i_2. Messages are exchanged in none, both or one of the two directions. Especially holds:

2. *A process doesn't wait for a message from a neighbour he received the first message from.*

For $M \in [M^0\rangle$ we get from i_2: $M_{nb2} + M_{vfi} + M_{wai} + M_{col} = M_{nb2} \cdot z + M_{vfi} \cdot z + M_{wai} \cdot z + M_{col} \cdot z = M \cdot i_2 = M_0 \cdot i_2 = \nu \cdot z = \nu$. Each token (q,r), initially on place $nb2$, lies always exclusively on one of the specified places. Particularly holds : $M_{vfi} \geq (q,r)$ implies $M_{wai} \not\geq (q,r)$. ∎

Using i_3 we prove for each token (r,q) on place vfi the existence of a token (q,r) on place wai.

3. *If q received the first message from r and had not sent it back, then r waits for a message from q.*

Assume that $M_{vfi} \geq (q,r)$. Using $M \cdot i_3 = M_0 \cdot i_3$, we conclude $M_{wai} \geq (q,r)$ or $M_{wai} \geq (r,q)$ because i_3 has exactly one negative entry at place wai, and the specified places are all initially unmarked. $M_{wai} \geq (q,r)$ can be ruled out (2). This yields $M_{wai} \geq (r,q)$. ∎

Using these invariant deductions, the *safety property* can be verified very easily:

Proposition 4.8 *Let $M \in [M^0\rangle$ be a reachable marking and a process r a node but not a leaf in G_M. Then r cannot send its last wave-message.*

Proof: Due to the premise there exists a process q such that $M_{vfi} \geq (q,r)$. Then $M_{wai} \geq (r,q)$ holds because of (3). By that and (1) the transitions M and N are not M-enabled and have not occured causally before in a mode $\beta(x) = r$. ∎

Analogously, we can show that the protocol is *live*, that means free of any deadlock. In [6] we considered maximal runs of the protocol which are acyclic Petri nets with unbranched places. Due to the lack of space a sketch of this proof is given arguing about markings and invariant properties. We will verify that the tree in fact gets reduced, i.e. processes become visited bottom up.

Proposition 4.9 *Let $M \in [M^0\rangle$ and q a leaf node of a maximally constructed path in G_M. Then for all $M' \in [M\rangle$ a reachable marking $M'' \in [M'\rangle$ exists with $M''_{vis} \geq q$.*

Proof: It holds $M_{vfi} \geq (q,q')$ for exactly one process q' (q is inner node) and $M_{vfi} \not\geq (q',q)$ for any process q' (q is a leaf). Because the forwarding and receipt of messages can be permanently activated we assume $M_{nb2} + M_{cha} = \breve{0}$ in the following. From i_1 we get $SEND(M_{wai} + M_{acc} \geq (\kappa - 1) \cdot q$. Transition M is M-activated or there exists any process r (which cannot be q') with $M_{wai} \geq (q, r)$. Assuming this, we get from i_3 : $M_{vfi} \geq (q, r)$ or $M_{vfi} \geq (r, q)$. Both cases are not possible, because G_M is a tree, and q is a leaf node.

The transition M must be enabled, and no other transition can consume the tokens from its preset. In a maximal protocol execution transition M will always occur in mode $\beta(x) = q$. ∎

The leafs of the spanning tree will send their last wave-messages. Their unique predecessors in the tree eventually become leafs if all descendants have sent their last wave-messages. At least, p itself is a leaf, and transition N is enabled in mode $\beta(x) = p$ analogously to transition M for all other processes such that p eventually finishes its wave.

4.2.2 Usage of the stable condition in the diffusion protocol

Both protocols are linked together now in a nice way (figure 10): the traversal has to respect the traffic regulations using red traffic lights as a delay. Both protocols can be performed concurrently. Only transitions M and N have in their presets the place *gre* to model the intended behaviour.

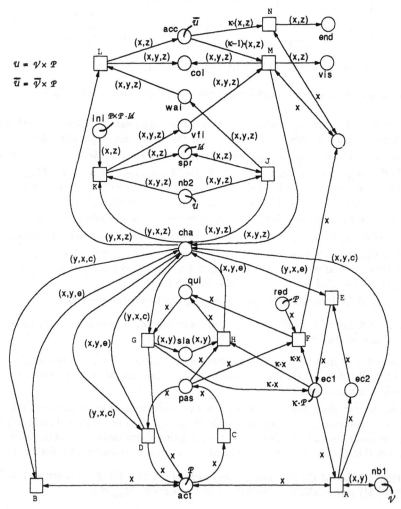

Fig.10 : Solution to the distributed termination problem

Moreover, each process p_i starts its own wave w_i and can be visited by each other wave. All tokens of the initial marking are increased by a third component which specifies the correspondence to a wave, i.e. the name of its starting process. This is respected by the arc inscriptions.

5 Conclusion

In the last ten years a lot of solutions to the distributed termination problem were proposed, but only a few have been proved formally. In the field of distributed algorithms informal solutions and intuitive reasoning to prove the correctness are highly unreliable. A rigorous proof requires the specification of the problem and the solution in a formal model for nonsequential behaviour. Petri nets turned out to be adequate for the modelling of distributed algorithms, and some of its analysis techniques could be used for formal verification.

Like [9] the solution satisfies the following quality properties:

• *Symmetry* : All processes should behave similar, in particular there is no leader.

• *Genericity* : No process knows anything about channels between other processes, and there is no predefined communication structure like a spanning tree or a Hamiltonian ring, on which a solution exclusively works.

• *Indulgence* : The underlying distributed computation must not be interrupted to establish a consistent global state.

All processes share a common, unique protocol, the solution protocols and the protocol for the distributed computation can work independently, and the spanning tree is constructed dynamically. Such a tree can be found underlying every graph (in contrast to Hamiltonian rings used in [2]) and must not be predefined as in [5]. Furthermore, the solution allows asynchronous communication, and there is no need for message passing in FIFO order. Future work is directed to a formal specification of such notions like symmetry, genericity and indulgence in the calculus of Petri nets.

References

[1] E.J.H. Chang: Echo Algorithms: Depth Parallel Operations on General Graphs. IEEE Transactions on Software Engineering, Vol. SE-8, No. 4, pp. 391–401 (1982)

[2] E.W. Dijkstra, W.H.J. Feijen, A.J.M. van Gasteren: Derivation of a Termination Detection Algorithm for Distributed Computations. Inform. Proc. Letters, Vol.16, No.5, pp.217–219 (1983)

[3] E.W. Dijkstra, C.S. Scholten: Termination Detection for Diffusing Computations. Inform. Proc. Letters, Vol.11, No.1, pp.1–4 (1980)

[4] H.Ehrig, B.Mahr: Fundamentals of Algebraic Specification 1. EATCS Monographs on Theoretical Computer Science, Vol.6 (1985)

[5] N. Francez: Distributed Termination. ACM Transactions on Programming Languages and Systems, Vol.2, No.1, pp.42–55 (1980)

[6] D.Gomm, R.Walter: Das Problem der verteilten Terminierung : Eine Lösung mit Petrinetzen. Universtät Bonn, Diplomarbeit (1989)

[7] W.Reisig: Petri Nets. EATCS Monographs on Theoretical Computer Science, Vol.4 (1985)

[8] W.Reisig: Petri Nets and Algebraic Specifications. TU München, Institut für Informatik, SFB-Bericht Nr.342/1/90B (1990)

[9] N.Shavit, N.Francez: A New Approach to Detection of Locally Indicative Stability. Lecture Notes in Computer Science, Vol.226 / L.Kott (ed.), pp.344–358 (1986)

Greedy Compression Systems

M. Loebl[*]

Department of Applied Mathematics
Faculty of Mathematics and Physics
Charles University
Prague
Czechoslovakia

Abstract:

The concept of compressions of trees encompasses many foundamental
problems of computer science. We define a greedy strategy consisting
in performing compressions from end-vertices of maximum distance
to the root.

We use a lexicorgaphic coding to obtain a lower bound for maximum
total length of greedy compression systems in form n. $\alpha(n)$, where
$\alpha(n)$ is the functional inverse to the Ackermann function. This
bound is optimal for balanced trees.

We also discuss other strategies with better bounds.

[*]The author is supported by Sonderforschungsbetreich 303 (DFG), of the
Institut für Diskrete Mathematik, Bonn, West Germany, and by the Alexander von Humboldt Stiftung.

1. Preliminaries

The operation which colepses trees called <u>compression</u>
encompasses many problems of computer science, like disjoint set
union problem and Davenport-Schinzel sequences. The trees
considered in this paper are rooted. <u>Compression</u> is defined as
follows: let T be a tree and let P be a path from an end-vertex
of T in the direction to the root. The <u>compression of T along</u>
<u>P</u> means to delete all the edges of P and to join each inner vertex
of P to the terminating vertex of P. This is illustrated on Fig.1.

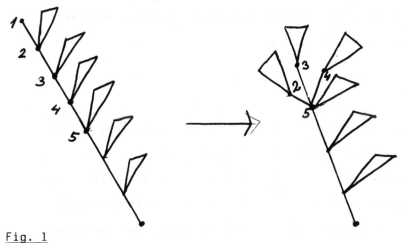

<u>Fig. 1</u>

A system $S = (C_1, C_2, \ldots, C_n)$ is called <u>compression system</u>
on T if each C_i is a compression of the tree T_i obtained from
T by performing compressions $C_1, \ldots, C_{i-1}$ $(T = T_1)$. Moreover
from each end-vertex of T goes exactly one compression of S, and
any compression of S starts in an end-vertex of T. Total length
of a compression system is $\sum_{i=1}^{n} |C_i|$, where $|C_i|$ is equal to
the number of edges of the path C_i. The total length of compression
systems will be considered as a function of $|T|$.

A strategy which chooses a compression of a tree is called <u>greedy,</u> if it schooses any compression which starts in an end-vertex of maximum distance to the root. The aim of this paper is to show that compression systems defined by a greedy strategy may have nonlinear total length even on (binary) balanced trees.

Theorem

Let k be a positive integer. Then there exists a balanced tree $T(k)$ and a greedy compression system $S(k)$ on $T(k)$ such that $|T(k)| \leq A(k)$ ($A(k)$ denotes the Ackermann function), and any compression from $S(k)$ has length k.

Method

We with use a coding of trees by k-dimensional vectors. We consider these vectors ordered lexicographically:
$(x_1, \ldots, x_k) < (y_1, \ldots y_k)$ iff $x_i < y_i$ for the first index i such that $x_i \neq y_i$. Lexicographical ordering may be successfully used to show that a given set contains a finite number of elements, by associating with all the elements vectorss which strictly decrease. The following observation will describe bounds obtained by this method. Let f be a function. Let $A_f(k, n)$ be a function defined as follows:
$A_f(1, n) = n$
$A_f(k, n) = A_f(k, n - 1) + A_f(k - 1, f(A_f(k, n - 1)))$

Observation

Let $s_1 < s_2 \ldots < s_n$ be k-dimensional strictly decreasing integer vectors. Let $f(i)$ denotes the sum of all elements of s_i. Then $m \leq A_f(k, f(1))$.

Remark

We remark that if f is a primitively recursive function then $A_f(k, n)$ is an Ackermann-type function.

We conclude this section by a definition of functional inverse. Let F be an integer function. Then functional inverse $F^{-1}(n)$ is defined by

$$F^{-1}(n) = \min \left\{ k; \ F(k) \gtrless n \right\}$$

2. Skeletons

Let T be a tree with each path from an end-vertex to the root not longer than k. The height of a vertex v is the distance of v to the root of T. The depth of a vertex v is the maximum distance from v to a descendant of v. We also denote by s(T, v) the number of sons of a vertex v in a tree T. The skelteton of a tree T is the (uniquelly determined) subtree C(T) of T stisfying:

(1) The end-vertices of C(T) are (some) and-vertices of T. The root of T belongs to C(T).

(2) Each pair v, w of vertices with the same height in C(T) have the same depth in C(T). Moreover any vertex of C(T) has the same distance to the end-vertices of C(T), which are its descendants.

(3) Let the vertices v, w have the same depth in C(T), say equal to i. Then s (C(T), v) = s (C(T), w) = s_i and s(T, v) = = s (T, w) = S_i. Here s_i and S_i are constants depending only on i. Further we put $s_i = S_i = \infty$ for all $i \lesseqgtr k$ and bigger than the depth of the root for C(T).

(4) The vector $W(C(T)) = (s_1, S_1, s_2, S_2, \ldots, s_k, S_k)$ is maximum in lexicographic ordering among all vectors $W(T')$ with subtrees T' satisfying (1) - (3).

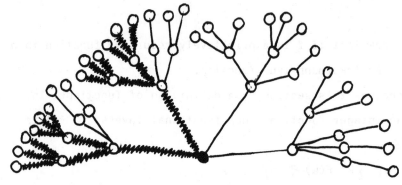

Fig. 2. (tree with skeleton : W(C(T)) = (3,3,2,4,2,4,   , . . .   )

We remark that it follows from (1) - (4) that the skeleton
is balanced and uniquelly determined. Finally we put D(T) =
= W(C(T)).

3. Proof of Theorem

We will construct a sequence of forests F_0, F_1, . . . , with
properties:

1. F_0 consists of discrete vertices,
2. The components of each F_i are isomorphic, and each path from
   an end-vertex to the root of the corresponding component
   has length less than k,
3. F_{i+1} is obtained from F_{i-} by performing two steps:
   A. First we stick to the roots of F_i a balanced forest of
      minimum height so that in the resulting componets a path
      of lenth k appears (see Fig. 3). Let the resulting forest
      ofter performing this operation be denoted by F'_{i+1}.
   B. Further we make the compressions of length k in F_{i+1}
      until all paths of lenght k disappear.

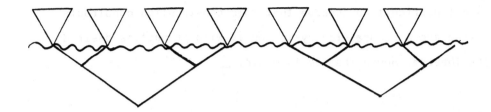

Fig. 3

This construction eventually terminates if all initial
end-vertices disappear. Let us denote by T_i a component of F_i.
Further we show that $D(T_{i+1}) < D(T_i)$ in the lexicographic
ordering ($D(T)$ was defined in section 2). In order to prove it we
examine the steps A and B. $D(T'_{i+1})$ is obtained from $D(T_i)$ by
replacing some " ∞ " by "2". Hence $D(T_i) > D(T'_{i+1})$. Hence
it is sufficient to prove the following: let T be a tree with
$D(T) = (\ . \ . \ . \ , c, \underbrace{\infty , \ . \ . \ . \ , \infty}_{\geq 0})$. Let T be obtained from
T by peforming one compression to the root of T. Then $D(\widetilde{T}) < D(T)$
or $D(\widetilde{T})$ is obtained from $D(T)$ by replacing the number "C" by a
bigger number. This is proved as follows. Let $C(T)$ be the skeleton
of T. Let $C(\widetilde{T})$ be the skoleton of $\widetilde{T}$. If $C(\widetilde{T})$ contains a noon-root
vertex of the performed compression then it is not difficult to
observe that $D(\widetilde{T}) < D(T)$. Otherwise $C(\widetilde{T})$ is a subtree of T satisfying (1) - (3) of the definition of the skeleton. Hence either
$D(\widetilde{T}) < D(T)$ or $C(T) = C(\widetilde{T})$ and $D(\widetilde{T})$ is obtained from $D(T)$ by
replacing the last integer in the vector by some other integre.
Hence the above claim is proved and thus $D(T_i) > D(T_{i+1})$.
Hence $D(T_1), D(T_2), \ . \ . \ . \ D(T_i), \ . \ . \ . \ .$ from a sequence of
2k-dimensional vectors strictly decreasing in the lexicographic
ordering. Hence our construction is finite and has at most $A(2k)$
steps (according to the observation in section 1). Moreover it

is not difficult to observe that this construction constructs
a tree and a compression system on it with properties desired in
the Theorem. Hence Theorem is prove. ☐

Remarks

1. The skeleton method was also used by Loebl and Matoušek in
   another setting (see /5/).
2. It follows from the result of Trjan (see /9/) that the lower
   bound obtained by the Theorem is best possible from balanced
   trees.

4. Other strategies

We proved in this paper that a greedy strategy leads to
compression systems with asymptotically maximum lenght on balance
trees. A natural question is whether there are interesting strategies
with better - perhaps linear - bahavior. This was studied by Loebl
and Nešetřil /7/. They defined a restriction to disjoint set
union problem called Local Postorder and also a procedure for solving
it based on tree compressions, with the property that the statement
"Total length of compressions defined by Local Postorder is nonlinear"
cannot be proved or disproved in Finete Set Theory. Local Postorder
was futher simplified by Loebl /10/.

References

/1/   Aho, A.V., Hopcroft, J.E., Ullman, J.D.(1974): The design
       and analysis of computer algoritms. Addison-Wesley, Reading

/2/   Galler, B.A., Fischer, M.J.(1964): An improved equivalence
       algorithm. Commun. ACM 7, 301 - 303

/3/   Hart, S., Sharir, M. (1986): Non-linearity of Davenport-
       -Schinzel sequences and of generalized path compression
       schemes. Combinatorica 6, 151-177 (See also Proc. 24th
       IEEE FOCS (1985), pp. 313 - 319)

/4/   Hopcroft, J.E., Ullman, J.D. (1973): Set merging algorithms.
       SIAM J. Comput. 2, 294 - 303

/5/   Loebl, M., Matoušek, J. (1987): Hercules versus Hidden
       Hydra Helper. KAM-series (submitted)

/6/   Loëbl, M., Nešetřil, J. (1988): Linearity and unprovability
       of the Set Union Problem Strategies (an extended abstract).
       Proceedings STOC Conference

/7/   Loebl, M., Nešetřil, J. (1989): Unprovability of Set Union
       Problem Strategies. Report No. 88528-OR, Institut für
       Operations Research, Bonn

/8/   Loebl, M., Nešetřil, J. (1989(: Linearity and unprovability
       of set union problem strategies: I. Linearity of on-line
       postorder. Technichal Report 89 - 04, University of Chicago
       (Submitted for publication)

/9/   Tarjan, R.E. (1975): Efficiently of a good but not linear
       set union algorithm. J. Assoc. Comput. Mach. 22, 215 - 225

/10/   Loebl, M. (1990): Partial Postorder, manuscript

A div(n) Depth Boolean Circuit for Smooth Modular Inverse

Michal Mňuk

Computing Center, Slovak Academy of Sciences

Dúbravská cesta 9, 842 35 Bratislava

Abstract

We present two families of Boolean circuits of depth $O(\log n)$ and size $n^{O(1)}$ (P uniform), and of depth $O(\log n \ \log\log n)$ and size $n^{O(1)}$ (log-space uniform) for computing the modular inverse of an n-bit integer, where the modulus has only small prime factors. In the case of P uniformity the circuits presented are asymptotically best possible.

1. INTRODUCTION

We consider the problem of parallel computing of the modular inverse of n-bit integers with the restriction that the modulus has only small prime factors, i.e. they are bounded by n^a, for some fixed positive a. The general problem of computing modular inverse plays an important role in the number theory. We present a family of Boolean circuits of depth $O(\log n \ \log\log n)$ for log-space uniformity, and of the optimal depth $O(\log n)$ for P uniformity which solves the problem stated above. This improves previous results – $O(\log^2 n \ \log\log n)$ – achieved by J. von zur Gathen, 1987, and – $O(\log n \ (\log\log n)^2)$ – achieved by T. Zeugmann, 1989, in both cases assuming the log-space uniformity.

2. PRELIMINARIES

Throughout this paper we denote by m an n-bit integer, p a prime dividing m (denoted by p|m), and e its multiplicity in m. We say m is n-smooth if $p \leq n^a$, for some fixed positive a, for any prime p dividing m. For any group G let G^* denote the group of all invertible elements of G. Let $\mathbb{Z}/m\mathbb{Z}$ denote the group of equivalence classes in the ring of integers $\mathbb{Z}$ modulo m. With every prime p we associate the p-adic field $\mathbb{Q}_p$ equipped with the non-archimedean norm $|\ |_p$. In particular, we use the notation $\mathbb{Z}_p = \{x \in \mathbb{Q}_p : |x|_p \leq 1\}$ for the ring of p-adic integers. The theory of p-adic fields may be found in [K]. Further we denote by div(n) the depth of a Boolean circuit with size $n^{O(1)}$ for n-bit integer division with remainder. In [BCH] the bound div(n)=O(log n) for P uniform Boolean families is achieved, and Reif has shown that div(n)=O(log n loglog n) for log-space uniform Boolean families (cf. [R]). Throughout this paper we consider only log-space and/or P uniform families.

3. SURVEY OF THE ALGORITHM

We start with a sketch of the algorithm in order to sum up crucial points and to emphasize main ideas on which the algorithm is based. Let m be an n-smooth integer and let $c \in (\mathbb{Z}/m\mathbb{Z})^*$. Our goal is to find the inverse b of c in $(\mathbb{Z}/m\mathbb{Z})^*$. The idea behind the algorithm is the same as in [vzG]. Several refinements, mainly in the second step, developed in this paper result in smaller depth, compared with [vzG] or [Z], of the circuit family.

Similarly as in the sequential case we use the decomposition of $(\mathbb{Z}/m\mathbb{Z})^*$ into unit groups of the form $(\mathbb{Z}/p^e\mathbb{Z})^*$, where p is a prime dividing m, and e its multiplicity in m, via Chinese Remainder Theorem. Due to the smoothness of m, all operations we need to perform in $(\mathbb{Z}/p\mathbb{Z})^*$ are almost trivial. Multiplicative inverses in these groups provide initial values which will be 'lifted' to inverses in $(\mathbb{Z}/p^e\mathbb{Z})^*$ by using the Hensel's Lemma. Putting the results together we obtain the solution of the problem stated above. The three main stages of the algorithm are the following ones:

1. Computing inverses in $(\mathbb{Z}/p\mathbb{Z})^*$;
2. Lifting them to inverses in $(\mathbb{Z}/p^e\mathbb{Z})^*$;
3. Putting the results together to get the inverse in $(\mathbb{Z}/m\mathbb{Z})^*$.

Now we describe these three steps of the algorithm in more details.

4. THE FIRST STEP OF THE ALGORITHM

Let p be a prime dividing m. Due to the n-smoothness of m, the relation $p \leq n^a$ is satisfied. Computing inverses in $(\mathbb{Z}/p\mathbb{Z})^*$ can be easily done by exhaustive search, whereby only multiplications and divisions of $\lceil \log n \rceil$-bit numbers are performed.

5. THE SECOND STEP OF THE ALGORITHM

We exhibit now the crucial idea of the algorithm. For the better clarity it is convenient to express the computations in this step in terms of p-adic fields. We start here with the inverse b_0 of c modulo p, $p|m$, obtained in the first step. Our goal is starting with b_0 to compute the inverse of c modulo p^e, where p^e is the exact power of p dividing m. Because of the natural embedding $\mathbb{Z} \rightarrow \mathbb{Q}_p$ both b_0 and c can be viewed as p-adic integers.

Our initial point is a p-adic integer $b_0 \in \mathbb{Z}_p$ with $|cb_0 - 1|_p < 1$, what means that b_0 is certain approximation of c^{-1} in $\mathbb{Z}_p$. Note, that $|c|_p = 1$ and c^{-1} in $\mathbb{Z}_p$ exists. Let $F(x) = cx - 1$ be a polynomial over $\mathbb{Z}_p$. Then we have a p-adic integer b_0 with $|F(b_0)|_p < 1$ or, in other words, $F(b_0) \equiv 0 \bmod p$. Moreover, the formal derivative $F'(x)$ of $F(x)$ is equal to c and therefore $F'(b_0) \not\equiv 0 \bmod p$. Under these conditions the Hensel's Lemma asserts the existence of a unique p-adic integer b^* with $F(b^*) = 0$ in $\mathbb{Q}_p$. We need to compute a p-adic approximation $\bar{b}$ of b^* with

$$|\bar{b} - b^*|_p < p^{-e}.$$

This can be achieved by exploiting the properties of the Newton method in the function field $Q_p(x)$. We define a rational function $f(x)=c-x^{-1}\in Q_p(x)$. Because $c\neq o$ mod p we may use $f(x)$ instead of $F(x)$ for determining of the root. For $x\neq 0$ the function $f(x)$ is differentiable and one can apply the Newton method in the same way as in the real analysis. The value b_0 obtained in the first step with

$$|cb_0-1|_p<1$$

provides the initial value for Newton iteration. Then we get the following recursion:

$$b_i\equiv-(cb_{i-1}-2b_{i-1})\ \text{mod}\ p^{2^i},\ 1\leq i\leq\lceil\log e\rceil. \tag{1}$$

From the precise analysis of the Newton method one may derive following facts:

$$|f(b_i)|_p\leq O(|b_{i+1}-b_i|_p^2)\ \text{and}$$

$$|b_i-b^*|\leq O(|b^*-b_0|_p^{2^i}).$$

The last two relations yield then the equation (1). From it we simply obtain (for $1\leq i\leq\lceil\log e\rceil$):

$$cb_i-1\equiv-(cb_{i-1}-1)^2\ \text{mod}\ p^{2^i},$$

that is

$$F(b_i)\equiv-(F(b_{i-1}))^2\ \text{mod}\ p^{2^i}.$$

Let $d=\lceil\log e\rceil$. Then

$$F(b_d)\equiv(-1)^d(F(b_0))^d\ \text{mod}\ p^{2^d}.$$

Using the fact that 'the structure of F' is formally the same as 'the structure of F^d', and that from given $F(b_d)$ the argument b_d can be computed quickly we get the main theorem:

THEOREM 1: *Let p^e be the exact power of a prime p dividing m, n be the length of the binary representation of m, $p\leq n^a$, for some fixed a, and $1\leq e\leq n$. Let b_0,c be p-adic integers, $p\nmid c$, and $cb_0-1\equiv0$ mod p. Then there exists a Boolean circuit of depth $\text{div}(n)$ which computes $\bar{b}\in(Z/p^eZ)^*$ with $c\bar{b}-1\equiv0$ mod p^e.*

Proof. We set

$$\bar{b}=\begin{cases}\sum_{i=1}^e\binom{e}{i}c^{i-1}b_0^i(-1)^{e-i}\ \text{mod}\ p^e,\ \text{e odd}\\\\(-1)\sum_{i=1}^e\binom{e}{i}c^{i-1}b_0^i(-1)^{e-i}\ \text{mod}\ p^e,\ \text{e even.}\end{cases}$$

We have to show $c\bar{b}-1\equiv0$ mod p^e. For odd e we have

$$c\bar{b}-1=\sum_{i=1}^{e}\binom{e}{i}c^{i}b_{0}^{i}(-1)^{e-i} \ -1=\sum_{i=0}^{e}\binom{e}{i}c^{i}b_{0}^{i}(-1)^{e-i}=$$

$$=(cb_{0}-1)^{e}\equiv 0 \bmod p^{e}$$

because $p|(cb_0-1)$. For even e this fact can be proved in the same way. The depth estimation is obvious since $e \leq n$ (cf. [BCH], [R]).

□

6. THE THIRD STEP OF THE ALGORITHM

In order to generalize the algorithm to composite moduli we use the Chinese remainder algorithm. First we recall some well-known problems connected with it (for reference, see [vzG]). Inputs are n-bit integers $a, a_1, \ldots, a_k, m, m_1, \ldots, m_k$, where $k \leq n$, and output is an n-bit number c:

GCD: $c = gcd(a, m)$;

MODINV: $\begin{cases} ac \equiv 1 \bmod m & \text{if } gcd(a, m) = 1 \\ c = 0 & \text{otherwise}; \end{cases}$

LAGRANGE: $c \equiv 0 \bmod m_2 \ldots m_k$

$c \equiv \begin{cases} 1 \bmod m_1 & \text{if } gcd(m_1, m_2 \ldots m_k) = 1 \\ 0 & \text{otherwise}; \end{cases}$

CHINREM: $c \equiv \begin{cases} a_i \bmod m_i & \text{if } gcd(m_i, m_j) = 1, \text{ for all } i \neq j \\ 0 & \text{otherwise}; \end{cases}$

FACTOR: compute all prime factors (with multiplicities) of m;

DIV: integer division with remainder.

Therein the following NC^1-reductions are stated (denoted by $\leq$):

$$CHINREM \leq LAGRANGE + GCD$$

$$LAGRANGE \leq MODINV + DIV.$$

We denote by "SMOOTH-" the condition that all moduli have only 'small' (in a sense of the second section) prime factors. With methods from [vzG], using the algorithm from Theorem 1 we easily obtain:

THEOREM 2: *The problems SMOOTH-LAGRANGE and SMOOTH-CHINREM can be solved by a log-space uniform family of Boolean circuits of depth O(log n loglog n), and by P uniform family of Boolean circuits of depth O(log n), both with polynomially bounded number of gates.*   □

Remark: Note, that the moduli m, m_i, $1 \leq i \leq k$, in all problems considered at this stage are powers of primes. Thus we only refer to problems the solution of which is already known.

7. THE MAIN RESULT

Putting together the results obtained in the previous sections we obtain

THEOREM 3: *There exists a log-space uniform family of Boolean circuits of depth $O(\log n \; \log\log n)$ with size $n^{O(1)}$, and a P uniform family of Boolean circuits of depth $O(\log n)$ with size $n^{O(1)}$ which computes SMOOTH-MODINV.*

Proof. <u>Algorithm</u>: Input: A positive n-smooth n-bit integer m and $c \in (\mathbb{Z}/m\mathbb{Z})^*$.

Output: $b \in (\mathbb{Z}/m\mathbb{Z})^*$ with $bc \equiv 1 \mod m$.

1. Determine all primes p_i dividing m, $1 \leq i \leq k$, and their multiplicities e_i.

2. For each i, $1 \leq i \leq k$, find $b_0^{(i)} \in (\mathbb{Z}/p_i\mathbb{Z})^*$ by exhaustive search such that $cb_0^{(i)} \equiv 1 \mod p_i$.

3. For each i, $1 \leq i \leq k$, compute $b^{(i)} \in (\mathbb{Z}/p_i^{e_i}\mathbb{Z})^*$ such that
$$cb^{(i)} \equiv 1 \mod p_i^{e_i}.$$

4. Compute $b \in (\mathbb{Z}/m\mathbb{Z})^*$ such that $b \equiv b^{(i)} \mod p_i^{e_i}$, for all $1 \leq i \leq k$.

Because of the n-smoothness of m, the factorisation in the step 1 can be easily done. The method for computing $b^{(i)}$ in the step 3 is provided by Theorem 1 as stated in Section 5. Computing $b \in (\mathbb{Z}/m\mathbb{Z})^*$ in the step 4 can be done by Chinese Remainder Theorem (cf. Theorem 2).

The proof of the correctness of the algorithm is an application of the Chinese Remainder Theorem. The depth estimate follows then from Theorems 1 and 2.

□

The algorithm improves the results obtained by J. von zur Gathen 1987 and also by T. Zeugmann 1989. According to [BCH] we have div(n)=O(log n) (P uniform) which is the best possible upper bound at all. Similar result has been shown in [LD] for finite fields with small characteristics.

REFERENCES

[BCH] P.W. BEAME, S.A. COOK and H.J. HOOVER, *Log depth circuits for division and related problems.* SIAM J. Comput., 15 (1986), pp. 994-1003.

[vzG] J. von zur GATHEN, *Computing powers in parallel.* SIAM J. Comput., 16 (1987), pp. 930-945.

[K]   N. KOBLITZ, *P-adic fields, p-adic analysis and dzeta functions.* Mir, Moscow, 1982.

[LD]   B.E. LITOW and G.I. DAVIDA, *O(log n) parallel time finite field inversion.* Proc. 3rd Aegean Workshop on Computing, 1988, Lecture Notes in Computer Science 319, Springer Verlag, pp. 74-80.

[R]   J. REIF, *Logarithmic depth circuits for algebraic functions.* SIAM J. Comput., 15 (1986), pp. 231-242.

[Z]   T. ZEUGMANN, *Improved parallel computations in the ring Z/p^a.* Journal of Information Processing and Cybernetics, 25 (1989).

Learning by Conjugate Gradients

Martin F. Møller

Computer Science Department, Mathematical Institute

University of Aarhus, Denmark

Abstract

A learning algorithm (CG) with superlinear convergence rate is introduced. The algorithm is based upon a class of optimization techniques well known in numerical analysis as the Conjugate Gradient Methods. CG uses second order information from the neural network but requires only O(N) memory usage, where N is the number of minimization variables; in our case all the weights in the network. The performance of CG is benchmarked against the performance of the ordinary backpropagation algorithm (BP). We find that CG is considerably faster than BP and that CG is able to perform the learning task with fewer hidden units.

1 Introduction

1.1 Motivation

In the recent years neural networks have shown themselves to be good alternatives to conventional methods used in classification tasks. Adaptive learning algorithms have been subject to intense investigation and many different algorithms have been suggested. These algorithms are often developed in a kind of *ad hoc* fashion with the local properties of a neural network as a basis for development. They usually have a very poor convergence rate or depend on parameters which have to be specified by the user, because no theoretical basis for choosing them exists. The values of these parameters are often crucial for the success of the algorithm. The aim of this paper is to develop a learning algorithm that eliminates some of these disadvantages.

In the development of the CG-algorithm we will abstract from the local properties of the neural network and look at the problem of learning in a more general way. From an optimization point of view learning in a neural network can be seen as being equivalent to minimizing a global error function, which is a multivariate function that depends on the weights in the network. This perspective gives some advantages in the development of effective learning algorithms because the problem of minimizing a function is well known in other fields of science, such as conventional numerical analysis.

Since learning in realistic neural network applications often involves adjustment of several thousand weights only optimization methods that are applicable to large-scale problems, are relevant as alternativ learning algorithms. The general opinion in the numerical analysis community is that only one class of optimization methods exists that are able to handle large-scale problems in an effective way. These methods are often referred to as the *Conjugate Gradient Methods* .

1.2. Notation

Let an arbitrary feedforward neural network be given. For convenience we will express all the weights in the network in vector notation. We assume that we have a global error function $E(w)$ attached to the neural network to our disposal and that we are able to calculate the gradient $E'(w)$ to this error function. One way of doing this is like in BP to propagate the error back through the network.

It might also be useful to recall that the error function $E(w)$ in a given point $(w+y)$ in $\Re^N$ can be expressed by the well known Taylor expansion

$$(1) \quad E(w+y) = E(w) + E'(w)^T y + \frac{1}{2} y^T E''(w) y + ...$$

Let $p_1,..,p_k$ be a set of non zero weight vectors in $\Re^N$. The set is said to be a *conjugate system* with respect to a nonsingular symmetric NxN matrix A if the following holds

$$(2) \quad p_i^T A p_j = 0 \quad (i \neq j, \, i = 1,..,k)$$

Let a set of linear restrictions be given by

$$(3) \quad q_i^T x = c_i \quad (i = 1,..., n-k, \, 1 \leq k \leq n)$$

where $q_1,...,q_{n-k}$ is a set of linear independent weight vectors. The set of points in $\Re^N$ which satisfy (3) is called a *k-plane* or π_k. A conjugate system $p_1,..,p_k$ and a point w_0 in weightspace represents a k-plane π_k given by π_k: $w = w_0 + \alpha_1 p_1 + ... + \alpha_k p_k$, $\alpha_i \in \Re$.

2 Optimization strategy

Most of the optimization methods used to minimize functions are based on the same strategy. The minimization is a local iterative process where you for each iteration minimize an approximation to the function in a neighbourhood of the current point in weightspace. The approximation is often given by a first or second order Taylor expansion of the function. The idea of the strategy is illustrated in the pseudoalgorithm presented below, which minimizes the error function E(w).

```
Algorithm Minimize E(w)
begin
    choose initial weight vector w₀.
    k:=0;
    while(E'(wₖ)≠0) do
    begin
        determine a search direction pₖ and a step length aₖ, so that
        E(wₖ+ aₖpₖ) < E(wₖ);
        wₖ₊₁:= wₖ + aₖpₖ;
        k := k+1;
    end;
    return wₖ as the desired minimum;
end.
```

Determining the next current point in this iterativ process involves two independent steps. First a *search direction* has to be determined, i.e in what direction in weightspace do we want to go in our search for a new current point. Once the search direction has been found we have to decide how far we want to go in the specified search direction, i.e we need to determine a *step length*.

If we set the search direction p_k to the negative gradient $-E'(w)$ and the step length a_k to a constant ε, then the algorithm equals the gradient descent algorithm. In the context of neural networks this is the BP-algorithm without momentum term. Minimization by gradient descent is based on the linear approximation $E(w+y) \approx E(w)+ E'(w)^T y$, which is the main reason why the algorithm often show poor convergence. Another reason is that the algorithm uses constant step length, which in many cases are insufficient and makes the algorithm less robust. Including a momentum term in the BP-algorithm is an attempt in an ad hoc fashion to force the algorithm to use second order information from the network. Unfortunately the momentum term is not able to speed up the algorithm considerable, but causes the algorithm to be even less robust, because of the inclusion of another user dependent parameter, *the momentum constant.*

3 The CG-algorithm

The Conjugate Gradient Methods are also based on the above general optimization strategy, but chooses the search direction and the step length more carefully by using information from the second order approximation $E(w+y) \approx E(w)+E'(w)^T y + \frac{1}{2}y^T E''(w)y$.

Quadratic functions have some nice properties that general functions do not necessarily have. Denote the quadratic approximation to E in a neighbourhood of a point w by $E_{qw}(y)$, so that $E_{qw}(y)$ is given by

(4) $E_{qw}(y) = E(w)+E'(w)^Ty + \frac{1}{2}y^TE''(w)y$

If the Hessian matrix $E''(w)$ is positive definite then $E_{qw}(y)$ has a unique global minimum point and there exist a minimum point for $E_{qw}(y)$ restricted to every k-plane π_k [Hestenes]. Furthermore does the following very important theorem hold for the quadratic function $E_{qw}(y)$.

Theorem 1 *Let y_{k+1} be the minimum point for $E_{qw}(y)$ restricted to the k-plane π_k. The (n-k)-plane π_{n-k} through y_{k+1} and conjugate to π_k contains the global minimum point y_0 for $E_{qw}(y)$ [Hestenes].*

We are now able to formulate the CG-algorithm in an informal way. Select an initial weight vector y_1 and a conjugate system $p_1,...,p_N$. Find successive minimum points for E_{qw} on the planes $\pi_1,...,\pi_N$, where π_k, $1 \leq k \leq N$, is given by π_k: $y = y_k+ \alpha_1p_1+...+ \alpha_kp_k$, $\alpha_i \in \mathfrak{R}$. If the global minimum point y_0 is not found in the k's iteration theorem 1 gives that the minimum point is to be found in the last (N-k) planes. The algorithm assures that the global minimum point for a quadratic function is detected in at most N iterations.

For each iteration k we have to determine a minimum point for E_{qw} restricted to a k-plane π_k. This is done recursively using theorem 2 below.

Theorem 2 *Let $p_1,...,p_N$ be a conjugate system and y_1 a point in weightspace. Let the points $y_2,...,y_{N+1}$ be recursively defined by the condition that for every k, $1 \leq k \leq N$, y_{k+1} is minimum for E_{qw} through the line $y = y_k+\alpha p_k$. Then y_{k+1} is given by*

$$y_{k+1} = y_k + a_kp_k \qquad where \qquad a_k = \frac{c_k}{d_k}, c_k = p_k^Tr_k, d_k = p_k^TE_{qw}''(y_k)p_k$$

and y_{k+1} minimizes E_{qw} restricted to the k-plane π_k given by $p_1,...,p_k$ [Hestenes].

The conjugate weight vectors $p_1,...,p_N$ can also be determined recursively by choosing p_{k+1} as the orthogonal projection of $r_{k+1} = -E_{qw}'(y_{k+1})$ on the (N-k)-plane π_{N-k}, i.e. p_{k+1} is chosen as the steepest descent vector to E_{qw} restricted to π_{N-k}. Theorem 3 shows how this is done.

Theorem 3 *Let p_1 be equal to the steepest descent vector $r_1 = -E_{qw}'(y_1)$. Define p_{k+1} recursively by*

$$p_{k+1} = -E_{qw}'(y_{k+1}) + b_k p_k = r_{k+1} + b_k p_k$$

*where y_{k+1} is the point generated in theorem 2 and $b_k = \dfrac{|r_{k+1}|^2 - r_{k+1} r_k}{c_k}$, $c_k = p_k^T r_k$.
Then p_{k+1} is the steepest descent vector to E_{qw} restricted to the $(N-k)$-plane π_{N-k} conjugate to the k-plane π_k given by y_{k+1} and $p_1,...,p_k$ [Hestenes].*

For each iteration we apply the above described algorithm to the quadratic approximation E_{qw} of the global error function E in the current point w in weightspace. The first version of the CG-algorithm is then

Algorithm CG-1 [Hestenes]
begin
    choose initial weight vector w_1;
    $p_1 := r_1 := -E'(w_1); k := 1;$
    while $(r_k \neq 0)$ do
    begin
      $s_k := E''(w_k)p_k;$
      $c_k := p_k^T r_k;$
      $d_k := p_k^T s_k;$
      $a_k := \dfrac{c_k}{d_k};$
      $w_{k+1} := w_k + a_k p_k;$
      $r_{k+1} := -E'(x_{k+1});$
      $b_k := \dfrac{|r_{k+1}|^2 - r_{k+1} r_k}{c_k};$
      if $(k \bmod N = 0)$ then $p_{k+1} := r_{k+1};$
      else $p_{k+1} := r_{k+1} + b_k p_k;$
      $k := k+1;$
    end;
    return w_k as the desired minimum;
end.

For each iteration in the algorithm we have to calculate and store the Hessian matrix $E''(w_k)$. Unfortunately we are not able to calculate the Hessian matrix because the neural network does not provide us with enough information. And even if we could calculate the Hessian we would run into storage problems because the Hessian matrix demand $O(N^2)$ memory usage. The solution to this problem is to estimate the $E''(w_k)p_k$ with

$$(5) \quad s_k = E''(w_k)p_k \approx \frac{E'(x_k + \sigma_k p_k) - E'(x_k)}{\sigma_k}, \quad 0 < \sigma_k \ll 1$$

We selected 10 different initial weight-vectors $w_1,\ldots,w_{10}$ and tested CG and BP with use of momentum term on the xor-problem with these same 10 initial weight vectors. The result is shown in table 1 below.

	CG-algorithm				BP-algorithm			
	#epo	minimum point			#epo	minimum point		
		g	l	f		g	l	f
w_1	23	●			292	●		
w_2	38	●			414	●		
w_3	27	●			439	●		
w_4	25	●			1453		●	
w_5	30	●			629	●		
w_6	31	●			408	●		
w_7	22	●			1365		●	
w_8	37	●			367	●		
w_9	30	●			365	●		
w_{10}	20	●			1600		●	
av.	28	–	–	–	858/416	–	–	–

table 1 The table shows 10 different tests on the xor-problem with CG and BP respectively. *#epo* indicates the amount of epoch learning iterations used before the algorithm terminated. *minimum point* indicates the type of the point found by the algorithm. There are three different types, *g* indicates a global minimum, *l* a local minimum or saddle-point and *f* indicates a non stationary point. *av.* indicates the average amount of learning epochs used. At the BP av. field there is two numbers displayed. 858 is an average over all 10 tests with BP including the tests that converged to a local minimum. 416 is an average over the 7 tests with BP that converged to a global minimum.

We observe that CG is considerably faster in all 10 tests, and on average about 15 times faster than BP. It is also interesting that BP converges to a local minimum 3 times out of 10 while CG finds a global minimum in all 10 tests.

Figur 4 below shows the error development for the test with initial weight vector w_3 with BP and CG respectively. We observe that the BP-curve oscillates in the first 60 iterations. The reason is to be found in the fact that BP uses constant step length, which implies that BP cannot guarantee a reduction of the error for each iteration. We also observe that the reduction in the error is very small from about 60 to 250 iterations. In this period the weights are pulled in almost opposite directions by the different patterns so that a weight have to go through a small ravine in weightspace before it can decide in which direction to go. This *ravine phenomenon* is not special for the xor-problem but is observed in many other learning tasks using BP.

When we look at the CG-curve we first observe that there is no oscillation. The CG-algorithm in fact assures that the error will be less than and in rare cases equal to the error in the preceding iteration. We also observe that the error is reduced with much

The algorithm is now direct applicable to a feedforward neural network and requires only $O(N)$ memory usage.

We tried the algorithm on a appropiate test problem and found that CG-1 in almost any test failed and converged to a non stationary point. The reason is to be found in the fact that CG-1 only works for functions with positive definite Hessian matrices. The Hessian matrix for the global error function E has shown to be indefinite in different areas of the weightspace, which explaines why CG-1 fails in the attempt to minimize E. The solution to this problem is to modify CG-1 so that it prevents the difficulties with the indefinite Hessian matrices. We have done that using a Levenberg-Marquardt approach in modifying the algorithm [Fletcher]. The idea is to introduce a scalar λ_k, which is supposed to regulate the indefiniteness of $E''(w_k)$. This is done by setting

$$(6) \qquad s_k = \frac{E'(x_k+\sigma_k p_k)-E'(x_k)}{\sigma_k} + \lambda_k p_k$$

and for each iteration adjusting λ_k looking at the sign of d_k, which directly reveal if $E''(w_k)$ is not positiv definite. The final CG-algorithm is then as follows

Algorithm CG
begin

    choose weight vector w_1; $\sigma_1>0$; $\lambda_1>0$; $\overline{\lambda}_1:=0$;
    $p_1:= r_1:= -E'(x_1)$; $k:=1$; *succes:= true;*
    while ($r_k{\neq}0$) do
    begin
      if(succes) then
      begin

        $\sigma_k:= \dfrac{\sigma}{|p_k|}$;

        $s_k:= \dfrac{E'(w_k+\sigma_k p_k)-E'(w_k)}{\sigma_k}$;

        $c_k:= p_k^T r_k$; $d_k:= p_k^T s_k$;
      end;

    $s_k:= s_k + (\lambda_k- \overline{\lambda}_k)p_k$;

    $d_k:= d_k+(\lambda_k- \overline{\lambda}_k)|p_k|^2$;
    if($d_k{\leq}0$) then
    begin

      $s_k:= s_k + (\lambda_k - 2\dfrac{d_k}{|p_k|^2})p_k$;

      $\overline{\lambda}_k:= 2(\lambda_k - \dfrac{d_k}{|p_k|^2})$;

      $d_k:= -d_k + \lambda_k|p_k|^2$; $\lambda_k:= \overline{\lambda}_k$;
    end;

$$a_k := \frac{c_k}{d_k};$$

$$\Delta_k := \frac{2d_k[E(w_k)-E(w_k+a_kp_k)]}{c_k^2};$$

if($\Delta_k \geq 0$) then
begin
   $w_{k+1} := w_k + a_kp_k;$
   $r_{k+1} := -E'(w_{k+1});$

   $b_k := \frac{|r_{k+1}|^2 - r_{k+1}r_k}{c_k};$

   if (k mod $N = 0$) then $p_{k+1} := r_{k+1};$
   else $p_{k+1} := r_{k+1} + b_kp_k;$

   if($\Delta_k \geq 0.75$) then $\lambda_k := \frac{1}{2}\lambda_k;$

   $\bar{\lambda}_k := 0;$ *succes:= true;*

  end else succes:= false; $\bar{\lambda}_k := \lambda_k;$
  if($\Delta_k < 0.25$) then $\lambda_k := 4\lambda_k;$
  $k := k+1;$
end;
return w_k as the desired minimum;
end.

At first sight the CG-algorithm looks complicated and seems to involve a lot of calculation work per iteration. But with a closer look we see that only the calls of the error function E(w) and of the derivative E'(w) take time. For each iteration there is one call of E(w) and two calls of E'(w), which gives a time complexity per iteration of $O(3N^2)$. When the algorithm is implemented this complexity can be reduced to $O(2N^2)$, because the calculation of E(w) can be built into one of the calculations of E'(w). In comparison with BP the CG-algorithm involves twice as much calculation work per iteration, since BP has a time complexity of $O(N^2)$ per epoch iteration. So CG has to perform the learning tasks in at least half as many iterations as BP in order to show that it is more effective than BP.

4. Test results

4.1 Toy problem

First we tested CG on the xor-problem, which is a well known small but complex problem often referred to in the litterature in the past.

larger steps per iteration than in the BP-curve. The reason is that CG chooses the search direction as well as the step length in each iteration much more carefully than BP using first and second order information from the neural network. The ravine phenomenon is not as destinct as in the BP-curve, but we observe an tendency in the first 8 iterations.

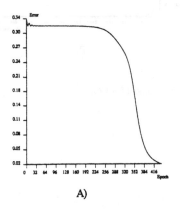

A)

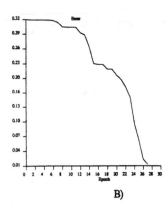

B)

fig.4 A) Error development for BP-test. B) Error development for CG-test. Both tests using initial weight vector w_3.

4.2 Practical problem

The results of the last experiment seemed very promising for CG. But we still need to know how CG behaves on large-scale practical problems requirering networks with thousands of weights. One such problem is the determination of bloodtypes of cattle. The blood is tested for reaction with 50 different antibodies. The 50 reactions can be split up in 10 different bloodtype systems and each of these systems has to be converted to what is called a phenotype. In one of our experiments we have tried to learn a neural network to convert the reactions belonging to the B-system, which is 26 out of the 50 reactions, to the right phenotypes. We used 500 different bloodtype reactions and there corresponding phenotypes as trainingset. We trained a network consisting of 26 input, 35 hidden and 26 output units, using CG as well as BP. In the runs with BP we had major difficulties setting the learning rate parameter. First when the learning rate was set to 0.01, BP stopped oscillating the error. We first ran the two algorithms for 500 iterations and compared results (see figure 7). We see that CG seems to have learned the task in about 150 iterations, while BP after 500 iterations still is far away from zero error. To see if BP was able to reduce the error as good as CG just using more iterations, we continued running with BP up til 5000 iterations. Figur 8 shows how well BP performed in these 5000 iterations.

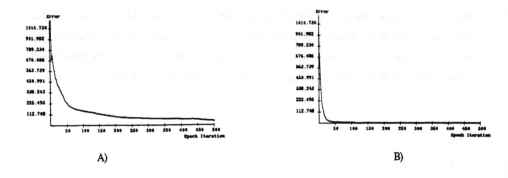

A)   B)

fig.7 A) Error development for BP. B) Error development for CG.

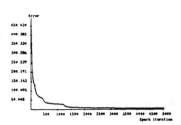

fig.8 Error development for BP during 5000 iterations.

We observe that still after 5000 iterations BP has not been able to reduce the error as much as CG had after 150 iterations.

The next experiment we did was to reduce the amount of hidden units in the network from 35 to 20 and then train with CG and BP again. We observed that CG still was able to perform the task, although not as good as with 35 hidden units. This time it took about 700 iterations to converge. The interesting thing is that BP could not perform the task, but converged to local minima or began to oscillate after a couple of thousand iterations. So it seems that when using CG as learning algorithm we are able to use networks with fewer hidden units. This is important because fewer hidden units in a network encourages the generalization ability of the network [Hinton].

5 Conclusions

Using a optimization approach in the development of adaptive learning algorithms we have introduced an alternative and more effective algorithm (CG) than ordinary backpropagation (BP). CG belongs to the class of Conjugate Gradient Methods, which shows superlinear convergence on most problems. CG can be viewed as a kind of second order backpropagation algorithm, because it like BP is based on the idea of propagating the error back through the network in order to get the information needed.

Through several experiments we find that CG is considerably faster than BP and that CG seems to be able to perform the learning tasks with fewer hidden units in the network, which raises the networks ability to generalize.

References

[Fletcher] Fletcher,R., Practical Methods of Optimization, Vol.1, Unconstrained Optimization, John Wiley & Sons, 1975.

[Gill] Gill, P., Practical Optimization, Academic Press inc., 1980.

[Hestenes] Hestenes, M., Conjugate Direction Methods in Optimization, Springer Verlag, New York, 1980.

[Hinton] Hinton, G., Connectionist Learning Procedures, Artificial Intelligence (1989), pp. 185-234.

[Madsen] Madsen, K., Optimering, hæfte 38, Numerisk Institut, DTH, 1984.

[Powell] Powell, M., Restart procedures for the Conjugate Gradient Method, Mathematical Programming, Vol. 12, pp. 241-254.

Monoids described by pushdown automata

Maryse Pelletier

LITP, Université Paris 6

4 Place Jussieu, 75230 Paris Cedex 05, France

Abstract

We define and study a family of monoids, called *(PR)-monoids*, of rather low complexity. A (PR)-monoid is a monoid the multiplication of which may be realized by a deterministic pushdown automaton. We prove that this family contains rational monoids, free groups and is closed under finitely generated submonoids and free products. We also consider other families of monoids of the same complexity than (PR)-monoids.

Introduction

We define a family of monoids the *complexity* of which is *not too high*. The complexity of the multiplication of a monoid is defined by Sakarovitch [13] in the following way. With every monoid, we may associate a function, called *description*, from a free monoid into itself. Such a description completely determines the initial monoid. The complexity of the monoid is defined as the complexity of its description. For instance, *rational monoids* [12] [13] have a low complexity since they are, by definition, described by rational functions. Sakarovitch [12] proves that the word problem is decidable in a monoid if and only if this monoid has a computable description.

We consider, in this paper, a family of monoids of complexity just a little higher than rational monoids: the monoids, called *(PR)-monoids*, the descriptions of which may be realized by deterministic pushdown automata. We prove that this family contains rational monoids and free groups. We study the rational subsets of (PR)-monoids. We prove that (PR)-monoids are closed under finitely generated submonoids and free products. We also consider other families of monoids which may be described by deterministic pushdown automata.

If X is a set, X^* denotes the free monoid generated by X. The free monoid X^* consists in the set of all sequences of finite length of elements of X, equipped with the concatenation. The identity element of X^* is the empty sequence, denoted by 1_{X^*}. We associate with each monoid a function from a free monoid into itself in the following way.

A *generating system* of a monoid M is a pair (X, α) such that α is a surjective morphism from X^* onto M. A *cross-section* of a monoid M for a generating system (X, α) is a subset T of X^* such that α is a bijection from T onto M. A mapping β from X^* into itself is a *description* of M for (X, α) if there exists a cross-section T such that β associates with each element of X^* its representative in T.

The *rational* monoids are described by rational functions. A rational function is realized by a finite automaton, i.e. an automaton with a finite set of states, which reads letters on an input alphabet and which writes a word on an output alphabet, for each input letter. For instance, free monoids, finite monoids are rational monoids.

The additive group $\mathbf{Z}$ is not described by a finite automaton: there is a problem of memory. In view to give other examples of non rational monoids, recall some definitions.

If X is an alphabet, we denote by $\overline{X}$ a copy of X, by $\bar{x}$ the letter of $\overline{X}$ which corresponds to the letter x of X and by $\widetilde{X}$ the set $X \cup \overline{X}$. For a letter z of $\widetilde{X}$, we use the following convention: $\bar{z} = \bar{x}$ if $z = x \in X$ and $\bar{z} = x$ if $z = \bar{x} \in \overline{X}$.

The *free group* generated by X (denoted by $F(X)$) is the quotient of $\widetilde{X}^*$ by the congruence generated by $z\bar{z} = 1$ for each $z \in \widetilde{X}$. The *Dyck's reduction* associates with each word of $\widetilde{X}^*$, its unique representative in $\widetilde{X}^* \setminus \widetilde{X}^*\{z\bar{z} \mid z \in \widetilde{X}\}\widetilde{X}^*$ (it is a description of the free group).

The *free involutive monoid* generated by X (denoted by $I(X)$) is the quotient of $\widetilde{X}^*$ by the congruence generated by $x\bar{x} = 1$ for each $x \in X$. The *Shamir's reduction* associates with each word of $\widetilde{X}^*$ its unique representative in $\widetilde{X}^* \setminus \widetilde{X}^*\{x\bar{x} \mid x \in X\}\widetilde{X}^*$ (it is a description of the free involutive monoid).

The *polycyclic monoid* generated by X (denoted by $P(X)$), is the Rees quotient of $I(X)$ by the ideal generated by $\{x\bar{y} \mid x, y \in X \text{ and } x \neq y\}$. If X is a singleton, the polycyclic monoid $P(X)$ is equal to the free involutive monoid $I(X)$ and is called bicyclic monoid. Otherwise, a cross-section of $P(X)$ in $\widetilde{X}^*$ is the set $\overline{X}^* X^* \cup \{x\bar{y}\}$ (where x and y are two distinct letters of X). The *stack reduction* associates with each word of $\widetilde{X}^*$, its unique representative in $\overline{X}^* X^* \cup \{x\bar{y}\}$. It is a description of the polycyclic monoid and it is equal to the composition of the Shamir's reduction and of a rational function from $\widetilde{X}^*$ into $\widetilde{X}^*$. We shall identify the non zero elements of $P(X)$ and their representatives in $\overline{X}^* X^*$.

Free groups, free involutive monoids, polycyclic monoids are not rational monoids. To realize their descriptions, we need the notion of functions realized by pushdown automata (pushdown automata are considered as transducers from the input alphabet into the stack alphabet).

1 (PR)-functions

The (PR)-functions are equal to the composition of functions realized by deterministic pushdown automata and of functions realized by finite automata. Nivat [8] [9] proved that functions realized by pushdown automata are equal to functions realized by rational transducers with values in a polycyclic monoid. Sakarovitch [11] extends this result to deterministic pushdown automata and rational subsequential transducers. We do not define (deterministic) pushdown automata (see [6] or [7]) but we define the equivalent notion of rational (subsequential) transducers.

DEFINITION 1.1 . — A rational *transducer* from X^* into a polycyclic $P(Z)$ is a triple (λ, μ, ν) where:

- $\lambda \in \text{Rat } P(Y)$, $\nu \in \text{Rat } P(Y)$
- μ is a morphism from X^* into Rat $P(Y)$.

A relation θ from X^* into $P(Z)$ is *realized* by a transducer (λ, μ, ν) if $f\theta = \lambda(f\mu)\nu$ for each $f \in X^*$. In this case, we write $\theta = (\lambda, \mu, \nu)$.

Two transducers are equivalent if they realize the same relation.

REMARK 1.1 . In fact, we have given the definition of transducers with *one state*. In general, transducers are defined with a set of states Q: λ is a row-vector $1 \times Q$, ν is a column-vector $Q \times 1$ and μ takes its values in matrices $Q \times Q$.

Nivat [8] proved that any transducer from X^* into $P(Z)$ with a set of states Q is equivalent to a transducer from X^* into $P(Z \cup Q)$ with one state.

Recall the classical generalization of the theorem of Kleene-Schützenberger:

THEOREM 1.1 . — *A relation from X^* into $P(Z)$ is rational iff it is realized by a rational transducer from X^* into $P(Z)$.*

To define subsequential transducers, we adopt the following convention: we identify the zero of $P(Z)$ and the empty set. There is no problem for the definition of rational sets since:

$$K \in \text{Rat } P(Z) \Longrightarrow K \setminus \{0\} \in \text{Rat } P(Z).$$

DEFINITION 1.2 . — A transducer (λ, μ, ν) from X^* into $P(Z)$ is *subsequential* if:

$$\forall f \in X^* \quad \text{Card}(\lambda(f\mu)) \leq 1 \text{ and } \text{Card}(\lambda(f\mu)\nu) \leq 1.$$

Remark that the relation realized by a (rational) subsequential transducer from X^* into $P(Z)$ is a (rational) function from X^* into $P(Z)$.

REMARK 1.2 . If (λ, μ, ν) is subsequential then λ is a singleton but the $x\mu$ and ν are not necessarily singletons, nor even finite sets. For instance, let $X = \{a, b\}$ and $Z = \{a, b, d\}$.

$$\begin{cases} \lambda &= d \\ a\mu &= \bar{d}da + \bar{a}aa + \bar{b}\,\bar{d}dba + \bar{b}\,\bar{b}bba + \bar{b}\bar{a}ab \\ b\mu &= \bar{d}db + \bar{b}\,\bar{b}bbb + \bar{a}^+\bar{b}\,\bar{d}dab + \bar{b}\bar{a}ab \\ \nu &= 1 \end{cases}$$

Then:

$$\lambda(f\mu) = \lambda(f\mu)\nu = \begin{cases} dab & \text{if } f \in X^*abX^* \\ df & \text{otherwise.} \end{cases}$$

(λ, μ, ν) is a rational subsequential transducer such that $b\mu$ is not finite.

DEFINITION 1.3 . — A function β from X^* into Y^* is a *(PR)-function* if $\beta = \theta\tau$ where $\theta = (\lambda, \mu, \nu)$ is a rational subsequential transducer from X^* into a polycyclic $P(Z)$, with values in Z^* and τ a rational function from Z^* into Y^*.

In this definition, we may assume that $\nu = 1$ or that θ is a transducer with a set of states Q.

EXAMPLE 1.1 .

- Any rational function from X^* into Y^* is a (PR)-function.

- The Dyck's reduction, the Shamir's reduction and the stack reduction are (PR)-functions.

  To avoid confusions, we define these reductions in monoids $(X \cup X')^*$. Convention: $y' = x'$ if $y = x \in X$ and $y' = x$ if $y = x' \in X'$. Let $d \notin X \cup X'$ and $Z = X \cup X' \cup \{d\}$. For each of these reductions, we build a rational subsequential transducer from $(X \cup X')^*$ into $P(Z)$, with values in Z^*.

  Dyck's reduction:
  $$\lambda = d,\ \nu = 1$$
  $$y\mu = \{\bar{z}zy \mid z \in Z \text{ and } z \neq y'\} + \overline{y'}.$$

  Shamir's reduction:
  $$\lambda = d,\ \nu = 1$$
  $$x\mu = x$$
  $$x'\mu = \{\bar{z}zx' \mid z \in Z \text{ and } z \neq x\} + \bar{x}.$$

  Stack reduction:
  $$\lambda = d,\ \nu = 1$$
  $$x\mu = x$$
  $$x'\mu = \{\bar{z}zx' \mid z \in X' \cup \{d\}\} + \bar{x}.$$

  It is sufficient to compose each of these transducers with the function which erases the letter d to obtain the reductions. □

2 (PR)-monoids

We use the class of (PR)-functions to define a new class of monoids.

DEFINITION 2.1 . — A monoid M is a *(PR)-monoid* if M has a (PR)-description for a generating system (X, α).

REMARK 2.1 . This definition does not depend upon the generating system.
Let $\beta = \theta\tau$ be a (PR)-description of M for (X, α), with $\theta = (\lambda, \mu, \nu)$. If (X', α') is another generating system of M, there exist morphisms ϕ from X^* into X'^* and ψ from X'^* into X^* such that $\phi\alpha' = \alpha$ and $\psi\alpha = \alpha'$. Then $\beta' = \psi\beta\phi$ is a description of M for (X', α'). Moreover $\beta' = \theta'\tau'$, with $\theta' = (\lambda, \psi\mu, \nu)$ and $\tau' = \tau\phi$. Hence β' is a (PR)-description of M.

EXAMPLE 2.1 .

- Any rational monoid is a (PR)-monoid.

- The free groups, free involutive monoids and polycyclic monoids are (PR)-monoids since Dyck's reductions, Shamir's reductions and stack reductions are (PR)-functions. □

3   Rationality

Recall that the Shamir's reduction preserves rationality, i.e. the image of a rational set is a rational set (cf. Benois [1] for Dyck's reduction, and Fliess [5]). It implies:

PROPOSITION 3.1 . — *Let θ be a rational relation from X^* into $P(Z)$, with values in Z^*. If $K \in \operatorname{Rat} X^*$, then $K\theta \in \operatorname{Rat} Z^*$.*

Proof. Since θ is a rational relation defined on a free monoid, θ preserves rationality. Let $K \in \operatorname{Rat} X^*$ then $K\theta \in \operatorname{Rat} P(Z)$. Since the Shamir's reduction preserves rationality, the stack reduction also preserves rationality. The rational subsets of $P(Z)$ are thus rational subsets of $\tilde{Z}^*$. It follows that $K\theta$ is a rational subset of $\tilde{Z}^*$. Since $K\theta \subset Z^*$, we have $K\theta \in \operatorname{Rat} Z^*$. ∎

This proposition implies that any (PR)-function preserves rationality. A (PR)-monoid has a description which preserves rationality hence [10]:

PROPOSITION 3.2 . — *The rational subsets of a (PR)-monoid are unambiguous and closed under boolean operations.*

We give now another formulation of a result proven by Ginsburg and Greibach [7]: they enounce this result in terms of pushdown automata and we enounce it in terms of rational subsequential transducers.

PROPOSITION 3.3 . — *Let θ be a rational subsequential transducer from X^* into $P(Z)$, with values in Z^*. If $K \in \operatorname{Rat} Z^*$ then $K\theta^{-1}$ is a deterministic context-free language.*

This proposition remains true for (PR)-functions, hence:

PROPOSITION 3.4 . — *Let M be a (PR)-monoid and (X, α) a generating system of M. If $R \in \operatorname{Rat} M$ then $R\alpha^{-1}$ is a deterministic context-free language.*

4   Closure properties

In this paper, we consider only two operations: submonoids and free products. To prove the closure of the family of (PR)-monoids by submonoids, we use the cross-section theorem of Eilenberg [4], as it is done for rational monoids. We prove that (PR)-monoids are closed by free products, unlike rational monoids. Other operations are studied in [10]: we have proven that a Rees quotient of a (PR)-monoid by a rational ideal is a (PR)-monoid and that a direct product of a (PR)-monoid by a finite monoid is a (PR)-monoid; we also conjectured that the family of (PR)-monoids is not closed under ideal extensions.

4.1   Submonoids

The closure of the family of (PR)-monoids by finitely generated submonoids is a consequence of two strong properties of (PR)-functions proven by Sakarovitch [11]. The first one is a generalization of the cross-section theorem of Eilenberg [4].

PROPOSITION 4.1 . — *Let θ be a rational function from X^* into $P(Z)$ then:*
$\forall R \in \operatorname{Rat} X^*, \exists S \in \operatorname{Rat} X^*$ *such that $S \subset R$ and θ is a bijection from S onto $R\theta$.*

For the definition and properties of rational subsequential transducers from X^* into Z^*, we refer to Berstel [2] (in fact they are functions realized by row-monomial transducers from X^* into Y^* with a set of states Q).

PROPOSITION 4.2 . — *Let θ be a rational subsequential transducer from X^* into $P(Z)$, with values in Z^*, and T be rational subset of X^* such that θ is injective on T. Then the restriction of θ to T is a rational subsequential function from X^* into Z^*.*

The (PR)-functions satisfy also these two properties. It allows to prove the following

PROPOSITION 4.3 . — *Any finitely generated submonoid N of a (PR)-monoid M is a (PR)-monoid.*

Proof. Let (X', α') a generating system of N. We extend it in a generating system (X, α) of M. Let β be a (PR)-description of M for (X, α). The two properties expressed above imply that there exists a rational subset T of X^* such that $T \subset X'^*$, the restriction β_T of β to T is a bijection from T onto $X'^*\beta$ and β_T is a rational function from X^* into X^*. $\beta\beta_T^{-1}$ is a (PR)-description of N. ∎

4.2 Free products

The *free product* of two monoids M and N, denoted by $M*N$, is equal to the monoid whose elements are the series $(u_1, \ldots, u_n)$, where the u_i are alternatively in $M \setminus \{1_M\}$ and $N \setminus \{1_N\}$ The product of two elements $(u_1, \ldots, u_n)$ and $(v_1, \ldots, v_p)$ is equal to:
(1) $(u_1, \ldots u_n, v_1 \ldots, v_p)$ if u_n and v_1 are not in the same monoid
(2) $(u_1, \ldots u_{n-1}, u_n v_1, v_2 \ldots, v_p)$ if u_n and v_1 are in the same monoid and if $u_n v_1$ is different from the identity of this monoid
(3) the product of $(u_1, \ldots, u_{n-1})$ and $(v_2, \ldots, v_p)$ if u_n and v_1 are in the same monoid and if $u_n v_1 = 1_M$ or 1_N.
We write $u = u_1 \ldots u_n$ instead of $u = (u_1, \ldots, u_n)$.

Sakarovitch [13] proves that *the free product of two rational monoids is a rational monoid if and only if at least one of the two monoids is a semigroup with adjoint identity.* If M and N are not semigroups with adjoint identity, there exist letters a, b (representatives of elements of M) and letters c, d (representatives of elements of N) which are not reduced in 1 and such that ab and cd are reduced in 1. We have thus to reduce in 1 the elements of the form $ac \ldots acdb \ldots db$, which is not possible with a rational function. The Shamir's reduction is the suitable object to do this.

In view to prove the closure of (PR)-monoids under free products, we give to any (PR)-monoid a (PR)-description $\beta = \theta\tau$ such that θ makes all the reductions in 1.

LEMMA 4.1 . — *Let M be a (PR)-monoid and (X, α) a generating system of M. There exists a (PR)-description $\beta = \theta\tau$ of M for (X, α) such that:*

$$u\alpha = 1 \iff u\beta = 1 \iff u\theta = 1.$$

Proof. There exists a (PR)-description β of M for (X, α) such that $1\beta = 1$. We have thus: $u\alpha = 1 \iff u\beta = 1$. There exist a subsequential transducer $\omega = (\xi, \psi)$ from X^* into a polycyclic monoid $P(Y)$ and a rational function v from Y^* from X^* such that $\beta = \omega v$.

Let $R_1 = 1v^{-1}$ then $R_1 \in \mathrm{Rat}\, Y^*$. Let $a_0 \notin Y$ and $(E, s, ., F_1)$ a deterministic automaton which accepts $a_0 R_1$.

Let $R_2 = Y^* \setminus R_1$ and $F_2 = E \setminus F_1$.

Let $Z = (Y \cup \{a_0\}) \times E$ and φ the morphism from Z^* into Y^* defined by:

$$\forall (z, t) \in Z \quad (z, t)\varphi = \begin{cases} z & \text{if } z \in Y \\ 1 & \text{if } z = a_0. \end{cases}$$

Let $a_1, \ldots, a_k \in Y$ such that $\xi = a_1 \ldots a_k$.

We build a transducer (λ, μ, ν) from X^* into $P(Z)$ in the following way.

$$\lambda = (a_0, s)(a_1, s.a_0) \ldots (a_k, s.a_0 a_1 \ldots a_{k-1})i \quad \text{if } \xi = a_1 \ldots a_k \in R_i;$$

$$x\mu = \{\overline{t}\,\overline{(y_1, t_1)} \ldots \overline{(y_l, t_l)}\,\overline{(z, t)}(z, t)(z_1, t.z) \ldots (z_n, t.zz_1 \ldots z_{n-1})j \mid$$
$$i, j \in \{1, 2\}, \overline{y_1} \ldots \overline{y_l} z_1 \ldots z_n \in x\psi \text{ and } t.zz_1 \ldots z_n \in F_j\}$$

Then:

$$\lambda(u\mu) = (a_0, s)(y_1, s.a_0) \ldots (y_m, s.a_0 y_1 \ldots y_{m-1})i$$
$$\text{iff}$$
$$\xi(u\psi) \in R_i \text{ and } \xi(u\psi) = y_1 \ldots y_m.$$

(Note that (λ, μ) is a subsequential transducer.)

$$\nu = \overline{1}\,\overline{R\varphi^{-1}}\,\overline{(a_0, s)} + \overline{2}.$$

Then $\theta = (\lambda, \mu, \nu)$ is a rational subsequential transducer and θ verifies:

$$u\theta = \begin{cases} 1 & \text{if } u\omega \in R_1 \\ (a_0, s)(y_1, s.a_0) \ldots (y_m, s.a_0 y_1 \ldots y_{m-1}) & \text{if } u\omega \notin R_1 \text{ and } u\omega = y_1 \ldots y_m \end{cases}$$

what implies: $u\theta = 1 \iff u\alpha = 1$.

Let $\tau = \varphi v$. Then $\beta = \theta \tau$. $\blacksquare$

THEOREM 4.1 . — *The free product of two (PR)-monoids is a (PR)-monoid.*

Proof. Let M and N be two (PR)-monoids. Let (X, α) be a generating system of M and (X', α') a generating system of N. Let γ be the morphism from $(X \cup X')^*$ into $M * N$ defined by:

$$z\gamma = \begin{cases} z\alpha & \text{if } z \in X \\ z\alpha' & \text{if } z \in X' \end{cases}$$

Then $(X \cup X', \gamma)$ is a generating system of $M * N$.

Let $\beta = \theta \tau$ a (PR)-description of M for (X, α) and $\beta' = \theta' \tau'$ a (PR)-description of N for (X', α') such that $\theta = (\lambda, \mu, \nu)$ is a subsequential transducer from X^* into $P(Z)$, $\theta' = (\lambda', \mu', \nu')$ is a subsequential transducer from X'^* into $P(Z')$ and:

$$\forall f \in X^* \quad f\alpha = 1 \iff f\theta = 1$$
$$\forall f \in X'^* \quad f\alpha' = 1 \iff f\theta' = 1.$$

Let χ the function of graph:

$$(1 \cup \hat{\tau}')(\hat{\tau}\hat{\tau}')^*(1 \cup \hat{\tau}).$$

($\hat{\tau}$ is the graph of τ.)

Let $d \notin Z \cup Z'$ and $\sigma = (\eta, \kappa, \rho)$ the following transducer from $(X \cup X')^*$ into $P(Z \cup Z' \cup \{d\})$:

$$\eta = d$$

$$z\kappa = \begin{cases} \bar{d}d\lambda(z\mu) + z\mu + \nu'\bar{d}d\lambda(z\mu) + \nu'D_{Z'}\lambda(z\mu) + \nu'(z\mu) & \text{if } z \in X \\ \bar{d}d\lambda'(z\mu') + z\mu' + \nu\bar{d}d\lambda'(z\mu') + \nu D_Z\lambda'(z\mu') + \nu(z\mu') & \text{if } z \in X' \end{cases}$$

$$\rho = \nu + \nu'$$

(where $D_Z = \{\bar{z}z \mid z \in Z\}$ and $D_{Z'} = \{\overline{z'}z' \mid z' \in Z'\}$).

This transducer is subsequential. Let ε be the function which erases the letter d. Then $\delta = \sigma\varepsilon\chi$ is a (PR)-description of $M * N$. ∎

5 Other families

We have studied the family of (PR)-monoids for the following reasons: it contains the rational monoids and the free groups, it is closed under free products and the complexity of (PR)-monoids is not too high. There exist other families of monoids of the same complexity than (PR)-monoids.

The first one is the family of *(P)-monoids*, described by *(P)-functions*. A *(P)-function* from X^* into Y^* is equal to the composition of a rational subsequential transducer from X^* into a polycyclic $P(Z)$, and of an *injective* rational function from Z^* into Y^*.

The family of (P)-monoids contains free groups, is closed under free products but does not contain rational monoids. For instance, let $X = \{a, b, c, x, y, z\}$ and $\equiv$ the congruence in X^* generated by:

$$ab^nc = \begin{cases} xy^nz & \text{if } n \text{ is odd} \\ xy^{2n}z & \text{if } n \text{ is even} \end{cases}$$

Let $M = X^*/\equiv$. Then M is a rational monoid and M is not a (P)-monoid. To prove this fact, we use the Proposition 4.2 and the characterization of rational subsequential functions between free monoids given by Choffrut [3].

Another family is the family of *(RP)-monoids*, described by *(RP)-functions*. A *(RP)-function* from X^* into Y^* is equal to the composition of a rational function from X^* into X'^* and of a (P)-function from X'^* into Y^*.

The family of (RP)-monoids contains rational monoids and free groups. I conjecture that it is not closed under free products. The family of (PR)-monoids does not contain the (RP)-monoids (we use the Proposition 3.4 to prove this assertion). I conjecture that the family of (RP)-monoids does not contain the (PR)-monoids

References

[1] Benois M. (1969), "Parties rationnelles du groupe libre", *C.R. Acad. Sci. Paris*, Ser. A 269, 1188-1190.

[2] Berstel J. (1979), "Transductions and Context-free Languages", Teubner, Stuttgart.

[3] Choffrut Ch. (1978), "Contribution à l'étude de quelques familles remarquables de fonctions rationnelles", Thèse Sci. math., Univ. Paris 6, Paris.

[4] Eilenberg S. (1974), "Automata, Languages and Machines", Vol. A, Academic Press, New York.

[5] Fliess M. (1971), "Deux applications de la représentation matricielle d'une série rationnelle non commutative", *Journal of Algebra*, 19, 344-353.

[6] Ginsburg S. (1966), "The Mathematical Theory of Context-free Languages", Mac Graw Hill.

[7] Ginsburg S., Greibach S. (1966), "Deterministic Context-free Languages", *Inform. and Control*, 9, 620-648.

[8] Nivat M. (1968), "Transductions des langages de Chomsky", *Ann. Inst. Fourier*, 18, 339-456.

[9] Nivat M. (1970), "Sur les automates à mémoire à pile", Proc. of International Computing Symposium, Bonn (W. Itzfeld, ed.); North Holland, 655-663.

[10] Pelletier M. (1989), "Descriptions de semigroupes par automates", Thèse de l'Université Paris 6.

[11] Sakarovitch J. (1979), "Syntaxe des langages de Chomsky", Th. Sc. Math., Univ. Paris 7.

[12] Sakarovitch J. (1981), "Description des monoïdes de type fini", *EIK*, 17, 417-434.

[13] Sakarovitch J. (1987), Easy Multiplications. I. The Realm of Kleene's Theorem, *Information and Computation*, Vol. 74, No. 3, 173-197.

OPTIMAL PARALLEL 3-COLOURING ALGORITHM
FOR ROOTED TREES AND ITS APPLICATION

Peter RAJČÁNI

Computing Center of the Slovak Academy of Sciences

Dúbravská cesta 9, 842 35 Bratislava, Czechoslovakia

Abstract

A new optimal parallel algorithm for 3-colouring rooted trees with maximum degree Δ is presented. The algorithm runs in $O(\Delta \log n/\log \log n)$ time on a CRCW PRAM using $O(\Delta \, n \log \log n/\log n)$ processors. This technique is used to develop optimal algorithms for several graph problems including $(\Delta+1)$-colouring of constant degree graphs, 7-colouring of planar graphs or finding a maximal independent set in a planar graph. The technique can be applied to expression tree evaluation as well and yields an optimal logarithmic time algorithm.

1. INTRODUCTION

Symmetry-breaking techniques introduced in [GPS] enable us to select a large set of inedpendent operations to be executed in parallel. Such technique was proposed by Goldberg et al. in [GPS]. It allows us to 3-colour a rooted tree in $O(\log^* n)$ time on a CREW PRAM using $O(n)$ processors. Goldberg et al. in [GPS] also posed a question if it is possible to find an optimal parallel algorithm within the same time bound .

We give an algorithm for 3-colouring rooted trees with maximum constant degree Δ in $O(\Delta \log n/\log \log n)$ time on a CRCW PRAM using $O(\Delta \, n \log \log n/ \log n)$ processors. This technique is used to construct algorithms listed below :

1. For graphs with maximum constant degree Δ we give CRCW PRAM algorithms for (Δ+1)-colouring and finding a maximal independent set (MIS) with running time $O(\Delta^2 \log n/\log \log n)$ using $O(\Delta\ n \log \log n/\log n)$ processors.

2. For planar graphs we give 7-colouring, MIS and maximal matching algorithms that run in $O(\log n)$ time on a CRCW PRAM and use $O(n/\log n)$ processors.

3. We give an $O(\log n)$ CRCW PRAM algorithm for expression tree evaluation that uses $O(n/\log n)$ processors.

The above algorithms are optimal in the sense that the product P.T is linear in the input size (T denotes the running time and P the number of processors).

The results give the first optimal algorithms for problems listed in cases 1 and 2 improving the processor bounds. The algorithm for expression tree evaluation is only of academical interest since optimal algorithms for this problem have previosly been found on an EREW PRAM, see [ADKP], [CV1], [GMT], [GR2], [KD].

Goldberg et al. in [GPS] proposed $O((\log \Delta)(\Delta^2 + \log^* n))$ time EREW PRAM algorithms for (Δ+1)-colouring and finding a maximal independent set for graphs with maximum degree Δ that use $O(n)$ processors. They also presented $O(\log n)$ time CRCW PRAM algorithms for 7-colouring, MIS and maximal matching in planar graphs that use $O(n)$ processors. Our algorithms for planar graphs, however, are optimal within the same time bound.

Another (Δ+1)-colouring algorithm for graphs with maximum degree Δ was proposed by Luby [Lu]. It runs in $O(\log^3 n \log \log n)$ time using a linear number of processors on a CREW PRAM. For the case of constant degree graphs, our algorithm is faster and uses less processors.

The best deterministic MIS algorithm was proposed by Goldberg and Spencer [GS]. It runs in $O(\log^3 n)$ time on an EREW PRAM using $O((m + n)/\log n)$ processors, where m is the number of edges in the input graph. Our algorithm is faster for the special case of planar graphs and constant degree graphs.

The paper is organized as follows. Basic definitions and the model of parallel computation are introduced in §2. The 3-colouring algorithm for rooted trees is given in §3. The applications to constant degree graphs, planar graphs and expression tree evaluation are presented in §§ 4, and 5 respectively. Concluding remarks are given in §6.

2. PRELIMINARIES

This section introduces the definitions and notation used throughout this paper. We consider an undirected graph $G = (V, E)$ with n vertices and m edges. The maximum degree of a graph is denoted by Δ. The subgraph of G induced by a set $V' \subseteq V$ is denoted by $G[V']$. A *vertex colouring* of a graph G is an assignment $c\colon V \to \mathbb{N} \cup \{0\}$ of nonnegative integers (colours) to the vertices of G such that no two adjacent vertices have the same colour. The colour of a vertex v is denoted by $c(v)$.

We say that a subset $I \subseteq V$ is *inependent* if no two vertices in I are adjacent. An independent set is maximal if it is not properly contained in another independent set of V.

A subset $M \subseteq E$ is a *matching* if the edges in M are node disjoint. A matching is maximal if by adding one more edge we obtain a non-matching set.

A *rooted tree* is the tree with a selected vertex r as the root and where each nonroot node knows which of its neighbours is its parent (i.e. for each $v \in V - \{r\}$ a function parent(v) is defined).

The model of parallel computation used is a concurrent-read concurrent-write (CRCW) parallel random access machine (PRAM) [CV2], [Hag]. A PRAM employs p synchronous processors having access to a common memory. A CRCW PRAM allows simultaneous access by more than one processor for reading and writing into a particular memory location in unit time. The write conflicts are assumed to be resolved arbitrarily (ARBITRARY CRCW PRAM).

We assume that input graphs are given by adjacency lists [GR1] and that the processors are assigned to the vertices and edges of the input graph. No particular processor allocation is specified, it will be apparent which processors are active in respective cases. Finally let us introduce a useful theorem that allows us to reduce the number of processors :

Theorem 2.1 (Brent) [CV2] *Any synchronous parallel algorithm taking time t that consists of a total of x elmentary operations can be implemented by p processors within a time of* $\lfloor x/p \rfloor + t$.

3. 3-COLOURING ROOTED TREE ALGORITHM

The 3-colouring rooted tree algorithm is inspired by the 3-colouring algorithm of Goldberg et al. [GPS] and by the 2-ruling set algorithm (a MIS algorithm for linked lists) by Cole and Vishkin [CV2].

The algorithm starts with an initial colouring given by processor numbers and proceeds in three steps. In the first step we reduce the number of colours to log n/log log n by applying twice the generalized deterministic coin tossing technique for rooted trees by Goldberg et al. [GPS]. In step 2 we reduce this colouring to a $(\Delta+1)$-colouring iterating through colours. For each vertex v with colour i we find the smallest colour $c \in \{0,1,..,\Delta\}$ that is not used by the neighbours of v and recolour v with this colour (procedure *RECOLOUR(v)*). The recolouring can be done in parallel since the vertices of one colour are independent. The implementation of step 2 follows the design proposed by Cole and Vishkin in [CV2]. Step 3 reduces the $(\Delta+1)$-colouring to a 3-colouring iterating through colours. In the ith iteration we shift down the current colouring (we mean by this recolouring each nonroot vertex with the colour of his parent and recolouring the root with any colour $c \in \{0,1,2\}$ different from its current colour, see [GPS]), and recolour each node of the colour i with the smallest colour $c \in \{0,1,2\}$ different from its neighbours' colours. After a shift of colours, the neighbours of any node have at most two different colours. Thus in each iteration the number of colours decreases by one as long as it is greater than three.

Algorithm *3-COLOUR*

Step 1: Start with an initial colouring given by processor numbers.
Apply twice the procedure by Goldberg et al. [GPS] to reduce the number of colours to log n/log log n.

Step 2: **for** $i = 0$ **to** $\log n/\log \log n - 1$ **do**

        begin

                for each $v, c(v) = i$ **in parallel do**

                        if $c(v) \notin \{0, 1, \ldots, \Delta\}$ **then** *RECOLOUR(v)* ;

        end;

Step 3: **for** $i = \Delta$ **to** 3 **step** -1 **do**

        begin

                shift down the colours;

                for each v, $c(v) = i$ **in parallel do**

                        recolour v with the smallest colour $c \in \{0, 1, 2\}$ not
used by v's neighbours;

        end;

Procedure *RECOLOUR(v)*

begin

    for each v', $v = \mathrm{parent}(v')$ **in parallel do** $x := 0$;

    for $j = 0$ **to** Δ **do**

        begin

             if $j = c(\mathrm{parent}(v))$ **then** $j := j + 1$;

             for each v', $v = \mathrm{parent}(v')$ **in parallel do**

                  if $j = c(v')$ **then** $x := 1$;

             if $x = 0$ **then** $c(v) := j$; **end;**

        end;

end;

Theorem 3.1 *A rooted tree $T = (V, E)$ with maximum constant degree Δ can be 3-coloured in $O(\Delta \log n/\log \log n)$ time on a CRCW PRAM using $O(\Delta \, n \log \log n/\log n)$ processors.*

Proof: It easy to see from the analysis above that the algorithm *3-COLOUR* indeed achieves a 3-colouring. According to Goldberg et al. [GPS] step 1 can be implemented in $O(1)$ time and $O(n)$ operations. The procedure *RECOLOUR(v)* terminates in at most Δ iterations. Due to the concurrent-write property each iteration takes $O(1)$ time. According to the complexity analysis by Cole and Vishkin in [CV2] the execution of the whole step 2 takes $O(\Delta \log n/\log \log n)$ time using $O(\Delta\, n \log \log n/\log n)$ processors on a CRCW PRAM. The shift of colours and recolouring in step 3 takes both constant time and $O(n)$ operations. Since each node has a maximum degree Δ, each iteration terminates in $O(\log n/\log \log n)$ time using $O(\Delta\, n \log \log n/\log n)$ processors (by Theorem 2.1). Step 3 terminates in at most $\Delta-2$ iterations. The theorem follows immediately. □

4. ALGORITHMS FOR CONSTANT DEGREE GRAPHS AND PLANAR GRAPHS

In this section, we give optimal algorithms for $(\Delta+1)$-colouring and MIS for constant degree graphs and optimal algorithms for 7-colouring, MIS and maximal matching for planar graphs. The algorithm for $(\Delta+1)$-colouring of graphs with maximum degree Δ follows the design proposed by Goldberg et al. in [GPS]. Their 3-colouring procedure, however, is replaced by our optimal one. Given a $(\Delta+1)$-colouring of a graph we can find an MIS of the graph iterating through colours [GPS]. The running time of these algorithms is dominated by the running time of the 3-colouring algorithm. Thus as a consequence of Theorem 3.1 we obtain:

Theorem 4.1 *A graph with maximum constant degree Δ can be coloured with $\Delta+1$ colours in $O(\Delta^2 \log n/\log \log n)$ time on a CRCW PRAM using $O(\Delta\, n \log \log n/\log n)$ processors.*

Theorem 4.2 *A maximal independent set of a constant degree graph can be found in $O(\Delta^2 \log n/\log \log n)$ time on a CRCW PRAM using $O(\Delta\, n \log \log n/\log n)$ processors.*

The 7-colouring algorithm for planar graphs uses the algorithm proposed by Goldberg et al. [GPS] which runs in $O(\log n)$ time using $O(n)$ processors on a CRCW PRAM. The algorithm uses a framework proposed by Hagerup in [Hag] and proceeds in three stages:

1. Iteratively reduce the size of the input graph to $n/\log n$. In the ith iteration remove the set V_1 that contains all vertices of degree six or less in $G[V - (V_1 \cup V_2 \cup \ldots \cup V_{i-1})]$ and colour $G[V_i]$ using the

algorithm for (Δ+1)-colouring of constant degree graphs (with Δ = 6).

2. Colour the remaining graph using the 7-colouring algorithm of Goldberg et al. [GPS].

3. Iteratively add the sets removed in the first stage. In each iteration recolour the nodes of $G[V - (V_1 \cup V_2 \cup \ldots \cup V_{i-1})]$ to maintain a 7-colouring.

Theorem 4.3 *The 7-colouring algorithm colours a planar graph with 7 colours and runs in $O(\log n)$ time on a CRCW PRAM using $O(n/\log n)$ processors.*

Proof: By Euler's formula [Har], in each iteration of the first stage the size of the input graph is reduced by a constant factor. Selection of the set V_1 takes constant time and $O(n)$ processors on a CRCW PRAM [GPS]. By Theorem 4.1 we conclude that one iteration of the first stage takes $O(\log n/\log \log n)$ time using $O(n \log \log n/\log n)$ processors. Adding and recolouring of the vertices in the ith iteration of the third stage takes $O(1)$ time and $O(n)$ operations since $G[V_1]$ is already 7-coloured and each vertex in V_1 is of degree six or less in $G[V - (V_1 \cup V_2 \cup \ldots \cup V_{i-1})]$. Since a planar graph can be 7-coloured in $O(\log n)$ time by $O(n)$ processors [GPS] according to [Hag] we complete the proof. □

Given a 7-colouring of a planar graph we can find an MIS of the graph iterating through colours [GPS]. Since only constant time is needed for each colour we obtain:

Corollary 4.1 *An MIS in a planar graph can be found in $O(\log n)$ time on a CRCW PRAM using $O(n/\log n)$ processors.*

The algorithm for maximal matching (MM) follows the same design as the 7-colouring algorithm using the maximal matching algorithm proposed by Goldberg et al. [GPS]. The algorithm proceeds in three stages:

1. Apply the first stage of the 7-colouring algorithm introduced above.

2. Apply an $O(\log n)$ time, $O(n)$ processors CRCW PRAM maximal matching algorithm by Goldberg et al. [GPS] to the reduced graph.

3. Iteratively add the sets V_1 removed in the first stage and compute an MM in $G[V - (V_1 \cup V_2 \cup \ldots \cup V_{i-1})]$ from the MM in $G[V - (V_1 \cup V_2 \cup \ldots \cup V_i)]$ using the algorithm by Goldberg et al. [GPS].

Theorem 4.4 *A maximal matching in a planar graph can be found in $O(\log n)$ time using $O(n/\log n)$ processors on a CRCW PRAM.*

5. EXPRESSION TREE EVALUATION

In this section we present an optimal algorithm for expression tree evaluation. An *expression tree* is the tree $T = (V, E)$ where each internal node stores an operator $(+, -, \times, :)$ and each leaf stores an integer. The problem is to compute the value of the expression tree without free preprocessing [MR]. We assume that the expression tree has a maximum constant degree Δ. This assumption is without loss of generality, since we can convert an expression tree to the equivalent binary tree [Hag].

We say a sequence of vertices $v_1, v_2, \ldots, v_k$ is a *chain* if v_{i+1} is the only child of v_i for $1 \le i < k$ and v_k has exactly one child which is not a leaf.

The expression tree evaluation algorithm can be obtained from the tree contraction algorithm by a proper interpretation of RAKE and COMPRESS operations, see [MR]. The tree contraction algorithm proceeds in two stages:

Procedure *Optimal Tree Contraction*

1.   **while** $|V| > n/\log n$ **do**
    begin
        1.1 Remove in parallel all leaves from T (RAKE);
        1.2 Apply the algorithm *3-COLOUR* to T;
        1.3 **for** $i = 0$ **to** 2 **do**
            begin
                for each $v \in V$, $c(v) = i$ **in parallel do**
                    if v and parent(v) belong to a chain and v has
                    different colour from parent(v) **then**
                        identify v with parent(v); (COMPRESS)
            end;
    end;

2.   Apply the tree contraction algorithm of Miller and Reif [MR] to the reduced tree.

Theorem 5.1 *The expression tree evaluation problem can be solved in O(log n) time on a CRCW PRAM using O(n/log n) processors.*

Proof: The algorithm is correct since we never remove two adjacent nodes from the tree. As described in [MR] using concurrent reads and writes we can determine if a vertex v belongs to a chain in constant time. Thus operations RAKE and COMPRESS take $O(1)$ time and $O(n)$ operations. By Theorem 3.1 step 1.2 takes $O(\Delta \log n /\log \log n)$ time and uses $O(\Delta n \log \log n/\log n)$ processors. Since T is coloured with three colours, the COMPRESS operation removes at least a half of vertices of each chain. Thus after simultaneous applying of the RAKE and COMPRESS operations the number of vertices decreases by a constant factor [MR]. Since the tree contraction problem and hence the expression tree evaluation problem can be solved in $O(\log n)$ time by $O(n)$ processors [MR], by [Hag] we complete the proof.□

6. CONCLUSION

An optimal 3-colouring algorithm for rooted trees of maximum constant degree Δ was presented. We have shown how to apply this technique to several graph problems and to the expression tree evaluation problem resulting in optimal algorithms for these problems. Our results give a positive answer to the question posed by Goldberg et al. in [GPS]. We believe that this technique may have applications in design of parallel algorithms. Our results motivate the following questions:

o   The 3-colouring algorithm works well on a CRCW PRAM.   Can we implement this algorithm on weaker models of computation (e.g. a CREW PRAM or an EREW PRAM) ?

o   Our technique works for rooted trees of a constant degree. Can we design an optimal 3-colouring algorithm for arbitrary rooted trees ?

Hierarchies over the context-free Languages

Klaus Reinhardt

Institut für Informatik, Universität Stuttgart

Azenbergstr.12, D-7000 Stuttgart-1

e-mail: reinhard@informatik.uni-stuttgart.dbp.de

Abstract　Alternation is a generalized principle of nondeterminism. The alternating turing machine is used to characterize the polynomial hierarchy. In this paper we show, that a hierarchy can be characterized with alternating pushdown automata, which we expect to be strict in contrast to a hierarchy with alternating finite automata or alternating space bounded automata. We describe a similar oracle hierarchy over the context-free languages, for which we construct complete languages. We show, that each level of the hierarchy with alternating pushdown automata is included in the corresponding level of the oracle hierarchy and that the logarithmic closure over both levels is the corresponding level of the polynomial hierarchy with one alternation less.

The principle of the alternation is also transfered to grammars. Hereby we prove, that the hierarchy with alternating context-free grammars is identical with the oracle hierarchy over the context-free languages and that in case of unbounded alternation context-free and context-sensitive grammars have the same power.

1　Alternating pushdown automata

In [LSL84] 2-way-pushdown automata without additional work tape $A\Sigma_k-2PDA$ are considered yielding the result $co\text{-}NTIME(n) \subseteq A\Pi_2-2PDA \subseteq co\text{-}NTIME(n^p)$ for a p and $NSPACE(n) \subseteq A\Sigma_k-2PDA \subseteq DSPACE(n^2)$ for $k \geq 2$. The reason for this is, that such a pushdown automaton can guess a word with unrestricted length into its pushdown store using an ∞-loop on existential states and after alternation test whether the guessed word is an accepting path of configurations. In contrast to that in this work we consider pushdown automata which stop on every path.

Definition　An alternating 1-way-pushdown automaton is a 9-tuple

$$A = (Z_e, Z_a, \Sigma, \Gamma, \delta, z_0, \$, E, R)$$

with the set of states $Z = Z_e \cup Z_a$ consisting of existential states Z_e and universal states Z_a, the input alphabet Σ, the pushdown alphabet Γ, the transition relation $\delta \subseteq (Z \times \Sigma \times \Gamma) \times (Z \times \Gamma^*)$, the start state z_0, the bottom symbol $\$$, the final states E, the rejecting states R, the configuration set $C_A = Z \times \Sigma^* \times \Gamma^*$, the start configuration $\sigma_A(x) = \langle z_0, x, \$ \rangle$ and the configuration transition relation $\langle z, x_1 x, gk \rangle \underset{A}{\vdash} \langle z', x, g'k \rangle$ if and only if $z, z' \in Z$, $k, g \in \Gamma^*$, $g \in \Gamma$, $g' \in \Gamma^*$ and $\langle z, x_1, g, z', g' \rangle \in \delta$. Let $\underset{A}{\overset{*}{\vdash}}$ be the reflexive and transitive closure of $\underset{A}{\vdash}$. If $z \in Z_a$, then a configuration $\langle z, x, k \rangle \in C_A$ is called a universal configuration, if $z \in Z_e$, then it is called an existential configuration, if $z \in R$ and $x = \lambda$, then the configuration is called rejecting, if $z \in E$ and $x = \lambda$, then it is called accepting. Let $l^i : C_M \to \{0, 1\}$ be the labeling function defined as

REFERENCES

[ADKP] K. Abrahamson, N. Dadoun, D. G. Kirkpatrick and T. Przytycka, "A simple parallel tree contraction algorithm", J. Algorithms, 10 (1989), pp. 287-302.

[CV1] R. Cole and U. Vishkin, "The accelerated centroid decomposition technique for optimal parallel tree evaluation in logarithmic time", Algorithmica, 3 (1988a), pp. 329-346.

[CV2] R. Cole and U. Vishkin, "Faster optimal parallel prefix sums and list ranking", Inform. and Comput., 81 (1989), pp. 334-352.

[GMT] H. Gazit, G. L. Miller and S. H. Teng, "Optimal tree contraction in an EREW model", in S. K. Tewkesbury, B. W. Dickinson and S. C. Schwartz, editors, Concurrent Computations: Algorithms, Architecture and Technology, Plenum Press, New York, 1988.

[GR1] A. Gibbons and W. Rytter, "Efficient parallel algorithms", Cambridge University Press, Cambridge, 1988.

[GR2] A. Gibbons and W. Rytter, "Optimal parallel algorithms for dynamic expression evaluation and context-free recognition", Inform. and Comput., 81 (1989), pp. 32-45.

[GPS] A. V. Goldberg, S. A. Plotkin and G. E. Shannon, "Parallel symmetry - breaking in sparse graphs", SIAM J. Disc. Math., 1 (1988), pp. 434-446.

[GS] M. Goldberg and T. Spencer, "Constructing a maximal independent set in parallel", SIAM J. Disc. Math., 2 (1989), pp. 322-328.

[Hag] T. Hagerup, "Optimal parallel algorithms on planar graphs", in J. H. Reif, editor, VLSI Algorithms and Architectures, Lecture Notes in Computer Science 319, Springer-Verlag, New York, Berlin, 1988, pp. 24-32.

[Har] F. Harary, "Graph theory", Addison Wesley, Reading, Mass., 1969.

[KD] S. R. Kosaraju and A. L. Delcher, "Optimal parallel evaluation of tree - structured computations by raking", in J. H. Reif, editor, VLSI Algorithms and Architectures, Lecture Notes in Computer Science, 319, Springer-Verlag, New York, Berlin, 1988, pp. 101-110.

[Lu] M. Luby, "Removing randomness in parallel computation without a processor penalty", in Proc. 29th Annual IEEE Symp. on Foundations of Computer Science, 1988, pp. 162-173.

[MR] G. L. Miller and J. H. Reif, "Parallel tree contraction and its application", in Proc. 26th Annual IEEE Symp. on Foundations of Computer Science, 1985, pp. 478-489.

follows:

$$l^0(\alpha) \quad := \quad \begin{cases} 1 \text{ if } \alpha \text{ is accepting} \\ 0 \text{ else} \end{cases}$$

$$l^{i+1}(\alpha) \quad := \quad \begin{cases} 1 & \text{if } \alpha \text{ is accepting,} \\ 0 & \text{if } \alpha \text{ is rejecting,} \\ \bigwedge\limits_{\alpha \vdash_{\overline{M}} \beta} l^i(\beta) & \text{if } \alpha \text{ an universal configuration,} \\ \bigvee\limits_{\alpha \vdash_{\overline{M}} \beta} l^i(\beta) & \text{if } \alpha \text{ is an existential configuration} \end{cases}$$

$$l^* \quad := \quad \sup_i l^i$$

An automaton M *accepts* x if $l^*(\sigma_M(x)) = 1$, that means $L(M) := \{x \in \Sigma^* \mid l^*(\sigma_M(x)) = 1\}$. $A1\Sigma_k PDA$ ($A1\Pi_k PDA$) is the set of languages which can be recognized by an alternating 1-way-pushdown automaton which starts in an existential (universal) state, changes the kind of states at most $k - 1$ times and stops on every path. In particular there are no ∞-loops on λ-transitions.

It holds that $A1\Sigma_0 PDA = A1\Pi_0 PDA = DCFL$ and $A1\Sigma_1 PDA = CFL$.

2 An oracle hierarchy with finite transducers

To define an oracle hierarchy over the context-free languages, we need a transducer, which can not calculate too much by itself (otherwise the oracle would be useless). For this reason the finite transducers according to [Ber79] are used:

Definition A finite transducer $T = (Z, \Sigma, \Gamma, \delta, z_0)$ is an automaton with a 1-way input tape with the input alphabet Σ, a 1-way output tape with the output alphabet Γ, a transition function $\delta : (Z \times \Sigma) \to (Z \times \Gamma^*)$ (or transition relation $\delta \subset (Z \times \Sigma) \times (Z \times \Gamma^*)$, if T nondeterministic) and a start state $z_0 \in Z$. $f_T(x)$ is the word, that is on the output tape, when T has scanned the word x on the input tape. (If T is a nondeterministic transducer then f_T is a relation.) $L \leq^f L'$ ($L \leq^{nf} L'$) means, that there is a deterministic (nondeterministic) finite transducer T with 1-way input tape and 1-way output tape with $x \in L$ if and only if there is a calculation $f_T(x) \in L'$.

Lemma 2.1 $\leq^f$ and $\leq^{nf}$ are transitive

Definition For a language L and a class of languages S we define

$$\begin{aligned} A\Pi_0 FT(L) \quad &:= \quad \{L' \mid L' \leq^f L\}, \\ A\Pi_k FT(L) \quad &:= \quad co\text{-}A\Sigma_k FT(L) \text{ and} \\ A\Sigma_{k+1} FT(L) \quad &:= \quad \{L' \mid \exists L'' \in A\Pi_k FT(L) \text{ with } L' \leq^{nf} L''\} \\ A\Sigma_k FT(S) \quad &:= \quad \bigcup_{L \in S} A\Sigma_k FT(L). \end{aligned}$$

For a regular language R all languages in $A\Sigma_k FT(R)$ are regular, because a finite automaton can simulate a finite transducer and test the output immediately.

For that reason a ground language for a hierarchy with the context-free languages as Σ_1-level should be a non-regular, deterministic context-free language, where all context-free languages can be reduced to by a nondeterministic finite transducer. We use L_{pp}, the language of pushdown protocols of computations, which end with an empty pushdown store. In this protocol an e stands before pushed characters and an a stands before popped characters. For an alphabet Σ the language L_{pp}^{Σ} is defined as follows:

Definition $\lambda \in L_{pp}^{\Sigma}$ and for all $x, y \in L_{pp}^{\Sigma}$ it holds $xy \in L_{pp}^{\Sigma}$ and $ewxaw^R \in L_{pp}^{\Sigma}$ for a $w \in \Sigma^*$. $L_{pp} := L_{pp}^{\{0,1\}}$.

It holds $A\Pi_0 FT(L_{pp}) \subseteq DCFL$, because a deterministic pushdown automaton can simulate a deterministic transducer and test directly wether its output is a pushdown protocol.

Lemma 2.2 $A\Sigma_1 FT(L_{pp}) = CFL$

Proof: '$\subseteq$': A nondeterministic pushdown automaton can simulate the transducer and test its output directly.
'$\supseteq$': Let $L \in CFL$ by the nondeterministic pushdown automaton $M = (Z, \Sigma, \Gamma, \delta, \$, z_0)$, which accepts with an empty pushdown store, so it holds $L \leq^{nf} L_{pp}$ by a transducer T, which simulates the pushdown automaton and guesses the characters popped by M. Hereby T produces a pushdown protocol. For an accepting calculation of M with empty pushdown store the output is in L_{pp} if the right contents of the pushdown store is guessed. ∎
From Lemma 2.2 and Lemma 2.1 it follows $A\Sigma_1 FT(L_{pp}) = A\Sigma_1 FT(DCFL) = A\Sigma_1 FT(CFL)$ and from that:

Corollary: $A\Sigma_k FT(L_{pp}) = A\Sigma_k FT(DCFL) = A\Sigma_k FT(CFL)$ for $k \geq 1$

Lemma 2.3 $A1\Sigma_k PDA \subseteq A\Sigma_k FT(L_{pp})$ *for all* $k \geq 1$

Proof: by induction using a technique more common than in Lemma 2.2. ∎

2.1 Further characterizations of the polynomial hierarchy

Definition It holds $L \leq^{log} L'$ ($L \leq^{Hog} L'$), if there is a logarithmic (1-way) transducer T with $x \in L$ if and only if $f_T(x) \in L'$. For a class of languages S we say

$$LOG(S) := \{Y \mid \exists X \in S \text{ with } Y \leq^{log} X\}.$$

Theorem 2.1 *For the k-th level of the polynomial hierarchy* Σ_k^P *it holds* $\Sigma_k^P = LOG(A1\Sigma_{k+1} PDA) = LOG(A\Sigma_{k+1} FT(L_{pp}))$ *for* $k \geq 1$.

Proof: $LOG(A1\Sigma_{k+1} PDA) \subseteq LOG(A\Sigma_{k+1} FT(L_{pp}))$ with Lemma 2.3.
$LOG(A\Sigma_{k+1} FT(L_{pp})) \subseteq \Sigma_k^P$: The logarithmic reduction and k nondeterministics reductions can be performed in polynomial time, the question to a language in CFL or $co-CFL$ on the last level can be answered directly in polynomial time according to [Sud78].
$\Sigma_k^P \subseteq LOG(A1\Sigma_{k+1} PDA)$: According to [Sto76] for odd (even) k the language of the true quantified boolean expressions in conjunctive (disjunctive) normalform with a change of quantifiers restricted by k is log-complete for Σ_k^p. Here the following variation of presentation is used:

$$BBF_k := \{ \ \exists 1^{l_k} \forall 0^{l_{k-1}} ... \exists 1^{l_1} \# c_1 \wedge c_2 \wedge ... c_m \mid k \text{ odd}$$
$$c_i \in \{p, n, 0\}^l \text{ and the formula}$$
$$\exists x_l, ... x_{l-l_k} \forall x_{l-l_k-1}, ... x_{l-l_k-l_{k-1}}, ... \exists x_{l_1}, ... x_1 C_1 \wedge C_2 \wedge ... C_m,$$
$$\text{with the clauses } C_i := \bigvee_{c_{ij}=p} x_j \vee \bigvee_{c_{ij}=n} \overline{x_j} \text{ is true}\}$$

$$\cup \{ \ \exists 1^{l_k} \forall 0^{l_{k-1}} ... \forall 1^{l_1} \# c_1 \vee c_2 \vee ... c_m \mid k \text{ even}$$
$$c_i \in \{p, n, 0\}^l \text{ and the formula}$$
$$\exists x_l, ... x_{l-l_k} \forall x_{l-l_k-1}, ... x_{l-l_k-l_{k-1}}, ... \forall x_{l_1}, ... x_1 C_1 \vee C_2 \vee ... C_m,$$
$$\text{with the clauses } C_i := \bigwedge_{c_{ij}=p} x_j \wedge \bigwedge_{c_{ij}=n} \overline{x_j} \text{ is true}\}$$

It holds $BBF_k \in A1\Sigma_{k+1}PDA$ by a pushdown automaton K_k, which enters an existential state reading a '$\exists$' and guesses for the following characters, which stand for a variable, a covering and push therefor 'p' or 'n' and enters an universal state reading '$\forall$' and guesses universally the covering for the following variables into the pushdown store. Reaching '#' in case of odd k an universal state is entered to choose universally the clause, which has to be tested by a simultaneous popping of the covering. A clause is satisfied, if a 'p' ('n') is popped while reading a 'p' ('n') from the input, so this literal of the clause is true in the covering and the machine can accept, if the length of the clause is correct.

If k is even and we have disjunctive normalform, the conjunction to test is guessed existentially and only accepted, if no 'p' comes together with an 'n'. An other transition of the last universal state on '#' tests the length of the conjunctions. ∎

$BBF_\omega \in DSPACE(n)$ according to [Sto76]. It even holds:

Theorem 2.2 $A1\Sigma_\omega PDA \subseteq DSPACE(n)$

Proof: Let $L \in A1\Sigma_\omega PDA$ by an alternating pushdown automaton P, so P can be simulated by a turingmachine using two stacks, one for the simulation of the pushdown store of P and the other for "backtracking"[1]. Because the pushdown automaton has no ∞-loop on λ-transitions, a path can only have linear length ([KoHo66], Theorem 2.22) and the contents of both stacks has only linear length. ∎

Theorem 2.3 $LOG(A1\Sigma_\omega PDA) = PSPACE$

Proof: '$\subseteq$' follows from Theorem 2.2.
'$\supseteq$': According to [Sto76] $BBF_\omega = \bigcup_k BBF_k$ is log-complete for $PSPACE$ and can be recognized by a pushdown auomat in analogy to that in Theorem 2.1, with the difference, that it can alternate into the same states at any time. ∎

This is stronger than the results of [JeKi89], where polynomial timebounded alternating pushdown automata with additional logarithmic work tape are used: $A\Sigma_{k+1}^L PDA_{pt} = \Sigma_k^p$ and $A\Sigma_\omega^L PDA_{pt} = \Sigma_\omega^p = PSPACE$. The strengthening consists of a separation of the logarithmic reduction from the calculation of the pushdown automaton.

L_{pp} provides computations, where there can be a pushing after a popping. The pushdown automaton from Theorem 2.1 recognizing BBF_k does not make use of this. For that reason we can take the language $L_{sp} = \{x \& x^R \mid x \in \{0,1\}^*\}$ of symmetric words as ground oracle to build an oracle hierarchy containig complete problems of levels of the polynomial hierarchy.

Theorem 2.4 $\Sigma_k^p = LOG(A\Sigma_{k+1}FT(L_{sp}))$

Proof: In analogy to Theorem 2.1 with the difference, that only pushdown automata are used, which can only once change from pushing to popping. ∎

Theorem 2.5 *If the polynomial hierarchy is strict, then the $A1\Sigma_k PDA$-hierarchy and the $A\Sigma_k FT(L_{pp})$-hierarchy are strict too.*

Proof: If $A1\Sigma_k PDA = A1\Sigma_{k+1}PDA$ or $A\Sigma_k FT(L_{pp}) = A\Sigma_{k+1}FT(L_{pp})$ held, then a language in Σ_k^p could be recognized by a polynomial timebounded Σ_{k-1}-maschine, which calculates the reduction of an input to $BBF_k \in A1\Sigma_{k+1}PDA$ rsp. $\in A\Sigma_{k+1}FT(L_{pp})$ and then simulates the k-times alternating pushdown automaton rsp. recognize the language in $A\Sigma_k FT(L_{pp})$. ∎

It is not known, whether the $A1\Sigma_k PDA$- and the $A\Sigma_k FT(L_{pp})$-hierarchies are strict. But in contrary to the polynomial hierarchy it can be shown, that the undermost two steps are strict. Because CFL is not closed under complement, we obtain

Corollary: $CFL \subset A1\Sigma_2 PDA \subseteq A\Sigma_2 FT(L_{pp})$

---

[1] Recovering the configuration before the visit of a subtree

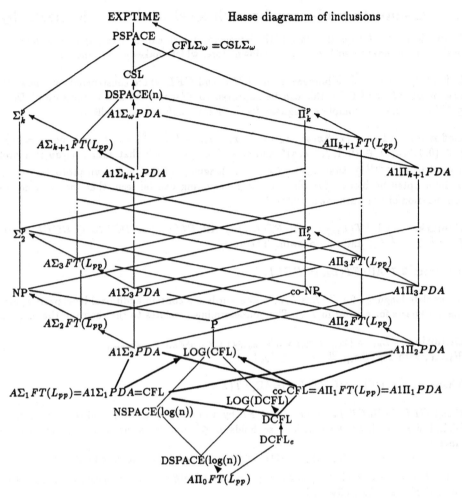

An arrow means, that the upper class is reachable by logarithmic reduction, thick lines mean strict inclusions.

2.2 Complexities of the undermost levels of the hierarchies

Theorem 2.6 $A\Pi_0 FT(L_{pp}) \subseteq DSPACE(log(n))$

Proof: $L_{pp} \in DSPACE(log(n))$ by following algorithm: test, whether there are as much characters behind an a as behind an e in the input (count the difference up and down), search for every ex in the input by counting the next ay on the same height and test, whether $y = x^R$. ∎
An oracle hierarchy with finite transducers can also reach complete problems of levels of the PH using languages in weaker complexity classes as ground language. For example the languages $L_= = \{a^n b^n \mid n \in N\} \in 1\text{-}DSPACE(log(n))$ and $L_{sb} = \{x \& x^R \mid x$ is a prefix of the concatenation of binary representations of all numbers $1\#10\#11\#100\#101...\} \in DSPACE(log(log(n)))$ yield the results $A\Sigma_k FT(L_{sp}) \subseteq A\Sigma_{k+1} FT(L_=)$ and $A\Sigma_k FT(L_{sp}) \subseteq A\Sigma_{k+1} FT(L_{sb})$ for $k \geq 1$.

2.3 Complete problems for each level of the oracle hierarchy

Definition $DCFL_e$ is the class of the languages, which can be recognized by a deterministic pushdown automaton with empty pushdown store, which makes no λ-transitions.

In [Sud78] $\leq^{log}$-complete languages for $DCFL$ and CFL where constructed; we show, that in case of $DCFL_e$ and CFL this can be improved to $\leq^f$-complete and in the case of $DCFL$ to $\leq^{Hlog}$-complete. As complete language for $DCFL$ we define L_{dv} as follows:

Definition $L_{dv} = \{x_0 \# x_1 \# ... x_n \mid x_0 x_{i_1} x_{i_2} ... x_{i_k} \in L_{pp}^{\{0,1,2,3\}}$ and there is no $x_l = ayz$ with $y \in \{0,1,2,3\}, z \in \{0,1,2,3,e,a\}^*$ and $i_j < l < i_{j+1}$, such that $x_0 x_{i_1} ... x_{i_j} ay$ is a prefix of a word in $L_{pp}^{\{0,1,2,3\}}.\}$, that means L_{dv} is the language of the pushdown protocols, which can be interrupted by blocks, for which at their beginning can be seen, that they can not be the continuation of the pushdown protocol.

Remark: $A\Pi_0 FT(L_{sp}) \subseteq A\Pi_0 FT(L_{pp}) \subseteq A\Pi_0 FT(L_{dv}) = DCFL_e \subseteq DCFL$ because of $L_{sp} \leq^f L_{pp} \leq^f L_{dv}$ and the following Theorem.

Theorem 2.7 $A\Pi_0 FT(L_{dv}) = DCFL_e$

A complete language for CFL is L_{nv}, whose words can contain additional blockparts apart from the blockparts for a word in L_{dv}. The nondeterminism relates to the choice of the blockparts.

Definition $L_{nv} = \{x_{0,1} \vee x_{0,2} \vee ... x_{0,n_0} \# x_{1,1} \vee ... \# x_{n,1} \vee ... x_{n,n_n} \mid \exists i_0, ... i_n$ with $x_{0,i_0} \# x_{1,i_1} \# ... x_{n,i_n} \in L_{dv}\}$.

Theorem 2.8 $CFL = A\Pi_0 FT(L_{nv}) = A\Sigma_1 FT(L_{nv})$

Proof: $CFL \subseteq A\Pi_0 FT(L_{nv})$: Let $L \in CFL$ by a nondeterministic pushdown automaton $M = (Z, \Sigma, \Gamma, \delta, z_0)$ without λ-transitions so holds $L \leq^f L_{nv}$ by a transducer T, calculating the function

$$f(b_1 ... b_n) = e2(e1)^{\varphi(\$)}(e0)^{\psi(z_0)} e3 \# g(b_1) ... g(b_n) a3$$

with $g(b) = a3 \# a1 \# a0 \# a2 x_{1,1} e3 \# a0 \# y_{1,2} \# ... \# a1 \# a0 \# y_{2,1} \# ... \# a0 \# y_{|\Gamma|,|Z|} \#$, $y_{i,j}$ is the concatenation of all $a2 x_{i,j} e3 \vee$ with

$$x_{i,j} = e2(e1)^{\varphi(d_1)} ... e2(e1)^{\varphi(d_n)}(e0)^{\psi(z')}$$

for $(z_i, b, c_j) \times (z', d_1 ... d_n) \in \delta$, in analogy to Theorem 2.7 with the difference, that for nondeterministic δ there is a choice between the $a2 x_{i,j} e3$.
$A\Sigma_1 FT(L_{nv}) \subseteq CFL$: A nondeterministic pushdown automaton can simulate the transducer and recognize L_{nv} guessing a blockpart between $\vee$ from every block between #'s and test whether this is in L_{dv}. ∎

Corollary: $A\Sigma_{k+1} FT(L_{pp}) = A\Sigma_{k+1} FT(L_{dv}) = A\Sigma_k FT(\overline{L_{nv}})$

We need the following Lemma for being able to insert additional tests in words of an oracle language.

Lemma 2.4 Let $L \in A\Sigma_k FT(L_{pp}) (\in A\Pi_k FT(L_{pp}))$ for $k \geq 1$ and without loss of generality $a, e, 0, 1 \notin \Sigma$, so $L' =: \{y_1 x_1 y_2 x_2 ... x_n y_m \mid x_1 x_2 ... x_n \in L, \forall j \; x_j \neq \lambda$ and $\forall i \; y_i \in L_{pp}\} \in A\Sigma_k FT(L_{pp}) (\in A\Pi_k FT(L_{pp}))$.

Theorem 2.9 For all k $A\Sigma_k FT(L_{pp})$ has complete languages for $\leq^f$.

Proof: by induction: $k = 0, 1\surd$

Let L_1 be complete for $A\Pi_k FT(L_{pp})$, so L_1' is too according to Lemma 2.4 and for every $L \in A\Sigma_{k+1} FT(L_{pp})$ it holds $L \leq^{nf} L_1$ by a nondeterministic transducer $M = (Z, \Sigma, \Gamma, \delta, z_0)$ and so we get

$$L \leq^f L_2 := \{ \ \# \vee x_{1,1} \vee x_{1,2} \vee ... x_{1,n_0} \# \vee x_{2,1} \vee ... \# \vee x_{n,1} \vee ... x_{n,n_n} \ | $$
$$\exists i_1, ... i_n, m \text{ with } e x_{1,i_1} x_{2,i_2} ... x_{n,i_n} a 0^m \in L_1'\}$$

by $M' = (\{z_0, \Sigma, \Gamma \cup \{\#, \vee, a, e, 0\}, \delta', z_0)$ with $\delta'(z_0, b) = (z_0, \#y)$, where y is a concatenation of all $\vee a 0^{\varphi(z_1)} c_1 ... c_k e 0^{\varphi(z_2)}$ with $((z_1, b), (z_2, c_1 ... c_k)) \in \delta$. (Let $\varphi(z_0) = 0$). It holds $v = v_1 ... v_n \in L$ if and only if there is a calculation of M on v with the series of states $z_0, ..., z_n$ and functional value $f_M(v) = c_{1,1} ... c_{1,k_1} c_2, 1 ... c_{n,k_n} \in L_1$ if and only if

$$eac_{1,1} ... c_{1,k_1} e 0^{\varphi(z_1)} a 0^{\varphi(z_1)} c_{2,1} ... c_{n,k_n} e 0^{\varphi(z_n)} a 0^{\varphi(z_n)} \in L_1' \text{ and}$$
$$\forall j < n \ ((z_{j-1}, v_j), (z_j, c_{j,1} ... c_{j,k_j})) \in \delta$$

if and only if $f_{M'}(v) \in L_2$ because $a 0^{\varphi(z_j - 1)} cj, 1 ... c_{j,k_j} e 0^{\varphi(z_j)}$ appears after the j-th $\#$ in $f_{M'}(v)$. It holds $L_2 \in A\Sigma_{k+1} FT(L_{pp})$ because of $L_1' \in A\Pi_k FT(L_{pp})$ and $L_2 \leq^{nf} L_1'$ by a transducer, which guesses a blockpart between $\vee$'s from each block between $\#$'s and copies it to the output tape, thereby a in the first blockpart and $e 0^{\varphi(z_n)}$ in the last blockpart is omitted, because ea and $e 0^{\varphi(z_n)} a 0^{\varphi(z_n)}$ are in L_{pp} as well as λ. The transducer can guess, which blockpart is the last, if it guesses wrong, it determines that at the next $\#$ and writes $e0a1$ to the output tape causing the output not to be in L_1. ∎

3 Alternating grammars

Transfering the principle of alternation to grammars, we have to consider strings of variables and terminal symbols of a derivation of a word by a grammar, which in the following we call *sentential forms*, instead of configurations of automata. In contrast to [Mor89] we take the reduction, that means the direction from the word to the start symbol as the direction of the alternation. Because there are no states which we could divide into existential and universal states, in the following definition the productions and variables of a grammar are divided into existential and universal productions and variables (not disjunctly). Instead of a labeling function for configurations we define sets of sentential forms for each level of alternation. A sentential form α is in a Σ-set, if there is a sentential form in the Π-set under that, from which α can be derived with universal productions; in the undermost level this sentential form must be the start symbol S. A sentential form β consisting only of existential variables and terminal symbols, is in a Π-set, if all sentential forms γ, from which β can be derived by universal productions, are in the Σ-set under that. For technical reasons γ has to be restricted to sentential forms consisting only of universal variables and terminal symbols and in the Π_1-level on the characters S and F.

Definition An alternating grammar G is an 8-tuple

$$G = (V, V_e, V_a, \Sigma, P_e, P_a, S, F) \text{ with } S, F \in V_e \cap V_a,$$

for $k > 0$ we define:

$$SenF\Sigma_0(G) := SenF\Pi_0(G) := \{S\}$$
$$SenF\Sigma_1(G) := \{\alpha \in (V_a \cup \Sigma)^* \mid S \overset{*}{\underset{P_e}{\Rightarrow}} \alpha\}$$
$$SenF\Pi_1(G) := \{\alpha \in (V_e \cup \Sigma)^* \mid \forall \beta \in \{S, F\}(\beta \overset{*}{\underset{P_a}{\Rightarrow}} \alpha \rightarrow \beta = S)\}$$
$$SenF\Sigma_{k+1}(G) := \{\alpha \in (V_a \cup \Sigma)^* \mid \exists \beta \in (V_e \cup \Sigma)^* \cap SenF\Pi_k(G) \text{ with } \beta \overset{*}{\underset{P_e}{\Rightarrow}} \alpha\}$$
$$SenF\Pi_{k+1}(G) := \{\alpha \in (V_e \cup \Sigma)^* \mid \forall \beta \in (V_a \cup \Sigma)^*(\beta \overset{*}{\underset{P_a}{\Rightarrow}} \alpha \rightarrow \beta \in SenF\Sigma_k(G)\}.$$

Because we presume, that S does not appear on the right side of productions in a grammar G, S is in every $SenF\Pi$-level and in every $SenF\Sigma$-level. Because of $S \in SenF\Pi_2(G)$ it holds that

$$
\begin{aligned}
SenF\Sigma_1(G) &= \{\alpha \in (V_a \cup \Sigma)^* \mid S \xRightarrow{*}_{P_e} \alpha\} \\
&\subseteq \{\alpha \in (V_a \cup \Sigma)^* \mid \exists \beta \in (V_e \cup \Sigma)^* \cap SenF\Pi_2(G) \text{ with } \beta \xRightarrow{*}_{P_e} \alpha\} \\
&\subseteq SenF\Sigma_3(G)
\end{aligned}
$$

from this we get

$$SenF\Sigma_{2k+3}(G) \supseteq SenF\Sigma_{2k+1}(G) \text{ and } SenF\Pi_{2k+2}(G) \supseteq SenF\Pi_{2k}(G)$$

for all k and so we can define the ω-set as union of all odd sets:

$$SenF\Sigma_\omega(G) := \bigcup_{k \text{ odd}} SenF\Sigma_k(G).$$

It would be interesting to know, whether we obtain the same results if we define the ω-set as union of all sets, the proof might be difficult for technical reason. Alternating languages can be defined as:

$$L\Sigma_k(G) := SenF\Sigma_k(G) \cap \Sigma^*$$

$$CFL\Sigma_k := \{L \mid \text{there is an alternating context-free grammar } G \text{ with } L\Sigma_k(G) := L\}$$

$$CSL\Sigma_k := \{L \mid \text{there is an alternating context-sensitive grammar } G \text{ with } L\Sigma_k(G) := L\}$$

The alternating languages $L\Pi_k(G)$, $L\Sigma_\omega(G)$, $CFL\Pi_k$, $CFL\Sigma_\omega$, $CSL\Pi_k$ and $CSL\Sigma_\omega$ can be defined analogously.

Corollary: $CFL = CFL\Sigma_1$

Remark: Alternating regular grammars can only produce regular languages.

3.1 Alternating context-free grammars

3.1.1 Examples for alternating grammars

a) It holds $L_p := \{a^p \mid p \text{ prim }\} = L\Pi_2(G)$ for the alternating grammar

$$
\begin{aligned}
G &:= (\{S,B,C,D,E,F,G,H\},\{S,F\},\{B\},\{a\},P_e,\{B \to a\},S,F) \text{ with} \\
P_e &:= \{ \quad S \to HC \mid ED \mid D \mid G \mid GB \mid GBG \\
&\qquad D \to B \mid BB \mid BCB \\
&\qquad C \to aC \mid BC \mid a \mid B \\
&\qquad E \to aEa \mid aE \mid aD \quad (* \text{ more } a\text{'s at the beginning } *) \\
&\qquad H \to aHa \mid Ha \mid Da \quad (* \text{ less } a\text{'s at the beginning } *) \\
&\qquad G \to Ga \mid a\},
\end{aligned}
$$

we get $SenF\Sigma_1(G) = \{\alpha \in \{B,a\}^{\geq 2} \mid \neg\exists n, m > 1 \; \alpha = (a^n B)^m\}$, because each sentential form containing a block of a's having a different length than the block of a's at the beginning of the sentential form can be derived from S. Only if the number of the a's is prime, no segmentation in blocks of the same length is possible and all sentential forms of $\{a, B\}^*$, from which a^p can be derived, must be in $SenF\Sigma_1(G)$.

b) It holds $L_q := \{a^{2^n} \mid n \in I\!N\} = L\Sigma_2(G)$ by the alternating grammar

$$
\begin{aligned}
G &:= (\{S,B,C,D,F,G\},\{S,F,B\},\{S,F\},\{a\},\{B \to a\},P_a,S,F) \text{ with} \\
P_a &:= \{ \quad F \to C \mid CG \mid GDB \mid GDBG \mid Ga \\
&\qquad C \to a \mid BCa \mid aCa \mid Ba \quad (* \; \#a \text{ in the block too big } *) \\
&\qquad D \to B \mid BDa \mid aDa \quad (* \; \#a \text{ in the block} = \#\text{characters before } B*) \\
&\qquad G \to B \mid a \mid BG \mid Ga\}.
\end{aligned}
$$

3.1.2 The equivalence of the oracle hierarchy and the hierarchy of alternating context-free grammars

To prove this equivalence, we show in the following Lemma, that for alternating grammars a Π-level is the set of the complements of the languages in the corresponding Σ-level.

Lemma 3.1 $CFL\Sigma_k = co\text{-}CFL\Pi_k$

The following Lemma shows another characterization of a Σ-level of the oracle hierarchy from the second level on, which is different to the reduction with a nondeterministic transducer to the underlying Π-level.

Lemma 3.2 If $\Sigma^* \supseteq L \in A\Sigma_{k+1}FT(L_{pp})$ for $k \geq 1$, then there is a $L_r \in A\Pi_k FT(L_{pp})$ with $L_r \subseteq \Delta^*$ and a relation $R \subseteq \Sigma \times \Delta$ with $x_1...x_n \in L$ if and only if $\exists y_1...y_n \in L_r$ and $\forall i \leq n \; \langle x_i, y_i \rangle \in R$

Theorem 3.1 $CFL\Sigma_k = A\Sigma_k FT(L_{pp})$

Proof: $CFL\Sigma_k \supseteq A\Sigma_k FT(L_{pp})$ by induction: $k = 1\checkmark$
Let $\Sigma^* \supseteq L \in A\Sigma_{k+1}FT(L_{pp})$ and according to the supposition of induction the language $\overline{L_r}$ according to Lemma 3.2 in $CFL\Sigma_k$ and according to Lemma 3.1 $L_r = L\Pi_k(G) \in CFL\Pi_k$ by the alternating grammar $G = (V, V_e, V_a, \Delta, P_e, P_a, S)$, so $L = L\Sigma_{k+1}(G') \in CFL\Sigma_{k+1}$ by the alternating grammar

$$G' = (V \cup \Delta, V_e \cup \Delta, V_a \cup \Delta, \Sigma, P'_e, P_a, S)$$

with $P'_e := P_e \cup \{D \to E \mid \langle E, D \rangle \in R \subseteq \Sigma \times \Delta\}$.
It holds $x_1...x_n \in L$ if and only if $\exists Y_1...Y_n \in L_r$ and $\forall i \leq n \; \langle x_i, Y_i \rangle \in R$ if and only if $\exists Y_1...Y_n \in SenF\Pi_k(G')$ and $Y_1...Y_n \underset{P'_e}{\overset{*}{\Rightarrow}} x_1...x_n$ if and only if $x_1...x_n \in SenF\Sigma_k(G')$.
$CFL\Sigma_k \subseteq A\Sigma_k FT(L_{pp})$: We have to show by induction, that $SenF\Sigma_k(G) \in A\Sigma_k FT(L_{pp})$ holds for $L = L\Sigma_k(G)$.
$k = 1$: $SenF\Sigma_1(G) \in CFL = A\Sigma_1 FT(L_{pp})$.
Conclusion from k to k+1: Let $L = L\Sigma_{k+1}(G)$ for the alternating grammar G, so according to Lemma 3.1 it holds

$$
\begin{aligned}
SenF\Pi_k(G) &= (V_1 \cup \Sigma)^* \setminus SenF\Sigma_k(G') \\
&= (V_1 \cup \Sigma)^* \cap \overline{SenF\Sigma_k(G')} \in A\Pi_k FT(L_{pp})
\end{aligned}
$$

because of $SenF\Sigma_k(G') \in A\Sigma_k FT(L_{pp})$ according to the supposition of induction. According to Lemma 2.4 there is a language $SenF\Pi_k(G)'$ with the property $SenF\Sigma_{k+1}(G) \leq^{nf} SenF\Pi_k(G)'$ by a transducer T, which guesses a sentential form in $SenF\Pi_k(G)$ and guesses, which character in the sentential form can be derived to which part. For every character Z it holds for the language $L_Z := \{\alpha \mid Z \underset{P_e}{\overset{*}{\Rightarrow}} \alpha\} \in CLF$ and so we get $L_Z \leq^{nf} L_{pp}$ by T_Z. For every guessed Z and the corresponding part of the input the transducer T inserts a reduction of this part by T_Z. Hereby $SenF\Pi_k(G)'$ tests the guessed sentential form in $SenF\Pi_k(G)$ and whether the input can be derived from the sentential form. According to Lemma 2.4 it holds $SenF\Pi_k(G)' \in A\Pi_k FT(L_{pp})$ and so we get $SenF\Sigma_{k+1}(G) \in A\Sigma_{k+1} FT(L_{pp})$. ∎

3.1.3 Reaching the context-sensitive languages with alternating context-free grammars

Theorem 3.2 $CSL \subseteq CFL\Sigma\omega$

Proof: Let $L \in CSL$ by the context-sensitive grammar $G' = (V, \Sigma, P, S)$, where all productions have the form $P_i = \alpha_i X_i \gamma_i \rightarrow \alpha_i \beta_i \gamma_i$. Then we can get $L = L\Sigma_\omega(G)$ for the alternating context-free grammar $G := (V_e \cup V_a \cup \{S^*\}, V_e, V_a, \Sigma, P_e, P_a, S', F)$ with

$$
\begin{aligned}
V_e &:= \{X' \mid X \in V\} \cup \{V_i \mid P_i \in P\} \cup \{F\}, \\
V_a &:= \{W_i \mid P_i \in P\} \cup V \cup \{S', F\}, \\
P_e &:= \{X' \rightarrow X \mid X \in V\} \cup \{V_i \rightarrow \beta_i \mid P_i \in P\} \cup \{S' \rightarrow S^* \mid S\} \cup \\
&\quad \{S^* \rightarrow S^* Z \mid Z S^* \mid Z \in V \cap \Sigma\} \cup \{S^* \rightarrow \alpha_i W_i \gamma_i \mid P_i \in P\}, \\
P_a &:= \{X \rightarrow X' \mid X \in V\} \cup \{X_i \rightarrow V_i \mid P_i \in P\} \cup \{W_i \rightarrow V_i \mid P_i \in P\}.
\end{aligned}
$$

The variables V_i and W_i represent the position of the X_i belonging to the production $P_i = \alpha_i X_i \gamma_i \rightarrow \alpha_i \beta_i \gamma_i$ in the sentential form. The production is simulated in the next Σ-level by the production $V_i \rightarrow \beta_i$. The universal production $X_i \rightarrow V_i$ tests, whether the sentential form can be derived and the universal production $W_i \rightarrow V_i$ tests, whether the context α_i and γ_i is given for the production P_i, because the set $Cont := \{\delta \alpha_i W_i \gamma_i \delta' \mid P_i \in P \text{ and } \delta, \delta' \in (V \cap \Sigma)^*\}$ is a subset of every $SenF\Sigma$-level. The grammar G can simulate one step of derivation by alternating twice. So we get

$$
\begin{aligned}
SenF\Pi_0(G) &= \{S'\}, \\
SenF\Sigma_1(G) &= \{S'\} \cup \{S\} \cup Cont, \\
SenF\Pi_2(G) &= \{S'\} \cup \{V_i \mid P_i = S \rightarrow \delta\}, \\
SenF\Sigma_3(G) &= \{S'\} \cup \{\beta \mid S \rightarrow \beta \in P\} \cup Cont \quad \ldots
\end{aligned}
$$

By induction it follows in general

$$
SenF\Sigma_{2k+1}(G, \{S'\}) = SenF\Sigma_{2k+2}(G, \{S'\}) = \{\alpha \mid S \overset{\leq k}{\underset{P}{\Longrightarrow}} \alpha\} \cup Cont
$$

and so we get $SenF\Sigma_\omega(G, \{S'\}) = \bigcup\limits_{k \text{ odd}} SenF\Sigma_k(G, \{S'\}) = \{\alpha \mid S \overset{*}{\underset{P}{\Longrightarrow}} \alpha\} \cup Cont$ for an optional number of alternations and so we get $L\Sigma_\omega(G) = L(G')$. ∎

Remark: It holds $CSL\Sigma_k = CSL$ because of [Imm88]/[Sze88].

This method can be generalized to alternating context-sensitive grammars.

Theorem 3.3 $CSL\Sigma_\omega = CFL\Sigma_\omega$

The proof is similar to the last proof, the same technique is used to simulate the existential productions, a complementary technique is used to simulate universal productions and additional productions, which represent transitions between the two simulations, simulate the alternation. The surprise of this result is, that for unboundedly alternating grammars the context is no factor.

With results from [Coo71] and [CKS81] we get

Corollary: $CFL\Sigma_\omega = CSL\Sigma_\omega = ASPACE(n) = DTIME(2^n) = A\Sigma_0^n PDA.$

The proof of $CSL\Sigma_\omega = ASPACE(n)$ is analogous to the proof of $CSL = NSPACE(n)$ in [HoUl79], where the alternating linear bounded automaton, which simulates the grammar, has to check before alternating, whether there are existential variables rsp. universal variables left. The grammar, which simulates the automaton, uses an existential variable for an existential state and a universal variable for an universal state.

Remark: This yields the assumption, that the alternating grammars we defined can generate more than the alternating grammars in [Mor89], where $LOG(ACFL) = PSPACE$ holds. Whereas in both cases P is the logarithmic closure over alternating linear languages, where only one variable can occur in a sentential form.

3.2 Alternating grammars without restrictions

Alternating turing machines can not recognize more than the recursively enumerable languages. The reason is, that only finitely much can be guessed, because a ∞-loop in universal states would produce an infinitely long path, which can not be in the finite accepting subtree. Alternating grammars do not have this restriction, for that they can give a further characterization of the arithmetic hierarchy from [Soare87], which is defined as oracle hierarchy, having the recursively enumerable languages as Σ_1-level. The arithmetic hierarchy can also be characterized with changing quantors leading a recursive set, the changing quantors can be simulated in every level of sentential forms by an alternating grammar with diminishing productions.

References

[Ber79] J. Berstel: Transductions and Context-Free Languages, Teubner 1979.

[CKS81] A.K. Chandra, D.C. Kozen, L.J. Stockmeyer; Alternation, Journ. of the ACM 28,1(1981), 114-133.

[Coo71] S.A. Cook: Characterizations of pushdown machines in terms of timebounded computers, Journ. of the ACM 18,1(1971), 4-18

[HoUl79] J.E. Hopcroft, J.D. Ullman: Introduction to Automata Theory, Languages and Computation, Addison-Wesley, 1979.

[Imm88] N. Immerman: Nondeterministic space is closed under complementation, SIAM Journ. Comput. 15, 5 (1988), 935-938.

[JeKi89] Birgit Jenner, Bernd Kirsig: Characterizing the polynomial hierarchy by alternating auxiliary pushdown automata. Theoretical Informatics and Applications, 1989, 87-99.

[KoHo66] A.J. Korenjak, J.E. Hopcroft: Simple deterministic languages, Conf. Rec. 7th Annual IEEE Symp. Switching and Automata Theory (1966), 36-46.

[LSL84] R.E. Ladner,L.J.Stockmeyer,R.J. Lipton: Alternation bounded auxiliary pushdown automata, Information and Control 62(1984), 93-108.

[Mor89] Etsuro Moriya: A grammatical characterization of alternating pushdown automata, TCS 67 (1989) 75-85.

[Sze88] R. Szelepcsenyi: The Method of forced enumeration for nondeterministic automata, Acta Informatica 26(1988), 279-284.

[Soare87] Robert I. Soare: Recursively Enumerable Sets and Degrees, Springer 1987.

[Sto76] L.J.Stockmeyer: The polynomial-time hierarchy, Theoret. Comp. Sci. 3 (1976), 1-22.

[Sud78] I.H. Sudborough: On the tape complexity of deterministic context-free languages, Journ. of the ACM 25, 3 (1978),405-414.

[Wra76] C. Wrathall: Complete sets and the polynomial-time hierarchy, Theoret. Comp. Sci. 3 (1976), 23-33.

A Hierarchy of Unary Primitive Recursive String-functions

Lila Santean*

Institute for Informatics
8-10 Miciurin blvd.
71316 Bucharest 1, Romania

Abstract

Using a recent result of G.Asser, an extention of Ackermann-Peter hierarchy of unary primitive recursive functions to string-functions is obtained. The resulting hierarchy classifies the string-functions according to their lexicographical growth.

1 Introduction

Let $\mathbf{N}$ be the set of naturals i.e. $\mathbf{N} = \{0, 1, 2, \ldots\}$. Consider a fixed alphabet $A = \{a_1, a_2, \ldots, a_r\}, r \geq 2$ and denote by A^* the free monoid generated by A under concatenation (with e the null string). The elements of A^* are called strings; if reffering to strings, " < " denotes the lexicographical order induced by $a_1 < a_2 < \ldots < a_r$. Denote by Fnc (respectively Fnc_A) the set of all unary number-theoretical (respectively, string) functions. By $I, Succ, C_m, Pd$ we denote the following number-theoretical functions:

$$
\begin{aligned}
I(x) &= x, \\
Succ(x) &= x + 1, \\
C_m(x) &= m, \\
Pd(x) &= x \doteq 1, \text{ where } x \doteq y = max\{x - y, 0\}, \\
&\quad \text{for all } x, m, y \in \mathbf{N}.
\end{aligned}
$$

By $I^A, Succ_i^A, C_u^A, \sigma, \pi$, we denote the following string-functions:

$$
I^A(w) = w,
$$

*Present address: Department of Mathematics, University of Turku, 20500 Turku, Finland

$$
\begin{aligned}
Succ_i^A(w) &= wa_i(1 \le i \le r), \\
C_u^A(w) &= u, \\
\sigma(e) &= a_1, \sigma(wa_i) = wa_{i+1} \text{ if } 1 \le i < r \text{ and } \sigma(wa_r) = \sigma(w)a_1 \\
\pi(e) &= e, \pi(\sigma(w)) = w, \\
&\quad \text{for all } w, u \in A^*
\end{aligned}
$$

Furtheron one uses the primitive recursive bijections $c : A^* \longrightarrow \mathbf{N}, \bar{c} : \mathbf{N} \longrightarrow A^*$ given by

$$
\begin{aligned}
c(e) &= 0, c(wa_i) = r \cdot c(w) + i, 1 \le i \le r, w \in A^*, \\
\bar{c}(0) &= e, \bar{c}(m+1) = \sigma(\bar{c}(m)), m \in \mathbf{N}.
\end{aligned}
$$

To each f in Fnc one associates the string-function $s(f) \in Fnc_A$ defined by $s(f)(w) = \bar{c}(f(c(w)))$ and for each g in Fnc_A one associates the number-theoretical function $n(g)$ defined by $n(g)(x) = c(g(\bar{c}(x)))$. It is easily seen that for every string-function g, $s(n(g)) = g$ and for every number-theoretical function f, $n(s(f)) = f$. For example, $s(Succ) = \sigma, n(I^A) = I, s(Pd) = \pi$. A mapping from Fnc^n to Fnc is called an operator in Fnc, and analogously for Fnc_A. We consider the following operators in Fnc and Fnc_A :

$$
\begin{aligned}
sub(f,g) &= h \Longleftrightarrow f, g, h \in Fnc, f(g(x)) = h(x); \\
diff(f,g) &= h \Longleftrightarrow f, g, h \in Fnc, h(x) = f(x) \dot{-} g(x); \\
it_x(f) &= h \Longleftrightarrow f, h \in Fnc, h(0) = x, h(y+1) = f(h(y)); \\
sub_A(f,g) &= h \Longleftrightarrow f, g, h \in Fnc_A, f(g(w)) = h(w); \\
\sigma - it_{A,w}(f) &= h \Longleftrightarrow f, h \in Fnc_A, h(e) = w, h(\sigma(u)) = f(h(u)).
\end{aligned}
$$

For every operator φ in Fnc, $s(\varphi)(f) = s(\varphi(n(f)))$, for every $f \in Fnc$; analogously, for every operator θ in Fnc_A, $n(\theta)(g) = n(\theta(s(g)))$, for every $g \in Fnc$. For example, $s(it_x) = \sigma - it_{A,c(x)}, n(\sigma - it_{A,w}) = it_{\bar{c}(w)}$.

2   Ackermann-Peter string-function

The primitive-recursive functions were introduced by Asser [1] and studied by various authors (see [4], [6], [8]). In order to study the complexity of such functions, we use as a measure of complexity the growth relatively to the lexicographical order. To this aim we use the string-version of the *Ackermann-Peter* unary function defined by *Weichrauch* [8]. The function, denoted by $A : A^* \longrightarrow A^*$, is given by means of the following three equations :

$$
\begin{aligned}
A_0(x) &= \sigma(x) & (1) \\
A_{n+1}(e) &= A_n(a_1) & (2) \\
A_{n+1}(\sigma(x)) &= A_n(A_{n+1}(x)). & (3)
\end{aligned}
$$

The following technical results concern the monotonicity properties of the function A; they generalize the monotonicity properties of the number-theoretical Ackermann-Peter function (see [4]).

Lemma 1 *For all naturals n and for all strings x over A^*, we have*

$$A_n(x) > x.$$

Proof. We proceed by induction on n.

For $n = 0$ we have $A_0(x) = \sigma(x) > x$. We assume that $A_n(x) > x$ and we prove the inequality $A_{n+1}(x) > x$ by induction on x.

For $x = e$, $A_{n+1}(e) = A_n(a_1) > e$. Suppose now that $A_{n+1}(x) > x$. We use (3) and the first induction hypothesis to get

$$A_{n+1}(\sigma(x)) = A_n(A_{n+1}(x)) > A_{n+1}(x).$$

Finally, by the second induction hypothesis, that is $A_{n+1}(x) \geq \sigma(x)$, we obtain $A_{n+1}(\sigma(x)) > \sigma(x)$. □

Lemma 2 *For all naturals n and for all strings x over A^*, we have:*

$$A_n(x) < A_n(\sigma(x)).$$

Proof. For $n = 0$,

$$A_0(x) = \sigma(x) < \sigma(\sigma(x)) = A_0(\sigma(x)).$$

Assume that $A_n(x) < A_n(\sigma(x))$. In view of (3) and lemma 1 we have

$$A_{n+1}(\sigma(x)) = A_n(A_{n+1}(x)) > A_{n+1}(x).$$

□

Corollary 1 *For all naturals n and all strings x, y from A^*, if $x < y$, then $A_n(x) < A_n(y)$.*

Lemma 3 *For all naturals n and for all strings x over A^*, we have*

$$A_n(x) < A_{n+1}(x).$$

Proof. We proceed by double induction on n and x.

For $n = 0$ we have

$$A_0(x) = \sigma(x) < \sigma(\sigma(x)) = A_1(x).$$

Assume now that $A_n(x) < A_{n+1}(x)$ and we prove that $A_{n+1}(x) < A_{n+2}(x)$ by induction on x.

For $x = e$, in view of (2) and the first induction hypothesis, we get

$$A_{n+1}(e) = A_n(a_1) < A_{n+1}(a_1) = A_{n+2}(e).$$

In view of a new induction hypothesis, $A_{n+1}(x) < A_{n+2}(x)$, we deduce the relations:

$$A_{n+1}(\sigma(x)) = A_n(A_{n+1}(x)) < A_n(A_{n+2}(x)) < A_{n+1}(A_{n+2}(x)) = A_{n+2}(\sigma(x))$$

(we have also used the first induction hypothesis, relation (3) and corollary 1). □

Corollary 2 *For all naturals n and m, and for all strings x in A^*, if $n < m$, then*

$$A_n(x) < A_m(x).$$

Lemma 4 *For all strings x of A^* we have: $A_2(x) = \sigma^{2c(x)+3}(e)$.*

Proof. We proceed by induction on x.

For $x = e$, in view of (2) we have

$$A_2(e) = A_1(a_1) = \sigma(\sigma(a_1)) = \sigma^3(e) = \sigma^{2c(e)+3}(e).$$

Assuming that $A_2(x) = \sigma^{2c(x)+3}(e)$, we prove that $A_2(\sigma(x)) = \sigma^{2c(\sigma(x))+3}(e)$. Indeed, using (3) and the equality $c(\sigma(x)) = c(x) + 1$, we get:

$$A_2(\sigma(x)) = A_1(A_2(x)) = A_1(\sigma^{2c(x)+3}(e)) = \sigma^{2c(x)+5}(e) = \sigma^{2c(\sigma(x))+3}(e).$$

$\square$

Lemma 5 *For all naturals k and $n \geq 1$, there exists a natural i (which depends upon k) such that*

$$A_n(\sigma^k(x)) < A_{n+1}(\pi^k(x)),$$

for every string x in A^* with $c(x) > i$.

Proof. We first notice that for every string x with $c(x) > 3k \div 1$, we have $\sigma^k(x) < A_2(\pi^{k+1}(x))$.

Indeed, by lemma 4 we have

$$
\begin{aligned}
A_2(\pi^{k+1}(x)) &= \sigma^{2c(\pi^{k+1}(x))+3}(e) = \sigma^{2(c(x) \div k \div 1)+3}(e) = \sigma^{2c(x) \div 2k+1}(e) \\
&> \sigma^{k+c(x)}(e) = \sigma^k(\sigma^{c(x)}(e)) = \sigma^k(x).
\end{aligned}
$$

Consequently, using corolary 1 and corollary 2,

$$A_n(\sigma^k(x)) < A_n(A_2(\pi^{k+1}(x))) < A_n(A_{n+1}(\pi^{k+1}(x))) = A_{n+1}(\pi^k(x)),$$

for all strings x with $c(x) > 3k \div 1$. In conclusion, we can take $i = 3k \div 1$. $\square$

Lemma 6 *For all naturals n and strings x in A^* we have*

$$A_{n+1}(x) = A_n^{c(x)+1}(a_1).$$

Proof. We proceed by induction on x.

For $x = e$, using (2) we obtain

$$A_{n+1}(e) = A_n(a_1) = A_n^{c(e)+1}(a_1).$$

Assuming that $A_{n+1}(x) = A_n^{c(x)+1}(a_1)$ we prove the equality

$$A_{n+1}(\sigma(x)) = A_n^{c(\sigma(x))+1}(a_1).$$

Indeed, using (3) we get:

$$A_n^{c(\sigma(x))+1}(a_1) = A_n^{c(x)+2}(a_1) = A_n(A_n^{c(x)+1}(a_1)) = A_n(A_{n+1}(x)) = A_{n+1}(\sigma(x)).$$

$\square$

The monotonicity properties of the string *Ackermann-Peter* function will be freely used in what follows.

3 A hierarchy of unary primitive recursive string-functions

We are going to define an increasing sequence $(C_n)_{n \geq 0}$ of string-function classes whose union equals the class of the one-argument primitive recursive string-functions.

Definition 1 We say that the function $f : A^* \longrightarrow A^*$ is defined by *limited iteration at e* (shortly, *limited iteration*) from the functions $g : A^* \longrightarrow A^*$ and $h : A^* \longrightarrow A^*$ if it satisfies the following equations:

$$
\begin{aligned}
f(e) &= e, \\
f(\sigma(x)) &= g(f(x)), \\
f(x) &\leq h(x),
\end{aligned}
$$

for every x in A^*.

Definition 2 For a natural n we define C_n to be the smallest class of unary primitive recursive string-functions which contains the functions A_0, A_n and is closed under composition, limited iteration and $s(diff)$ (the string-function operation corresponding to the arithmetical difference).

Lemma 7 *For all naturals n, the class C_n contains the functions C_e^A, I^A, π and the functions $l_i (1 \leq i \leq r)$, sg and $\overline{sg}$ defined by:*

$$
\begin{aligned}
l_i(w) &= a_i, 1 \leq i \leq r, \\
sg(w) &= \begin{cases} e & \text{if } w = e \\ a_1 & \text{if } w \neq e \end{cases} \\
\overline{sg}(w) &= \begin{cases} a_1 & \text{if } w = e \\ e & \text{if } w \neq e, \end{cases} \\
&\quad \text{for all } w \in A^*.
\end{aligned}
$$

Proof. It follows from the following equalities:

$$
\begin{aligned}
C_e^A &= s(diff)(A_0, A_0) \\
l_i &= A_0^i(e), 1 \leq i \leq r \\
I^A &= s(diff)(A_0, l_1) \\
\overline{sg} &= s(diff)(l_1, I^A) \\
sg &= s(diff)(l_1, \overline{sg}) \\
\pi &= s(diff)(I^A, l_1)
\end{aligned}
$$

and from the definition 2. $\qquad \square$

Theorem 1 *For all naturals n, $C_n \subseteq C_{n+1}$.*

Proof. We shall prove by induction on n that for all natural numbers n and $k, A_n \in C_{n+k}$.

If $n = 0$, by definition 2, $A_0 \in C_m$, for every natural m. Assume that $A_n \in C_{n+k}, \forall k \in \mathbf{N}$. We shall prove that $A_{n+1} \in C_{n+k+1}, \forall k \in \mathbf{N}$.

Assertion: For every string $x, A_{n+1}(x) = f(\sigma(x))$, where

$$
\begin{aligned}
f(e) &= e, \\
f(\sigma(x)) &= A_n(g(f(x))), \text{ and} \\
g(x) &= s(\mathit{diff})(\sigma(x), sg(x)).
\end{aligned}
$$

The equalities will be proved by induction on the string x. If $x = e$, from the definitions of the functions A_n and $s(\mathit{diff})$ we deduce:

$$
\begin{aligned}
f(\sigma(e)) &= A_n(g(f(e))) = A_n(g(e)) = A_n(s(\mathit{diff})(\sigma(e), sg(e))) \\
&= A_n(s(\mathit{diff})(a_1, e)) = A_n(a_1) = A_{n+1}(e).
\end{aligned}
$$

Supposing now that $A_{n+1}(x) = f(\sigma(x))$, we shall show that $A_{n+1}(\sigma(x)) = f(\sigma^2(x))$.

Indeed,

$$
\begin{aligned}
f(\sigma(\sigma(x))) &= A_n(g(f(\sigma(x)))) = A_n(g(A_{n+1}(x))) \\
&= A_n(s(\mathit{diff})(\sigma(A_{n+1}(x)), sg(A_{n+1}(x)))) \\
&= A_n(s(\mathit{diff})(\sigma(A_{n+1}(x)), a_1)) \\
&= A_n(\bar{c}(\mathit{diff}(c(\sigma(A_{n+1}(x))), c(a_1)))) \\
&= A_n(\bar{c}(\mathit{diff}(c(A_{n+1}(x)) + 1, 1))) \\
&= A_n(\bar{c}(c(A_{n+1}(x)))) = A_n(A_{n+1}(x)) \\
&= A_{n+1}(\sigma(x)).
\end{aligned}
$$

Using now definition 2, lemma 7, the induction hypothesis and the relations

$$
f(x) = A_{n+1}(\pi(x)) \leq A_{n+1}(x) \leq A_{n+k+1}(x), x \in A^*,
$$

we deduce that A_{n+1} is in C_{n+k+1} being obtained from functions belonging to C_{n+k+1}, using composition, limited iteration and $s(\mathit{diff})$. $\qquad\square$

Lemma 8 *For all naturals n and all functions f in C_n, there exists a natural k such that $f(x) < A_n^k(x)$, for every string x in A^*.*

Proof. We shall make use of the inductive definition of C_n.

If $f(x) = A_0(x)$ then

$$
f(x) < A_0(A_0(x)) \leq A_n(A_n(x))
$$

and we can take $k = 2$.

If $f(x) = A_n(x)$, then

$$
f(x) \leq A_n(A_n(x))
$$

and we can also take $k = 2$.

If $f(x) < A_n^p(x)$ and $g(x) < A_n^q(x)$, for all strings x in A^* then

$$(f \circ g)(x) = f(g(x)) < A_n^p(g(x)) < A_n^{p+q}(x)),$$
$$s(\text{diff})(f,g)(x) \leq f(x) < A_n^p(x).$$

Finally, if f is obtained by limited iteration from g and h, $h(x) < A_n^k(x)$, then $f(x) \leq h(x) < A_n^k(x)$. $\qquad\square$

Theorem 2 *For every class $C_n, n \geq 1$, and every f in C_n, there exists a natural i (depending upon f) such that $f(x) < A_{n+1}(x)$ for every string x in A^* satisfying $c(x) \geq i$.*

Proof. Assume that f is a function in $C_n, n \geq 1$. In view of lemma 8, we can find a natural $k \geq 2$ (which depends upon f) such that, for every string $x, f(x) < A_n^k(x)$. We shall show that the requested inequality holds for $i = 3k$.

From the monotonicity properties of *Ackermann-Peter* string-function, one can deduce the following relations:

$$A_n^k(x) = A_n^{k-1}(A_n(x)) \leq A_n^{k-1}(A_n(\sigma^{k-1}(x))) < A_n^{k-1}(A_{n+1}(\pi^{k-1}(x))),$$

for every string x with $c(x) > 3k \div 1$.

Intermediate step: $A_{n+1}(x) = A_n^{k-1}(A_{n+1}(\pi^{k-1}(x)))$, for every string x with $c(x) \geq k$.

We shall prove the equality by induction on x. If $c(x) = k$, then we have

$$\begin{aligned}
A_n^{k-1}(A_{n+1}(\pi^{k-1}(x))) &= A_n^{k-1}(A_{n+1}(\pi^{k-1}(\sigma^{c(x)}(e)))) \\
&= A_n^{k-1}(A_{n+1}(\pi^{k-1}(\sigma^k(e)))) = A_n^{k-1}(A_{n+1}(a_1)) \\
&= A_n^{k-1}(A_n^2(a_1)) = A_n^{k+1}(a_1) = A_n^{c(x)+1}(a_1) \\
&= A_{n+1}(x).
\end{aligned}$$

If the equality holds for x, we can prove that

$$A_{n+1}(\sigma(x)) = A_n^{k-1}(A_{n+1}(\pi^{k-1}(\sigma(x)))).$$

Indeed,

$$\begin{aligned}
A_n^{k-1}(A_{n+1}(\pi^{k-1}(\sigma(x)))) &= A_n^{k-1}(A_{n+1}(\sigma(\pi^{k-1}(x)))) \\
&= A_n^{k-1}(A_n(A_{n+1}(\pi^{k-1}(x)))) \\
&= A_n(A_n^{k-1}(A_{n+1}(\pi^{k-1}(x)))) \\
&= A_n(A_{n+1}(x)) = A_{n+1}(\sigma(x)),
\end{aligned}$$

and the intermediate step is proved.

Returning to the proof of the theorem, we can now write

$$f(x) < A_n^k(x) < A_n^{k-1}(A_{n+1}(\pi^{k-1}(x))) = A_{n+1}(x),$$

for all strings x with $c(x) \geq 3k \div 1$ and taking $i = 3k \div 1$, the proof is finished.

$\qquad\square$

Theorem 3 *The set $\bigcup_{n=0}^{\infty} C_n$ coincides with the set of **unary** primitive recursive string-functions.*

Proof. We shall make use of the characterization of the set of unary primitive recursive string-functions obtained in [5], namely as the smallest class of unary string-functions which contains σ and is closed under the operations

$$sub, \sigma - it_{A,e}, s(\text{diff}).$$

It is obvious that every function in $\bigcup_{n=0}^{\infty} C_n$ is primitive recursive. For the converse inclusion, all that remains to be proved is reduced to the closure of $\bigcup_{n=0}^{\infty} C_n$ to $\sigma - it_{A,e}$.

We shall show that if $f \in \bigcup_{n=0}^{\infty} C_n$ is obtained by pure iteration from $g \in \bigcup_{n=0}^{\infty} C_n$, there exists a function $h \in \bigcup_{n=0}^{\infty} C_n$ such that f is obtained by limited iteration from g and h and, therefore, f is in $\bigcup_{n=0}^{\infty} C_n$.

Indeed, let f be obtained by pure iteration from g in $C_m, m > 0$. We shall prove, by induction on the string x that f is majorized by A_{n+1}.

If $x = e$, we have $f(e) = e < A_{n+1}(e)$.

Supposing that $f(x) < A_{n+1}(x)$ and using the definition and the monotonicity properties of Ackermann-Peter function, we get:

$$f(\sigma(x)) = g(f(x)) < A_n(f(x)) < A_n(A_{n+1}(x)) = A_n(\sigma(x)).$$

$\square$

Theorem 4 *The function $\overline{A} : A^* \longrightarrow A^*$ defined by $\overline{A}(w) = A_{c(w)}(w)$ is not primitive recursive.*

Proof. Assume, on the contrary, that $\overline{A}$ is primitive recursive. From theorem 3 we get a natural n such that $\overline{A} \in C_n$. By theorem 2, there exists a natural i such that $A(x) < A_{n+1}(x)$ for every x with $c(x) \geq i$. Let x be a string satisfying the condition $c(x) = n + i + 1$. We arrive at a contradiction since

$$\overline{A}(x) = A_{c(x)}(x) = A_{n+i+1}(x) < A_{n+1}(x)$$

(see corollary 2). This completes the proof of the theorem. $\square$

4 Acknowledgements

We are grateful to Dr. Cristian Calude for drawing our attention to these problems and for many helpful remarks.

References

[1] G.Asser. Rekursive Wortfunktionen *Z.Math. Logik Grundlag.Math.* 6(1960), 258-278.

[2] G.Asser. Primitive recursive word-functions of one variable, in E.Borger (ed.), *Computation Theory and Logic*, LNCS 270, Springer 1987, 14-19.

[3] G.Asser. Zur Robinson Charakterisierung der Einstelligen Primitiv Rekursiven Wortfunktionen, *Z.Math.Logik Grundlag.Math.*, 34(1988), 317-322.

[4] C.Calude. *Theories of Computational Complexity*, North-Holland, Amsterdam, New-York, Oxford, Tokio, 1988.

[5] C.Calude, L.Santean. On a Theorem of Gunter Asser, *Z.Math.Logik Grundlag.Math.*, 1990.

[6] F.W.v.Henke, K.Indermark, G.Rose, K.Weichrauch. On Primitive Recursive Wordfunctions, *Computing* 15(1975), 217-234.

[7] M.Tatarim. Darboux property and one-argument primitive recursive string-functions,*Revue Roumaine des Mathematiques Pures et Appliques*, 1987, 79-94.

[8] K.Weichrauch. Teilklassen primitiv-rekursiver Wortfunktionen, *Berichte der GMD* 91(1974), 1-49.

MINIMIZING PICTURE WORDS

Patrice SÉÉBOLD

I.U.T. de Calais, dept. inform., C.N.R.S. - U.A. 369, L.I.F.L., Université de Lille1
59655 Villeneuve d'Ascq Cédex, France

Karine SLOWINSKI

C.N.R.S. - U.A. 369, L.I.F.L., Université de Lille1
59655 Villeneuve d'Ascq Cédex, France

Abstract: With any word over the alphabet $D = \{ r, \bar{r}, u, \bar{u} \}$, we associate a connected picture in the following manner : the reading of each letter of this word induces a unit line : r ($\bar{r}$, u, $\bar{u}$ resp.) stands for a right (left, up, down resp.) move. We present a rewriting system which allows to obtain, from any word over D, all the words describing the same picture. Particularly, we give an algorithm to find in finite time, a minimal word describing a given picture : this word represents the shortest way to draw this picture "without pen-up".

Introduction

A *picture word* is a word over the alphabet $D = \{ r, \bar{r}, u, \bar{u} \}$. With any picture word, we associate a connected picture as follows : the reading of each letter of the word induces a unit line : r ($\bar{r}$, u, $\bar{u}$ resp.) stands for a right (left, up, down resp.) move. This method can be compared with the encoding established by Freeman [Fr] to facilitate the processing of geometric configurations by computer. In this paper, we study the set of all the words describing a given picture and we are particularly interested in the formation of a minimal word : this word represents the shortest way to draw this picture "without pen-up". Such results can be helpful, for example, to improve the use of plotter pen or in such domains as graph theory or pattern recognition. This approach (the description of pictures by words) which allows to use results and techniques from the formal language theory (See [Ha], [Sa]), was initiated by Maurer, Rozenberg and Welzl [MRW]. They established many results about different classes of picture languages and they in particular introduced the concept of "retreat" which was studied by Hinz [Hi] and is the starting point of our work. More precisely, we construct a rewriting system which allows to obtain, from a given word describing a picture, all the words describing the same picture and to find algorithmly a minimal word.

Our results complete recent works. Gutbrod [Gu], in particular, supplied a similar system permitting to get all the words describing a same picture. However, his system has not the notion of irreducible word and thus, does not allow to realize an algorithm to find a minimal word. As for Brandenburg and Dassow [BD], they introduced a rewriting system able to reduce words but not to minimize them. Note that Brandenburg [Br] showed, using graph theory, that it is possible to compute a minimal word for a given picture in polynomial time (but he did not give an algorithm to achieve this). Moreover, our results seem to remain true (and we use the same system) even if we increase the number of elementary moves in the plane or if we consider spaces having more than two dimensions.

This paper is organized as follows : after preliminaries (section 1) and basic notions for the construction of picture languages (section 2), we introduce the rewriting system in section 3 and establish, in section 4, the main results. We conclude with some open questions.

1 - Preliminaries -

We assume the reader to be familiar with the basic formal language theory (see [Ha], [Sa]), and we just remind him of several notations. Let A, be a finite set called *alphabet*. The elements of A are *letters* and finite strings over A are *words*. A* is the semi-group generated by A with the operation of concatenation (the neutral element is the empty word ε). For a word w over A, $|w|$ denotes its *length*, ie the number of letters of this word (in particular, $|\varepsilon| = 0$) and, for any $x \in A$, $|w|_x$ is the number of occurrences of the letter x within w is written. A word $w' \in A*$ is a *factor* (*left factor* resp.) of the word $w \in A*$ if there exist $w_1 \in A*$ ($w_1 = \varepsilon$ resp.) and $w_2 \in A*$ such that $w = w_1 w' w_2$.

2 - Basic notions -

Let Z^2, the cartesian plane and $D = \{ r , \bar{r} , u , \bar{u} \}$, a four letter alphabet. With each letter from D, we associate a unit move in Z^2 as follows: r ($\bar{r}$, u, $\bar{u}$ resp.) induces a unit move to the right (left, up down resp.). Thus, we define a morphism δ (non injective) which associates with any word over D, an integer pair representing the associated move in Z^2:

$$\delta : (D, .) \rightarrow (Z \times Z , +)$$
$$r \rightarrow (1 , 0)$$
$$\bar{r} \rightarrow (-1 , 0)$$
$$u \rightarrow (0 , 1)$$
$$\bar{u} \rightarrow (0 , -1)$$

A *segment* $t_{i,j}$ is the portion of straight line between the points (i, j) and (i, j) + δ(t)   (t ∈ { r , u }). An *oriented segment* $x_{i,j}$ is the oriented trace of the move between the points (i, j) and (i, j) + δ(x)   (x ∈ D).

We associate with any word over D, a unique picture as follows:
- The word is read, letter by letter, from left to right.
- The starting point is the point (0,0).
- For each letter, we draw the associated oriented segment whose ending point is the starting point of the next segment.

For any word w ∈ D*, S(w) ($\overrightarrow{S(w)}$ resp.) is the set of (oriented resp.) segments of the picture associated with w. The drawn picture of w, *dpic(w)*, is the pair (S(w),δ(w)) and if the starting and ending points have no importance, we call it basic picture of w denoted by *bpic(w)*. In the following, we use the word *picture* instead of *drawn picture*.

Even if a given segment is drawn several times, it appears only once in the picture. Thus, a given drawn (or basic) picture is associated with an *infinite number* of words over D.

For any segment $t_{i,j}$ ∈ S(w), w ∈ D*, $mult_w(t_{i,j})$ denotes the multiplicity relative to the word w of this segment (ie the number of passages on this segment, independently of the direction, during the tracing of the associated picture). The notation $\overrightarrow{mult}_w(x_{i,j})$ is used for the multiplicity relative to the word w of the oriented segment $x_{i,j}$.
P(w) denotes the segments' polynomial of the picture associated with w as follows :
$$P(w) = \sum_{S(w)} mult_w(t_{i,j}) \cdot t_{i,j}$$
A word w ∈ D* is *irreducible* if for any $t_{i,j}$ ∈ S(w) we have $mult_w(t_{i,j})$<=2 (ie the picture is drawn with at most two passages on each segment).
A word w ∈ D* is *minimal* if there is no word, strictly shorter than w describing the same picture.
Remark: In general, there are *several* irreducible words and minimal words which describe a given picture.

Example: The words w1, w2, w3 and w4 describe the same picture.

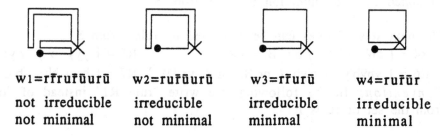

w1=rr̄ruȓūurū	w2=ruȓūurū	w3=rȓurū	w4=ruȓūr
not irreducible	irreducible	irreducible	irreducible
not minimal	not minimal	minimal	minimal

3 - The rewriting system S -

We introduce in this section a rewriting system S which allows to obtain from any word w over D, all the words of D* describing the same picture (in particular, *all* the irreducible words and *all* the minimal words).

Definitions : Let X, be an alphabet. A *rewriting system* S_R over X is a subset of X*×X*. Each element $(u,v) \in S_R$ is called a rule and is denoted by u → v. One step derivation relation $\underset{S_R}{\Rightarrow}$ is defined by :

$$(\ xuy \underset{S_R}{\Rightarrow} xvy \quad \forall x \in X^*, \forall y \in X^*) \Leftrightarrow (u,v) \in S_R$$

$\underset{S_R}{\overset{*}{\Rightarrow}}$ denotes the transitive and reflexive closure of $\underset{S_R}{\Rightarrow}$.

If $w \underset{S_R}{\overset{*}{\Rightarrow}} v$, $w \in X^*, v \in X^*$, we say that *w is an ancestor of v* (by S_R)
or *v is a descendant of w* (by S_R).
(For further details about rewriting system, see [Ja])

Let $w \in D^*$, *inv(w)* denotes the *inverse of w* defined by
$$inv(\varepsilon) = \varepsilon \quad inv(r) = \bar{r} \quad inv(\bar{r}) = r \quad inv(u) = \bar{u} \quad inv(\bar{u}) = u$$
if w = w'x with w'∈ D* and x∈ D   inv(w) = inv(x) inv(w')
Convention: In the following, we write $\bar{w}$ instead of inv(w), $w \in D^*$.

A *ring* is a word b over D such that δ(b) = (0,0) (the starting and ending points of the picture are the same). We note B = { b ∈ D* / δ(b) = (0,0) }

We define the rewriting system S over D as R1 ∪ R2 ∪ R3 ∪ R4
with
$$R1 = \{ b \to \bar{b} \ / b \in B \}$$
$$R2 = \{ x\bar{x}x \to x \ / x \in D \}$$
$$R2' = \{ x \to x\bar{x}x \ / x \in D \}$$
$$R3 = \{ bb \to b \ / b \in B \}$$

Property : S *preserves pictures* (ie for any word v descendant of w, we have δ(w)=δ(v) and S(w)=S(v))
Remark: Gutbrod [Gu] introduced a similar system working on the words. We easily show that every transformation of his system can be simulated by a combination of rules from S.

The next sets of rules can be simulated by rules from S :
R4 = { bb' → b'b / b ∈ B, b'∈ B }   R5 = { yȳy → y / y∈ D* }
R6 = { ybȳb'y → b'yb / b∈ B, b'∈ B, y∈ D* } R7 = { b → bb / b ∈ B }
Convention: In the following, we write "rule R1" instead of "one rule from the set of rules R1".

4 - The main results -

Using our system S, we show the three next results : first, from any word $w \in D^*$ we can derive a minimal word m and we give an algorithm (theorem 1). Then, for any word $w \in D^*$ our system S allows to obtain all the words from D^* describing the same picture (proposition 2). Finally, we extend the system S and we show that it is possible to get a minimal word in terms of basic picture (theorem 2). The system S will be implicit for any derivations.

THEOREM 1: From any word $w \in D^*$, we can derive a minimal word m.

First we show that from any word w we can derive an irreducible word p [cor. 1.2] and then, from p we can derive a minimal word m [cor. 3.3]. To do this, we establish several intermediate results.

Lemma 1 : Let $w \in D^*$. For any segment $s \in S(w)$ such that $mult_w(s) \geq 3$, we can derive from w, a word w' verifying:
$$mult_{w'}(s) = mult_w(s) - 2$$
$$mult_{w'}(t) = mult_w(t) \text{ for any } t \in S(w), t \neq s$$
$$(\text{ therefore, } |w'| = |w| - 2)$$

Proof: Let $w \in D^*$, and $s \in S(w)$ be a segment such that $mult_w(s) \geq 3$. Assume $w = x\ a_1\ y\ a_2\ z\ a_3\ v$ with $x \in D^*$, $y \in D^*$, $z \in D^*$, $v \in D^*$ and $a_1 \in D$, $a_2 \in \{a_1, \bar{a}_1\}$, $a_3 \in \{a_1, \bar{a}_1\}$ where a_1, a_2 and a_3 represent in this order the 3 first passages on s. Four cases are possible, depending on the values of a_2 and a_3. These four cases are similar, so we establish the result only for one of them.
For instance, suppose $a_2 = \bar{a}_1$ and $a_3 = a_1$: $w = x\ a_1\ y\ \bar{a}_1\ z\ a_1 v$ with $x \in D^*$, $y \in B, z \in B, v \in D^*, a_1 \in D$ (we also have $a_1\bar{a}_1 \in B$ and $\bar{a}_1\ z\ a_1 \in B$).
w is rewritten as follows :

$w = xa_1y\bar{a}_1za_1v \quad \Rightarrow \quad xa_1\bar{a}_1za_1yv \quad \Rightarrow \quad xza_1\bar{a}_1a_1yv \quad \Rightarrow \quad xza_1yv = w'$
$\qquad\qquad\qquad\quad R4 \qquad\qquad\qquad R4 \qquad\qquad\qquad R2$

Remark: R4 is simulated only by R1 which does not change the multiplicity of segments. As R2 is just used once, only the multiplicity of s decreases by 2. Consequently, $|w'| = |w| - 2$. ♦

Corollary 1.1: Each minimal word is irreducible.

Corollary 1.2: From any word w∈ D*, we can derive an irreducible word.

The next result is not used to prove theorem 1, but it is interesting because it indicates that every picture can be drawn with *at most* one passage in each direction on each segment.

Proposition 1 : From any word w ∈ D* can be derived a word t verifying:
$$\forall \ s \ \in \ \overrightarrow{S(t)}, \quad \overrightarrow{mult_t}(s) \leq 1$$

Proof: We assume that $w = x_1 \ x_2 \ ... \ x_n$ with $x_i \in D$, $1 \leq i \leq n$, is irreducible [cor. 1.2]. We construct a word $t = y_1 \ y_2 \ ... \ y_n$ as follows : we read w, letter by letter, from left to right. For each letter x_i , we give to y_i the value of x_i and :
- if x_i induces a segment of multiplicity 1 or if x_i induces the second passage on a segment, we read the next letter.
- if x_i induces the first passage on a segment of multiplicity 2, we transform the part of w not yet read, so that the second passage on this segment will be drawn in the opposite way.♦

Lemma 2 : Two words q and q' ∈ D* have the same polynomial of segments if and only if q' is a descendant of q by R1.

Proof : The necessary condition is proved by induction over $n=|q|=|q'|$.
. For n=0 ou n=1, the claim is obvious.
. Assume the claim holds for any p ∈ N, p>1. We will show it also holds for n=p+1. Two cases are possible:
. q and q' start with the same letter x. So, $q=xq_1$ and $q'=xq'_1$ with $q_1 \in D^*$, $q'_1 \in D^*$. By induction hypothesis, we have $q=xq_1 \overset{*}{\underset{R1}{\Rightarrow}} q'=xq'_1$.
. or we have $q=xq_1$ and $q'=yq'_1$ with $x \neq y$ $x \in D$, $y \in D$, $q_1 \in D^*$, $q'_1 \in D^*$. Let t, the segment induced by y during the tracing of the picture associated with q'. We set $q=v_1x'v_2$, $x' \in D$; x' represents the first passage on t during the tracing of the picture associated with q. We have : eitheir v_1 is a ring or v_1x' is a ring. In both cases, we show that q can be rewritten as follows: $q \overset{*}{\underset{R1}{\Rightarrow}} yq_0$, $q_0 \in D^*$, and by induction hypothesis, $q \overset{*}{\underset{R1}{\Rightarrow}} yq_0 \overset{*}{\underset{R1}{\Rightarrow}} yq'_1=q'$♦

Corollary 2.1: If two words q and q' ∈ D* have the same polynomial of segments then $\delta(q) = \delta(q')$.

To establish the following result, we need some further notions. We call:

. *node*, an element of $\mathbf{Z}^2$.
. *path*, a sequence of segments $S_1S_2...S_n$ such that there exists a sequence of nodes $N_0N_1...N_n$ verifying $S_k=\{N_{k-1},N_k\}$, $k\in[1,n]$ (it is unique).
  - A path is a *cycle* if $N_0 = N_n$.
  - A path is *eulerian* if it includes each segment exactly once.
. *circuit*, an eulerian cycle.
  - Two circuits are *disjointed* if they have no common segment.
    (But they may have common nodes).

A word w *describes a path* C if for any left factor w' of w, we have $|w'|=k$, $N_0 + \delta(w') = N_k$ where $N_0\ N_1\ ...\ N_n$ is the sequence of nodes associated with C.

Properties: The word w describing a circuit C is unique.If C is a cycle, $w \in B$. If C is eulerian, $\forall\ s \in S(w)\quad mult_w(s) = 1$.

For any $p \in D^*$ and $q \in D^*$, $S(p,q)$ denotes the set of segments whose multiplicities relative to p and to q are different.

Lemma 3 :   Let p and q two irreducible words over D, describing the same picture. The segments in $S(p,q)$ constitute disjointed circuits.

Proof: Let S_1, a segment from $S(p,q)$. Set $S_1 = \{ N_0 , N_1 \}$.
We construct a path $S_1\ S_2\ ...\ S_k$ with elements from $S(p,q)$ as follows:
- starting from N_0
- not including the same segment twice
    One can always go away from a node with a segment not yet used: indeed, we easily verify that for each node N, the set of segments from $S(p,q)$ which have N as an extremity, have an even number of elements. By construction, this path is eulerian.
- ending in N_0 . By construction, this path is a cycle.
Thus, we just have constructed a circuit. As long as the segments from $S(p,q)$ have not been all used, we choose a segment from $S(p,q)$ not yet used, and we start again the same process. By construction, all these circuits are disjointed. ♦

Corollary 3.1: Let $p\in D^*$, p irreducible. For any circuit C from $S(p)$, an irreducible word $q\in D^*$ can be derived from p such that: . $\forall\ s \in C\quad mult_q(s) = mult_p(s)\ mod\ 2\ +1$.
                    . $\forall\ s \notin C\quad mult_q(s) = mult_p(s)$.

Proof: Let p, an irreducible word over D and C, a circuit $S_1 S_2 ... S_n$ from S(p). $N_0 N_1 ... N_n$ is the sequence of nodes associated with C. Set $p = x_1 a_1 x_2 a_2 ... x_n a_n x_{n+1}$ with $\forall$ i$\in$ [1 , n+1] , $x_i \in D^*$ and $\forall$ i$\in$ [1 , n], a_i induces the first passage on a segment of C.

We show that we can derive p as follows :

$$p \overset{*}{\Rightarrow} p_n = x_1 a_1 x_2 a_2 ... x_k e_n \bar{e}_n a_k x_{k+1} ... a_n x_{n+1}$$

with k $\in$ [1 , n] and e_n describes the path $S_1 S_2 ... S_n$.

As $S_1 S_2 ... S_n$ is a circuit, $e_n \in B$ and p_n can be derived by R1 and R3 as follows : $x_1 ... x_k e_n \bar{e}_n a_k x_{k+1} ... a_n x_{n+1} \Rightarrow x_1 ... x_k e_n a_k x_{k+1} ... a_n x_{n+1} = p'$

p' can be derived as follows : for any segments s$\in$ C such that $mult_{p'}(s) = 3$, we apply lemma 1. Thus, we obtain a descendant q verifying:

$\forall$ s $\in$ C if $mult_p(s) = 1$ then $mult_q(s) = 2$.

if $mult_p(s) = 2$ then $mult_q(s) = 1$.

and $\forall$ s $\notin$ C $mult_p(s) = mult_q(s)$. ♦

Corollary 3.2: For any irreducible words p and q over D describing the same picture, q is a descendant of p by S.

Corollary 3.3: From any irreducible word p$\in$ D*, we can derive a minimal word.

Theorem 1 is a direct consequence of corollary 1.2 and corollary 3.3 and has two interesting corollaries.

Corollary 1: From any word w $\in$ D*, we can derive a minimal word in finite time.

Proof: The different steps of theorem 1 are summarized in the following algorithm: let w $\in$ D*, we set n=| w | .

1st step : From w, we derive an irreducible word p [cor. 1.2]: for each segment, we apply rule R1 at most twice and rule R2 at most once. The number of segments is bounded by n, so we get p in finite time. .

2nd step : In S(p), we look for a circuit C such that the number of segments with multiplicity 2 is greater than the number of segments with multiplicity 1 in C. The number of segments being finite, this investigation needs finite time. If such a circuit exits, we apply corollary 3.1 and obtain a word p', descendant of p, verifying |p'| < |p| . We start it again taking p' instead of p. Since |p| strictly decreases at each step, the process is finite and the last word is minimal.♦

Corollary 2: From any word w $\in$ D*, we can derive a minimal word m' verifying: $\forall$ s $\in$ $\overrightarrow{S(m')}$, $\overrightarrow{mult_{m'}}(s) \leq 1$

We saw in section 2, that there is an infinite number of words describing the same picture. We are interested in knowing if, from any word over D, we can get by S all the words describing the same picture.

Proposition 2 : For any word w ∈ D*, the set of descendants of w by S (denoted $W_s(w)$) is the set of all the words over D describing the same picture as w.

Proof:

. Since S preserves pictures, we have $W_s(w) \subset \{ v \in D^*/dpic(v)=dpic(w) \}$
. From any words v and w over D such that dpic(v)=dpic(w), we can derive irreducible words w' and v' [cor. 1.2]. Since S preserves pictures, we have dpic(w') = dpic(v') and so, v' is a descendant of w' [cor. 3.2]. To derive v' from v, we only use R1 and R2 [cor. 1.2], thus v can be derived from v' using R1 and R2'.
Consequently, w can be rewritten as follows : $w \overset{*}{\Rightarrow} w' \overset{*}{\Rightarrow} v' \overset{*}{\Rightarrow} v$
and we deduce $W_s(w) \supset \{ v \in D^* / dpic(v) = dpic(w) \}$ ♦

In the first part, we were interested in giving a rewriting system S and an algorithm to derive from a word w over D, a minimal word describing the same picture, starting and ending points being fixed. We extend our work and completing S, we define now a system S' which preserves basic pictures. The aim is to get an equivalent tracing, independently from the starting and ending points. To do this, we complete S with two transformations introduced by Gutbrod [Gu]:

$$T6 = \{ w_1w_2 \rightarrow w_1w_2\overline{w}_2 \ / \ w_1 \in D^*, \ w_2 \in D^* \}$$
$$T7 = \{ w_1w_2 \rightarrow \overline{w}_1w_1w_2 \ / \ w_1 \in D^*, \ w_2 \in D^* \}$$

THEOREM 2: From any word w ∈ D*, we can derive by the system S'=S∪T6∪T7, a word m minimal in the sense of basic pictures

Example :

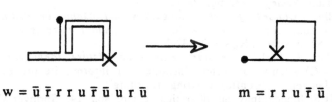

$w = \overline{u} \, \overline{r} \, r \, r \, u \, \overline{r} \, \overline{u} \, u \, r \, \overline{u}$ $m = r \, r \, u \, \overline{r} \, \overline{u}$

Proof: Since T6 and T7 allow to change the starting and ending points of a picture, it is enough to compute a minimal word for each configuration and to keep the shortest of them.

Conclusion

In this paper, we have defined a rewriting system S and an algorithm which allow to get from any word over D, all the words from D* describing the same picture and in finite time, a minimal word describing this (drawn or basic) picture. That is to say, from a given (drawn or basic) picture, our algorithm computes in finite time the shortest way to draw this picture without "pen-up". If we extend our work joining other elementary moves in the plane, the preceding results remain true using the *same* system S. In this case, a minimal word could be a word such that the length of the tracing is minimal. We only need to associate with each letter the length of the segment induced by it. We show analogously that a minimal word describing a given picture can be computed in finite time. In the same way, the generalization to the third (or more) dimension should not be a problem.

Now, if we add to our alphabet letters which induce invisible lines, these letters will simulate the drawing with "pen-up" (see [HW]). In this case, does there exist a similar rewriting system which allows to obtain all the words describing any given picture (not necessary connected) ? Is there a "clever" algorithm to find a minimal word describing this picture. How to choose the "best" invisible lines to minimize the tracing ?

Acknowledgments The authors would like to thank M. Latteux for very useful discussions and for helpful ideas during the preparation of this work.
This work was partially supported by the Programme de Recherche Coordonnée "Mathématiques et informatique" of the Ministère de la Recherche et de la Technologie.

References

[BD] :   F.J. Brandenburg, J. Dassow : *Reduction of picture words.*
Univ. Passau MIP 8905, 1989 (Tech-report).

[Br] :   F.J. Brandenburg : *On minimal picture words.*
Univ. Passau MIP 8903, 1989 (Tech-report).

[Fr] :   H. Freeman : *On the encoding of arbitrary geometric configurations.*
Ire transactions on electronic computers 10 (2) 1961, 260-268.

[Gu] :   R. Gutbrod : *A transformation system for generating description languages of chain code pictures.* TCS 68 (3) 1989, 239-252.

[Ha] :   M. Harrison : "Introduction to formal language theory" (1978).
Addison-Wesley, reading, Mass.

[Hi] :   F. Hinz : *Classes of picture languages that cannot be distinguished in the chain code concept and deletion of redundant retreats.*
Proc. STACS 89, LNCS 349, 132-143.

[HW] :   F. Hinz, E. Welzl : *Regular chain code picture languages with invisible lines.* Graz univ. of techn., institute fuer inform., Report 252, (1988).

[Ja] :   M. Jantzen : "Confluent string rewriting".
EATCS Monographs on theoritical comp. sc., 14. Springer-Verlag, (1988).

[MRW] :   H.A. Maurer, G. Rozenberg, E. Welzl : *Using string languages to describe picture languages.* Inform. Contr. 54 (1982), 155-185.

[Sa] :   A. Salomaa : "Formal languages" (1973). Academic Press , London.

Remarks on the frequency-coded neural nets complexity

Peter Škodný

VUSEI-AR, Dúbravská 3, 842 21 Bratislava
Czechoslovakia

Abstract: Some of the basic models of the neural nets are presented. Short introduction to the neural net computation and complexity theory is given and the frequency-coded neural net are explored. It is shown that it has the same computational power as the Hopfield net and belongs to second machine class.

1. Introduction

Most of the research done in the complexity theory of the neural net in recent time is oriented on the Hopfield neural network (6), Boltzmann machines (1), or spin glasses (2). Other types of the neural net, like frequency-coded neural network (4) or competition based nets are often outside of interest. In what follows we shall concentrate our attention on the computational properties of the frequency-coded neural networks and their relation to Hopfield like neural nets.*

First, in the section 2, we will briefly review the basic models of the neural nets which are used in our discussion. Then, in the section 3, basic definitions and recently obtained results on the neural net complexity theory will be introduced. In the following section 4, will be presented our results concerning properties of the frequency-coded neural net. It will be shown that any frequency-coded neural network is equivalent to Hopfield one and that its computational power is the same as that of Hopfield nets. The last section 5, will make conclusions.

2. Preliminaries

2.1 Basic definitions

Generally, the neural net consists of two sets, a set of so-called neurons and a set of interconnections. The neuron is an abstract processing device which is named after the brain neuron. The neuron has two states, which depend on the states of the other neurons in the net. Formally, the neural net consisting of the neurons and interconnections can be defined in the following way:

---

* In our paper we will consider the net and the network as the synonyms.

Definition 2.1.1. *A neural network is a 7-tuple $M = (V, C, I, O, A, w, h)$, where*
— *V is a finite set of neurons*
— *$C \subseteq V \times V$ is a set of oriented interconnections among neurons*
— *$I \subseteq V$ is a set of input neurons*
— *$O \subseteq V$ is a set of output neurons*
— *$A \subseteq V$ is a set of initially active neurons, $A \cap I = \emptyset$*
— *$w : C \to Z$ is a weight function; Z is the set of all integers*
— *$h : V \to Z$ is a threshold function*

The ordered pair (V, C) forms an oriented graph that is called an interconnection graph (pattern) of M. ∎

M will be called *symmetric* if its interconnection pattern is an undirected labeled graph. Symmetric neural network are often termed *Hopfield neural network* since it was Hopfield who as the first observed special properties of this neural net type. M will be called *simple* or *asymmetric* if its interconnection pattern is simple. If the simple neural net interconnection pattern is acyclic then it will be called *neural circuit*. Neural circuits are often called *feedforward neural networks*.

Each neuron (*node, processor,* or *processing unit*) $u_i \in V$ can enter two different *states*: 0 (inactive) or 1 (active) as characterized by its *output* x_i. There is a so-called *threshold value* $t_i \in Z$ assigned by the function h to each neuron u_i. Each neuron has an arbitrary number of input and output *connections(links, interconnections)* that are labeled by *weights*. The *total input* to each neuron u_i at any moment is given by the sum $h_i = \sum_{j=1}^{n} a_{i,j} x_j$, where $a_{i,j} \in Z$ is the weight (assigned by the function w) of the u_i's input connection leading from u_j to u_i, x_j is the state of u_j at a given moment and n is the total number of neurons in the network.

2.2 The neural net computation

Formally, a *computation* of the neural network $M = (V, C, I, O, A, w, h)$ on input $x \in B^n$ is defined as follows. Initially, the input processors of M are placed into states which encode x. That is, if $I = \{u_1, \ldots, u_n\}$ then processor u_i is placed in the active state if $x_i = 1$. The processors of A are also placed in the inactive state. The computation then begins.

Time is measured by dividing it into discrete intervals. During each interval some or all processors are given the opportunity to update their states. The state of individual processor $u \in V$ is updated according to the definition of the particular neural network model. Let $S(u, t)$ is the state of processor u at time t. Then we should say that processor $u \in V$ is *stable* at time t if $S(u, t) = S(u, t - 1)$, otherwise we should say that $S(u, t)$ is *unstable*.

Suppose $U \subseteq V$, and $U = \{u_1, u_2, \ldots, u_m\}$ for some $m \in N$. The state of U at time t is defined to be string $S(u, t) = S(u_1, t) S(u_2, t), \ldots, S(u_m, t)$. A *configuration* of M at time t is defined to be $S_M(t) = S(V, t)$. The computation is said to be *terminated* by the time t if it has reached a stable configuration, that is, $S_M(t) = S_M(t + 1)$. The termination is often replaced with *halting, reaching a stable state, converging.*

In the previous paragraphs the basic definitions of the neural net computation were given, but it was not exactly defined which processors to be update their state within specified interval. Two modes of computation are generally accepted.

1. *Sequential mode,* in which a single processor updates its state within each interval. This processor may be chosen at random, or according to some deterministic rule.

2. *Parallel mode*, in which at least two processors update their state during each interval. Each processor could decide randomly and independently whether to update, this is called *random parallel* operation or all processors could update simultaneously, this is called *fully parallel* operation.

A computation is called *productive* if at least one unstable processor is updated in each interval.

Hopfield (6) has shown that the sequential computation of the symmetric neural net will always halts after final number of steps and that the computation of a such type of the neural network can be characterized as a process of a *minimization* of a certain *energy function E* which takes the form

$$E = -\frac{1}{2} \sum_{i=1}^{n} \sum_{j=1}^{n} a_{ij} x_i x_j + \sum_{i=1}^{n} t_i x_i$$

with the meaning of individual symbols as described in previous section.

2.3 The Boltzmann machines

The Boltzmann machine is a special kind of the symmetric neural network with the probability embodied into the neuron behavior.

Definition. 2.3.1. *A discrete Boltzmann machine is a symmetric neural network, where to each neuron $u_n \in V$ and discrete time t a so-called temperature function $\tau_n : V \times N \to N$ assigns a "temperature".* ∎

The state of each neuron is updated as follows. The total input to the kth neuron u_k in time $t > 0$ is given similarly as in the section 2.1. Then u_k is active in time t with some probability $p(\Delta E_{k,t})$. Typically, in literature the probability function p takes the form

$$p_k = \frac{1}{1 + e^{-\Delta E_{k,t}/T}}$$

where T is parameter that acts like temperature and $\Delta E_{k,t}$ is the energy gap between the states of the kth neuron in time t.

2.4 The frequency-coded neural net

The frequency-coded (or pulse-coded) neural network is based on early works at Sandia Laboratories by Iben Browning (3). Some of the findings together with practical applications of this model are given in the works of Dress [DRE87b]. The frequency-coded neural net (shortly FCNN) activity differs from that performed by the Hopfield model.

Definition 2.4.1 *A discrete frequency-coded neural network is a asymmetric neural network, where to each neuron $u_k \in V$ and discrete time t a output function $x_k : V \times N \to \{0,1\}$ assigns the output value. The output function x_k takes the form*

$$x_k(t+1) = h(\sum_{i=1}^{n} w_{ki} x_i(t) + c^{\beta \Delta t} + \alpha p_k(t))$$

where c, β are constants characterizing spontaneous increasing of the neuron internal potential , $\alpha p_k(t)$ is the probability that the kth neuron will be random firing in time t, Δt is time since last neuron firing. The remaining symbols have the same meaning as in the previous sections. ∎

In the opposite of the neuron model as defined in the section 2.1, the neuron model used in the FCNN can enter three states *active*, *nonactive*,and the *refractory period state*, during which is prevented from updating. The length of this period is typically few clock cycles. The state of neuron updates as follows. Initially the neuron enters nonactive state and the sensitivity of the neuron inputs is exponentially increasing (due to $e^{\beta t}$ additional factor in the output function). If the sum $\sum_{i=1}^{n} w_{ki}x_i + e^{\beta t}$ exceeds the threshold value the neuron enters active state for one clock cycle, which is followed with the refractory period. The neuron can also enter the active state anytime during the nonactive state with the probability $p_k(t)$.

3. On the neural networks complexity

3.1 Size of the neural network

Conventional computational models are characterized with time and space used during the computation. In the neural net complexity theory there are two measures which can characterize the amount of hardware needed to implement neural net M which we will consider here. One is a number of nodes $|V|$, the *size* of M, and the other is

$$\sum_{u,v \in V} |w(u,v)|$$

which we will call the *weight* of M. The size S(n) of neural net M is taken as the worst case size of M over all inputs of length n.

3.2 Running time of the neural network

The *running time*(or *time requirement*) of M on input $x \in B^n$, $\tau(M,x)$ is defined to be the smallest t such that the computation has terminated by time t. The *output* of M is defined to be $S(O, \tau(M,x))$. Running time $T(n)$ of M is taken as the worst-case running time over all inputs of length n.

A neural network M_2 is said to be f(t)-*equivalent* to M_1 iff for all inputs x, for every computation of M_1 on input x which terminates in time t there is a computation of M_2 on input x which terminates in time f(t) with the same output.

A neural network M_2 is said to be *equivalent* to M_1 iff it is t-*equivalent* to it.

3.3 Computational power of neural networks

A complexity theory which would answer questions concerning the computational power of the neural network was emerging slowly. Only in the last few years some important results for neural net complexity theory were obtained (7),(8), (9).

These results were proved for the models of neural nets similar to Hopfield neural net and Boltzmann machines only and it was shown (9) that these machines belong to a so-called second machine class that embodies machine allowing for unrestricted parallelism. Computational power of other neural net types is not yet known.

4. Frequency-coded neural network simulation

In what follows we will show the equality of the frequency-coded neural networks and Hopfield type neural net. Main differences between FCNN and Hopfield model could be summarized in the following points:

1. Processor should fire randomly or if the threshold value is exceeded.
2. Structure of the net is varying during the computation due to refractory period.

We will call the processor $u_i \in N$ *deterministic* if its function is nonstochastic function of its inputs otherwise we will call it *nondeterministic*. We will call FCNN *nondeterministic* if it has at least one nondeterministic processor. FCNN will be called *deterministic* if all of its processors are deterministic.

Lemma 4.1 *Let N_1 be deterministic frequency-coded neural net of size $S(N)$ and running time $T(n)$. Then there is equivalent nondeterministic FCNN N_2 of size $S(n)^{O(1)}$ and running time $O(T(N))$.* ∎

Proof(Sketch) Each processor $u_i \in N_2$ can be replaced with the pair of nodes $u_i^{(1)}$ and $u_i^{(2)}$, where

$u_i^{(1)}$ is the deterministic processor with one more input and the same threshold output function as the original u_i has. The node $u_i^{(2)}$ is the nondeterministic processor with no inputs which creates random input to $u_i^{(1)}$. The weight of the connection $(u_i^{(1)}, u_i^{(2)})$ is 1. Following these instructions we get the net N_2' of size $2S(n)$ and running time $T(n)$. In (8) it is shown that given a Boltzmann machine B_1 with deterministic processors and random inputs it is possible to produce a new machine B_2 which is deterministic and equivalent to B_1 with only polynomial more processors. Each nondeterministic processor with threshold value k and s inputs in the Boltzmann machine with size $S(n)$ is replaced by $2Z(n)^2 + 1$ random inputs, equality processors and AND processors, and a single OR processor. The key is to provide random input for each possible probability. Using the same approach we could remove random inputs and we get a new net of polynomial size and constant running time which can simulate N_1.

Lemma 4.2 *Let N_1 be Hopfield type neural network of size $S(n)$ and running time $T(n)$. Then there is equivalent deterministic frequency-coded neural net N_2 of size $O(S(n))$ and running time $O(T(n))$.* ∎

Proof(Sketch) Every processor of the FCNN N_2 could be replaced with a chain of auxiliary processors of the same type as it is displayed on fig.1.

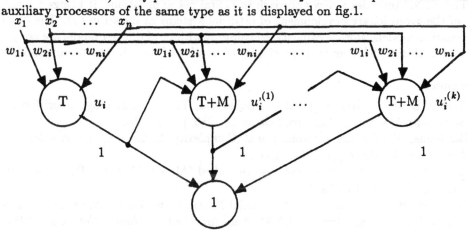

$u_i, u_i^{(i)}$ ... nodes with the refractory period
T ... threshold value
$M = \sum_{j=1}^{n} |w_{ij}|$

Figure 1. Refractory period elimination

This chain will eliminate influence of the refractory period on the net activity. Each processor of the chain is sequentially activated if the previous one fired. So during the whole refractory period at least one processor in the chain is active. Number of auxiliary processors depends on the refractory period length. The modified asymmetric net is size of $O(\tau_R S(n))$ and running time $O(T(n))$, where $\tau_R = max(t_{R_1}, \ldots, t_{R_n})$, t_{R_i} is refractory period of the processor $u_i \in N_2$. Wiedermann (9) has shown that it is possible to simulate asymmetric neural network by the symmetric one of constant size and constant running time. Using his approach we get symmetric neural network which can simulate N_1.

Theorem 4.1 Let N_1 be Hopfield type neural network of size $S(n)$ and running time $T(n)$. Then there is equivalent frequency-coded neural net N_2 of size $S(n)^{O(1)}$ and running time $O(T(n))$. ■

Proof(Sketch) Using lemmas 4.1 and 4.2 we can construct the FCNN N_2 of polynomial bounded size and constant time which will simulate N_1.

From the theorem 4.1 it is clear the computational power of the frequency-coded neural nets is the same as that of the Hopfield nets, and complexity results obtained on this model are valid for the FCNN too. So FCNN belongs to the same class of computational machines as the Hopfield net, Boltzmann machines and spin glasses.

5. Conclusion

In the paper we have presented a link between "standard" neural net and the frequency-coded one of which not all properties are yet explored. Experimentally obtained results on the FCNN model shown that it may have some features different from the conventional neural nets. We have shown the computational power of the FCNN is the same as that of the second class machine if we assume bounded fan-in, so it doesn't create a new class of computational devices.

The FCNN provides a new approach to neural net applications, it brings a possibility of the evolutionary development of artificial systems as shown in (5). The exact mathematical models, storage capacity, learning algorithms of this net model are not yet known , but this model gives to us possibility of creation of the self-developing machine.

References

(1) Ackley, D. N. — Hinton, G. E. — Sejnowski, T. I.: A Learning Algorithm for Boltzmann Machines. *Cognitive Science* 9, 1985, pp. 147–169

(2) Barahona, F.: On the Computational Complexity of Ising Spin Glass Models. *J. Phys. A.* 15, 1982, pp. 3241–3253

(3) Browning, I.: A Self-Organizing System Called "Mickey Mouse". Panomaric Research,Inc., Palo Alto, Calif.

(4) Dress, W. B. : Frequency-Coded Artificial Neural Networks: An Approach To Self-Organizing Systems. *Proc. IEEE 1st Ann. Int. Conf. on Neural Net.*, USA, 1987

(5) Dress, W. B. : Darwinian Optimization Of Synthetic Neural Systems. *Proc. IEEE 1st Ann. Int. Conf. on Neural Net.* , USA, June 1987

(6) Hopfield, J. J.: Neurons with Graded Response Have Collective Computational Properties Like Those of Two–state Neurons. *Proc. Natl. Acad. Sci. USA*, 1984, pp. 3088–3092

(7) Parberry, I.: A Primer on the Complexity Theory of Neural Networks. *Research Report CS-88-38*, Dept. of Comp. Sci., The Pennsylvania state university, October 1988

(8) Parberry, I. — Schnitger, G.: Relating Boltzmann Machines to Conventional models of Computations. *Neural Networks*, **2**, 1989

(9) Wiedermann, J.: On the Computational Efficiency of Symmetric Neural Networks. *Proc. 14-th Symp. on Math. Found. of Comp. Sci.*, *MFCS'89*, LNCS Vol. **379**, Springer Verlag, Berlin, 1989, pp. 545–552

Picture Generation Using Matrix Systems

Ralf Stiebe

Technische Universität Magdeburg, Sektion Mathematik

Universitätsplatz 2, DDR-3024 Magdeburg

0. Introduction

The concept of picture generation using grammars is extensively
studied. A well-known approach is to use chain code picture languages where each letter of an alphabet is interpreted as a command for
a plotter. In this paper we shall investigate another method which
was introduced by the Siromoneys [Si]. By means of a context-free
regular matrix system a picture is generated as follows.
First using a context-free grammar a word is generated in horizontal
direction. Then from every letter of this word we derive a word in
vertical direction using a right-linear grammar.
This paper is organized as follows. In the first section we present
the necessary definitions. In section 2 we will compare CF-RM systems
and generalized chain code picture languages. In the sections 3 and 4
decision problems are studied for some geometrical or graph-theoreti-
cal properties as it was done in [DH] for generalized chain code
picture languages. The decidable problems are contained in section 3
while the undecidable problems are investigated in section 4.

1. Definitons

Throughout the paper we assume that the reader is familiar with the
basic concepts of formal language theory ([HU],[DP]).
First we want to recall the definitons of a picture and of a chain
code picture language. Let (m,n) be a point of the grid Z^2 over the

set Z of integers, and let $b \in \pi = \{u,d,r,l\}$. Then we set

$$u((m,n)) = (m,n+1), \quad d((m,n)) = (m,n-1),$$

$$r((m,n)) = (m+1,n), \quad l((m,n)) = (m-1,n).$$

By $\langle z,b(z)\rangle$ we denote the unit line connecting z and $b(z)$. In the sequel we define a __picture__ as a finite set of these unit lines. Now we associate with a word over $\pi_\uparrow = \pi \cup \{\downarrow,\uparrow\}$ a triple (p,z,r) where p is a picture, z is a point, and r gives the state pen-up or pen-down, in the following inductive way:

i) $t(\lambda) = (\emptyset,(0,0),\downarrow)$,

ii) if $t(w) = (p,z,r)$, then

$$t(wb) = (p,z,\downarrow) \quad \text{if } b =\downarrow$$
$$= (p,z,\uparrow) \quad \text{if } b =\uparrow$$
$$= (p,b(z),\uparrow) \quad \text{if } r =\uparrow \text{ and } b \in \pi$$
$$= (p \cup \langle z,b(z)\rangle, b(z),\downarrow) \quad \text{if } r =\downarrow \text{ and } b \in \pi. \quad \bullet$$

If $t(w) = (p,z,r)$, then p is the picture of w, which we denote by $\text{pic}(w)$. Clearly, a picture p can be seen as a graph g where p is the set of edges, the set $\{z:\langle z,b(z)\rangle \in p\}$ is the set N of nodes. The width of a picture p is defined as follows:

$$\text{width}(p) = \max\{m_1- n_1: (m_1,m_2),(n_1,n_2) \in N \text{ for some } m_2,n_2 \}.$$

Let G be a grammar generating a language $L(G)$ over $\pi_\uparrow$. Then we set

$$\text{Pic }(G) = \{\text{pic}(w): w \in L(G)\}.$$

The set $\text{Pic}(G)$ is the __generalized chain code picture language__ generated by G. A generalized picture language B is called context-free if $B = \text{Pic}(G)$ for some context-free grammar G.

A __CF-regular matrix system__ is defined as a pair $G = (G_1,G_2)$ where $G_1= \langle V_1,I_1,P_1,S_0\rangle$ is a context-free grammar. V_1 is the set of horizontal non-terminals, $I_1=\{S_1,\ldots,S_k\}$ is the set of horizontal terminals (intermediates), P_1 is the set of horizontal rules and $S_0\in V_1$ is the start symbol.

$G_2= \underset{i}{\cup} G_{2i}$, $i \in \{1,\ldots,k\}$, where $G_{2i} = \langle V_{2i},I_2,P_{2i},S_i\rangle$ are right-linear grammars with $V_{2i}\cap V_{2j}= \emptyset$ for $i \neq j$.

The derivation proceeds as follows: First a string $S_{i_1}\ldots S_{i_n}$ over I_1 is generated using the horizontal production rules of P_1. Then from every letter S_{i_j} a word $a_{1j}a_{2j}\cdot\cdot a_{r_jj}$ is derived using the rules of G_{2i_j}. These n words are written in vertical direction. They form a matrix $A = [a_{ij}]$ with $j=1,\ldots,n$, $i = 1,\ldots,r_j$. The set of all matrices generated by $G, L(G)$, is called a __CF-regular matrix language__ (CF-RML). If G_1 is a regular grammar the according set is a REG-RML. Further for each $a \in I_2$ there exists a picture pic(a) with $pic(a) \subseteq N_q^2 \times N_q^2$, $N_q = \{0,\ldots,q\}$. Let $t_{ij}(pic(a))$ be defined in the following way: $((a_1,a_2),(b_1,b_2)) \in pic(a)$ iff

$((a_1+(j-1)q, a_2-iq),(b_1+(j-1)q, b_2-iq)) \in t_{ij}(pic(a))$.

Note that $t_{ij}(pic(a))$ means that the picture is shifted iq unit lines down and $(j-1)q$ lines to the right. Now for a matrix $A \in L(G)$ a picture can be constructed in this way:

$$pic(A) = \bigcup_{a_{ij} \in A} t_{ij}(pic(a_{ij})).$$

In the sequel we shall identify pictures which can be transformed to each other by shifts.

For a CF-RMS G we set $Pic(G) = \{pic(A) : A \in G(L)\}$. The set $Pic(G)$ is called a __CF-RM picture language__ (CF-RMPL).

2. CF-RML and generalized chain code picture languages

__Theorem 1:__ Let $G = (G_1, G_2)$ be a CF-RMS. Then there exists a context-free picture grammar H such that:

$$Pic(H) = Pic(G).$$

We will give here a sketch of the proof. We consider the context-free grammar $H = (N, \pi_{\updownarrow}, P, S_0)$ where

$N = V_1 \cup V_2$

P is defined in the following way :

$A \to w \in P \iff A \to w \in P_1$

$A \to p(a)B{\uparrow}u^q{\downarrow} \iff A \to aB \in P_{2i}$ for some $i \in \{1..k\}$

$A \to p(a){\uparrow}r^q u^q{\downarrow} \iff A \to a \in P_{2i}$ for some $i \in \{1,..,k\}$

$p(a) \in \pi_{\updownarrow}^*$ is a word that describes the picture pic(a) with the start point $(0,0)$, the end point $(0,-q)$ and the final state pen-down.

It is easy to see that $Pic(H) = Pic(G)$.

<u>Theorem 2:</u> There are regular chain code picture languages L such that there is no CF-RMS G with   Pic(L) = Pic(G).

One example is the language L = $\{d^k r^l d^m : k, l, m > 0\}$.

Proof. Assume there is a CF-RMS G such that Pic(L) = Pic(G). The picture pic($d^{(N+1)q} r^{3q} d$) is contained in Pic(L) (N denotes the number of vertical nonterminals $|\cup V_{2i}|$). Now there is a column such that the picture of it is pic(r^q). Let this column be derived from the intermediate S_i, it consists of the vertical word $w_1 a w_2$, where w_1, w_2 are words over the set I_2, a is a letter of I_2, and we have: $|w_1| > N$, pic(x) is the empty picture for x$\in$ $w_1 w_2$, and pic(a)= pic(r^q). According to the well-known pumping lemma it can be shown that L(G_{2i}) contains a word $w_1' a w_2$ with $|w_1'| <$N. Thus, if we substitute the column by the vertical word w_1', we obtain a picture that is not contained in Pic(L).

Since the family of regular chain code picture languages is not contained in the family of CF-RMPL, all problems investigated in [DH] have to be considered again.

3.Some decidable problems

In this section we shall consider the subpicture problem and some similar questions. The subpicture problem deals with the question whether or not a given picture is a subpicture of some picture of a given language.

<u>Theorem 3:</u> For CF-RML the subpicture problem is decidable.

Proof. We reduce the subpicture problem to the question whether a word is a subword of some word of a context-free language. Let p be a picture with mq-r < width(p) $\leq$ mq, 0$\leq$r < q. We assume that there is a matrix A such that pic(A) contains p as a subpicture. Then there is a matrix A' contained in A with l columns , l $\in$ {m,m+1,m+2}, such that pic(A') contains p as a subpicture. It is not difficult to show the following fact. If $S_{i_1} \ldots S_{i_l}$ generates A' then from this string can be derived a matrix A" of the size [l,K] that contains p as a subpicture, where K is a constant. Hence, we have to investigate for each

string over I_1 of length l whether or not it generates a matrix of
the size [l,r], r < K such that the picture of this matrix contains p
as a subpicture. If there is not a string with this property the
question whether or not p is a subpicture of some picture generated
by the CF-RMS can be answered negatively. In the other case we have
to investigate whether or not one of these strings is contained as a
subword in some word $w \in L(G_1)$. Since this question is decidable the
subpicture problem is decidable, too.

Note that the questions whether or not a graph can be edge-coloured
by k colours, $k \in \{1,2,3\}$, and whether or not a graph is regular of
degree k, $k \in \{1,2\}$, can be reduced to the problem whether or not one
of some certain pictures is contained in this graph as a subpicture.
Thus we obtain:

Theorem 4: It is decidable whether or not all pictures generated by a
    CF-RMS i) can be edge-coloured by k colours, $k \in \{1,2,3\}$.

        ii) are regular of degree $k, k \in \{1,2\}$.

4. Some undecidable problems for REG-RMS

Before we investigate the undecidable problems we want to present the
scheme for the undecidability proofs. It is similar to the method
used in [KS] to show undecidability of the equivalence problem for
regular chain code picture languages.

The basic idea is to simulate a run of a linearly bounded automaton
by a regular grammar. The system $G = (G_1, G_2)$ will be chosen such that
G_1 is a grammar where each word $w \in L(G_1)$ corresponds to a run of
the linearly bounded automaton on a probably defect Turing tape.

G_2 is defined such that there is a picture described by a matrix of
L(G) with a certain property if and only if no defects of the Turing
tape occur in the run that corresponds to the word generated by G_1.

We consider a linearly bounded automaton $M = (Q, \{0,1,t\}, q_0, \mathcal{S}, F)$ in
normal form. The input words consist of letters from $\{0,1\}$ while t is
the endmarker. A regular grammar to describe a run of M is

$H = (Q \times \{r,1\}, I, P, (q_0, r))$ where $I = \{ \overrightarrow{r_i}\overrightarrow{w_j}, \overleftarrow{r_i}\overleftarrow{w_j}, RL, LR: i,j \in \{0,1\}\}$.

P contains the following rules:

$(q,1) \rightarrow \lambda$ for $q \in F$,

$(q,1) \rightarrow \overleftarrow{r_i}\overleftarrow{w_j}(q',1)$ if $\delta(q,i) \ni (q',j)$, $i,j \in \{0,1\}$,

$(q,1) \rightarrow LR(q',r)$ if $\delta(q,t) \ni (q',t)$

$(q,r) \rightarrow \overrightarrow{r_i}\overrightarrow{w_j}(q',r)$ if $\delta(q,i) \ni (q',j)$, $i,j \in \{0,1\}$,

$(q,r) \rightarrow RL(q',1)$ if $\delta(q,t) \ni (q',t)$.

For the sake of convenience we set Right = $\{\overrightarrow{r_i}\overrightarrow{w_j}: i,j \in \{0,1\} \}$

Left = $\{\overleftarrow{r_i}\overleftarrow{w_j}: i,j \in \{0,1\} \}$

Obviously, a word $w \in L(H)$ describes a run without defect if and only if it is of the form $w = u_1 RL v_1 LR u_2 RL v_2 .. u_{n-1} RL v_{n-1} LR u_n RL$

with   i) $u_k \in \text{Right}^+$ $k = 1,\ldots,n$

ii) $v_k \in \text{Left}^+$ $k = 1,\ldots,n-1$

iii) $|u_k| = |v_k| = |u_{k+1}|$, $k = 1,\ldots,n-1$

iv) If the m-th letter of $\text{rev}(u_k)$ is $\overrightarrow{r_i}\overrightarrow{w_j}$ then the m-th letter of v_k is $\overleftarrow{r_j}\overleftarrow{w_x}$, $i,j,x \in \{0,1\}$.

v) If the m-th letter of $\text{rev}(v_k)$ is $\overleftarrow{r_i}\overleftarrow{w_j}$ then the m-th letter of u_{k+1} is $\overrightarrow{r_j}\overrightarrow{w_x}$, $i,j,x \in \{0,1\}$.

For a word w we denote by $\text{rev}(w)$ the word that we obtain when w is written in reverse direction. If L is a given language we define:

$\text{Rev}(L) = \{ w: \text{rev}(w) \in L \}$

Now let us consider the undecidable problems.

<u>Theorem 5:</u> It is undecidable whether or not, for a REG-RML L, Pic(L) contains a connected picture.

Proof. We consider the REG-RMS $G = (G_1, G_2)$ where

$L(G_1) = AL(H)E$, H as above,

and G_2 is defined such that

$L(A) = \{x(\{d_0, d_1\}z)^+ v\}$

$L(E) = \{v(v\{b_0, b_1\})^+\}$

$L(LR) = \{x(\{a_0, a_1\}z)^+ y\}$

$L(RL) = \{x(z\{a_0, a_1\})^+ y\}$

$L(\overrightarrow{r_i}\overrightarrow{w_j}) = \{v(v\{c_0, c_1\})^* b_i b'_j (\{c_0, c_1\}v)^* w\}$

$L(\overleftarrow{r_i}\overleftarrow{w_j}) = \{v(v\{c_0, c_1\})^* b'_i b_j (\{c_0, c_1\}v)^* w\}$

$L(x: x \in I)$ denotes the language generated by the grammar of G_2 with the start symbol x.

The symbols are replaced by the following pictures.

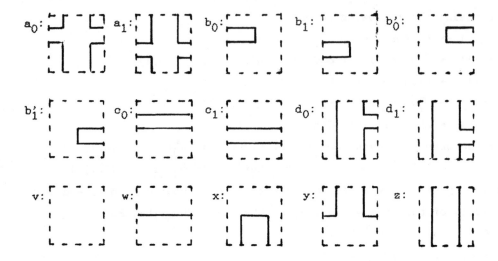

We assume that there exists a connected picture in B(G). The horizontal word from which the according matrix is derived should be

$$w = Au_1(RL)v_1(LR)u_2(RL)v_2(LR)\ldots u_n(RL)v_n(LR)u_{n+1}(RL)E$$

First we will show that the lengths of the columns of the according matrix are equal. We consider the columns generated by A, and the first RL, respectively. A connection between these columns exists if and only if the y's of them stand in the same row like the w's in the columns between them. This means that both columns as well as the ones between them are of the same length. In the same way it can be shown that the columns between two columns generated by RL, and LR, respectively, have the same length, and finally all columns of the matrix have the same length, say $r = 2m+2$. Now we regard the picture that is derived from the horizontal subword $v_l LRu_{l+1}$, $l \in \{1,\ldots,n\}$. In the second row of the column generated from LR we find the symbol a_{i_1}, $i_1 \in \{0,1\}$. In the neighbouring right (left) column the symbol b_{i_1} (b'_{i_1}) has to appear. This means that the first letter of u_{l+1} is $\overrightarrow{r_{i_1}}\overrightarrow{w_x}$ while the first letter of $\mathrm{rev}(v_1)$ is $\overleftarrow{r_y}\overleftarrow{w_{i_1}}$. It is also easy to see that remaining columns in the second row contain only v's. By induction it can be shown for the 2k-th row ($k \in \{2,\ldots,m\}$): In the column derived from LR stands the symbol a_{i_k}, in the (k-1) columns left (right) from this column we find c_{i_k}, in the k-th column right (left) stands b_{i_k} (b'_{i_k}), and in the other columns we find v. Thus we have for $k \in \{2,\ldots,m\}$: If $|u_{l+1}| \geqslant k$ ($|v_1| \geqslant k$), then the

k-th letter of u_{1+1} (rev(v_1)) is $\vec{r}_{i_k}\vec{w}_x$ ($\overleftarrow{r}_y\overleftarrow{w}_{i_k}$). As shown above, the
(2m+2)-th row is the last one for all columns. Hence, we find in this
row the symbol y if the column is derived from LR, and w otherwise.
Now we want to consider the columns derived from the first letter of
v_1 (the last letter of u_{1+1}). These columns contain in their 2m-th
row the symbol b_i' (b_i) or c. If the letter is c then the picture is
disconnected, hence these columns have to contain the letter b_i' (b_i)
in their 2m-th row. Since in the 2m-th row the symbol b_i' (b_i)appears
only in the m-th column left (right) from the column derived from LR,
the words u_{1+1} and v_1 are of the same length m. Thus we have
obtained for the subword $v_1 LR u_{1+1}$: $|u_{1+1}| = |v_1|$, and u_{1+1}, v_1 sa-
tisfy condition v). In the same way it can be shown that, for a sub-
word $u_1 RL v_1$, holds: $|u_1| = |v_1|$, and u_1, v_1 satisfy condition iv).
We have shown: If a picture is connected then the horizontal word
from which the matrix is derived satisfies the conditions i) - v).
It can also be shown that from any horizontal word that satisfies
these conditions we can derive a matrix such that the picture of the
matrix is connected (as an example see figure 1).Thus we have reduced
the question whether or not a given REG-RMPL contains a connected
picture to the question whether or not there exists a run without
defect of the linearly bounded automaton.As an accepting computation
of the linearly bounded automaton corresponds to a run without defect
and as the emptiness problem is undecidable for languages accepted by
linearly bounded automata we obtain undecidability for the existence
of a connected picture.
Using the same method by modifications of the REG-RMS G and of the
pictures belonging to the terminals we obtain:
Theorem 6: It is undecidable whether or not a given REG-RM picture
language contains

     i) a regular graph of degree k = 1,2.

    ii) a 2-connected graph.

   iii) a circle.

    iv) a Eulerian graph (cycle).

    v) a Hamiltonian graph (cycle).

   vi) a graph that can be edge-coloured by k colours, k=1,2,3.

Figure 1:

A connected picture derived from a word that corresponds to a run without a defect

$$w = A\overrightarrow{r_0}\overrightarrow{w_1}\overrightarrow{r_1}\overrightarrow{w_0}\overrightarrow{r_0}\overrightarrow{w_0}(RL)\overleftarrow{r_0}\overleftarrow{w_1}\overleftarrow{r_0}\overleftarrow{w_0}\overleftarrow{r_1}\overleftarrow{w_1}(LR)\overrightarrow{r_1}\overrightarrow{w_0}\overrightarrow{r_0}\overrightarrow{w_1}\overrightarrow{r_1}\overrightarrow{w_0}(RL)E$$

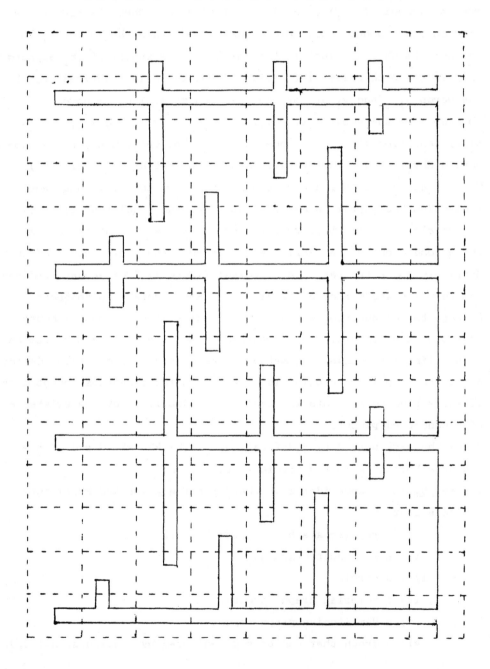

Theorem 7: It is undecidable whether or not all pictures of some given REG-RM picture language are

      i) connected.

      ii) 2-connected.

The universal subpicture problem is the question if a given picture p is a subpicture of all pictures of a picture language. For pictures consisting of only one line it is trivially decidable. In the other case it can be shown by the same method as above:

Theorem 8: For any picture p, consisting of more than one line, it is undecidable whether or not p is a universal subpicture of some given REG-RM picture language.

6. References

[DH] Dassow, J., and Hinz, F., Decision Problems and Regular Chain Code Picture Languages

[DP] Dassow, J., and Paun, G., Regulated Rewriting in Formal Language Theory, Akademie-Verlag Berlin, 1989

[HU] Hopcroft, J. E., and Ullman, J. D., Introduction to Automata Theory Languages, and Computation. Addison Wesley Publ. Co., 1979.

[KS] Kim, C., and Sudborough, I. H., The Membership and Equivalene Problem for Picture Languages. Theor. Comput. Sci. 52 (1987) 177-192

[Si] Siromoney, G., R. Siromoney, and K. Krithivasan, Abstract Families of Matrices and Picture Languages. Computer Graphics and Image Processing 1 (1972) 284-307

Representing Heuristic-Relevant Information for an Automated Theorem Prover

Christian B. Suttner

Forschungsgruppe Künstliche Intelligenz
Technische Universität München
Augustenstr. 46 Rgb, D-8000 München 2
E-mail: suttner@tumki.informatik.tu-muenchen.dbp.de

Abstract

A promising approach to attack the problem of combinatorial explosion faced in automated theorem proving is to employ search guiding heuristics. Our system, which is able to learn such heuristics automatically, uses evaluation functions to rate different choices for continuation during a proof. In this paper, we will focus on the content and representation of the input to these evaluation functions.

1 Introduction

Automated theorem proving still lacks the capability to handle the enormous search space usually encountered during the search for a proof. A method to attack this dilemma is the use of heuristics to guide the search. For this the decision-relevant information and its representation are fundamental issues. Moreover, in our case the automatic acquisition of heuristics is a primary goal. This means that a learning system has to select and combine parts of the available empirical information appropriately and in an efficient way (both in terms of learning time and heuristic decision speed). As a result, restrictions apply for the representations both for the information and for the heuristics. However, before discussing further issues a short introduction to the problem shall be supplied (see e.g. [CL73] for an introduction to theorem proving).

Given a theorem and a set of axioms, the task of an automated theorem prover is to show that the theorem is a logical consequence of the axioms. In a refutation based system, this is done by adding the negation of the theorem to the axioms and proving the unsatisfiability of the resulting formula. Here, formulas are assumed to be in clausal normal form. On the upper right of Figure 1 an example formula is shown (each line represents a *clause* consisting of a set of *literals*, a literal being either an *atom* or a *negated atom*; the first line shows the negation of the theorem).

The goal is to obtain heuristics for SETHEO (see [LBSB]), a theorem prover which is based on the *model elimination* refutation procedure ([Lov68]). For our purposes, it is sufficient to regard the search for a proof as the exploration of an AND/OR tree specified by a formula. An example of such a tree is given in Figure 1. Obviously decisions at OR-nodes[1] have a great impact on the search effort. Thus we will consider heuristics which

---

[1] Nodes at which different continuations of the proof are possible. These possibilities are called the OR-branches, and proving any one OR-branch is sufficient to complete a proof for the subgoal specified by its parent OR-node (compare surrounded area in Figure 1).

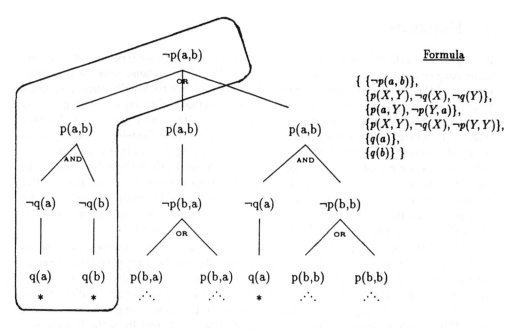

Formula

$$\{ \{\neg p(a,b)\},$$
$$\{p(X,Y), \neg q(X), \neg q(Y)\},$$
$$\{p(a,Y), \neg p(Y,a)\},$$
$$\{p(X,Y), \neg q(X), \neg p(Y,Y)\},$$
$$\{q(a)\},$$
$$\{q(b)\} \}$$

Figure 1: *A partial model elimination tree for the formula given on the right. A '*' denotes a closed branch of the tree. The surrounded area marks a proof for the formula.*

order the available choices at an OR-node according to estimates of their provability. Ideally, the choice which has the shortest proof is tried first, which usually reduces the search space spanned by the subgoal (the predicate at the OR-node) enormously (in Figure 1 this is achieved by choosing the leftmost branch).

In our learning system, a connectionist network together with a backpropagation learning procedure ([RHW86]) is used to obtain evaluation functions. This is done by employing empirical knowledge extracted from former proofs. Briefly, the decisions at OR-nodes made in some training proofs together with the respective feature-values are used to define a pattern association task. The purpose is to classify a given choice by the similarity of its feature-values to those values which occurred in decisions made in the training proofs. A more detailed description of the approach and results on the improvement obtained by learned heuristics are presented in [SE90].

In the following, some basic definitions and a classification scheme are presented. Then, a detailed description of features which already lead to successful heuristics is given (Section 3). Finally, in Section 4 we discuss promising extensions which are subject to further research.

Related Work. Feature-based evaluation functions have a long tradition in AI, especially in game-playing. Learning of such heuristics goes back to Samuels work on playing checkers ([Sam59], [Sam67]). Applications to the field of automated theorem proving are found in [SF71] and [OMW76]. More recently, hand-coded heuristics using features are shown in [BES+81]. Related results of preliminary experiments in the present context are given in [ESS89].

2   Features

An important part of the information to be encoded is the syntactic structure of a formula
(consisting of a set of clauses). In predicate logic, literals of a clause may contain many
terms, and the terms may have arbitrary sizes. One approach to describe such a structure
would be to employ a grammar for well-formed formulas and to represent formulas by
their parse-trees. However, as input to evaluation functions and because of efficiency
reasons fixed length representations are much more desirable. Therefore we use features
to encode interesting aspects of clause occurrences in a simple and concise way. A clause
occurrence is a copy of a clause together with additional information (e.g. about the
current location in the search tree). A feature of a clause occurrence is a property of this
occurrence which is assumed to contribute to the task of a heuristic in some way (for
example the number of literals in a clause). To avoid coding and utilization problems,
we further require that a feature is representable by a single number.

At each OR-node, a set of clauses is available for selection. However, unit clauses
is always given priority over non-unit clauses (similar to the unit preference strategy
for resolution theorem provers). Therefore unit clauses are not subject to a heuristical
evaluation, and in the following clauses are assumed to have non-empty bodies. A heuristic then is an ordering mechanism which arranges the (remaining) choices available
at an OR-branch according to the ratings these choices attained from the learned evaluation function (The evaluation function is called for each clause occurrence with its
feature-values as input).

Classification.   For efficiency purposes, it is useful to classify features with respect to
their availability. Some features attain a constant value for a given clause, while others
depend on the specific situation at proof-time. Therefore the following classification is
proposed:

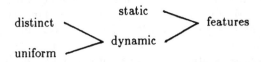

Static features attain invariate values for a given clause, i.e. the values do not change
during a proof. Thus they can be computed in advance and their computational complexity is not of crucial concern. These features mainly encode aspects of the syntactic
structure of a clause (e.g. the number of literals in a clause).

All features not being static, i.e. calculable only at run-time, are called *dynamic*.
Being computed whenever they are needed at an OR-branch, their computational complexity is of direct influence to the overhead caused by the heuristic.

Distinct dynamic features usually have different values for different clause occurrences available for selection. Clearly, this follows the intuitive expectations about the
task to select between clauses. They are able to supply additional information concerning syntactic structures captured with static features (e.g. taking into account run-time
instantiations of variables). Other uses are to maintain clause-specific histories (e.g. how
often a certain clause was used).

Uniform dynamic features are attributes of the OR-branch (environment) itself rather than the clauses. The values attained are therefore the same for all choices given. Since these features are independent of the clauses, they need to be calculated only once for a branch.

3 Examples for Features

In the following most of the features currently available in our system are presented. Obviously, the selection of features is crucial for the quality of heuristics attainable by any learning method. However, in most cases the "worth" of a specific feature cannot be evaluated without taking into account possible combinations with other features. Since the goal is to derive such combinations automatically and intuition concerning complex relationships is quickly exceeded, the criteria for the selection of features are not as restrictive as they would be for the development of heuristics by hand. Thus, in the following, annotations to features do not necessarily denote their actual and only "effect", but are suggestions why they might be useful. The word "number" will be encountered frequently and may be abbreviated by the symbol '#'.

3.1 Static Features

Component counts (of a clause). The following features are grouped further according to the syntactic components involved.

Literals
- ⋄ the number of literals
  tells how many subgoals will need to be solved
- ⋄ the number of negative literals
  allows in combination with the (# of literals) identification of (non-)Hornclauses

Predicates
- ⋄ the number of different predicate symbols
  together with the (# of literals) repeated occurrences of predicates are recognized
- ⋄ the number of duplicated predicates (predicate symbols occurring more than once)
  (# of predicates being repetitions) = (# of literals) − (# of different predicates) + (# of duplicated predicates)

The above features contain enough information to partially reconstruct the predicate structure of the original clause (except for the ordering and identity of predicates): Assume (# of literals) = 4, (# of negative literals) = 2, (# of different predicates) = 2, (# of duplicated predicates) = 1. Here are the only possible structures for the original clause (using dummy identifiers):
$$\{ p(\ldots), q(\ldots), \neg p(\ldots), \neg p(\ldots) \}$$
$$\{ p(\ldots), p(\ldots), \neg q(\ldots), \neg p(\ldots) \}$$

Functional terms
- ⋄ the number of constant occurrences (0-ary functions)

⋄ the number of function occurrences (non 0-ary-functions)

Variables

⋄ the number of variables
⋄ the number of distinct variables
⋄ the number of variables in the head
⋄ the number of distinct variables in the head

Example: (# variables) = 4, (# distinct variables) = 2, (# variables in head) = 2, (# distinct variables in head) = 2; then assuming the clause structure { p(...), ¬q(...), ¬r(...) } gives: { p(X,Y), ¬q(X), ¬r(Y) }

It should be noted that the head of a clause is a very special literal of the clause. In terms of logic programming, variables in the head handle both input and output parameter passing for predicates. Furthermore, they show how these I/O links are connected to the subgoals of the clause. Therefore they deserve particular attention.

Interconnections between literals (via shared variables). All these features determine how tight the literals of a clause are bound together, and to which degree instantiations will have effects on other literals. As an example, a large number of relationships may propose a high probability that backtracking will be required, since instantiations will have many consequences (note that such considerations apply for goal reordering as well).

Here are two possible types of interconnections:

• head to body (e.g. p(X) :- q(X).)
• body to body (e.g. ... :- p(X), q(X).)

Remark: In the theory of relational databases, these links represent joins with respect to the attributes specified through the position of the variables (this comparison leads to the investigation of common query optimization heuristics, as for example the "selection before join" heuristic).

The features below attempt to capture these aspects. The numbers in parentheses are the respective feature-values for the following example:

$$p(X,Y,Z) :- q(X,Y), q(Y,Z).$$

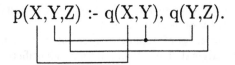

Relations with respect to variables

⋄ the number of variables connecting two literals (2†)

---

†Value of the feature for the example shown above.

⋄ the number of variables connecting three literals or more[2] (1)

⋄ the number of variables connecting the head with subgoals (3)

Relations with respect to predicates
Above we considered how many variables caused certain types of links. Now we count the links themselves.

⋄ the number of predicates connected to exactly one other predicate (0)

⋄ the number of predicates connected to exactly two other predicates (3)

⋄ the number of predicates connected to exactly three or more predicates (0)

⋄ the number of predicates connected with the head (2)

Relationships between clauses. Expanding subgoals without performing unification allows estimates on the search space spanned by a clause (see Figure 2 for explanation):

⋄ the average number of subgoals to be solved one proof-tree level deeper

⋄ the average number of subgoals to be solved two proof-tree levels deeper

⋄ the minimum number of subgoals to be solved until a success is reached

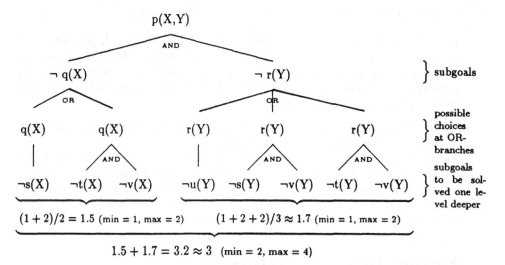

Figure 2: *Explaining the measurements for the "explosiveness" of a predicate.*

3.2   Distinct Dynamic Features

Clause history

⋄ the number of uses of a clause so far

---

[2]Interesting aspects are often splittable into smaller parts, which allow to derive more detailed information. Since arbitrarily continued splits are undesirable, it is useful to introduce catch-all features ("x items or more").

Run-time instantiations

◇ the number of variables in the head of the calling subgoal becoming specialized (a variable is *specialized* through unification, if it is matched with a term not being a variable; this is more rigid than instantiation)

◇ the number of variables in the head of the clause to be rated becoming specialized

3.3 Uniform Dynamic Features

Proof Status

◇ the current depth in the proof-tree

Run-time instantiations

◇ the number of instantiated variables in the calling subgoal

◇ the number of uninstantiated variables in the calling subgoal

These features attain the same values for each of the possible choices. At first sight, using such features seems to be counterintuitive. Our intention is to differentiate between clause occurrences in order to derive an improved arrangement of the choices. Uniform dynamic features may contribute to this goal in two different ways:

- Instead of differentiating clauses, they can be used to distinguish (proof-tree) situations. This allows for example to select between different heuristics depending on the situation. Similarly, they can be used to parameterize heuristics, achieving a changing behaviour with respect to branch attributes (e.g. heuristics depending on the current depth in the proof-tree).

- By supplying additional information, these features can improve the conclusions drawn from other (non-uniform) features alone.
  As an example, a heuristic may use the number of variables in the head of a clause. However, the significance of different values for different clauses may be overestimated unless run-time instantiations in the calling subgoal are taken into consideration. Thus, adding the number of uninstantiated variables of the calling subgoal may reduce supposed differences between choices.

4 Further Issues on Features

4.1 Simple vs. Complex Features

All features presented so far are rather simple in structure. However, complex features can be defined through functional combinations of such simple features (e.g. by forming ratios[3]). They can be used either to reduce the number of features to be dealt with or to supply the heuristic with "preprocessed" features (possibly in addition to the component features used). Creation of such "new" features can remove the burden for a learning

---

[3]For ratios precautions need to be taken to avoid division by 0 and to prevent loss of information in case that integer division is used. Example: ((# of constants) * 10)/(# of variables + 1)

scheme to find these combinations on its own. Furthermore, a particular learning method may be restricted in the class of functions it allows to be learned (e.g. if only linear combinations of features are possible). In this case the use of features being nonlinear combinations of other features can enhance the representational power of the functions. For some examples of complex features see [BES+81].

4.2 Evaluating Features

The usefulness of a feature can depend on the formula. While a given feature may be a good clause descriptor in one case, its value might be the same for all clauses in an other case:

- A static feature may attain the same constant value for all clauses of a certain formula.
  Example: The number of functions in a clause for a formula not containing any functions.

- A static or distinct dynamic feature may attain the same value for all clause occurrences of OR-branches (but the value may be different for different branches). In other words, the feature behaves as a *uniform* feature.
  Example: The number of variables in the clause-head becoming specialized, if all weakly unifiable literals are syntactically equal with respect to variables (modulo renaming).

- Features may be totally (or highly) correlated (for certain formulas).
  Example: For a formula in Hornclause logic, the number of literals of a clause is equal to the number of negative literals plus one.

Such features do not contribute to heuristics and can be eliminated to improve learning efficiency. A program was created that performs such analysis (for linear correlations) automatically ([Sut89]). For an improved assessment of the worth of certain features it is possible to evaluate features based on information from the learning scheme (e.g. by inspecting the weights attached to features by a connectionist network). Also, statistical analysis based on the defined learning task allows to derive estimates on a features contribution to heuristic decisions.

4.3 Syntax and Semantics

Our aim is to select clauses which can be used to complete a proof quickly. Clearly, this task involves to consider the semantics of a formula. However, most features considered are of syntactic nature. Thus the question arises how good the decision can be made if it is based on such features only. Another question is what the features presented so far contribute under this aspect.

As an example for such a consideration we examine the explosiveness of a clause (i.e. the induced number of subproblems on deeper levels of the proof-tree; see Figure 2). This information may be used to select from choices that lead to a proof the one that might do so faster. However, it does not help to find out which choices lead to a proof and which do not. Obviously, heuristics using such features do not perform explicit semantic analysis of the problem at all. What they can give is an evaluation of the choices (identified by their attributes) based on empirical knowledge which combinations of such attributes have lead to success in former cases. Thus all semantic capability of the heuristics is contained in the prior knowledge (i.e. training proofs) used for their development. The role of the features is to capture as many aspects of the relevant information as possible.

Marking Interesting Clauses. Features can be used to describe semantic properties of clauses simply by stating the presence or absence of a certain property. Examples for interesting cases are:

- recursive clauses
- clauses defining a transitive (associative, ...) relation
- equality axioms, equational theories clauses

Marking Clauses by Hand. Up to now the values for features have been derived automatically. Another possibility are user-specified values for special features. This allows to pass user intuition about the problem on to the heuristic (e.g. accentuating clauses which are believed to be crucial for a proof).

Domain-specific Features. Depending on the domain of application (e.g. group theory), certain information may be well known to be interesting. As an example, proofs in a theory may often contain specific combinations of functions. Then features capturing the presence of certain functions in clauses allow to direct clause selection based on empirically desirable function combinations.

4.4 Experimental results

Heuristics have been learned for a particular benchmark formula (Schubert's Steamroller, [Sti86]). Generally, their application lead to a reduction of the required search effort up to an exponential factor both in terms of inference-count and proof-time. For a more detailed analysis see [SE90], which also illuminates the dependency between heuristic perfomance and the relationship of training proofs to the theorem to be proven.

5 Summary

In this paper the information employed by a system capable of learning heuristics was presented. While it is already possible to obtain successful heuristics with the set of features presented here, further investigations will include more detailed analysis on the usefulness of individual features. Besides the information itself, its representation was discussed. This is a crucial issue as well because it might greatly influence the effectiveness of a particular machine learning scheme. Finally, by using a larger set and especially by employing more semantics related features a great potential for increased heuristic performance is available.

Acknowledgements. Thanks to Peter Baumgartner, Ulrich Furbach, and Wolfgang Ertel of the AI research group for reading drafts and making valuable suggestions.

References

[BES+81] K. Bläsius, N. Eisinger, J. Siekmann, G. Smolka, A. Herold, and C. Walther. The Markgraf Karl Refutation Proof Procedure. In *Proceedings of the Seventh International Joint Conference on Artificial Intelligence*, Vancouver, 1981.

[CL73] C.-L. Chang and R.C.-T. Lee. *Symbolic Logic and Mechanical Theorem Proving*. Academic Press, 1973.

[ESS89] W. Ertel, J. Schumann, and C.B. Suttner. Learning Heuristics for a Theorem Prover using Back Propagation. In *Proceedings of the 5. ÖGAI-Conference*, Igls, Austria, 1989. Springer.

[LBSB] R. Letz, S. Bayerl, J. Schumann, and W. Bibel. SETHEO: A High-Performance Theorem Prover. *to appear in: Journal of Automated Reasoning*.

[Lov68] D.W. Loveland. Mechanical Theorem-Proving by Model Elimination. *Journal of the ACM*, 15(2), 1968.

[OMW76] R. Overbeek, J. McCharen, and L. Wos. Complexity and Related Enhancements for Automated Theorem-Proving Programs. *Comp. & Maths. with Appls.*, 2(1-A), 1976.

[RHW86] D.E. Rumelhart, G.E. Hinton, and R.J. Williams. Learning Internal Representations by Error Propagation. In *Parallel Distributed Processing*, 1986.

[Sam59] A.L. Samuel. Some Studies in Machine Learning Using the Game of Checkers. *IBM Journal*, 1(3), 1959.

[Sam67] A.L. Samuel. Some Studies in Machine Learning Using the Game of Checkers, II. *IBM Journal*, 11(6), 1967.

[SE90] C.B. Suttner and W. Ertel. Automatic Acquisition of Search Guiding Heuristics. In *Proceedings of the 10. International Conference on Automated Deduction (CADE)*. Springer, 1990.

[SF71] J.R. Slagle and C.D. Farrell. Experiments in Automatic Learning for a Multipurpose Heuristic Program. *Comm. of the ACM*, 14(2), 1971.

[Sti86] M.E. Stickel. Schubert's Steamroller Problem: Formulations and Solutions. *Journal of Automated Reasoning*, 2:89–101, 1986.

[Sut89] C.B. Suttner. Learning Heuristics for Automated Theorem Proving. Diploma Thesis, Technical University Munich, May 1989.

A new method for proving lower bounds in the model of algebraic decision trees

Kristel Unger

Karl-Weierstraß-Institut für Mathematik

Mohrenstr. 39

Berlin

1086

G.D.R.

1. Introduction

Computational geometry makes often use of algebraic decision trees. For examples compare e.g. with [PS]. On the one hand, this is caused by the fact that many algorithmic problems can be solved in the framework of this model. On the other hand, there exists a method by [SY] (resp. the initiating work [DL]) how to prove lower bounds in this model.

The following results present a method for proving lower bounds which differs essentially from the method given in [SY]. It provides lower bounds which could not be proved up to now with the help of the already known method.

[U] formulates the method in a general way, here it will be presented for the concrete example of constructing the convex hull of d-dimensional finite point sets improving the lower bound $\Omega(n\log n)$, known up to now, to $\Omega(dn\log n)$.

2. Definition of the algorithmic problem and the computational model

Problem CH_d resp. EP_d:

Given a set P of n points from $\mathbb{R}^d$ construct the facial lattice of the convex hull resp. the set of extreme points of P.

The convex hull of a set P is the smallest convex set containing P. A set in $\mathbb{R}^d$ is convex iff P contains with any two points also the finite line connecting the two points. The facial lattice is a finite description of the convex hull of a finite point set. To illustrate the concept of this lattice we note that the convex hull in three dimensions consists of points (0-dimensional, these are the extremal points or vertices), edges (1-dimensional) and faces (2-dimensional). Note, that lower dimensional elements of the lattice are the intersection of higher dimensional elements.

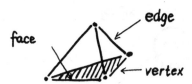

P will be represented as sequence $\langle P_1, \ldots, P_n \rangle$ = $\langle (x_{11}, \ldots, x_{1d}), \ldots, (x_{n1}, \ldots, x_{nd}) \rangle \in \mathbb{R}^{dn}$.

Definition:

k-th order algebraic decision trees (k-ADT) are ternary decision trees with internal nodes marked by polynoms of maximal degree k and with the input P as argument. The internal nodes dispose of three out-edges marked by "<", "=", resp. ">" according to the outcome of testing the value of the polynom against 0. The leaves of the tree are marked by answers, i.e. for CH_d resp. EP_d by descriptions of convex hulls. □

The path leading from the root of a k-ADT T to a leave for input P is denoted by T_P, l_P denotes the corresponding leaf. A tree T solves CH_d resp. EP_d iff for all P l_P is marked by the correct answer.

The definition of k-ADT's can be found in [SY] and [PS]. [SY] gave also a method how to prove lower bounds in this computational model. This method bases on the fact that the input space is partitioned into the classes of inputs with the same answer. Fixing one answer a, this set consists of a number of connected components. Informally, one connected component is surrounded by inputs with other answers. The number w(a) of connected components according to the answer a must be reproduced by the number of connected components according to the signs of the polynoms tested on all paths leading to leaves marked

with the answer a. The later number can be given as term depending on the height h of a k-ADT T. This estimation bases on a number theoretical theorem of Milnor and Thom. It holds
$w(a) \leqslant 3^h \cdot k \cdot (2k-1)^{n+h-1}$. Compare with [PS].

Observe, that this method does not consider the concrete form of the tested polynoms. The method introduced here tries to show what kind of polynoms and how many of that kind has to be tested in a tree correctly solving the concrete problem.

To illustrate this concepts with a trivial example we show a tree solving EP_d for n=3 and d=1, i.e. $P=\langle x_1, x_2, x_3 \rangle$.

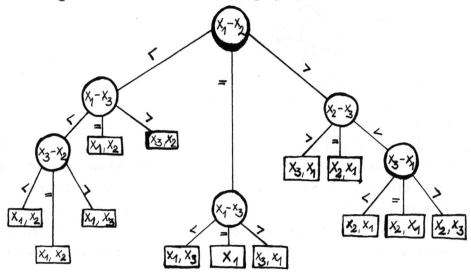

3. The lower bound $\Omega(dn\log n)$ for CH_d

3.1 About the half of the points determines a maximally rich convex hull

Let us fix the $M := \lfloor \frac{n}{2} \rfloor$ last points of the input in such a way that these points determine a convex polyeder with $t = \Omega(M^{\lfloor d/2 \rfloor})$ many faces $F_1, \ldots, F_t$. (Faces are the (d-1)-dimensional elements of the convex hull.) That it is possible to place M points in this way is a result of V. Klee (1966), compare [PS, p.92].

In any k-ADT solving CH_d let us replace the M points by their values from the procedure above. Obviously, the structure of the tree is the same as before. The new tree solves CH_d under the condition that $P_1, \ldots, P_M$ are fixed as above. Lower bounds for this restricted problem are also valid for the original problem.

$m := \lceil \frac{n}{2} \rceil$, $R = \langle P_1, \ldots, P_m \rangle$. $H_1, \ldots, H_t$ denotes the hyperplanes containing the faces $F_1, \ldots, F_t$. $h_1(V)=0, \ldots, h_t(V)=0$ are the according linear equations. For convenience, the origin 0 of the coordinate system is placed in the interior of the fixed convex hull. Furthermore, let $h_1(0)<0, \ldots, h_t(0)<0$.

$\mathcal{M}$ denotes the set of all functions $6:\{1,\ldots,m\} \longrightarrow \{1,\ldots,t\}$, i.e. 6 places points on faces. $s:=\#\mathcal{M}=t^m=\Omega(n^{\lfloor d/2 \rfloor}{}^{n/2})$.

$\mathcal{F}^6 := F_{6(1)} \times \cdots \times F_{6(m)}$.

3.2 The concept of related functions

Definition:

X is an argument from $\mathbb{R}^a$, $X=(x_1, \ldots, x_a)$. We call Y (b-)part of X iff $Y=(y_1, \ldots, y_b)=(x_{i_1}, \ldots, x_{i_b})$ with $1 \leq i_1 < \ldots < i_b \leq a$. □

Definition:

$u: \mathbb{R}^a \longrightarrow \mathbb{R}$, polynom and $v: \mathbb{R}_b \longrightarrow \mathbb{R}$, polynom, both nontrivial. We call u related with v in Y part of X, $(u \leftrightarrow v[Y])$ iff $\forall Z \in \mathbb{R}^b$ $[v(Z)=0 \Longrightarrow \forall X \in \mathbb{R}^a (Y=Z \Longrightarrow u(X)=0)]$. □

With other words u is related with v in Y iff u takes the value 0 for any argument X where Y (part of X) determines v to be 0, independently of the remainder part of X. This seems to be a very strong definition, but it is efficient for the aim of these considerations.

$u > -\langle \{v_1[Y_1], \ldots, v_w[Y_w]\}$ denotes the fact that u is not related with any v_i in Y_i ($1 \leq i \leq w$).

Lemma:

$u(X)$ is a nontrivial polynom. $v_1(Z), \ldots, v_w(Z)$ are linear functions (not necessarily different) and $Y_1, \ldots, Y_w$ are parts of X with $v_1(Y_1) \neq v_j(Y_j)$ ($1 \leq l < j \leq w$) and $u \leftrightarrow v_l[Y_l]$ ($1 \leq l \leq w$). Then holds $u(X) = u_1(X) \prod_{l=1}^{w} [v_l(Y_l)]^{\alpha_l}$ with $u_1(X)$ polynom, $u_1 > -\langle \{v_l[Y_l] : l=1, \ldots, w\}$ and α_l positive integer ($1 \leq l \leq w$) and $\deg u \geq \sum_{l=1}^{w} \alpha_l \geq w$. □

3.3 There are a lot of essential inputs

Assertion:

We claim that for any fixed k-ADT T correctly solving CH_d resp. EP_d and for any $6 \in \mathcal{M}$ there exists a so-called essential input $R^6 \in \mathbb{R}^{dm}$, i.e. for any i ($1 \leq i \leq m$) there exists a node on the path $T_R 6$ where a function related with $h_{6(i)}$ in P_i is tested against 0.

Proof:

Any polynom $g(R)$ can be given as

$$g(R) = g_1(R) \Pi_{i=1}^{m} [h_{6(i)}(P_i)]^{\alpha_i} \text{ with } \alpha_i \geq 0, \text{ integer and}$$

$g_1 >-< \{h_{6(i)}(P_i) : i=1,\ldots,m\}$.

We refer to $g_1(R)$ as "nowhere related part" (nr-part) of g.

$G_1 := \{g_1(R) :$ There is a testfunction $g(R)$ in T with $g_1(R)$ as nr-part.$\}$

$K_f := \{R \in \mathbb{R}^{dm} : f(R)=0\}$ denotes the so called 0-level-set of f.

$K := \mathcal{F}^6 \setminus \cup_{f \in G_1} K_f$.

It holds $K \neq \emptyset$. Verbal, the union of 0-level-sets of finite many nr-parts cannot represent the whole facet product $\mathcal{F}^6$.

While the representation of g is principally determined by its nature as a polynom, the non-emptyness of K follows essentially from the continous nature of g and $\mathcal{F}^6$.

Now, fix $R^k \in K$. We claim that R^k is essential.

From definition follows that $g_1(R^k) \neq 0$ for all $g_1 \in G_1$. Because G_1 is finite, there exists an environment U' of R^k where the sign of any $g_1 \in G_1$ does not change. Suppose now that there is an index i for which there is no test on $T_R k$ related to $h_{6(i)}$ in P_i.

R^+ and R^- rises from R^k by perturbating P_i in U' above resp. below the hyperplane $H_{6(i)}$. Obviously, the convex hull of R^+ contains P_i, but the convex hull of R^- does not contain P_i. On the other hand, $T_R+ = T_R k = T_R-$. Indeed, nr-parts on $T_R k$ do not change their sign in U' and the perturbation of R_i has no effect to hyperplane-tests in other arguments than R_i and, by assumption, there is no related test for $h_{6(i)}(P_i)$. Therefore, the assumption indicated the contradiction that inputs with different answers lead to the same leaf in a correct k-ADT. By this, R^k is an essential input. □

3.4 The lower bound $\Omega(d n \log n)$ follows from the high number of essential inputs

Assertion:

The hight h_T of any k-ADT correctly solving CH_d or EP_d is at least $\frac{1}{2}\log_3 s$ where $s := \#M = t^m$.

Proof: (indirect)

Suppose, $h_T < \frac{1}{2}\log_3 s$. Then T possesses at most $\sqrt{s}$ leaves. Therefore, there exists at least one leaf to which at least $\sqrt{s}$ essential inputs lead. But, the path according to this leaf contains, as any path in T, at most $\frac{1}{2}\log_3 s$ nodes. Therefore, maximally $\frac{k}{2}\log_3 s$ "relation tests" can be done on this path (follows from lemma in section 3.2). In detail, if i_1 many relation tests for $P_1,\ldots,$ and i_m many relation tests for P_m are done on this path, maximally $i_1 \cdot \ldots \cdot i_m$ many different essential inputs can use this path.

We know, $i_1 + \ldots + i_m \leqslant \frac{k}{2}\log_3 s$. Under this condition $i_1 \cdot \ldots \cdot i_m$ is maximally for $i_1 \approx \ldots \approx i_m \approx \frac{k}{2m}\log_3 s$. Therefore, the maximal value of the product $i_1 \cdot \ldots \cdot i_m$, i.e the maximal number of essential inputs on this path is $\Theta((\frac{k}{2m}\log_3 s)^m)$, which is $o(\sqrt{s})$. We got a contradiction to the fact that the path under consideration is used by more than $\sqrt{s}$ essential inputs. $\square$

From the definition of t (section 3.1) follows

Theorem:

It holds the lower bound $\Omega(d n \log n)$ for CH_d and EP_d in the model of k-ADT's. $\square$

But, one has to note that the gap between this lower bound and the best known upper bound is still tremendous, .e.g. the best known upper bound for EP_d (d$\geqslant$3) is $\Theta(n^2)$ in the worst case, [E].

4. Other lower bounds obtained with similar considerations

Significant parts of the proof above, i.e. fixing a part of the input, the existence of essential inputs and the connection between the number of essential inputs and the lower bound, can be reformulated in a more general way. This requires an extended formalism which can be found in [U].

By this general method, the lower bound could be reproduced for the

d-dimensional ε-closeness problem. This is an already known result.
The problem of ε-closeness is treated as one of the fundamental
problems in computational geometry, compare e.g. [PS].

Problem ε-C_d:

Determine if there are two points in an n elementary point set P from
R^d where the distance under the maxima norm is not greater than ε.

An algorithm solving this problem in the model of 1-ADT's with worst-
case-costs θ(dnlogn) is known from the literature, [PS,pp.93]. One
guesses that sorting the input in all d dimensions occurs necessarily
in any correct agorithm and dominates the costs. But, just the method
introduced here could not improve the lower bound to Ω(dnlogn).
Therefore, ε-C_d stands rather as example illustrating that the new
method is at least such efficient as the method from [SY].

Another example where the method proves lower bounds which could not
be obtained in another way are

Problem R-n_1 (R-En_1):

Given a set P of n points from the plane, where there are only up to
(resp. exactly) n_1 different x-coordinates, construct the convex hull
of P.

Here holds the lower bound Ω(nlogn_1).

The general method and the results concerning ε-C_d, R-n_1 and R-En_1 can
be found in [U] with more details.

References
[DL] Dobkin,D.P. and R.Lipton: On the complexity of computations
     under varying sets of primitives, J.Comp.Syst.Sci. 18(1979),
     pp.86-91.
[E] Edelsbrunner,H.: Algorithms in Computational Geometry,
     Springer 1987.
[PS] Preparata,F.P. and M.I.Shamos: Computational Geometry - an
     Introduction, Springer 1985.
[SY] Steele,J.M. and A.C.Yao: Lower bounds for algebraic decision
     trees, J.Algorithms 3(1982), pp.1-8.
[U] Unger,K.: Obere und untere Schranken für Probleme der algorithmi-
     schen Geometrie in problemspezifischen Modellen (Ph.D. Thesis),
     Berlin 1990.

Area Time Squared and Area Complexity of VLSI Computations Is Strongly Unclosed Under Union and Intersection

Juraj WACZULÍK

Institute of Computer Science, Comenius University

842 15 Bratislava, Czechoslovakia

Abstract

The communication complexity is an abstract complexity measure intensively investigated in the last few years. Since it provides lower bounds on the area (A) and area time squared (AT^2) complexity measures of VLSI computations, the main interest is in proving lower bounds on communication complexity of specific languages. We present a new combinatorial technique in order to establish a nontrivial lower bound on communication complexity of a specific language. Our lower bound provides the first, constructive proof of the fact, that communication complexity is strongly unclosed under union and intersection, and (what is the main point) this lower bound proves that AT^2 and A complexity of VLSI circuits is strongly unclosed under their Boolean operations.

1 Introduction

The communication complexity C was defined as an abstract complexity measure in [19]. It provides direct lower bounds on the area ($A \geq C$) and area time squared ($AT^2 \geq C^2$) complexity measures of VLSI circuits [6,7,12] and on the area complexity of Boolean circuits ($A^B \geq C$) [18].

So, the main interest in the investigation of communication complexity is in developing lower bound proof techniques providing nontrivial lower bounds on communication complexity of languages [1,2,4,12,13,14,17,19]. We use a new combinatorial argument in order to prove the lower bound $\Omega\left(\frac{n}{\sqrt{\log^3 n}}\right)$ on the communication complexity of a specific language. Since we construct this language as union of two languages $G1$ and $W0$ with constant communication complexity we obtain a constructive proof of the fact that the complexity classes defined by bounded communication complexity are strongly unclosed under union and intersection. The main result of our paper is that the complexity classes defined by bounded area (A) and area time squared (AT^2) and A complexities of VLSI computations are strongly unclosed under union and intersection which follows from the fact that $G1$ and $W0$ can be recognized in $AT^2 \in O(n \log^3 n)$ and $A \in O(1)$. The same unclosure property is obtained for the area complexity of Boolean circuits despite of the fact that the combinational complexity does not have this property.

Our paper is organised as follows. Section 2 contains the basic definitions. In section 3 we prove the strong uncloseness of communication complexity. In the proof we use the new combinatorial technique. The following sections contain the results for A and AT^2 measures of VLSI circuits and for measure A^B of Boolean circuits.

2 Definitions

We shall use the definition of VLSI circuit from Hromkovič's paper [7]. According to this definition we can imagine a VLSI circuit as an directed graph embedded in a square lattice. There are processors placed in graph vertices and graph edges represent their mutual interconnection. Values of input variables come in a circuit through input processors and values of output variables come out of output processors. VLSI circuit operates in machine cycles. According to the values assigned to the input edges on time t each processor computes output values of its function and assigns these values to its output edges in time $t + 1$.

The area complexity $A(R)$ of a VLSI circuit R equals to the area of the minimal rectangle comprising the whole circuit.

The time complexity $T(R)$ of VLSI circuit R is the time t in which the value of the last output variable came out of the circuit.

Let $L \subset \{0,1\}^*$ be a language. The set $L_n = L \cap \{0,1\}^n$ for $n \in N$ is called the n-th level of a language L.

Let R is a VLSI circuit with n input variables $x_1, \ldots, x_n$ and one output variable y. We say that r recognizes L_n if $y = 1$ iff the word $x_1 \ldots x_n \in L_n$. Let $\{R_n\}_{n=1}^\infty$ be a sequence of VLSI circuits and R_n recognizes L_n then the sequence $\{R_n\}_{n=1}^\infty$ recognizes a language L. The area complexity of a language L is a function $A(L)_{(n)} = \min_{R_n}\{A(R_n)\}$, where R_n recognizes L_n.

The complexity measures $T(L)_{(n)}$ and $AT^2(L)_{(n)}$ are defined in the same way.

Definition of communication complexity:

Informally, the communication complexity was defined in [19] as follows. Suppose that a language $L \subset \{0,1\}^*$ must be recognised by two distant computers. Each computer receives a half of the input bits, and the computation proceeds using some protocols (one for each level) for communication between the two computers. The minimum number of bits that has to be exchanged in order to recognize $L \cap \{0,1\}^n$ successfully, minimized over all partitions of the input bits into two equal parts, and considered as a function of n, is called the communication complexity of L.

$\pi_{2n} = (S_I, S_{II})$ is a partition of the set $\{1, \ldots, 2n\}$ into two sets such that $S_I \cup S_{II} = \{1, \ldots, 2n\}$, $S_I \cap S_{II} = \emptyset$ and $\mid S_I \mid = \mid S_{II} \mid = n$.

Let us have a partition $\pi_{2n} = (S_I, S_{II})$ and a word $x \in \{0,1\}^{2n}$, $x = x_1 \ldots x_{2n}$. A word x is called an input word, a word $x_I = x_{k_1} \ldots x_{k_n}$, $k_i < k_{i+1}$, $k_i, k_{i+1} \in S_I$ for $i = 1, \ldots, n-1$ is called an input for the word x, restricted to the set S_I. x_{II} is defined in the same way.

Function $\Phi_n : \{0,1\}^n \times \{0,1,\$\}^* \longrightarrow \{0,1\}^* \cup \{accept, reject\}$ we call a communication function if it fills the prefix freeness property: If $c \in \{0, 1, \$\}^*$ then for each $Y, Y' \in \{0, 1\}^n$, $Y \neq Y'$, $\Phi_n(Y, c)$ is not the proper prefix $\Phi_n(Y', c)$.

A computation of the communication function Φ_n on a word x for a partition π_{2n} is a string $c = c_1\$ \ldots \$c_k\$c_{k+1}$, where $k \geq 0$, $c_1 \ldots c_k \in \{0,1\}^*$ and $c_{k+1} \in \{accept, reject\}$ such that for each $j \in \{0, \ldots, k\}$ we have:

If j is even then $c_{j+1} = \Phi_n(x_I, c_1\$ \ldots \$c_j)$, where x_I is the input restricted to the set S_I for the word x.

If j is odd then $c_{j+1} = \Phi_n(x_{II}, c_1\$ \ldots \$c_j)$, where x_{II} is the input restricted to the set S_I for the word x.

The length of a computation is $| c_1 \ldots c_k |$.

We say that a communication function Φ_n recognizes a level L_{2n} for a partition π_{2n} if the computation of a communication function Φ_n on a word w ends with accept iff $w \in L_{2n}$.

Let L be a language, Φ_n be a communication function and π_{2n} be a partition. We introduce signs as:

$C(L_{2n}, \pi_{2n}, \Phi_n)$ is a communication complexity of the $2n$-th level of a language L for a fixed partition π_{2n} and given communication function Φ_n which recognizes L_{2n} for a partition π_{2n}. $C(L_{2n}, \pi_{2n}, \Phi_n)$ is equal to the length of the longest accepting computation Φ_n on words $w \in \{0,1\}^{2n}$ for a partition π_{2n}.

$C(L_{2n}, \pi_{2n})$ denotes the communication complexity of the $2n$-th level of a language L for a fixed partition π_{2n}. $C(L_{2n}, \pi_{2n}) = \min_{\Phi_n} C(L_{2n}, \pi_{2n}, \Phi_n)$, where Φ_n is an arbitrary function, which recognizes L_{2n}.

$C(L_{2n})$ is the communication complexity of the $2n$-th level of a language L. $C(L_{2n}) = \min_{\pi_{2n}} C(L_{2n}, \pi_{2n})$, where π_{2n} is an arbitrary partition.

$C(L)_{(n)} = C(L_{2n})$ is the communication complexity of a language L.

3 Closure Properties of Communication Complexity

Languages, according to their communication complexity, form the respective complexity classes. The main subject of paper is the investigation of the closure properties of these classes. In [15] there is a proof that for a fixed partition the communication complexity of union (intersection) of two languages is not greater than the sum of the communication complexities of these languages. It is known that the communication complexity of a language and of its complement is the same.

In this section we show that for any arbitrary partition the communication complexity is strongly unclosed under union and intersection. Let us define two languages having its communication complexities constant and we prove that the union of these languages has the communication complexity at least $\Omega\left(\frac{n}{\sqrt{\log^3 n}}\right)$. For the intersection we shall prove the same result. Let $k \geq 1$ be a constant and $n = 2^{2k(2m+1)}$, where $m \in N$. For $i = 0, \ldots, n^{(1-1/(2k))}$ and $j = 1, \ldots, n^{1/(2k)}$ we define the following sets:

$$K_n^i = \left\{ in^{1/(2k)} + 1, in^{1/(2k)} + 2, \ldots, in^{1/(2k)} + n^{1/(2k)} \right\}$$
$$L_n^j = \left\{ j, j + n^{1/(2k)}, \ldots, j + \left(n^{(1-1/(2k))} - 1 \right) n^{1/(2k)} \right\}$$

Let $w \in \{0, 1\}^n$, $w = w_1 \ldots w_n$. Let $K_n^i(w)$ $(L_n^j(w))$ denote a word formed of bits of a word w which indices are in the set K_n^i (L_n^j) in a given order. Using K_n^i and L_n^j we define sets $G_n, W_n \subset \{0,1\}^n$ in the following way:

$$G_n = \left\{ w \mid K_n^i(w) \in \{0^{n^{1/2k}}, 1^{n^{1/2k}}\}, \ 0 \leq i \leq n^{(1-1/(2k))} - 1 \right\}$$

$$W_n = \Big\{ w \mid L_n^j(w) = v_1 v_1 \ldots v_{2^b} v_{2^b}; v_r \in \{0,1\}^{2^{b-a-1}}, 1 \leq r \leq 2^a,$$

$$\text{where } b = \log n^{(1-1/(2k))}, \ a = j \bmod b, \ 1 \leq j \leq n^{1/(2k)} \Big\}$$

Informally, the sets G_n and W_n can be described as follows:

Let the bits of a word of the length $n = 2^{2k(2m+1)}$ be arranged following its indices from up to down and from left to right, into the form of a rectangle with the sides $n^{1/(2k)}$ and $n^{(1-1/(2k))}$. (bit with number $n^{1/(2k)}$ is in the left down corner) A word belongs to G_n iff the same values are in the columns of the rectangle.

A word belongs to W_n iff vv-words only are in the lines of the rectangle. In the first line there is one vv-word, in the second line there are two vv-words, ... , in the i-th 2^i vv-words, and so on until the vv-words have length two. This form is repeated in the next lines, to the last line. The set W_{64} for $k = 1$ is illustrated on the figure: Using G_n

w				w			
w_1		w_1		w_2		w_2	
a_1	a_1	a_2	a_2	a_3	a_3	a_4	a_4
w'				w'			
w_1'		w_1'		w_2'		w_2'	
a_1'	a_1'	a_2'	a_2'	a_3'	a_3'	a_4'	a_4'
w''				w''			
w_1''		w_1''		w_2''		w_2''	

and W_n we define languages G and W in the following way:

$$G = \left\{ w \mid w \in G_n, n = 2^{2k(2m+1)}, \ m \in N \right\}$$

$$W = \left\{ w \mid w \in W_n, n = 2^{2k(2m+1)}, \ m \in N \right\}$$

<u>Theorem 3.1</u>: Let $G1 = \{ w11 \mid w \in G \}$ and let $W0 = \{ w00 \mid w \in W \}$. Then

$$C(G1)_{(n)} = C(W0)_{(n)} = O(1) \text{ and } C(G1 \cup W0)_{(n)} = \Omega \left(\frac{n^{(1-1/(2k))}}{\sqrt{\log^3 n}} \right)$$

<u>Proof</u>: of the first part of the assertion is a trivial one. For each level of the language $G1$ ($W0$) we can easily found a partition for which the communication complexity of $G1$ ($W0$) equals one.

The lower bound of the communication complexity of the language $G1 \cup W0$ is obtained using the sets W_n and G_n.

Lemma 3.2:

$$C((G1 \cup W0)_{n+2}) \geq \min_{\pi_n} (\max\{(C(G_n, \pi_n), C(W_n, \pi_n))\}) - 4$$

Proof: Let π_{n+2} be the partition such that

$$C((G1 \cup W0)_{n+2}) = C((G1 \cup W0)_{n+2}, \pi_{n+2}).$$

Without loss of generality we assume that

$$C(G1_{n+2}, \pi_{n+2}) \geq C(W0_{n+2}, \pi_{n+2})$$

Let us have a communication function $\Phi_{n/2+1}$ which recognizes $(G1 \cup W0)_{n+2}$ for the partition π_{n+2}. Using $\Phi_{n/2+1}$ we can construct a communication function $\Phi'_{n/2+1}$ which recognizes $G1_{n+2}$ for the partition π_{n+2} with the communication complexity is greater by two than $C((G1 \cup W0)_{n+2}, \pi_{n+2}, \Phi_{n/2+1})$. The computation of function $\Phi'_{n/2+1}$ will proceed in the following way. If the two last bits of a word are units computers will exchange a unit. Otherwise one of the computers claims *reject*. Further the computation proceeds according to the original communication function $\Phi_{n/2+1}$. This construction of $\Phi'_{n/2+1}$ can be done for each communication function $\Phi_{n/2+1}$. Hence

$$C((G1 \cup W0)_{n+2}) \geq \min_{\pi_{n+2}} (\max\{C(G1_{n+2}, \pi_{n+2}), C(W0_{n+2}, \pi_{n+2})\}) - 2$$

Let $\pi_{n+2} = (S_I, S_{II})$. There exists a partition $\pi_n = (Z_I, Z_{II})$ such that $\mid Z_I \cap S_I \mid + \mid Z_{II} \cap S_{II} \mid \geq n - 1$. It can be easily proved that the communication complexity of $G1_{n+2}$ $(W0_{n+2})$ for the partition π_{n+2} is greater than the communication complexity G_n (W_n) for the partition π_n diminished by two (the same idea as for $\Phi'_{n/2+1}$). Hence

$$\min_{\pi_{n+2}} (\max\{C(G1_{n+2}, \pi_{n+2}), C(W0_{n+2}, \pi_{n+2})\}) \geq \min_{\pi_n} (\max\{C(G_n, \pi_n), C(W_n, \pi_n)\}) - 2$$

Further we shall show for any partition that the communication complexity for at least one of the sets G_n, W_n is great. Let π_n^p be a partition that there exists a set $V \subset \{1, \ldots, n^{(1-1/(2k))}\}$, $\mid V \mid = p$ such that for each $i \in V$ $K_n^i \in S_I$ or $K_n^i \in S_{II}$ holds. We shall express the communication complexity of G_n by parameter p.

Lemma 3.3: Let $1 \leq p \leq n^{(1-1/(2k))}$ and π_n^p be a partition. Then

$$C(G_n, \pi_n^p) \geq n^{(1-1/(2k))} - p.$$

Proof: is done by a standard technique of communication protocols. Let there exist a communication function which for π_n^p recognizes G_n with the communication complexity less than $n^{(1-1/(2k))} - p$. It means that, there exist at most $2^{(n^{(1-1/(2k))}-p}} - 1$ different accepting computations. Hence there exist at least two different words $u, v \in G_n$ such that the communication function has the same computations on these words and a set K_n^i exists such that $K_n^i \not\subset S_I$, $K_n^i \not\subset S_{II}$ and $K_n^i(u) \neq K_n^i(v)$. Let q be a word such that $q_I = u_I$ and $q_{II} = v_{II}$. Then the communication function will accept this word. This is a contradiction because $q \notin G_n$.

Further we shall deal with a relation between parameter p and the communication complexity of W_n. Let us refer to each two bits of a word, that must be equal in order the word belongs to W_n, as to a couple. A couple is partitioned if one of its bits belongs to S_I and another one to S_{II}.

<u>Fact 1:</u> Let x couples be partitioned for a partition $\pi_n = (S_I, S_{II})$. Then $C(W_n, \pi_n) \geq x$.

<u>Fact 2:</u> Let π_n^p be a partition and let $p = n^{(1-1/(2k))}$. Then

$$C(W_n, \pi_n^p) \geq \left\lceil \frac{n^{1/(2k)}}{b} \right\rceil \binom{b}{(b-1)/2}, \text{ where } b = \log n^{(1-1/(2k))}.$$

<u>Proof:</u> Let us consider a word of length n as a rectangle. The partition π_n^p has an interesting property. It parts lines of the rectangle by the same way. For the bits of each column hold, that all belong to S_I or all to S_{II}. Let γ_p denote this partition. We shall prove that, for any arbitrary partition γ_p, the sum of the number of couples partitioned in the particular types of vv-words is big enough. We shall construct a graph as follows:

We assign a vertex to each bit from set $\{1, \ldots, p\}$. We shall connect two vertices by an edge iff they form a couple in some type of vv-words. The partition γ_p parts vertices in the graph into two sets each one having $\frac{p}{2}$ elements. The number of partitioned couples, for the partition γ_p, is equal to the number of those edges in the graph which have not their end vertices in the same set. The graph we have defined is isomorphic with the Boolean cube $B_{\log p}$. So we may use Harper's result in [5] where the isoperimetrical problem for Boolean cubes is solved. According to this paper, any arbitrary set M containing $\frac{p}{2}$ vertices of the cube $B_{\log p}$ has at least $\binom{\log p}{(\log p - 1)/2}$ bound vertices. A bound vertex has at least one neighbouring vertex, which does not belong to the set M. From the previous facts it follows that $\binom{\log p}{(\log p - 1)/2}$ is also the lower bound for the sum of the partitioned couples in the particular types of vv-words. The number of lines containing each type of vv-words is at least $\left\lceil \frac{n^{1/(2k)}}{\log n^{(1-1/(2k))}} \right\rceil$. Let $n^{(1-1/(2k))}$ be substituted for p and let us use the Fact 1. Thus we obtain our assertion which completes the proof.

Using Fact 2 we obtain a bound on the communication complexity of W_n, for an arbitrary value of parameter p.

<u>Lemma 3.4:</u> Let $p \in \{0, \ldots, n^{(1-1/(2k))}\}$ and let π_n^p be a partition. Then

$$C(W_n, \pi_n^p) \geq \left\lceil \frac{n^{1/(2k)}}{b} \right\rceil \binom{b}{(b-1)/2} - (n - pn^{1/(2k)}), \text{ where } b = \log n^{(1-1/(2k))}.$$

<u>Proof:</u> We use the idea that a small change of the partition causes just a small change of the communication complexity:

<u>Fact 3:</u> Let $M_{2d} \subset \{0,1\}^{2d}$ be an arbitrary set. Let $\gamma_{2d} = (S_I, S_{II})$, $\gamma'_{2d} = (S'_I, S'_{II})$ be partitions and $| S_I \cap S'_I | + | S_{II} \cap S'_{II} | = 2d - 2x$ holds. Then

$$| C(M_{2d}, \gamma_{2d}) - C(M_{2d}, \gamma'_{2d}) | \leq 2x.$$

Proof: Without loss of generality we can assume that $C(M_{2d}, \gamma_{2d}) \geq C(M_{2d}, \gamma'_{2d})$. Let Φ_d be a communication function which recognizes M_{2d} for the partition γ'_{2d}. A communication function which recognizes M_{2d} for the partition γ_{2d} will be constructed in the following way. At first computers exchange values of these bits which they do not know for the partition γ_{2d}, but they know them for the partition γ'_{2d}. Further the computation proceeds according to the original communication function Φ_d.

For each partition $\pi_n^p = (S_I, S_{II})$ there exists a partition $\pi_n^q = (Z_I, Z_{II})$, $q = n^{(1-1/(2k))}$, such that $\mid S_I \cap Z_I \mid + \mid S_{II} \cap Z_{II} \mid \geq pn^{1/(2k)}$. Using Facts 2. a 3. we obtain the assertion of lemma 3.4.

Now we can complete the proof of Theorem 3.1. Following Lemmas 3.2, 3.3, 3.4 we have:

$$C\left((G1 \cup W0)_{n+2}\right) \geq \min_p \max \left\{ n^{(1-1/(2k))} - p \ ; \ \frac{n^{1/(2k)}}{b} \binom{b}{(b-1)/2} + pn^{1/(2k)} - n \right\}$$

where $b = \log n^{(1-1/(2k))}$ a $0 \leq p \leq n^{(1-1/(2k))}$. The minimalization according to parameter p is equivalent to the minimalization over all partition. The communication complexity of W_n is directly proportional to the parameter p and the communication complexity of G_n is indirectly proportional to p so that the minimal maximum of these two functions is in their intersection. The value of the maximum is

$$\frac{1}{n^{1/(2k)} + 1} \left[\frac{n^{1/(2k)}}{b} \right] \binom{b}{(b-1)/2}$$

Using Stirlig's formula for bound of factorial we obtain the following asymptotic bound:

$$C(G1 \cup W0)_{(n)} = \Omega \left(\frac{n^{(1-1/(2k))}}{\sqrt{\log^3 n}} \right)$$

This completes the proof of Theorem 3.1.

Theorem 3.5: Let $P = \{0,1\}^* - G1$ and $Q = \{0,1\}^* - W0$. Then

$$C(P)_{(n)} = C(Q)_{(n)} = O(1) \text{ and } C(P \cap Q)_{(n)} = \Omega \left(\frac{n^{(1-1/(2k))}}{\sqrt{\log^3 n}} \right)$$

Proof: Communication complexity of a language and of its complement are equal. We have:

$$C(P \cap Q)_{(n)} = C(\overline{P \cap Q})_{(n)} = C(\overline{P} \cup \overline{Q})_{(n)} = C(G1 \cup W0)_{(n)}$$

Note 3.6: The bounds proved in Theorem 3.1 and 3.5 depend on parameter k. We assumed that k is an arbitrary constant in definitions of G and W. If the value of k comes up to infinite, our bound will be improved:

$$\lim_{k \to \infty} \Omega \left(\frac{n^{(1-1/(2k))}}{\sqrt{\log^3 n}} \right) = \Omega \left(\frac{n}{\sqrt{\log^3 n}} \right)$$

This note is valid for the assertions of the next chapters, too.

4 Closure Properties of AT^2 Complexity

Lipton and Sedgewick proved in their work [16] (for a model with unbounded indegree of processors), that there exist languages with measure $AT^2 \in O(n)$ and the union of these languages has $AT^2 \in \Omega(n^2)$. We prove a similar result for the languages $G1$ and $W0$.

Theorem 4.1:

$$AT^2(G1)_{(n)} = AT^2(W0)_{(n)} = O(n \log^3 n) \text{ and } AT^2(G1 \cup W0)_{(n)} = \Omega\left(\frac{n^{(2-1/k)}}{\log^3 n}\right)$$

Proof: of the first part of assertion is not difficult. We do not present if here because of the lack of place. The second part of the assertion follows from theorem 3.1 and from the relation $AT^2 \geq C^2$ [6].

Theorem 4.2:

$$AT^2(P)_{(n)} = AT^2(Q)_{(n)} = O(n \log^3 n) \text{ and } AT^2(P \cap Q)_{(n)} = \Omega\left(\frac{n^{(2-1/k)}}{\log^3 n}\right)$$

5 Closure Properties of Area Complexity of Boolean Circuits

The exact definition of Boolean circuit is in [21]. The area complexity (A^B) of Boolean circuit is defined in the same way as the area complexity of VLSI circuit. A^B is equal to the area of the minimal rectangle comprising the whole Boolean circuit embedded in the square lattice. We shall prove strong uncloseness of A^B under union and intersection. It is interesting that the combinational complexity of Boolean circuits does not have this property.

Theorem 5.1:

$$A^B(G1)_{(n)} = A^B(W0)_{(n)} = O(n \log n) \text{ and } A^B(G1 \cup W0)_{(n)} = \Omega\left(\frac{n^{(2-1/(2k))}}{\sqrt{\log^3 n}}\right)$$

Theorem 5.2:

$$A^B(P)_{(n)} = A^B(Q)_{(n)} = O(n \log n) \text{ and } A^B(P \cap Q)_{(n)} = \Omega\left(\frac{n^{(2-1/(2k))}}{\sqrt{\log^3 n}}\right)$$

The correctness of these two assertions follows from the facts:

1. We can construct Boolean circuits which recognize $G1_n, W0_n, P_n, Q_n$ and have the area complexity $O(n \log n)$. The construction is not presented here for the lack of place.

2. The relation between the measure A^B and the communication complexity is given by $A^B \geq nC$ [18].

6 Closure Properties of Area Complexity

In [3] a proof of strong uncloseness of the area complexity of VLSI circuits is given. There are two languages of constant area complexity defined and there is given a proof that the area complexity of the union the languages is $\Omega\left(\sqrt{n}\right)$. Using communication complexity we shall prove a stronger result for languages $G1$ and $W0$.

Theorem 6.1:

$$A(G1)_{(n)} = A(W0)_{(n)} = O(1) \text{ and } A(G1 \cup W0)_{(n)} = \Omega\left(\frac{n^{(1-1/(2k))}}{\sqrt{\log^3 n}}\right)$$

Proof: VLSI circuits which recognize $G1_n$ and $W0_n$ with the area complexity $O(1)$ are not presented there for the lack of place. The second part of the assertions follows from theorem 3.1 and from the relation $A \geq C$ [6].

Theorem 6.2:

$$A(P)_{(n)} = A(Q)_{(n)} = O(1) \text{ and } A(P \cup Q)_{(n)} = \Omega\left(\frac{n^{(1-1/(2k))}}{\sqrt{\log^3 n}}\right)$$

References

[1] AHO,A.V. – ULLMAN,J.D. – YANAKAKIS,M.: On notions of information transfer in VLSI circuits. In: Proc. 15th ACM STOC, ACM 1983, pp. 133–139.

[2] ĎURIŠ,P. – GALIL,Z. – SCHNITGER,G.: Lower bounds on communication complexity. In: Proc. 16th ACM Symp. on Theory of Computing, ACM 1984,pp. 81–91.

[3] GUBAŠ,X. – WACZULÍK,J.: Closure properties of the complexity measures A and AT². ŠVOČ 1987, section VLSI and computer graphics. Comenius University, Bratislava 1987, (in Slovak) 25 p.

[4] HAJNAL,A. – MAASS,W. – TURAN,G.: On the communication complexity of graph properties. In: Proc. 20th Annual ACM STOC, ACM 1988, pp. 186–191.

[5] HARPER,L.H.: Optimal numbering and isoperimetrical problems on graphs. Journ. of combinatorial theory, 1966, v. 1, no. 1 pp. 385–393.

[6] HROMKOVIČ,J.: Lower bound techniques for VLSI algorithms. In: Proc. IMYCS'86, Hungarian Academy of Sciences, Budapest 1986, pp. 9–19.(also in: Treds, Techniques, and Problems in Theoretical Computer Science (Alica Kelemenová Jozef Kelemen Eds.), Lecture Notes in Computer Science 281, Springer-Verlag, Berlin 1987, pp.2–25.)

[7] HROMKOVIČ,J.: Same complexity aspects of VLSI computations. Part 1. A framework for the study of information transfer in VLSI circuits. Computers and Artificial Intelligence, Vol. 7, 1988, No. 3, 229–252 pp.

[8] HROMKOVIČ,J.: Same complexity aspects of VLSI computations. Part 2. Topology of circuits and information transfer. Computers and Artificial Intelligence, Vol. 7, 1988, No. 4, 289–302 pp.

[9] HROMKOVIČ,J. - PARDUBSKÁ,D.: Same complexity aspects of VLSI computations. Part 3. On the power of input bit permutation in tree and trellis automata. Computers and Artificial Intelligence, Vol. 7, 1988, No. 5, 397–412 pp.

[10] HROMKOVIČ,J. - PARDUBSKÁ,D.: Same complexity aspects of VLSI computations. Part 4. VLSI circuits with programs. Computers and Artificial Intelligence, Vol. 7, 1988, No. 6, 481–495 pp.

[11] HROMKOVIČ,J.: Same complexity aspects of VLSI computations. Part 5. Nondeterministic and probabilistic VLSI circuits. Computers and Artificial Intelligence, Vol. 8, 1989, No. 2, 169–188 pp.

[12] HROMKOVIČ,J.: Same complexity aspects of VLSI computations. Part 6. Communication complexity. Computers and Artificial Intelligence, Vol. 8, 1989, No. 3, 209–255 pp.

[13] HROMKOVIČ,J.: The advantages of new approach to defining the communication complexity for VLSI. In: Theoretical Computer Science 57, 1988, pp. 97–111.

[14] JIRÁSKOVÁ,G.: Chomski hierarchy and communication complexity. In: Machines, Languages and Complexity. Lecture Notes in Computer Science 381, Springer-Verlag, Berlin 1989, pp.12–18.

[15] KURCABOVÁ,V.: Communication complexity. Master thesis, Dept. of Theoretical Cybernetics, Comenius University 1985 (in Slovak) 60 p.

[16] LIPTON,R.J. - SEDGEWICK,R.: Lower bound for VLSI. In: Proc. 13th Annual ACM STOC, ACM 1981, pp. 300–307.

[17] LOVÁSZ,L. - SAKS,M.: Lattices mobius functions and communication complexity. In: Proc. 29th Annual Symposium on FOCS 1988, pp. 81–90.

[18] LOŽKIN,S.A. - RYBKO,A.I. - SAPOŽENKO,A.A. - HROMKOVIČ,J. - ŠKALIKOVA,N.A.: An approach to lower bound of area complexity of Boolean circuits. In: Mathematical problems in computation theory, Banach Center Publication, Vol. 21, PWN Polish Scientific Publishers, Warsaw 1988 pp. 503–512 (in Russian), extended version in English accepted for publication in Theoretical Computer Science.

[19] PAPADIMITRIOU,C.H. - SIPSER,M.: Communication complexity. J. Comp. Syst. Sci., Vol. 28, 1984, pp. 260–269.

[20] THOMPSON,C.D.: Area-time complexity for VLSI. In: Proc. 11th Annual ACM STOC, ACM 1979, pp. 81–88.

[21] WEGENER,I.: The Complexity of Boolean Functions. John Wiley & Sons and B. G. Teubner 1987.

Decision Procedure for Checking Validity of PAL Formulas

Igor Walukiewicz

Institute of Informatics

Warsaw University

00-901 Warszawa POLAND

Abstract: The aim of propositional algorithmic logic (PAL) is to investigate properties of simple nondeterministic while-program schemes on propositional level. We present algorithm for checking validity of PAL sequents based on a finite Gentzen-type axiomatiaztion, which reaches lower complpexity limit. Additionally we obtain small model theorem for PAL.

1 Introduction

Propositional algorithmic logic (PAL) was constructed by Mirkowska [4] as a propositional counterpart of algorithmic logic (AL) [7]. The aim of PAL is to investigate the properties of simple nondeterministic while-programs build upon the set of atomic actions on a propositional level abstracting from values of variables, functions etc. As opposed to PDL there are two not dual modalities. Modality ◇ means (as in PDL) "there exists successful execution" and modality □ which means "all executions are successful". With these two we are able to construct formulas expressing important properties of programs like : termination, looping, partial and total correctness.

Lifting theorem brings another reason to investigate such logic. It is a theorem which says that tautologies of PAL become tautologies of AL after replacing program variables by programs and propositional variables by formulas [4]. Existence of easy to implement decision procedure for PAL can help in attempts to construct automated prover based on AL.

Because of existence of strong modality □ it was not obvious that small model theorem holds or that there exists finite axiomatization for PAL. It is well known fact that PAL like PDL with loop construct does not enjoy collapsed model property i.e. the property which says that if a formula α is unsatisfied in some structure than it is unsatisfied in a structure which is constructed by merging states satisfying the same subformulas of α. The small model theorem for PDL with loop-construct was proved by Street [8] and for deterministic PAL by Chlebus[1] but there still remained a question if the same theorem holds for unrestricted PAL.

Infinite axiomatization of PAL was presented in Mirkowska [4]. Attempts to give finite Gentzen type axiomatization of PDL where done by Nishimura [5][6]. Decision procedure for deterministic PAL was presented by Chlebus in [1]. In this paper we present procedure for unrestricted PAL which checks validity of PAL sequents and exhibits counterexample if sequent is not valid. Additionally as a corollary we obtain the small model theorem.

2 Syntax and Semantics

The syntax of PAL is based upon two sets of symbols: V_0 the set of propositional variables, and Π_0 the set of atomic programs. We will use $p, q, ..$ for elements of V_0 and $A, B, ..$ for elements of Π_0.

From V_0 we construct the set of open formulas F_0 as usual propositional formulas i.e, $V_0 \in F_0$ and if $\alpha, \beta \in F_0$ then $\alpha \wedge \beta, \alpha \vee \beta, \neg \alpha \in F$.

Given sets F_0 and Π_0 the set Π of programs is generated by the following grammar:

$$\Pi ::= \Pi_0 \mid \Pi; \Pi \mid \text{if } F_0 \text{ then } \Pi \text{ else } \Pi \text{ fi} \mid \text{either } \Pi \text{ or } \Pi \text{ ro} \mid \text{while } F_0 \text{ do } \Pi \text{ od}$$

Finally we define the set of formulas F:

$$F ::= F_0 \mid F \vee F \mid F \wedge F \mid \neg F \mid \Diamond \Pi F \mid \Box \Pi F$$

We will often write o which will mean any modality i.e. $\Box$ or $\Diamond$.

Formulas of PAL will be interpreted in so called Kripke structures which have form $< S, R, \rho >$ where:

- S is a non empty set of so called states,

- R is a function assigning to each atomic program $A \in \Pi_0$ a binary relation $R(A)$ on S

- ρ assigns to each state $s \in S$ the subset of V_0

Intuitively R gives interpretation of atomic programs as an actions changing states ρ gives expresses which propositional variables are true in a given state. Mapping ρ is easily extended to all members of F_0 in usual propositional sense. In order to extend relation R to all programs in Π we will provide the notion of execution.

2.1 Definition

— Given structure $\Im =< S, R, \rho >$ define one step of execution relation *rel* between configurations, i.e. pairs (state,program):
1. $(s, A; Rest) \triangleright (s', Rest)$ where $A \in \Pi_0$ and $(s, s') \in R(A)$,
2. $(s, \text{if } \gamma \text{ then } K \text{ else } L \text{ fi}; Rest) \triangleright (s, K; Rest)$ if $\gamma \in \rho(s)$ and $(s, L; Rest)$ otherwise,
3. $(s, \text{either } K \text{ or } L \text{ ro}; Rest) \triangleright (s, K; Rest)$ and $(s, \text{either } K \text{ or } L \text{ ro}; Rest) \triangleright (s, L; Rest)$,
4. $(s, \text{while } \gamma \text{ do } K \text{ od}; Rest) \triangleright (s, K; \text{while } \gamma \text{ do } K \text{ od}: Rest)$ if $\gamma \in \rho(s)$ and $(s, Rest)$ otherwise.

Where Rest is possibly empty sequence of programs $K_1; K_2; ..; K_n$.

—*Execution* of program K from state $s_0 \in S$ is an sequence of configurations $(s_i, L_i)_{i \in I}$

such that $s_0 = s$, $L_0 = K$ and $(s_i, L_i) \triangleright (s_{i+1}, L_{i+1})$. We will call execution *successful*, if it is finite and its last element is of the form (s, ε), state s will be called the *final state* of execution.

— If $\alpha = \circ K_1(..(\circ K_n \beta)..)$ and β is not of the form $\circ L\gamma$ then *realization of program in formula* α *from state* s $(Rel(\alpha, s))$ is the shortest successful execution of program $K_1; ..; Kn$ from state s. $\qquad\qquad\qquad\qquad\qquad\qquad\qquad\qquad\qquad\qquad\qquad\qquad\qquad\qquad\qquad\qquad\qquad\quad$ □

Now we are ready to formulate the notion of satisfiability of a GPAL formula α in state s of structure $\Im$ ($\Im, s \models \alpha$):

1. $\Im, s \models \alpha$ iff $\alpha \in \rho(s)$, for $\alpha \in F_0$

2. if $\alpha = \diamond K\beta$ then $\Im, s \models \alpha$ iff there exists successful execution of program K from state s and in it's final state t, $\Im, t \models \beta$

3. if $\alpha = \square K\beta$ then $\Im, s \models \alpha$ iff every execution of program K is successful and in every final state t, $\Im, t \models \beta$

4. In case of propositional connectives as usual.

We will say that the formula α is $\Im - valid$ iff for all states $s \in \Im$, $\Im, s \models \alpha$. Finally we will say that α is valid, $\models \alpha$ iff for all structures $\Im$, $\Im \models \alpha$.

3 Sequents and Refutation Trees

Sequent is an ordered pair of finite sets of formulas, we will denote sequent as $\Gamma \to \Delta$ and call set Γ the predecessor of a sequent and Δ the successor of $\Gamma \to \Delta$.

In this section we are going to characterize validity of PAL sequents by syntactic objects called refutation trees. This tree will be obtained by reducing sequent in the root, hence first of all we have to define reduction relations.

3.1 Definition

— *Strong reduction relation* $\Longrightarrow$ between pairs of sequents is the smallest relation satisfying following conditions:

1. $\neg\alpha, \Gamma \to \Delta \Longrightarrow \Gamma \to \Delta, \alpha$
2. $\Gamma \to \Delta, \neg\alpha \Longrightarrow \alpha, \Gamma \to \Delta$
3. $\alpha \wedge \beta, \Gamma \to \Delta \Longrightarrow \alpha, \beta, \Gamma \to \Delta$
4. $\Gamma \to \Delta, \alpha \wedge \beta \Longrightarrow \Gamma \to \Delta, \alpha$ and $\Gamma \to \Delta, \beta$
5. $\alpha \vee \beta, \Gamma \to \Delta \Longrightarrow \alpha, \Gamma \to \Delta$ and $\beta, \Gamma \to \Delta$
6. $\Gamma \to \Delta, \alpha \vee \beta \Longrightarrow \Gamma \to \Delta, \alpha, \beta$
7. $\circ(K; L)\alpha, \Gamma \to \Delta \Longrightarrow \circ K(\circ L\alpha), \Gamma \to \Delta$
8. $\Gamma \to \Delta, \circ(K; L)\alpha \Longrightarrow \Gamma \to \Delta, \circ K(\circ L\alpha)$
9. $\circ$if γ then K else L fi $\alpha, \Gamma \to \Delta \Longrightarrow \gamma, \circ K\alpha, \Gamma \to \Delta$ and $\circ L\alpha, \Gamma \to \Delta, \gamma$
10. $\Gamma \to \Delta, \circ$if γ then K else L fi $\alpha \Longrightarrow \gamma, \Gamma \to \Delta, \circ K\alpha$ and $\Gamma \to \Delta, \circ L\alpha\gamma$
11. $\circ$while γ do K od $\alpha, \Gamma \to \Delta \Longrightarrow \alpha, \Gamma \to \Delta, \gamma$ and $\gamma, \circ K(\circ$while γ do K od $\alpha), \Gamma \to$
12. $\Gamma \to \Delta, \circ$while γ do K od $\alpha \Longrightarrow \Gamma \to \Delta, \gamma, \alpha$ and $\gamma, \Gamma \to \Delta, \circ K(\circ$while γ do K od

13. $\diamond$either K or L ro $\alpha, \Gamma \to \Delta \implies \diamond K\alpha, \Gamma \to \Delta$ and $\diamond L\alpha, \Gamma \to \Delta$

14. $\Gamma \to \Delta, \diamond$either K or L ro $\alpha \implies \Gamma \to \Delta, \diamond K\alpha, \diamond L\alpha$

15. $\Box$either K or L ro $\alpha, \Gamma \to \Delta \implies \Box K\alpha, \Box L\alpha, \Gamma \to \Delta$

16. $\Gamma \to \Delta, \Box$either K or L ro $\alpha \implies \Box\Gamma \to \Delta, \Box K\alpha$ and $\Gamma \to \Delta, \Box L\alpha$

—We define family of *weak reduction relations* $\overset{A}{\longmapsto}$ for $A \in \Pi_0$ in a similar way:

1. $\diamond A\beta, \Gamma \to \Delta \overset{A}{\longmapsto} \{\alpha : \Box A\alpha \in \Gamma\}, \beta \to \{\alpha : \diamond A\alpha \in \Delta\}$

2. $\diamond A\gamma, \Gamma \to \Delta, \Box A\beta \overset{A}{\longmapsto} \{\alpha : \Box A\alpha \in \Gamma\} \to \{\alpha : \diamond A\alpha \in \Delta\}, \beta$ $\Box$

We will call sequent $\Gamma \to \Delta$ *strongly unreducible* iff there is no $\Sigma \to \Omega$ such that $\Gamma \to \Delta \implies \Sigma \to \Omega$ additionally if there is no $\Sigma \to \Omega$ and atomic program A such that $\Gamma \to \Delta \overset{A}{\longmapsto} \Sigma \to \Omega$ then we will call $\Gamma \to \Delta$ *unreducible*. *Axiom* will be called such sequent $\Gamma \to \Delta$ that $\Gamma \cap \Delta \neq \emptyset$. If $\Sigma \to \Omega$ is unreducible and not an axiom then we will call it *simply refutable*. Let us now state some remarks concerning both reduction relations:

3.2 Lemma

For any structure $\mathfrak{I} = \langle S, R, \rho \rangle$ and state s if $\mathfrak{I}, s \not\models \Gamma \to \Delta$ then:

— if $\Gamma \to \Delta$ is reducible by strong reduction then there exists $\Sigma \to \Omega$ such that $\Gamma \to \Delta \implies \Sigma \to \Omega$ and $\mathfrak{I}, s \not\models \Sigma \to \Omega$

— if $\Gamma \to \Delta \overset{A}{\longmapsto} \Sigma \to \Omega$ then there exists state t such that $(s,t) \in R(A)$ and $\mathfrak{I}, t \not\models \Sigma \to \Omega$.
$\Box$

Another important property of both reductions is that they do not add new formulas to the sequent i.e. if $\Gamma \to \Delta$ is reduced to $\Sigma \to \Omega$ then all formulas in $\Sigma \to \Omega$ are subformulas of $\Gamma \to \Delta$. To be more precise

3.3 Definition

Fisher-Ladner closure of formula α, $FL(\alpha)$ is the smallest set of formulas such that:
(1) $\alpha \in FL(\alpha)$
(2) if $\beta \in FL(\alpha)$ and $\beta \to$ can be reduced to $\Sigma \to \Omega$ then all formulas from $\Sigma \to \Omega$ belong to $FL(\alpha)$.

3.4 Proposition

— For any formula α, $|FL(\alpha)| = O(|\alpha|)$ where $|\alpha|$ is number of symbols on α
— For any sequent $\Gamma \to \Delta$, the set $FL(\Gamma \to \Delta) = \{ \Sigma \to \Omega : \Sigma \to \Omega$ is obtained by application of some number of weak or strong reductions to $\Sigma \to \Omega \}$ is finite and $|FL(\Gamma \to \Delta)| = O(2^{|\Gamma \to \Delta|})$.
$\Box$

To define the notion of refutation tree we need one more definition:

3.5 Definition

— Given a sequence of sequents $(\Gamma_i \to \Delta_i)_{i \in I}$, such that $\Gamma_i \to \Delta_i \hookrightarrow \Gamma_{i+1} \to \Delta_{i+1}$, where $\hookrightarrow$ is either $\Longrightarrow$ or $\xmapsto{A}$ for some atomic program A we define:

— Family of *trace relations* $S_{i,i+j}$ $(i+j \in I, i, j > 0)$ as follows:

1. if formula $\alpha \in \Gamma_i$ is not reduced by the weak reduction applied to $\Gamma_i \to \Delta_i$ then $(\alpha, \alpha) \in S_{i,i+1}$

2. if formula $\circ K\alpha \in \Gamma_i$ and reduction applied to $\Gamma_i \to \Delta_i$ reduced it to the formula of the form $\circ M\beta$ then $(\circ K\alpha, \circ M\beta) \in S_{i,i+1}$

3. $S_{i,i+j} = S_{i,i+j-1} \circ S_{j-1,j}$ $(j > 1)$

— *Trace* of any formula $\alpha \in \Gamma_i$ to be a sequence $(\alpha_j)_{j \in J}$ such that $\alpha_j \in S_{i+j}$.

— *Loop node* as such element $i \in I$ that there exists $j < i$, $\Gamma_i \to \Delta_i = \Gamma_j \to \Delta_j$, and $S_{j,i} = \emptyset$. $\qquad\qquad\qquad\qquad\qquad\qquad\qquad\qquad\qquad\qquad\qquad\qquad\qquad\qquad\qquad\square$

3.6 Definition

Refutation tree for a sequent $\Gamma \to \Delta$ will be a pair $< T, L >$ where T is a finite tree and L labeling of nodes of T with sequents such that:

1. label of the root of T is $\Gamma \to \Delta$

2. if n is internal node labeled with $\Gamma \to \Delta$ which is strongly unreducible then there are exactly as many sons of n as there are possible sequents $\Sigma \to \Omega$ such that $\Gamma \to \Delta \xmapsto{A} \Sigma \to \Omega$ for some A. Labels of this sons are exactly those assumptions.

3. if n is internal node labeled with $\Gamma \to \Delta$ which is reducible by strong reduction relation then:

   (a) if $\Gamma \to \Delta = \circ$while γ do K od $\alpha, \Sigma \to \Omega$ or $\Gamma \to \Delta = \Sigma \to \Omega, \circ$while γ do K od α and there is ancestor of current node n labeled with the same sequent $\Gamma \to \Delta$ such that we reached current node from n using only strong reduction and have already reduced formula $\circ$while γ do K od α on this way, then the only son of current node is labeled with $\alpha, \Sigma \to \Omega$ or $\Sigma \to \Omega, \alpha$ respectively.

   (b) otherwise the label of the only son of the current node is labeled with arbitrary sequent $\Sigma \to \Omega$ such that $\Gamma \to \Delta \Longrightarrow \Sigma \to \Omega$.

4. if n is a leaf then either n is a loop node or is labeled with simply refutable sequent.

We will often refer to label of node n as $L(n)$, $\Gamma(n)$ will denote predecessor of sequnet which is label of n and $\Delta(n)$ it's successor. $\qquad\qquad\qquad\qquad\qquad\qquad\square$

The most difficult clause 2.a in this definition is to avoid infinite repetitions of reductions of program which behaves like empty program in the context of whole sequent. This rule says that if we are to reduce the same program second time than we know that it behaves like an empty program hence we can reduce it at all.

In the rest of this section we will show that sequent $\Gamma \to \Delta$ is unsatisfiable iff there exists refutation tree for $\Gamma \to \Delta$. First let us deal with left to right implication.

3.7 Lemma

For any sequent $\Gamma \to \Delta$, if $\not\models \Gamma \to \Delta$ then there exists refutation tree for $\Gamma \to \Delta$.

Proof

Form assumption $\not\models \Gamma \to \Delta$ follows that there exists structure $\Im = < S, R, \rho >$ and state s_0 such that $\Im, s_0 \not\models \Gamma \to \Delta$. We will construct refutation tree $\Re$ for $\Gamma \to \Delta$ assigning to each node n of it state s of $\Im$ such that $\Im, s \not\models L(n)$. With the root n_0 of $\Re$ we associate state s_0. For any internal node n of $\Re$ with associated state s such that $\Im, s \not\models L(n)$ we proceed in a following way:

— If $L(n)$ is not strongly unreducible then from lemma 3.2 follows that there exist sequent $\Sigma \to \Omega$ such that $L(n) \Longrightarrow \Sigma \to \Omega$ and $\Im, s \not\models \Sigma \to \Omega$. Hence we can take as a label of the only son of n, m sequent $\Sigma \to \Omega$ and associate with node m the same state s. We will do this in all cases but when rule 13 is applicable to $L(n)$ and both possible results of reduction are unsatisfied in s. In this case we choose this result of reduction were realization of program in new formula (i.e. obtained by reduction of formula in $L(n)$) is shorter. Additionally we have to remember about rule 2.a from definition of refutation tree but it is easy to see that if we are to apply such rule then the only son obtained by it's application is still unsatisfiable in the same state as father.

— If $L(n)$ is strongly unreducible then from lemma 3.2 follows that for every possible $\Sigma \to \Omega$ and program A, such that $L(n) \overset{A}{\longmapsto} \Sigma \to \Omega$ there exist state t such that $(s, t) \in R(A)$ and $\Im, t \not\models \Sigma \to \Omega$. Of course we can take t as a state associated with son of n labeled by $\Sigma \to \Omega$ but again we face the problem of nondeterminizm. It does matter what state we choose only in one case, when we reduce formula of the form $\Diamond A\alpha \in \Gamma(n)$. In this case we choose state t to be this one which is next in $Rel(s, \Diamond A\alpha)$.

Structure $\Re$ constructed in such way clearly satisfies all conditions lied on refutation tree but one which requires $\Re$ to be finite. Our $\Re$ may have infinite paths but we will show that on every infinite path we can find a loop node. To do this we show by induction on formula α that:

(*) For every node n, formula $\alpha \in \Gamma(n)$ and path P from node n every trace of α is finite.

— if α is propositional variable or of the form $\beta \vee \gamma, \beta \wedge \gamma, \neg\beta$ then for any $m \in P$ at most pair $(\alpha, \alpha) \in S_{n,m}$. It is easy to observe that pair $(\alpha, \alpha) \in S_{n,m}$ as long as only strong rules are applied between n and m, but we can apply strong rules only finitely many times before we obtain strongly unreducible sequent. Hence we finally reach node $m \in P$ such that L(m) is strongly unreducible, it's easy to observe that there is no formula δ such that $(\alpha, \delta) \in S_{n,m'}$ for any node m' which is descendant of m.

— if $\alpha = \Diamond K\beta \in \Gamma(n)$ then let us assume conversely that the trace of α form node n is infinite. From induction hypothesis we obtain that every trace of formula β is finite hence there must be infinite sequence of formulas $\Diamond M_i\beta$, $i \in I$ such that $(\alpha, \Diamond M_i\beta) \in S_{n,m_i}$. It is easy to observe that $(s_i, M_i)_{i \in I}$,where s_i are stares associated with nodes m_i, is an execution of program K from state s associated with node n. It is easy to prove that this execution is prefix of the $Rel(\alpha, s)$ which is finite because $\Im, s \not\models \Diamond K\beta$.

— if $\alpha = \Box K\beta \in L(n)$ then as in previous case if we assume conversely than it follows that there must be an infinite execution of program K form state associated with node n. Contradiction with assumption that $\Im, s \models \Box K\beta$.

Now let us take any infinite path P of $\Re$. From lemma 3.4 follows that there are only finitely many different sequents which can occur as a labels in $\Re$. Hence there must be sequent $\Gamma \to \Delta$ which occurs infinitely many times on P. From $(*)$ follows that there must be two occurrences of $\Gamma \to \Delta$, n and m such that $S_{n,m} = \emptyset$ hence m is a loop node. $\square$

Let us turn to right to left implication, that is we are to show that given a refutation tree of $\Gamma \to \Delta$ we can construct structure in which it is unsatisfiable. To do so we will first introduce some helpful notation:

3.8 Definition

— Given an refutation tree $\Re = < T, L >$ we define a *strong successor* relation $\succ$ between pairs of nodes from T, $n \succ m$ iff one of following conditions hold:

- m is a son of n in tree T and $L(n) \Longrightarrow L(m)$

- n is an leaf and loop-node and m is an ancestor of n such that $L(m) = L(n)$ and $S_{m,n} = \emptyset$.

— $\succ^*$ will mean reflexive and transitive closure of $\succ$
— $\Gamma^*(s) = \{\Gamma(t) : t \succ^* s\}$, $\Delta^*(s) = \{\Delta(t) : t \succ^* s\}$ $\square$

Equipped with this notation we will define the notion of canonical structure:

3.9 Definition

Given a refutation tree $\Re = < T, L >$ we define canonical structure $\Im = < S, R, \rho >$ in a following way:

- $S = \{n \in T : L(n) \text{ strongly unreducible sequent}\}$

- $(s, t) \in R(A)$ iff there exists son of s, r such that $L(s) \overset{A}{\longmapsto} L(r)$ and $r \succ^* t$.

- $p \in \rho(s)$ iff $p \in \Gamma(s)$ $\square$

And finally we show that in canonical structure the root of refutation tree is unsatisfied.

3.10 Lemma

If sequent $\Gamma \to \Delta$ has a refutation tree $\Re = < T, L >$ then it is unsatisfied in canonical structure $\Im = < S, R, \rho >$ build from $\Re$.
Proof
First of all let us introduce new concept which will be very helpful in this proof

3.10.1 Definition

For a state s of $\Im$ and formulas $\circ K\alpha \in \Gamma^*(s)$ $(\circ K\alpha \in \Delta^*(s))$, we define *traced execution* of program K to be such an execution $(s_i, M_i)_{i \in I}$ of K from s, that every formula $\circ M_i\alpha \in \Gamma^*(s_i)$ $(\circ M_i\alpha \in \Delta^*(s_i)$ respectively). $\square$
The usefulness of this notion is shown by following lemma:

3.10.2 Lemma

For a state s of $\Im$ and formula $\circ K\alpha \in \Gamma^*(s)$ any traced execution of program K is successful and in it's final state t formula $\alpha \in \Gamma^*(t)$.
Proof
Suppose conversely that there exists infinite traced execution of K. Then it easy follows that there must exist on it at least one loop node s and corresponding to it node n such that $S_{n,s} = \emptyset$, contradiction with definition of loop node. $\qquad\square$

Thesis of the lemma 3.10 will follow from next fact which we will prove by induction on structure of formula α:

$$(**) \quad \text{if } \alpha \in \Gamma^*(s) \text{ then } \Im, s \models \alpha \text{ and if } \alpha \in \Delta^*(s) \text{ then } \Im, s \not\models \alpha.$$

— If $\alpha \in \Gamma^*(s)$ is a propositional variable then it's easy to observe that $\alpha \in \Gamma(s)$ hence from definition of ρ, $\Im, s \models \alpha$.

— Other cases with propositional connectives and dual one for $\alpha \in \Delta^*(s)$ follow immediately from the form of rules.

— if $\Box K\alpha \in \Gamma^*(s)$ then it easily follows from definition of canonical structure and form of the reduction rules that every execution of program K from state s is traced. Then $\Im, s \models \Box K\alpha$ follows from lemma 3.10.2 and induction hypothesis.

— if $\diamond K\alpha \in \Gamma^*(s)$ then we observe that there exists traced execution of K from s. Then as in case above we obtain that $\Im, s \models \diamond K\alpha$.

— if $\Box K\alpha \in \Delta^*(s)$ then we show that there exists a traced execution of K from s. If it is successful then in it's final state t, $\beta \in \Delta^*(t)$, but from induction hypothesis $\Im, s \not\models \alpha$ hence $\Im, s \not\models \Box K\alpha$.

— if $\diamond K\alpha \in \Delta^*(s)$ then we observe that every execution of K from state s is traced. Hence in final state of every successful execution formula $\beta \in \Delta^*(t)$.

From fact $(**)$ it immediately follows that in state s such that $n_0 \succ^* s$ sequent $\Gamma \to \Delta$ is unsatisfied, where n_0 is the root of refutation tree T. $\qquad\square$

We can summarize results of this section in a following theorem.

3.11 Theorem

Sequent $\Gamma \to \Delta$ is not valid iff there exists refutation tree for $\Gamma \to \Delta$.

4 Algorithm

Equipped with characterization proved in previous section we present algorithm for checking validity of PAL sequents. The main part of the algorithm will be procedure *Prove* which given a sequent and a path from root of the tree to the current node, will attempt to find part of refutation tree for it using DFS search.

$Prove(\Gamma \to \Delta, P)$:

1. if $\Gamma \to \Delta$ is an axiom then return false

2. if $\Gamma \to \Delta$ is simply refutable sequent then return $\Gamma \to \Delta$

3. if $\Gamma \to \Delta$ is a loop node on path P then return $\Gamma \to \Delta$

4. if there are two nodes on P, n_1, n_2 labeled with $\Gamma \to \Delta$ such that $S_{n_1,m} = S_{n_1,n_2}$ where m is the current node and $\{\Sigma \to \Omega : \Sigma \to \Omega$ label of ancestor of $n_2\} \supseteq \{\Sigma \to \Omega : \Sigma \to \Omega$ label of a node between n_2 and m$\}$ then return false

5. if on path P condition 2.a from definition of refutation tree is satisfied then let $\Sigma \to \Omega$ be the sequent as desired by this rule. Make call $Prove(\Sigma \to \Omega, P \circ \Gamma \to \Delta)$ and if it returns part of refutation tree, return it with added new root labeled $\Gamma \to \Delta$, otherwise return false

6. if $\Gamma \to \Delta$ is strongly unreducible sequent then call $Prove(\Sigma \to \Omega, P \circ \Gamma \to \Delta)$ for every $\Sigma \to \Omega$ and A such that $\Gamma \to \Delta \xrightarrow{A} \Sigma \to \Omega$ then:

   (a) if one of this calls returned false then return false.

   (b) otherwise return tree with root labeled $\Gamma \to \Delta$ and roots of all returned by procedure calls trees as it's sons.

7. if none of above cases hold then:

   (a) if there exists sequent $\Sigma \to \Omega$ such that $\Gamma \to \Delta \implies \Sigma \to \Omega$ and call $Prove(\Sigma \to \Omega, \Gamma \to \Delta)$ succeeded (i.e. it returned part of the tree) then return tree with root labeled $\Gamma \to \Delta$ and then root of returned tree as its only son

   (b) otherwise return false.

To show partial correctness of above algorithm we have to prove

4.1 Proposition

If there exist refutation tree for $\Gamma \to \Delta$ then there exist refutation tree without nodes satisfying condition (4) of above algorithm.
Proof
Let refutation tree $\Re$ and node m, satisfying condition (4) will be given. Then let us throw away part of $\Re$ between nodes n_2 and m. Obviously after this operation all conditions lied on refutation tree remain satisfied. □

It is easy to observe that call $Prove(\Gamma \to \Delta, \varepsilon)$ returns either false or refutation tree for $\Gamma \to \Delta$. From proposition 4.1 follows that if false is returned than we can be sure that there is no refutation tree for $\Gamma \to \Delta$ and hence from lemma 3.7 follows that sequent is valid. Otherwise following construction from definition 3.9 we can exhibit structure and state in which sequent $\Gamma \to \Delta$ is false.
It only remains to show that above algorithm always stops. First let us observe that all sequents that may occur during execution of $Prove(\Gamma \to \Delta, \varepsilon)$ belong to set $FL(\Gamma \to \Delta)$. Because of condition (4) the length of each path is less than the number of trace relations multiplied by the number of possible sequents i.e. $|FL(\Gamma \to \Delta)|$ hence by proposition 3.4 is finite and bounded by exponential function. From conditions (6) and (7) follows that degree of every node is bounded and less than there can be formulas to reduce hence

less than $O(n)$. Finally we obtain that the size of whole search space and complexity of algorithm is bounded by double exponential function in size of $\Gamma \to \Delta$.

It is well known that the lower bound on decidability problem for both deterministic PDL and PAL is 2^{cn} for some constant c (see Harel [3]). To reach this bound we have to somehow refine our algorithm. Modification arises from the observation that we can compactificate refutation tree to the DAG like structure which will have the same properties as refutation tree but will be at most exponential in the size of a input sequent.

4.2 Definition

— Given a refutation tree $\Re$ it's node n we will say that this node *finishes formula* $\alpha \in \Gamma \to \Delta$ iff there is no leaf m of $\Re$ and formula β such that $(\alpha, \beta) \in S_{n,m}$. $Fin(n)$ will denote the set of formulas finished by node n.

—Given a refutation tree $\Re$ we define *refutation dag* to be structure obtained by sequential applications of following rule:

> if on the left of a node n (i.e previous in infix numbering and not on a same path) there exists node m such that $L(n)=L(m)$ and $Fin(n) \subseteq Fin(m)$ delete subtree with root n from refutation tree and connect father of n to m.

□

Clearly lemma 3.10 still holds for refutation dag hence sequent is valid iff there is no refutation dag of it. It is easy to see that every sequent $\Gamma \to \Delta$ can occur at most as many times as there are possible subsets of formulas in $\Gamma \to \Delta$. Because there can be at most $O(n)$ formulas in $\Gamma \to \Delta$ hence there can be at most exponential number of occurrences of any sequent. Hence the size of whole structure is bounded by $O(2^{cn})$ where n is the size of the input sequent. Algorithm for constructing refutation dag is almost the same as for refutation tree. We have to preserve the invariant that what is to the left of current node is refutation dag.

We can summarize results of this section in following theorems:

4.3 Theorem Decidability

Validity of PAL formulas is decidable in $O(2^{cn})$ time for appropriate constant c. □

4.4 Theorem Small Model

For every not valid PAL formula α there exist model $\Im$ such that $\Im \not\models \alpha$ and size of $\Im$ is less then $O(2^{c|\alpha|})$. □

References

1. Chlebus, On the Decidability of Propositional Algorithmic Logic, *Zeitschr. f. math. Logik* 28, 247–261 (1982)

2. Fisher M. J. and Ladner R. E., Propositional dynamic logic of regular programs, *J. Comput. Syst. Sci.* 18 194–211.

3. Harel D., Dynamic Logic, *Handbook of Philosophical Logic* Vol 11, 197–604 (1984)

4. Mirkowska G., PAL — propositional algorithmic logic, *Fund Informaticae 4*, 675–760. Also in Lecture Notes in Computer Science, Vol 125, Springler-Verlag pp.23–101 (1981)

5. Nishimura H., Sequential Method in Propositional Dynamic Logic, *Acta Informatica 12*, pp. 377–400 (1979)

6. Nishimura H., Semantical Analysis of Constructive PDL, *Publ. Res. Inst. Math. Sci. Kyoto Univ.* (1981)

7. Salwicki A., Formalized algorithmic languages, *Bull. Acad. Polon Sci. Ser Sci. Math. Astron. Phys. 18*, pp. 227–232 (1970)

8. Street R.S., Propositional dynamic logic of looping and converse is elementary decidable, *Inf. and Control 54* pp. 121–141. (1982)

9. Walukiewicz I. Gentzen Type Axiomatization of PAL to appear in *Proceedings of MFCS 90*, Springler-Verlag.

Vol. 408: M. Leeser, G. Brown (Eds.),Hardware Specification, Verification and Synthesis: Mathematical Aspects. Proceedings, 1989. VI, 402 pages. 1990.

Vol. 409: A. Buchmann, O. Günther, T. R. Smith, Y.-F. Wang (Eds.), Design and Implementation of Large Spatial Databases. Proceedings, 1989. IX, 364 pages. 1990.

Vol. 410: F. Pichler, R. Moreno-Diaz (Eds.), Computer Aided Systems Theory – EUROCAST '89. Proceedings, 1989. VII, 427 pages. 1990.

Vol. 411: M. Nagl (Ed.), Graph-Theoretic Concepts in Computer Science. Proceedings, 1989. VII, 374 pages. 1990.

Vol. 412: L. B. Almeida, C. J. Wellekens (Eds.), Neural Networks. Proceedings, 1990. IX, 276 pages. 1990,

Vol. 413: R. Lenz, Group Theoretical Methods in Image Processing. VIII, 139 pages. 1990.

Vol. 414: A.Kreczmar, A. Salwicki, M. Warpechowski, LOGLAN '88 – Report on the Programming Language. X, 133 pages. 1990.

Vol. 415: C. Choffrut, T. Lengauer (Eds.), STACS 90. Proceedings, 1990. VI, 312 pages. 1990.

Vol. 416: F. Bancilhon, C. Thanos, D. Tsichritzis (Eds.), Advances in Database Technology – EDBT '90. Proceedings, 1990. IX, 452 pages. 1990.

Vol. 417: P. Martin-Löf, G. Mints (Eds.), COLOG-88. International Conference on Computer Logic. Proceedings, 1988. VI, 338 pages. 1990.

Vol. 418: K.H. Bläsius, U. Hedtstück, C.-R. Rollinger (Eds.), Sorts and Types in Artificial Intelligence. Proceedings, 1989. VIII, 307 pages. 1990. (Subseries LNAI).

Vol. 419: K. Weichselberger, S. Pöhlmann, A Methodology for Uncertainty in Knowledge-Based Systems. VIII, 136 pages. 1990 (Subseries LNAI).

Vol. 420: Z. Michalewicz (Ed.), Statistical and Scientific Database Management, V SSDBM. Proceedings, 1990. V, 256 pages. 1990.

Vol. 421: T. Onodera, S. Kawai, A Formal Model of Visualization in Computer Graphics Systems. X, 100 pages. 1990.

Vol. 422: B. Nebel, Reasoning and Revision in Hybrid Representation Systems. XII, 270 pages. 1990 (Subseries LNAI).

Vol. 423: L. E. Deimel (Ed.), Software Engineering Education. Proceedings, 1990. VI, 164 pages. 1990.

Vol. 424: G. Rozenberg (Ed.), Advances in Petri Nets 1989. VI, 524 pages. 1990.

Vol. 425: C. H. Bergman, R. D. Maddux, D. L. Pigozzi (Eds.), Algebraic Logic and Universal Algebra in Computer Science. Proceedings, 1988. XI, 292 pages. 1990.

Vol. 426: N. Houbak, SIL – a Simulation Language. VII, 192 pages. 1990.

Vol. 427: O. Faugeras (Ed.), Computer Vision – ECCV 90. Proceedings, 1990. XII, 619 pages. 1990.

Vol. 428: D. Bjørner, C. A. R. Hoare, H. Langmaack (Eds.), VDM '90. VDM and Z – Formal Methods in Software Development. Proceedings, 1990. XVII, 580 pages. 1990.

Vol. 429: A. Miola (Ed.), Design and Implementation of Symbolic Computation Systems. Proceedings, 1990. XII, 284 pages. 1990.

Vol. 430: J. W. de Bakker, W.-P. de Roever, G. Rozenberg (Eds.), Stepwise Refinement of Distributed Systems. Models, Formalisms, Correctness. Proceedings, 1989. X, 808 pages. 1990.

Vol. 431: A. Arnold (Ed.), CAAP '90. Proceedings, 1990. VI, 285 pages. 1990.

Vol. 432: N. Jones (Ed.), ESOP '90. Proceedings, 1990. IX, 436 pages. 1990.

Vol. 433: W. Schröder-Preikschat, W. Zimmer (Eds.), Progress in Distributed Operating Systems and Distributed Systems Management. Proceedings, 1989. V, 206 pages. 1990.

Vol. 434: J.-J. Quisquater, J. Vandewalle (Eds.), Advances in Cryptology – EUROCRYPT '89. Proceedings, 1989. X, 710 pages. 1990.

Vol. 435: G. Brassard (Ed.), Advances in Cryptology – CRYPTO '89. Proceedings, 1989. XIII, 634 pages. 1990.

Vol. 436: B. Steinholtz, A. Sølvberg, L. Bergman (Eds.), Advanced Information Systems Engineering. Proceedings, 1990. X, 392 pages. 1990.

Vol. 437: D. Kumar (Ed.), Current Trends in SNePS – Semantic Network Processing System. Proceedings, 1989. VII, 162 pages. 1990. (Subseries LNAI).

Vol. 438: D. H. Norrie, H.-W. Six (Eds.), Computer Assisted Learning – ICCAL '90. Proceedings, 1990. VII, 467 pages. 1990.

Vol. 439: P. Gorny, M. Tauber (Eds.), Visualization in Human-Computer Interaction. Proceedings, 1988. VI, 274 pages. 1990.

Vol. 440: E.Börger, H. Kleine Büning, M. M. Richter (Eds.), CSL '89. Proceedings, 1989. VI, 437 pages. 1990.

Vol. 441: T. Ito, R. H. Halstead, Jr. (Eds.), Parallel Lisp: Languages and Systems. Proceedings, 1989. XII, 364 pages. 1990.

Vol. 442: M. Main, A. Melton, M. Mislove, D. Schmidt (Eds.), Mathematical Foundations of Programming Semantics. Proceedings, 1989. VI, 439 pages. 1990.

Vol. 443: M. S. Paterson (Ed.), Automata, Languages and Programming. Proceedings, 1990. IX, 781 pages. 1990.

Vol. 444: S. Ramani, R. Chandrasekar, K.S.R. Anjaneyulu (Eds.), Knowledge Based Computer Systems. Proceedings, 1989. X, 546 pages. 1990. (Subseries LNAI).

Vol. 445: A. J. M. van Gasteren, On the Shape of Mathematical Arguments. VIII, 181 pages. 1990.

Vol. 446: L. Plümer, Termination Proofs for Logic Programs. VIII, 142 pages. 1990. (Subseries LNAI).

Vol. 447: J.R. Gilbert, R. Karlsson (Eds.), SWAT 90. 2nd Scandinavian Workshop on Algorithm Theory. Proceedings, 1990. VI, 417 pages. 1990.

Vol. 448: B. Simons, A. Spector (Eds.), Fault-Tolerant Distributed Computing. VI, 298 pages. 1990.

Vol. 449: M. E. Stickel (Ed.), 10th International Conference on Automated Deduction. Proceedings, 1990. XVI, 688 pages. 1990. (Subseries LNAI).

Vol. 450: T. Asano, T. Ibaraki, H. Imai, T. Nishizeki (Eds.), Algorithms. Proceedings, 1990. VIII, 479 pages. 1990.

Vol. 451: V. Mařík, O. Štěpánková, Z. Zdráhal (Eds.), Artificial Intelligence in Higher Education. Proceedings, 1989. IX, 247 pages. 1990. (Subseries LNAI).

Vol. 452: B. Rovan (Ed.), Mathematical Foundations of Computer Science 1990. Proceedings, 1990. VIII, 544 pages. 1990.

Vol. 453: J. Seberry, J. Pieprzyk (Eds.), Advances in Cryptology – AUSCRYPT '90. Proceedings, 1990. IX, 462 pages. 1990.

Vol. 454: V. Diekert, Combinatorics on Traces. XII, 165 pages. 1990.

Vol. 455: C. A. Floudas, P.M. Pardalos, A Collection of Test Problems for Constrained Global Optimization Algorithms. XIV, 180 pages. 1990.

Vol. 456: P. Deransart, J. Maluszyński (Eds.), Programming Language Implementation and Logic Programming. Proceedings, 1990. VIII, 401 pages. 1990.

Vol. 457: H. Burkhart (Ed.), CONPAR '90 – VAPP IV. Proceedings, 1990. XIV, 900 pages. 1990.

Vol. 458: J. C. M. Baeten, J. W. Klop (Eds.), CONCUR '90. Proceedings, 1990. VII, 537 pages. 1990.

Vol. 459: R. Studer (Ed.), Natural Language and Logic. Proceedings, 1989. VII, 252 pages. 1990. (Subseries LNAI).

Vol. 460: J. Uhl, H.A. Schmid, A Systematic Catalogue of Reusable Abstract Data Types. XII, 344 pages. 1990.

Vol. 461: P. Deransart, M. Jourdan (Eds.), Attribute Grammars and their Applications. Proceedings, 1990. VIII, 358 pages. 1990.

Vol. 462: G. Gottlob, W. Nejdl (Eds.), Expert Systems in Engineering. Proceedings, 1990. IX, 260 pages. 1990. (Subseries LNAI).

Vol. 463: H. Kirchner, W. Wechler (Eds.), Algebraic and Logic Programming. Proceedings, 1990. VII, 386 pages. 1990.

Vol. 464: J. Dassow, J. Kelemen (Eds.), Aspects and Prospects of Theoretical Computer Science. Proceedings, 1990. VI, 298 pages. 1990.